Giving Women

Giving Women

Alliance and Exchange in Victorian Culture

JILL RAPPOPORT

OXFORD
UNIVERSITY PRESS

OXFORD
UNIVERSITY PRESS

Oxford University Press, Inc., publishes works that further
Oxford University's objective of excellence
in research, scholarship, and education.

Oxford   New York
Auckland   Cape Town   Dar es Salaam   Hong Kong   Karachi
Kuala Lumpur   Madrid   Melbourne   Mexico City   Nairobi
New Delhi   Shanghai   Taipei   Toronto

With offices in
Argentina   Austria   Brazil   Chile   Czech Republic   France   Greece
Guatemala   Hungary   Italy   Japan   Poland   Portugal   Singapore
South Korea   Switzerland   Thailand   Turkey   Ukraine   Vietnam

Copyright © 2012 by Oxford University Press, Inc.

Published by Oxford University Press, Inc.
198 Madison Avenue, New York, New York 10016

www.oup.com

Oxford is a registered trademark of Oxford University Press

Library of Congress Cataloging-in-Publication Data
Rappoport, Jill.
Giving women : alliance and exchange in Victorian culture / Jill Rappoport.
    p.   cm.
Includes bibliographical references and index.
ISBN 978-0-19-977260-5 (hardcover : acid-free paper) 1. English literature—19th
century—History and criticism. 2. English literature—Women authors—History and criticism.
3. Generosity in literature. 4. Women and literature—England—History—19th century.
5. Literature and society—England—History—19th century. 6. Women in literature. 7. Women and
literature—England—History—20th century. 8. Literature and society—England—History—20th
century. I. Title.
PR468.W6R37 2011
820.9′352209034—dc22   2011004978

1 3 5 7 9 8 6 4 2

Printed in the United States of America
on acid-free paper

CONTENTS

ACKNOWLEDGMENTS

Substantial institutional support has made this book possible. I am particularly grateful to the Monticello College Foundation Fellowship, which funded a valuable semester of research and writing at the Newberry Library. The University of Virginia provided the President's Fellowship and Mellon-supported interdisciplinary dissertation seminar that launched the project; Winchester Fellowships from Wesleyan University enabled me to consult archives for chapter five; a Penn Humanities Forum Mellon Research Fellowship helped me to write chapter six; and Villanova University sponsored my revisions of this project with five years of generous assistance, including a Research Support Grant and a Summer Research Fellowship.

Many people have given time and energy to this project, and I am deeply thankful to everyone who wanted it to succeed. Some have been part of this process from its beginning to its end, reading multiple drafts at multiple stages: Alison Booth, Herbert Tucker, Michael Genovese, Sarah Hagelin, Ann L. Rappoport, Hallie Smith Richmond, and Jolie Sheffer. I hope you all know how much your friendship, encouragement, and suggestions have meant to me.

There have been so many other thoughtful readers and advisers along the way. At the University of Virginia, where it began: Stephen Arata, Karen Chase, Michael Levenson, Rei Magosaki, Jerome McGann, Alison Milbank, Daniel Siegel, Chloe Wigston Smith, and members of a fantastic nineteenth-century workshop group that included Peter Capuano, Paul Fyfe, Michael Lewis, Heather Morton, and David Sigler. In Philadelphia: Seth Koven, Lynn Lees, and the rest of the rigorous Delaware Valley British Studies Seminar; many colleagues at Villanova University, especially Evan Radcliffe, Cristina Cervone, Heather Hicks, Marylu Hill, Jean Lutes, Timothy McCall, and Deborah Thomas; members of the Penn Humanities Forum including Genevieve Abravanel, Judith Brown, and Michael Gamer; and Ellen Malenas Ledoux, Rachel Buurma, and Sharrona Pearl. In Chicago: Jim Grossman, Diane Dillon, Bruce Calder, Deborah Cohen, Leon Fink, Paul Gehl, Jen Hill, Alejandra Irigoin, Craig Koslofsky, Scott Nelson, Susan

O'Donovan, and Dana Rabin. Still others have lent support at various stages, in numerous ways: Amanda Claybaugh, Jay Clayton, Mary Jean Corbett, Julie Crowell, Lana Dalley, Frank Genovese, Susan Genovese, Eileen Gillooly, Jordana Greenwald, Janet Gusdorff, Katherine Harris, Samantha Kennedy, Sharon Marcus, Rachel Mundy, Paul Rappoport, Rachel Teukolsky, Stephanie Kuduk Weiner, and Joanne van der Woude. In workshops and at conferences, other colleagues responded to early versions of these chapters with insights and suggestions. Thanks are due, also, to the generous community of scholars who respond to queries posted on VICTORIA-l, and to my students, especially three smart and hard-working research assistants: Laura DeFurio, Benjamin Raymond, and Emily Veale. This project would not have been possible without the hard work and patience of archivists and librarians. Special thanks go to Judith Olsen of Villanova University's Falvey Library and Lew Purfoy of the University of Virginia. At the Salvation Army International Heritage Centre at the William Booth College in London, Army archivist Gordon Taylor, archive assistant Karen Thompson, and photographic archivist Alex von der Becke were particularly generous with their time and materials, as were others at the Bodleian, the British Library, the Newberry Library, the Women's Library, and the University of Pennsylvania Van Pelt Library. This project began out of a conviction that giving did not necessarily entail giving *up*; I owe my early speculation on what it meant to be a "giving woman" to opportunities provided by many people and programs, including Charles Stamm at CHS, Frank Kuan and Chris Lanser at Wesleyan's Office of Community Services, and the Caring Institute.

Many thanks to Shannon McLachlan and Brendan O'Neill at Oxford University Press for seeing potential in this project and for working with me to see it through. The book benefits from the efforts of Jenny Wolkowicki and the rest of her production team at OUP as well as from the extremely helpful feedback of the Press's three anonymous reviewers. I am very grateful for their encouragement and detailed suggestions. All remaining missteps are my own.

Portions of this book were published in earlier stages. A version of chapter three first appeared in *Victorian Literature and Culture* 36:1 (2008) as "Conservation of Sympathy in *Cranford*"; chapter four is reprinted with permission from *SEL Studies in English Literature 1500–1900* 50:4 (Autumn 2010). I am grateful to the editors for allowing me to reprint these materials.

With love for all my family, I dedicate this book to Michael Genovese, my toughest critic and best friend, and to Isaac Edward Genovese, who reminds us to laugh. They make the everyday give and take of our life together a joy.

Giving Women

Introduction

"Accept them, lady—to me they are valueless. I will never wear jewels more."
"You are then unhappy," said Rowena, struck with the manner in which Rebecca uttered the last words. "O remain with us [. . .], and I will be a sister to you." —Walter Scott, *Ivanhoe* (1819)

. . .

"[A] present has many faces, has it not? and one should consider all before pronouncing an opinion as to its nature." —Charlotte Brontë, *Jane Eyre* (1847)

. . .

"If you'll be true to me, Lucy, in this business, I'll make you the hand-somest present you ever saw in your life. I'll give you a hundred guinea brooch;—I will, indeed." [. . . .]
"You mean thing!" said Lucy. "I didn't think there was a woman so mean as that in the world.[. . . .] Pick up what I hear, and send it you in letters,—and then be paid money for it!" —Anthony Trollope, *The Eustace Diamonds* (1873)[1]

Jane Eyre's cautious deliberation over presents is only one of many Victorian attempts to contemplate the dangers and pleasures of gift exchange for women of the middling classes. As this brief sampling suggests, gifts throughout nineteenth-century British literature and culture set the terms for kinship, threaten heroines with obligations they cannot repay, and create conditions for bribes. Such disparate scenes as Scott's, Brontë's, and Trollope's reveal a far more nuanced understanding of how giving can define relationships than those that currently influence either literary scholarship or theories of exchange. Gifts and giving pervade the nineteenth-century popular imagination, but our studies of the Victorians have not yet assessed their significance, either to the women who are frequently depicted as objects and agents of exchange or to the broader society reflected and shaped by them. Through giving, women engaged in and helped to fashion cultural discourses on female intimacy, property law, religious social action, and scientific discovery.

Popular images of feminine altruism, such as the one privileged by Charles Dickens's novel *Bleak House* (1853),[2] serve as useful models both for how Victorian studies and gift theories have previously treated the subject of giving and for how even the period's most canonical fiction opens up a much broader set of options for women than those that currently inform our critical understanding. Dickens's portrait of Esther Summerson, to which I shall return throughout this Introduction, evokes two prevalent but problematic views of Victorian women's giving: that women's primary gift exchanges were imagined as selfless acts of charity or sacrifice and that marriage was seen as the most frequent or desirable outcome of these exchanges. As we will see, however, women took control of gift-giving to forge their own diverse alliances.

Esther's sympathetic approach to charity—unlike Mrs. Pardiggle's showy "business" of visiting the urban poor and Mrs. Jellyby's "telescopic philanthropy," which ignores domestic problems in favor of colonial missions—offers a more "natural" progression of gendered care from home to a wider sphere. "I thought it best to be as useful as I could, and to render what kind services I could, to those immediately about me; and to try to let that circle of duty gradually and naturally expand itself" (128). She immediately befriends and nurses the neglected children of the Jellyby household; in contrast to Mrs. Pardiggle's "systematic" district rounds (130), this work is simply heaven-sent: "It rained Esther" (84). Whether offering a sympathetic ear to her new friends or forfeiting her own health in order to help a small-pox-ridden pauper, Esther is one mid-century exemplar of the "giving women" who filled the pages of Victorian literature: naturally dutiful, self-effacing, and (at least seemingly) at odds with more radical proponents of women's rights.

She is also a gift. Dickens's paradigm requires feminine self-sacrifice. Despite her love for Allan Woodcourt, Esther prepares to surrender her feelings and, in an effort to be a grateful ward, give herself in marriage to her guardian, Mr. Jarndyce. Jarndyce passes this gift along, transferring his fiancée to Woodcourt in a move that makes Esther the object rather than the agent of gift-giving. "'Allan,' said my guardian, 'take from me a willing gift [...]. Take with her the little home she brings you. [...] Allan, take my dear'" (966). In this second figuration of giving, Dickens makes Esther the gift between men that secures their connection. His literary transfer of a woman enacts a form of gift exchange familiar to theorists of kinship. As scholars from Claude Lévi-Strauss to Eve Sedgwick have observed, "giving women" in marriage creates reciprocal obligations that have typically served men's interests.[3]

As this book demonstrates, however, and as even *Bleak House* ultimately suggests, the relational identities available to "giving women" far exceed these limited interpretations of Victorian women as gifts or selfless givers. A broader perspective on giving offers a more nuanced understanding of how the Victorians imagined kinship and agency. Even when Esther is gift rather than giver, she nevertheless exerts some influence on the exchange. More than just an object passed between men, she is (by her own account) "willing." It is difficult to assess the degree of choice that even a "willing" woman had in such cases, of course. Nineteenth-century conduct books such as those of Sarah Stickney Ellis defined women as "relative creatures"—relative to the husbands and other men whose interests they served—and writers from the nineteenth century to the present day have found women's disproportionate appearance of "selflessness" dangerous because of the second-order identity this cultural mandate seems to assign them.[4] Exalted as a gendered duty, ideological pressures to give can threaten women's autonomy.[5] But Victorian discourses of giving also reveal the ways in which women shaped the language and goals of these ideologies, imagining and enacting their own exchanges.[6]

When we shift critical focus from the unequal exchanges of philanthropy and patriarchal marriage to the peer alliances women established with one another through gift-giving, we recover a complex history of bourgeois women's strategies for achieving economic agency during a period when most lacked property rights and professional opportunities.[7] Through gifts that ranged from small tokens to their own bodies, women entered into volatile and profitable economic negotiations of power and created diverse forms of community. Their personal gift transactions expanded kinship circles, served as the bases for larger civic coalitions, and established both the reach and the limits of these alliances. By empowering female authors and their fictional protagonists to build networks within a political landscape that denied them the benefits of enfranchisement, gift exchanges radically reconstructed women's private relationships and public activism in the nineteenth century. Gift-giving provides a crucial lens for seeing how women redefined the primary allegiances of their everyday lives, forged extended communities of reader-activists, and launched social and political campaigns.

Indeed, *Bleak House*, which seems simply to offer a masculine fantasy of "giving women," actually affords Esther much more agency as a giver than the passivity of her "rain[ing]" goodness might initially suggest. Esther's first-person account of her praiseworthy selflessness directs our reading of those acts and sets her own private generosity against other women's increasingly public, professionalized gifts of charity. Critical of them, competing against them, Esther's narration aligns her gifts with self-interest by positioning her as the most competent giver. Here and across Victorian literature and culture, altruism and self-assertiveness go hand-in-hand. In their expectation that givers not only *will* but also *should* get something back, the texts I discuss insist that a gift is also a debt. They thus offer an important counterpoint to Stefan Collini's argument that Victorian intellectuals better known for "self-interest and rational calculation" were equally "obsess[ed] with the role of altruism."[8] The inverse is also true. Along similar lines, but to different effect, I am arguing that when we look closely at those discourses most frequently associated with altruism—charity and sacrifice, sisterhood and maternity—we also find both self-interest and rational calculation.[9] Gift-giving thus ruptures the "exhaustive polarity between egoism and altruism" by which Collini characterizes the period and demands that we re-evaluate our assumptions about Victorian women and exchange.[10]

I. Women Giving

The economic and legal disenfranchisement of women during most of the nineteenth century, along with the rise of industrial capitalism and its discontents, make the period from 1820 through World War I particularly fertile for the analysis of alternative economic practices.[11] If, as David Cheal observes, large-scale control of others through gifts is found most frequently only where other, "more effective forms of domination do not exist," then we should understand Victorian women's gifting as a subversive way to direct social networks and establish civic authority that otherwise remained beyond their reach.[12] As material possessions acquired new moral, social, and national meaning for the Victorians, women found ways to shape and benefit from those meanings.[13]

The nineteenth century saw the rise of charity as an increasingly professional occupation that allowed middle-class women to expand the ideological and practical reach of their domestic "sphere."[14] Partly for this reason, literary and cultural historians typically approach women's gifts through the study of philanthropy. This book takes up several key movements in the history of British women's public activism: the abolitionist cause of the 1820s and '30s; the mid-century emergence of the Anglican "sister of charity"; the slum efforts of the early Salvation Army in the 1870s and '80s; and the biological "altruism" of late-century eugenic reforms. However, I also discuss the continuities of these activist movements with fictional treatments of women's more intimate, private exchanges. The importance and variety of women's gift practices that existed alongside the marketplace and pervaded the popular imagination went well beyond philanthropy and public activism.

The texts I examine speak to a growing interest in the motivations and consequences of women's lateral transactions, which are distinct from top-down gifts of charity.[15] In *Jane Eyre* and Elizabeth Barrett Browning's *Aurora Leigh* (the subjects of Chapter 2), women use financial gifts to circumvent property law and construct new family ties, while Elizabeth Gaskell's novella *Cranford*, drawing on contemporary scientific models, shows how the circulation of symbolic gifts—sympathy and secrets—can sustain a whole community of single women (see Chapter 3). Horizontal exchanges such as these extend the scope of women's giving and its place in the multifaceted nineteenth-century economy. Although recent scholarship has begun to account for the ways in which women have benefited from and been implicated in traditional markets as well as in volunteerism, capitalist and charitable models still present an incomplete vision of economics in literary history, particularly with regard to women's roles.[16] This book expands our conception of women's gift practices in order to better understand women's economic contributions and to re-evaluate the literary and social traditions that reflected and produced them. By exploring the ways in which women imagined, constructed, and galvanized communities, I show how gift practices developed into the burgeoning women's movements of the nineteenth and twentieth centuries.[17]

Methodologically speaking, I find cross-disciplinary approaches to the ideals and dangers of reciprocity valuable because they enable us to see how women used depictions of gift exchange to assert economic agency and take advantage of the power and prestige that giving promised. Literary studies of gift exchanges reveal continuities with but also sharp departures from the possibilities presented by anthropological theories derived from life study. For instance, although Marcel Mauss spends little time on women's economic agency, his observation that gifts are never one-sided, central to most current discussions of gift transactions, including my own, is absent from many critical accounts of nineteenth-century charity.[18] Despite their voluntary appearance, gifts require that we look beyond the donation side of the equation to assess the process of acceptance as well as the material or symbolic payback.

While for some theorists this obligatory return makes the gift nothing more than a self-canceling fiction that attempts to conceal its underlying contract,[19] Victorian literature is frequently quite frank about the expectation that gifts will be reciprocated. In Trollope's *The Eustace Diamonds* (1873), for example, when Mrs. Hanbury Smith sends Mrs. Carbuncle's niece a wedding present of lesser value than the one that Mrs. Carbuncle gave to this friend years before, Mrs. Carbuncle reminds her of the discrepancy, only to learn that Mrs. Hanbury Smith "quite acknowledge[s] the reciprocity system, but do[es]n't think it extends to descendants,—certainly not to nieces."[20] This satirized exchange only slightly exaggerates earlier nineteenth-century literature's more earnest depiction of women using and manipulating gift-giving as an economic system.

Such gifts, which allow women to assert claims over property and friends, are clearly not the impossibly "pure" gifts of Derridean philosophy.[21] Although my approach owes much to this and other theories of the gift, *Giving Women* is ultimately far more about the dynamic action—and *reaction*—of giving than it is about what constitutes a gift. Whether or not a gift "can" exist seems to me to be the wrong question to ask when faced with the countless representations of giving women that appear in Victorian literature and culture. Instead, I am interested in the historical specificity and stakes of these representations. The particular traits of diverse gift objects ranging from illustrated books to mysterious silver pennies bear importantly on local claims (see Chapters 1 and 4, respectively), but they must be located in and interpreted as part of a larger tradition of women's giving.

Throughout the nineteenth century, gift and market economies coexisted, each informed by and influencing perceptions of the other.[22] If Mrs. Carbuncle and Mrs. Hanbury Smith are ready to tally their reciprocal gifts down to the last shilling, however, Trollope's novel adamantly maintains that they are doing so outside the legal obligations and protections afforded by commerce: "[N]ot even can a Mrs. Carbuncle exact payment of such a debt in any established court [. . .]."[23] Despite demanding a balanced account, gift circulation can be distinguished from typical market contracts through its frequent extension over indeterminate periods of time and beyond two parties.[24] Even though givers receive countergifts, returns may be asymmetrical and indirect; in literature of the nineteenth century, givers frequently find that their rewards are deferred. This larger sense of gift circulation compels us to look beyond the partners most explicitly implicated in a given transaction and instead examine the dynamic networks these offerings construct, a strategy particularly well-suited to tracing the imagined and largely self-contained communities presented by literature.

Gift circulation that finds its way back to an original source resembles market ideas of "credit" by ensuring a later return on an initial outlay.[25] The texts I examine consistently highlight the intersections of gift and market systems and women's fluid movement between them. As I discuss in Chapter 1, literary annuals, commercially marketed and sold as gifts, offer one example of these closely knit economies. The subject of Chapter 5—the Salvation Army's call for donations, which were then put in the service of working-class women's consumerism— similarly suggests the close relationships between these two ideologically distinct systems of exchange. Despite even this contemporary recognition of their overlap, echoed by recent criticism, Victorians writing in the wake of gloomy pronouncements that "Cash Payment has become the sole nexus of man to men!" often decry the purportedly "asocial" trade of commodities in markets.[26] They privilege gift transactions as the more social form of exchange by illustrating how interpersonal relationships determine and are determined by the values and meanings of gifts.[27] These social interactions are not necessarily more equalizing. As Mauss and others have shown, while mutual, egalitarian exchanges empower donors by strengthening bonds among social "equals," unequal, patronizing transactions benefit donors by keeping recipients in debt, under obligations they cannot afford.[28] In Victorian literature, the lines between obligation and empowerment are never static, and frequently blurred.

Again, *Bleak House* provides a model for both versions of the gift relationship, while also showing how gift-giving opens up additional possibilities for women's alliances. In the Pardiggle and Jellyby charities, the "great show" of giving (130; 133) takes precedence over the beneficiaries of their gifts. Such conspicuous expenditure, the offering of gifts so large that they cannot be repaid, becomes the functional equivalent of sacrifice, endowing its donor with prestige but indebting and often antagonizing the recipient with the knowledge of her obligation.[29] Unequal exchange provokes the anger that Mrs. Pardiggle's cottagers feel when she makes an excessive display of hard work and offers them utterly inappropriate gifts. It also establishes rivalry, as we see in the exhibition of Esther's selflessness, which Dickens sets against the other women's more openly calculated offerings. These aggressively one-sided transactions follow a line of Victorian condescension that stretches from the humiliating charity school of *Jane Eyre* through the aborted interclass wedding of Elizabeth Barrett Browning's *Aurora Leigh* (see Chapter 2 of this volume).[30] They afford their donors status—Esther records that "[t]he people even praise Me [...] and make so much of me that I am quite abashed" (988–989)—but create distanced relationships between donor and recipient. Mrs. Jellyby's efforts for the natives of Borrioboola-Gha are not likely to see immediate returns from the left bank of the Niger.

Such labor does create networks of givers, however. Mrs. Jellyby receives as many as "two hundred letters respecting Africa in a single day" (57). Significantly, this correspondence allows her to establish a working community and, at least in some circles, affords her a sense of professional identity, despite Dickens's clear preference for Esther's less professional but more praiseworthy gifts. As we have seen, the novel also, and more conservatively, presents alliance formation as the result of heterosexual marriage transactions. Esther, as the gift that joins Jarndyce and Woodcourt, is Jarndyce's expression of gratitude for Woodcourt's "inestimable services" (961). In return, Jarndyce gains a second home ("Let me share its felicity sometimes, and what do I sacrifice? Nothing, nothing") (966).[31]

By establishing Esther as one gift among others in this transaction, the scene accords with Mauss's record, which names women and children—along with "banquets, rituals, military services [...] and fairs"—among the goods and services ceremonially exchanged as gifts.[32] Dickens's passage makes explicit the imbalanced expectations of patriarchal exchange; Jarndyce sacrifices "nothing." Turning Esther into the link "between men" that opens Woodcourt's home to him, Jarndyce's gift produces an extended family. Insofar as Esther is merely the "conduit" to male relationships, this gift exchange appears to rely on the heteronormative "traffic in women" that, as theorists since Gayle Rubin and Luce Irigaray have observed, typically benefits men at women's expense.[33] But Victorian women's gifts produced a much wider range of roles than those of the dutiful daughter or devoted wife. Just as Mrs. Jellyby's working community suggests the possibility that women might use exchange to create networks of their own, Esther's gift practices make her more than the object of a marriage transaction. The novel establishes additional patterns of alliance formation that gift theories do not yet account for.

In addition to receiving the general acclaim and husband that fit neatly into theoretical accounts of conspicuous expenditure and heterosexual exchange,

Esther constructs equally important ties with women through gifts.[34] Her close connections to Caddy Jellyby and Ada Clare suggest that, here and elsewhere, giving can establish female community as an alternative or supplement to the patriarchal family. At times, this intimacy helps to facilitate the marriages that, according to Sharon Marcus, were frequent outcomes of female friendships in Victorian fiction.[35] Yet marriage was not the only form of kinship or closure that nineteenth-century women derived from gifts. Much more than a means to heterosexual union, these exchanges between women provide alternative structures, not only for women's kinship and community formation but also for literary design. Whether as pairs, small groups, or larger networks, women's alliances frequently have greater narrative force than the heterosexual romance plots in which they sometimes culminate. In addition to establishing a network of mutually giving women, *Bleak House* demonstrates how such a community might reproduce itself. Both Ada and Caddy essentially produce children for Esther. She names and mothers Ada's son, who will think of her as one of his "two mamas" (988), while Caddy's "little Esther" is Esther's goddaughter as well as her namesake (768). The surrogate children they present to her by the novel's end receive more attention than her two biological daughters, shifting the priorities of kinship and storytelling away from heterosexual procreation and toward women's elective affiliation. By keeping female transactions firmly in focus as ends in themselves, we can see how giving offers structures for both family and narrative plot that do not depend solely upon marriage. My attention to women's giving thus joins recent scholarly efforts to challenge familiar conceptions of Victorian kinship.[36] Mapping out these nonconventional relationships shows how the meeting of gift theory and Victorian literature can benefit both. Seen through the lens of "giving women," narratives such as *Bleak House* provide new ways to think about the benefits and purposes of gendered exchange, even as interdisciplinary gift theories broaden our understanding of the literary traditions in which these exchanges appear.

As we will see, the patterns I am tracing in *Bleak House* are part of a much larger phenomenon. Across nineteenth-century literature and culture, gifts promised to make women the agents of wide-ranging alliance formation. Their alliances were frequently though not always figured through the language of "sisterhood." Far more than a natural or biological relationship, "sisterhood" extended the horizontal axis of familial sisterhood outward, using its (imagined) spheres of equivalence to reach beyond the local economies and hierarchies of home.[37] Simultaneously private and public, generous and competitive, nineteenth-century sisterhood served as a flexible shorthand for a range of elective affiliations including political unions, religious affiliation, and the romantic or sexual relationships that, as Martha Vicinus reminds us, in some cases mimicked heterosexual courtship rituals through gifts of letters, jewelry, and photographs.[38] In the homosocial community of single women in *Cranford* surreptitiously sucking oranges in private, the homoerotic celebration of sisters kissing each other in "Goblin Market," and the erotics of sexual sacrifice itself in fin-de-siècle eugenics, physical and immaterial transactions among women in this book disrupt kinship structures and marriage plots alike, removing male desire entirely or subordinating it to female desire.[39]

Gifts extend female alliances in *Bleak House* and the writing of many of Dickens's contemporaries, but they also circumscribe community. Mrs. Pardiggle's working-class cottagers, Mrs. Jellyby's Africans, and even the two ridiculed philanthropists themselves remain outside the intimate social network Esther establishes. The economic practices that forged women's alliances determined who could be party to an exchange, what the nature of that exchange would be, and what relationships it would produce. Each chapter of *Giving Women* attends to the ways that the networks some women create rely on and also reproduce inequalities. Class status differentiates women from one another throughout the entire book, most obviously in *Aurora Leigh* (Chapter 2) and Salvation Army journalism (Chapter 5). Racial inequalities come to the foreground in my first and last chapters, which address how gift strategies advanced abolition and eugenics, respectively. Other differences among women repeatedly shape the narratives that I discuss, too. When a sexual "fall" distinguishes between two sisters in Rossetti's "Goblin Market," for instance, the gift practices that allow one to reclaim the other are rooted in specific religious economic traditions (see Chapter 4). Finally, diverse political beliefs and strategies make the use of sacrificial gifts in campaigns for women's suffrage extremely divisive by the turn of the century, as I show in the epilogue. Forcing us to see the exclusionary tactics of alliance formation as well as the alliances themselves, domestic fiction and eugenic pamphlets alike create group identities by determining the limits of gift exchange.[40]

II. Gifts of Writing

The works treated here all present multiple scenes of exchange, establishing models of giving that, as I note above, frequently depart from anthropological traditions or the literary criticism based on these accounts. They also make gifts more than subject matter. The process and products of writing are themselves frequently implicated in gift exchange. Narrators such as *Bleak House*'s Esther highlight the significance of authorship to nineteenth-century experiences of giving. Apparently undergoing "a great deal of difficulty" as she begins to write her story (27), Esther labors to construct the vision of giving that the novel applauds; in this formulation, writing itself becomes a sacrificial offering, one part of this orphan's extreme and putatively one-sided attempt to "do some good to some one, and win some love to myself if I could" (39).[41] Narrative enters into exchange here. Indeed, when we discuss literature's *reception*, the very term reminds us that audiences are on the receiving end of a transaction that exceeds the commercial purchase of a book.[42]

Thus writing offered Victorian women one more way to claim the role of giver. For this reason, I focus primarily on female writers in the chapters that follow.[43] Whether they emphasized their work's material circulation as a gift or compelled readers to read themselves (as readers, recipients, or givers) in depictions of exchange;[44] whether they directly appealed to audiences for contributions to a cause or capitalized more subtly on perceptions of readers' reciprocal obligations; whether they explicitly referred to their work as a gift or experimented with narrative and linguistic patterns that formally mimicked experiences of giving, the work that they performed as authors was on a continuum with the nonliterary work that they performed as public activists.

Popular writing reflected, enacted, and shaped women's giving. Accordingly, "literary" and "social" strategies intermingle and support each other in this book.[45] The texts I take up are wide-ranging: canonical fiction and verse appear alongside once-popular but now more obscure annuals, "new woman" novels, and a significant degree of archival materials—newspapers and pamphlets, illustrations and photographs. This variety allows me to assess the broad cultural stakes of women's gift-giving, to consider the specific ways in which distinct genres engaged with it, and to highlight the continuities between print and activist movements for a period that saw the two as intimately connected.

Nineteenth-century writers acknowledged that literature could act as a gift by engaging and cultivating readers' feelings. George Eliot's professed indebtedness to art for its "benefit" of extending human sympathy is only one of the better known examples.[46] More recently, Rachel Ablow has suggested that Victorian literature sought to "influence" readers as nineteenth-century wives were thought to influence their husbands, in theory if not always in practice, by restoring mercenary, market-driven men to the moral values of a less competitive domestic sphere.[47] Although this analogy misses the way that Victorian readerships, like Victorian relationships, could be constructed along lines of exchange that did not privilege heterosexual marriage, the idea of literature's feminized, redemptive influence is relevant here. By this account, Victorian fiction in general joins *Bleak House*'s heroine in making use of symbolic gift practices that offer an alternative to market economies: both aim to "win some love" through doing "good" and encourage "kindness instead of self-interest."[48]

Insofar as literature works as a gift to influence feelings or attempt to "win love," it creates an "imagined community" of feeling analogous to the alliances that Victorian women were establishing through gifts.[49] In *Jane Eyre*, as we will see, reading provides the basis for Jane's intimacy with Mary and Diana Rivers, an intimacy which drives subsequent gift exchanges. In nonfictional cases, too, as the records of the Salvation Army and the militant suffragette Women's Social and Political Union show, groups of Victorian women gave their reading communities credit for the social work that they performed.[50] However, feelings experienced through reading have never automatically constituted common action; I share Suzanne Keen's critical suspicions regarding an easy leap from readerly empathy to altruistic action.[51] For many of the writers discussed here, the production of specific communities of women, rather than altruism, was the key task.[52] As a gift and by virtue of its diverse strategies for representing gifts, literature developed the meaning of exchanges that would support women's attempts to forge and mobilize coalitions.

Of course, even as women were writing about gift communities, using their own work to target and consolidate audiences of giving women, and treating literature itself as a gift, they were increasingly benefiting from their roles as professional writers. Supporting themselves and their families as never before, female editors, novelists, poets, and journalists were placing their "gifts" on the literary market at least partly in order to profit from commercial transactions. At a time when many women still published anonymously, pseudonymously, or under the auspices of their married names, the construction of writing as a gift eased women's way into the literary marketplace by making their economic ambitions and successes appear more conventionally feminine. But the depiction of literature as a gift was more than simply a mask for women's commercial ventures. Allowing writers to situate their work within a long line of gift exchanges, it connected them to a larger publishing tradition, invited readers to compare fictions and rhetorics of gift-giving with their own practical experiences of exchange, and established a community of readers and activists defined by their imagined relationship to giving.

III. Organization of the Book

This book's six chapters and epilogue are organized in two parts. Part I (Balanced Accounts) demonstrates how single women used gift exchange to construct intimate communities out of scarcity; Part II (Much Obliged) emphasizes the ways in which those alliances were deployed on a larger scale, as groups of women used extreme gifts of sacrifice to further social and national agendas in times of more conspicuous consumption.

In Part I, gift-giving most frequently appears as the mutual, lateral action of individual subjects. The texts considered in Chapters 1 through 3 put this form of giving in the service of nontraditional, egalitarian kinship formation. Whereas Marshall Sahlins's mapping of social relations onto a spectrum of reciprocities suggests that the closest kin are too generous to look for their return gifts,[53] these nineteenth-century narratives imply instead that close female relationships depend upon the reciprocal exchanges Sahlins associates with more distanced relations, such as trade transactions. Mutual exchanges, more than unilateral acts of benevolence, foster and sustain relationships within literary annuals of the 1820s and '30s, Charlotte Brontë's *Jane Eyre*, Elizabeth Barrett Browning's *Aurora Leigh*, and Elizabeth Gaskell's *Cranford*.[54] These texts frequently eschew top-down charity (along with the people who might enter into such exchanges) in favor of more egalitarian relationships that hinge upon the presentation and return of gifts. They feature female donors who create gift communities in their own image and find forms of practical subsistence through gifts. Those with any income or inheritance gain community support by sharing their monetary means; others exchange symbolic gifts of sympathy and secrets in order to enter into community.[55] Stressing scenes of privation and hunger, these texts evoke the dire economic conditions single women of the middling classes faced as increasingly "redundant" members of society and suggest that those women required some assurance of a return. The balanced exchanges portrayed by these narratives offer single women the possibility of generous action without risking the scarce resources they possess. Gift-giving allows them to secure, sustain, and reproduce communities. These texts further attempt to incorporate readers into these networks by calling attention to books' status as gifts and to the reciprocal acts demanded by their reception.

While Part I emphasizes the local formation of community through balanced exchanges, the texts of Part II assume the existence of that community and celebrate sacrifice. Using excessive, seemingly asymmetrical gifts to further civic agendas, women—defined collectively—create spectacles of loss: they deprive themselves of food and clothing, submit themselves to insult and torture, and prepare to give up life itself in order to galvanize social networks. This section highlights the religious valence of women's gift practices as giving becomes part of a more communal ethos. During the second half of the century, women gained additional property rights, entered new professions, and found new outlets for consumer desires. They increasingly had more to give. In Christina Rossetti's narrative poem "Goblin Market" and Anna Jameson's lecture "Sisters of Charity"; in Salvation Army periodicals; and in eugenic novels and pamphlets by late-century New Women including Sarah Grand, Ménie Muriel Dowie, and Charlotte Perkins Gilman, women transformed these economic opportunities into empowering displays of expenditure, even as the language of sacrifice insulated them from accusations of self-interest.[56] Chapters 4 through 6 examine women's social alliances (Anglican and evangelical religious sisterhoods, societies for civic and racial "reform") and show how they used affective and material gifts to make narratives of salvation out of Christian service, slum work, and even eugenics. Appraising gifts as the remedy to an inhumane market or the means for entering it, late-century writers and reformers negotiated the competing value systems of gift and market economies. Their texts register new interest in women's social and financial profits as they simultaneously disavow them through depictions of sacrifice: Rossetti details her heroine's brutal victimization at the goblins' market, while suffragette newspapers glory in the physically taxing hunger strikes of imprisoned protestors.

Attending to the gift practices that established and mobilized communities of women throughout the nineteenth century forces us to rethink assumptions about even the most familiar texts by providing an alternative narrative history of the early women's movement, one that resists simple linear progression. These feminist discourses stress gender "difference" in contrast to other emerging discourses of shared "rights" that have found greater favor in more recent political movements and critical accounts of Victorian women's fiction and activism. They emphasize the unique potential of women's gifts to forge alliances and reform communities. As this book demonstrates, however, the emphasis on sexual "difference" in traditions of giving actually converged with and intensified women's arguments for greater social, economic, and political rights. For the writers discussed in the following pages, women's giving linked such apparently disparate forms of authority as domestic networks and colonial missions. *Bleak House* satirizes the public, political woman; after Mrs. Jellyby's charitable effort in Borrioboola-Gha fails, she takes up "the rights of women to sit in Parliament" and, we are to understand, makes this cause as ridiculous as her earlier project (795). Although Dickens finds both professionalism and parliamentary politics at odds with women's more traditional domestic roles, the works I explore in the rest of this book demonstrate the breadth of possible politics centered in women's giving. With their shared basis in profitable gifts, the formation of women's domestic ties and the political struggle for women's suffrage had far more in common than *Bleak House* overtly acknowledges. In the years before suffrage, traditions of giving at the heart of Victorian feminism authorized women's diverse social interventions. This book reveals the power of these gifts while also bringing them to account, by recognizing, as Jane Eyre once did, that "a present has many faces."

BALANCED ACCOUNTS

CHAPTER 1

Literary Offerings

When the British literary annual *Forget Me Not* (*FMN*) debuted for the 1823[1] holiday season, it changed the face of nineteenth-century publishing. Dozens of British and American imitators competed to present the public with the most elaborately illustrated and elegantly bound books. These 300- to 400-page volumes included tales of adventure and romance, lyric poetry, dramatic scenes, and travel essays; they were widely read but also valued for their silk covers, gilt edges, and engravings.[2] Luxury items selling for between twelve shillings and three pounds each, they were a triumph of the literary marketplace, earning an estimated £100,000 per season for their publishers during their peak years in the 1830s, supporting such well-known authors and editors as Felicia Hemans, William Wordsworth, Letitia Elizabeth Landon, and Alfred Tennyson, and providing less familiar writers with reliable sources of income and audience.[3]

The fact that annuals were such a commercial success may make them a surprising choice for the first chapter of a book such as this one, which explores the alternative economic action of women's gift exchange. But annuals, like many profitable ventures throughout the nineteenth century, blur the boundaries between market and gift economies. Although literary critics and historians have emphasized the annuals' sales over their gift status,[4] at every level of their material production and circulation these books traded on their classification as Christmas and New Year's gifts.[5] Despite the technical distinction between "annuals," which were published serially, and "gift books," which were not,[6] both were regularly marketed and given as presents. Through prefaces, short-stories, poems, and engravings that stress annuals' unique position to mediate gift exchange, the genre repeatedly weighs in on the significance of giving and promises to help receptive readers identify appropriate beneficiaries.

Literary annuals also showcase the increasing agency of middling women as givers in the first half of the nineteenth century. Recent scholarship appears to confirm popular and critical assumptions that the majority of annuals were owned by women.[7] Paula R. Feldman's preliminary study of the volumes' inscriptions indicates that women were the most frequent recipients of these gifts. Male family members were the most frequent givers, but Feldman also notes that "[m]ore than a quarter of these annuals were given by females—a surprisingly high ratio considering what we thought we knew."[8] Annuals were not simply the objects of courtship rituals they were once thought to be, and women were not merely their passive recipients.[9] Beyond this written evidence of some women's physical gift transactions, however, and in addition to the fact that women, as authors and editors, were responsible for much of the literary content of these volumes, annuals more consistently gender gift exchange as feminine by depicting female givers within the volumes and by suggesting that the best kind of reader response might involve women placing their own volumes (or other offerings) in circulation. As I argue, annuals not only shaped the way women imagined giving by modeling scenes and styles of exchange but, by cultivating a larger ethos of generosity for this publishing enterprise, also positioned readers as gift recipients, placing them under the burdens and benefits of gift exchange.[10] As gifts, annuals created a reading community and urged that community to engage in reciprocal efforts—either by passing along the gift of the annual itself or by engaging in the other kinds of exchange it promoted. Annuals are thus a key site for exploring how women's literature helped to construct, not just represent, the giving subjects and networks that this book explores.[11]

I. Benevolent Books, Receptive Readers

The preface to the 1830 *Forget Me Not* proudly advertises its engravings, not because of their beauty, quality, or subject matter but because of the annual's generous transmission of them:

> We rejoice to see that the selfish satisfaction of locking up master-pieces of art for the exclusive gratification of the possessors, is giving way to a more liberal feeling, which induces proprietors of such productions to communicate to others some portion of the pleasure which they afford [. . .]. (*FMN* [1830]: vi)[12]

By making art and literature available to a large audience, annuals such as the *Forget Me Not* claim to be as "liberal" as they are commercially successful. Unlike "selfish" owners who refuse to share their art, these costly yet open-handed productions allegedly produce a "salutary moral tendency" through their generosity, uniting "simplicity of style with elevation of sentiment" (*Friendship's Offering* [1832]: v). The preface to the 1831 *Friendship's Offering* (*FO*) similarly declares that it will not only "impress the mind" and "assist in forming the taste" but also help to "improv[e] the heart" (*FO* [1831]: v–vi). For editors who here equate "liberal" display with moral and aesthetic merit, the classification of annuals as gifts extends from their very production to the holiday distribution that follows. Along these lines, the editor of the 1826 *Literary Souvenir* (*LS*) thanks writers who "have so obligingly favoured me with their contributions" (*LS* xi), promoting the idea that generous gift transactions, not competitive trade, drives the annual market.[13]

Generosity seems to inhere in many of the contributions themselves. James Montgomery often prefaces his poems for the annuals with notes suggesting that they assist in the charitable causes they depict.[14] In the 1830 *Forget Me Not*, for example, "Garden Thoughts" is "[w]ritten on occasion of a ladies' bazaar, in aid of the church missionary society, being held in the garden-grounds of a benevolent family resident on the banks of the Yorkshire Ouse" (*FMN* [1830]: 256). He introduces "An Every-Day Tale" in the 1833 *Forget Me Not* similarly, as a poem "[w]ritten in behalf of a society for relieving distressed females in the first month of their widowhood, to save their little households from being broken up before they can provide means for their future maintenance" (*FMN* [1833]: 115). The motive behind a third poem, "A Cry from South Africa," is equally generous: "These lines were written for the Rev. Barnabas Shaw, of Cape Town, in aid of his appeal to British benevolence to enable him to build a place of worship there for the slaves, of whom there are about forty thousand in the Colony" (*FO* [1830]: 37). Each preamble gives its poem credit for substantial philanthropic action. The poems are written "on occasion," "in behalf of," and "for," datives which could indicate nothing more than the theme or inspiration of each "given" poem. But correlation turns rhetorically into causation; the length and detail of the clauses that follow shift the emphasis from the literary act of writing "in behalf of" to the activist work of saving, relieving, or providing for poor distressed widows and slaves. Generous efforts are ascribed to the poems themselves as much as to the "ladies' bazaar" that enacts them. Here and throughout the annuals, writing is figured as a wide-ranging act of benevolence.

The expectation that these generously constructed books would circulate as equally generous gifts appears in presentation plates that eagerly prompted givers' inscriptions.[15] In the *Forget Me Not*, for example, the image of an open scroll, draped with flowers and ribbon, underscores the importance of text to gift and solicits a gift message by including four blank lines after the single word "*To.*" Like other gifts, annuals established or intensified relationships at least in part by creating an obligation to reciprocate. Promoting the intimacy imagined by such titles as *Friendship's Offering* or *Affection's Gift*, they assign to readers the responsibility to *Forget Me Not*, to *Remember Me*, or to join in a *Pledge of Friendship*. Recipients could discharge this obligation by acknowledging the gift, a reciprocal gesture which at least temporarily "remember[s]" the giver, whether or not any affection follows.

But if annuals are doubly gifts—given to "friends" and also constructed as generous, gift-giving objects themselves—even deep friendship for the giver only fulfills part of a recipient's obligation. Implicit in the annuals' professions of generosity is another debt. These books, sharing liberally, demand that readers give in return. Whereas the holiday transaction itself might be limited to a specific giver and recipient, the symbolic exchange between an avowedly benevolent book and its reader could potentially extend community further, as the annual encourages the kind of gift giving that it also describes. When the annuals offer up scenes of effective giving, they actively solicit social action and show how readers can pass the gift along. Inscribing their readers as recipients, they also conscript them into an imagined network of gift-giving women.[16]

According to some annual authors, the task of becoming an appropriately receptive and reciprocating reader can be fairly straightforward: for a start, she can give away the book that urges the action in the first place.[17] Self-referential stories hint that annuals best serve their benevolent function when they change hands frequently. In Eliza Leslie's "The Souvenir," for instance, which appeared in *The Pearl, or, Affection's Gift* for 1830, an annual becomes the object of repeated gift transactions.[18] Amelia, who is "delight[ed]" to receive the richly illustrated, "elegant" volume as a Christmas gift (108), nevertheless determines that its engravings would be of greater value to her brother's friend, a talented but poor young artist who lacks models for his drawing. She asserts her rights to the gift and then uses it to claim the role of giver: "'When we receive a present, does it not become our own? [...] And we are at liberty to do exactly what we please with it?'" (113). Desirous of "giving it away" to make the artist "happy," and enjoying the "power to offer [...] anything of consequence" (113, 114), she also fears the impropriety of a direct transaction with an unknown boy. Amelia thus presents the "Souvenir" to her brother while expressing her pointed hope that he, too, will give it away as soon as possible: "I do not *insist* on you keeping it for ever [...]. You may give it away again [...]. Indeed, I would rather you should give it away than not— and as soon as possible, too—this very day, if you choose" (115). Changing hands half a dozen times throughout the story to eventually reach the artist, this "Souvenir" signals to readers its importance as a circulating holiday present, the agency (though tentative) of its female owner in this process, and the similar role a reader of the similarly titled tale might hold. The annual (in this case, its "liberal" display of engravings in particular) benefits both men and women, despite— or even because of—the fact that it is initially given to a young lady. The artist's status as the good friend of Amelia's brother underscores the horizontal nature of intimate giving; this is not charity. He will reciprocate by copying the annual's engravings for her. This mediated relationship also reminds us that—as I discuss further with respect to Elizabeth Gaskell's *Cranford*, in chapter three—women could enjoy the "power" and pleasure of gift transactions even when these gifts were indirect exchanges.[19]

Similarly urging readers to share their annuals, Barbara Hofland's "The Gipsy Mother," from the 1835 volume of *The Amulet*,[20] agrees that doing so can have important social consequences. The short story focuses on the aftermath of an affair between a gypsy woman, Ayeshe, and an English farmer, William Hughes, whose prejudiced conception of her family's idleness, ignorance, and immorality prevents him from marrying her (*Amulet* [1835]: 182).[21] After Ayeshe departs with their child in an attempt to free William for higher pursuits, he encounters his first literary annual: the 1833 volume of *The Amulet*, left open on a table in a clergyman's home. Reading in it a story parallel to his own, he experiences the kind of "improve[d . . .] heart" and "impress[ed . . .] mind" that *Friendship's Offering* had earlier associated with the genre. His encounter shows how annuals can motivate action. He begins where the clergyman's daughter, Anna, left off, on the second page of a story called "Grace Huntley":

> William read, and read, not only with his eyes, but his mind, his very soul; audible sobs, quick gushing tears, succeeded; [. . .]. Grace Huntley on the one hand, and his own infant child on the other, possessed him wholly; and at length, dropping the book, he exclaimed, "And did *she* do this?—a poor, weak, trembling, and loving woman! [. . .] and shall I suffer my innocent babe to become the associate of the vile from its birth? No! I will rather search every corner, from sea to sea, to seek and snatch it from perdition; and God grant I may save its mother also!" (*Amulet* [1835]: 187)

This self-referential fiction demonstrates the annual's targeted response. It invites readers to identify with the scene, experience similar sympathy, and see how literature can benefit society by evoking feeling.[22] More than straightforward didacticism, it presents the ensuing action as a necessary reaction to fictional characters as much as to William's "own infant child." The answer to his question ("did *she* do this?") is not merely emulation but also obligation; his dramatic declaration implies that he must act *because* Grace Huntley acted, not simply *as* she once did. His resolution thus responds to a character whose action the passage never entirely spells out but might have been familiar to the annual's first readers, who indeed could have encountered her story in the 1833 *Amulet*.[23] If William can hold onto the story's lesson even as he lets the book fall, it will apparently "possess[. . .] him wholly" in return. It is a two-sided exchange. Annuals, directly addressing readers in lengthy prefaces and literally inscribing them in stories such as this one, solicit and at times even demand a reciprocal action.

William's receptive reading requires the annual's circulation. As Lewis Hyde reminds us, gifts necessarily move.[24] This *Amulet*, like the "Souvenir" of the previous story, changes hands, passing from Anna's to William's before the gift's "issue" (William's tears and intended action) finally promises to benefit Ayeshe and her child.[25] As it turns out, despite his receptive reading, William does not actually have to "seek" or "snatch." The gift-giver in this story is the clergyman's daughter, who is a page ahead of William both in reading the *Amulet*, which she has shared with him, and in resolving the story of the gypsy mother whom, we learn, she has already taken under her wing. By possessing and passing along her annual, a young woman can apparently awaken and "improv[e ...] the heart"; but her job as the annual's recipient does not end there. The task of "sav[ing]" Ayeshe is hers; the most meaningful transactions of this story occur between women, suggesting that even the simple gifts of "a poor, weak, trembling, and loving woman" can be more effective than William's more robust claims to "search" and "save."[26]

Notwithstanding this clear preference for feminine gifts, the story firmly distinguishes between its benefactress and her less privileged recipient, limiting the ranks of "giving women" even as it extends possible membership in that group to its readers. These women are not equal. It is telling that Ayeshe's earlier attempt to benefit William entailed her disappearance. She now repays the clergyman's daughter's aid and religious instruction with "veneration and gratitude" because, as an unmarried gypsy mother, "fallen" and poor, she apparently has nothing else to give (191). The imbalanced exchange creates relations of obligation.[27]

Ayeshe's indebted status is both challenged by and also mirrored in the story's visual prompt. The engraving that accompanies and most likely preceded "The Gipsy Mother" depicts a nursing mother and baby, a pairing often understood iconographically to represent the virtue *caritas*, with the woman as the selfless giver of milk, child, and life (see Figure 1.1).[28] Yet this interpretation, which would emphasize Ayeshe's role as a "giving woman," is complicated by the image's class coding. Although the exposed female form would not have been out of place among illustrations that typically appealed to a mixed audience's erotic desires as much as to their fashion consciousness and sympathetic interest,[29] the hunched "Gipsy Mother," who disregards the breast she bares to both reader and feeding infant, stands out among other images of gracefully elongated ladies clad in contemporary dress, partially draped classical figures, rustic girls, and even other variations on the same theme (see Figure 1.2).[30] Any reading of this "Mother" as a giving agent is undercut by the narrative's emphasis on her role as a charitable object in need of salvation. The clergyman's daughter, not Ayeshe, is the source of the story's gifts. Like other literature in the annuals, "The Gipsy Mother" is more committed to creating a community of receptive middle-class readers and givers than it is to extending that community beyond its target audience. Readers are asked, *as* readers, to identify with this story's givers, changing their hearts, sharing their own books, or assisting other women.

Despite Ayeshe's status as the object of others' gifts, she is not entirely removed from their community. According to the Victorian double standard that held a woman solely responsible for her sexual indiscretions, the best possible charity for a "fallen" woman was marriage.[31] In order to make Ayeshe a fitting wife for William, the story transforms her. With the aid of the clergyman's

Figure 1.1 "THE GIPSY MOTHER" (*The Amulet*, 1835) Reprinted in *The Imperial*, 1839
Special Collections, University of Virginia Library

daughter, she converts to Christianity, rejects the "usual arts of her people," and Anglicizes her name to acknowledge and honor her "young benefactress." As the newly christened "Anna," Ayeshe appears to be "altered exceedingly for the better." William now sees her with "a delight he had never known before; for, under the improving hand of her female friend [. . . .] [t]he gipsy-cloak and head-gear were discarded for the neat and delicately clean habiliments of the Sussex peasantry [. . .]" (*Amulet* [1835]: 190). Hofland's story, eager to show how annuals can shape gift practices, endorses charity across what it calls the "great gulf" of class and race but reserves both "female friend[ship]" and marriage for someone who resembles the clergyman's daughter. Whitewashing Ayeshe with a new religion, appearance, and name ensures that, though gifts might occasionally be extended to the poor or the fallen, the community they form will take the image of the givers. In the closing words of the tale, Ayeshe/Anna is "no longer a gipsy-mother" (191).[32]

Figure 1.2 "THE GIPSY MOTHER"
Fisher's Drawing Room Scrapbook, 1840
Rare Book and Manuscript Library University
of Pennsylvania

Hofland is ultimately ambivalent about the success or sufficiency of this transformation; the new family is quickly shipped off to Canada, far from the clergyman's giving daughter and the annual's first readers.[33] Like other authors in the annuals, she prioritizes a reading network capable of mutual giving over less egalitarian relationships between donors and needy recipients. By removing the gypsy mother from England, her story also expresses anxiety about unequal gifts (and their ability to create Annas from Ayeshes). Similar anxiety about one-sided giving appears in Mary Shelley's tale for the 1837 *Keepsake,* "The Parvenue." The narrator, who has risen in the world by marrying a lord, rehearses a debate we will see again in *Jane Eyre* and *Aurora Leigh* when she sets "patrician charity [. . .], which consists of distributing thin soup and coarse flannel petticoats" against her own earnest "payments of my debts to my fellow-creatures"

(*Keepsake* [1837]: 214–215). Creating a fairly straightforward binary of condescending and "just" approaches to giving, Shelley then undercuts it by burdening the narrator with a family whose incessant requests for aid eventually estrange her from her husband. In the limitless "debts" that "The Parvenue" feels obliged to repay, her gifts, like the patrician charity she dislikes, become dangerously asymmetrical. Estranging her from her husband, these gifts also fail to sustain real intimacy with her blood relations, who take advantage of her too-giving ways.[34] Shelley's story reminds readers that gift-giving requires a degree of self-interest.

This is an important caution for women who, like Shelley's narrator, treat every request as an obligation. It also speaks to the annuals' interest in maintaining social hierarchies. The same impulse that keeps Ayeshe from being welcomed into William's parish and causes trouble between the "Parvenue's" wealthy husband and her own needy family leads Geraldine Jewsbury, in her tale for the 1830 *Forget Me Not*, "The Boor of Brocken," to label an ambitious but chastened cottage-dweller as "Fit only for the station to which thou wert born" (*FMN* [1830] 199). Givers in the annuals do sometimes cross class lines, but they rarely dissolve them. Critical of the ruling classes' patronage (as many middle-class reformers were), annual writers nevertheless found it difficult to assert egalitarian values and also maintain the class authority in which they were clearly invested.[35] Thus they mapped giving along both horizontal and vertical lines, onto an unstable grid of similarities and differences. While many social reformers attempted to confront the overwhelming numbers of those in need by categorizing the poor as either "deserving" (like Ayeshe) or "undeserving" (like Jewsbury's dissatisfied cottage-dweller),[36] literature in the annuals frequently reconciles an attachment to hierarchy with the growing preference for lateral gifts by tweaking the definition of deserving.

To this end, recipients often prove deserving not through merit but through a kind of familiarity effected through transformation or recognition. Rather than forge entirely new connections, gifts in the annuals either mold recipients to resemble their benefactors (as we saw with Ayeshe) or reveal pre-existing ties between giver and recipient.[37] This pattern allows literary annuals to have it both ways: they emphasize generous sentiment and action but don't require readers to imagine reaching too far. As a result, they keep the focus on practices of middle-class giving. Although they frequently lose sight of the consequences of these gifts for the poor by privileging balanced exchanges, this strategy emphasizes donors, bolstering readers' self-identification as givers and enabling them to imagine forms of exchange that do not require great wealth. It is a trade-off which speaks to the way that the early empowerment of some women was bound strictly by class and race,[38] but it also reminds us that the "domestic" literature of the annuals was more than an antidote to men's mercenary, public lives.[39] Gift exchanges in the annuals suggested ways for select women to move beyond

the presumably private sphere of their reading and engage, however problemati-
cally, in community formation.

II. Gifts of Freedom

Literary critics and cultural historians continue to distinguish between the content of the annuals and "topics of many of the periodicals and newspapers of the
day," denying annuals' investments in "politics, current events, radical social
opinions."[40] Yet the gifts that these books embody, describe, and invite allow
readers to address pressing civic affairs. Not only do they solicit sympathetic interest for worthy causes but, by offering gift practices as a solution to social problems, they also make community action homologous to the acts of reader reception
discussed above. In their suggestion that the gift of an annual can resemble gifts
of serious social change, they highlight the public implications of women's private
actions and give their mostly female readers access to important political debates,
such as abolitionism.[41] At the same time, however, the annuals use debates about
slavery primarily in order to advance the interests of their own readers, emphasizing the profit and community available to white readers and activists through—
and frequently at the expense of—their gifts to slaves.

Slavery makes a regular appearance within the annuals. There, abolition, like
charity, is positioned as a gift through a shared rhetoric of compassion and benevolence.[42] An introductory essay in the *Remember Me!* (*RM*) for 1825, for example,
praises England's munificent prohibition of the slave trade, noting that "Slavery,
it is probable, will also soon be abolished in our islands, by the same active benevolence of Wilberforce, best of men" (*RM* [1825]: xviii). In the 1830 *Friendship's
Offering*, the speaker of the anti-slavery poem "The African" contrasts the greedy
world "Of slavery and of pain" with "generous England," where "At last [. . .] They
took away my chain" (*FO* [1830]: 177). And again, in "The Bechuana Boy,"
Thomas Pringle denounces the slave trade as well as the religious hypocrisy of the
"Christians" who participate in its immoral economy:

> The white men gathered round;
> And there, like cattle from the fold,
> By Christians we were bought and sold,
> Midst laughter loud and looks of scorn,—
> And roughly from each other torn. (*FO* [1830]: 33)

The slave boy of this poem, seeking an alternative economy of "human sympathy,"
stands "rejoicingly" in the presence of an English "chief" who will presumably
offer it (*FO* [1830]: 33). In all of these examples, abolition (like the annuals
themselves) is "benevolen[t]," "generous," and "sympath[etic]." By rhetorically

opposing it to the market transactions of slavery ("like cattle [. . .] bought and sold"), the poems proffer abolition as a gift, not a right.[43] This seemingly generous gift has its own rewards, as abolition continues to serve British interests. In exchange for the fact that the English man of this last example "Scornest not the captive's grief," that same captive offers his voluntary servitude: "Then let me serve thee—as thine own—" (33). In such a case, benevolence turns out to be good for business—a fantasy shared (notwithstanding very different consequences) by the competitive, commercial genre of annuals claiming an ethos of generosity and by a nation that prided itself on the "generous" abolition of the slave trade while still importing slave-grown sugar from British colonies in the West Indies.[44] Gifts and markets intersect here in their shared emphasis on advantageous returns. As a gift, abolition was an intimate, personal offering through which writers could simultaneously acquit select "English" characters of British colonial abuses and imagine an expanding public sphere that profited from slaves even as it emancipated them.[45]

This generosity privileges female slaves but requires the near erasure of their bodies or a firm denial that they might have—or desire—any existence independent of European interests. In "The Planter: A West Indian Story" (*FO* 1831), the Englishman John Vivian arrives incognito to inspect his land, which turns out to be the rightful (though temporarily lost) property of Sophie Halstein, daughter of a West Indian quadroon. Sophie catches John's eye because "[s]he was lovely, graceful, virtuous, intellectual, accomplished, modest" (*FO*, 243). A "model for women," Sophie is also modeled after nearly every other English heroine described in the annuals, both in character and in her almost white appearance: "she had a particle—(scarcely apparent, indeed, but still there *was* a particle or two)—a few drops of blood of a warmer tinge than what loiters through the pallid cheeks of an European" (*FO* [1831]: 243). When the vicious manager, unaware of John's identity as landowner, claims Sophie as a slave and orders "eight or ten black slaves" to "[s]eize upon that woman, in the name of your master" (*FO* [1831]: 249, 250), John rushes to her rescue, revealing his identity as master and offering conditional liberty to those slaves: "Obey me, as you value the liberty which every man on my estate shall have if he deserve it" (*FO* [1831]: 251).

John's spontaneous offer of liberty responds to Sophie's particular plight as a woman and possible slave, rather than any longstanding belief in abolition; it is in his immediate interest to protect the woman he loves. The final sentence of the story highlights the gift's sustained power to gratify the giver. "'After all,—the greatest pleasure in the world,' said Vivian, one day to his wife, 'is *conferring* pleasure; and the greatest pleasure which one can confer, is to give *Freedom* to one's fellow-man'" (*FO* [1831]: 252, emphasis in original). As a unilateral "gift," abolition becomes the prerogative of an individual, land-owning Englishman, rather than of the slave violence hinted at by the threat of "advancing negroes."[46] The story subordinates abolitionists' questions of parliamentary reform and human rights to individual benevolence and a white community's shared delight in its power to bestow gifts.

Also missing from the conclusion of this anonymously authored tale is further commentary regarding the racial status of this "wife," whose mixed blood appears not to hinder their marriage. The story explicitly narrates the emancipation of John's "fellow-man" but also, and more subtly, emancipates the octoroon, whose lack of legal protections threaten her body and property. When John initially offers to liberate the slaves, the offer is contingent upon Sophie's release. By extending freedom to all of them, the gift underscores their similar subjection. So, too, does the fact that their narratives have similar endings. Both Sophie and the slaves will serve John by continuing to enrich him, Sophie by bringing property to the marriage, and the (freed) slaves by voluntarily continuing to cultivate the land.

The wrongfully and illegally enslaved woman is clearly privileged in this scenario: the imprecise number of "black" male slaves ("eight or ten") makes them indistinguishable from each other but distinct from Sophie, whose skin is simply "of a warmer tinge"; the drama of her own unjust enslavement effectively makes their captivity a more matter-of-fact condition; and they are the figured as the perpetrators, rather than victims, of violence. The freedom offered also differs. Sophie regains rights to her estate and her body instantly.[47] The slaves, in contrast, can expect to receive freedom only gradually, "in the course of time," and selectively, "if [t]he[y] deserve it."[48]

Thus Sophie is both the privileged wife of a gift-giving Englishman and also a nearly enslaved, racially mixed woman who benefits from these gifts. On the one hand, the story ultimately makes her racial status inconsequential with regard to her ability to hold property and marry an Englishman—a radical move. On the other hand, and in order to do so, it erases any residual trace of her otherness—a move which suggests the author's difficulty representing a free, propertied black woman and stresses her similarity to the Englishwomen for whom the story makes her a model and mirror: the wives, daughters, and sisters of those bestowing the "gift" of abolition. Ultimately calling attention to her physical, social, and legal difference from the male slaves, the story asks readers to recognize themselves or a close relation in her predicament and to sympathize with risks they might share—of sexual assault, servitude, and disinheritance. The "gift" of freedom is extended to a non-white woman, a potential slave in this story, but the woman who receives that gift is so quickly transformed into the wealthy wife of John Vivian that the gift finally appears unnecessary; his parting discourse on pleasure seems to forget that his wife ever benefited from such a transaction. This forgetfulness on the part of the story, like the transformation of Hofland's "Gipsy Mother," again emphasizes the action of gift-giving over the status of the recipient and reminds the annual's readers that giving, which can entail emancipation, provides pleasure and other profits for givers as well as freedom for the enslaved.

Through gifts of freedom to (and, as we will see, also by) women, annuals modeled the strategies of recognition that would become so important to women's reciprocal exchanges and alliance formation in the following decades.

Although the abolitionist implications of these gift strategies were relatively conservative, putting gift practices rather than rights discourses at the center of anti-slavery writing afforded white, middle-class women a voice in movements over which they had no legal sway.[49] John Vivian's observation that "the greatest pleasure which one can confer, is to give *Freedom* to one's fellow-man" would not have been unfamiliar to the annuals' mostly female audience; women had been active in the twenty-year effort to abolish the slave trade (finally achieved in 1807), signing petitions and abstaining from slave-grown sugar in protest. Between 1825 and 1833, dates which correspond to the annuals' peak in popularity, at least seventy-three new women's anti-slavery societies revitalized these efforts, joining a national movement to abolish the institution of slavery itself.[50] Ladies' associations now took the lead in determining national anti-slavery policy, supporting immediate abolition, for instance, when men's organizations were still pressing for more gradual, ameliorative remedies.[51] Like the author of "The Planter: A West Indian Story," they were particularly urgent when presenting the case of female slaves, to whom they claimed affinity. They made joint cases for abolition and women's rights by focusing on the sexually victimized female slave's body. Yet the alliance between white and black women was precarious, as a number of scholars have demonstrated. Not only did it rest upon slaves' victimization, but it underplayed their specific suffering and asserted the superiority of white, Anglo-American women over black women and men.[52]

Abolitionist images and slogans reflect the difficulty of creating balanced exchange out of imbalanced social relations. The familiar 1787 Wedgwood design bears the profile of a single male slave, who kneels before heaven to solicit the "gift" of freedom.[53] Thousands of these jasperware cameos were cast and distributed for free. Markers of generosity through their distribution as much as through the possibility of freedom they depicted, they "came with the particular obligation that they should be given in turn to others."[54] In 1828, female abolitionist societies asserted their own ability "to give *Freedom*" by adopting a modified version of this design. Their version included a second figure, a white woman who stands before the kneeling female slave, visually taking the place of heavenly succor.[55] Circulating this medallion, abolitionist women asked (on behalf of female slaves) "Am I not a Woman and a Sister?" Anne Mellor, Jean Fagan Yellin, and others have rightly emphasized the hierarchical implications of these seemingly egalitarian images.[56] The gift of liberty, here and elsewhere, is an unequal exchange, one that writes racial subordination into the very representation of "sisterhood." But it is also a gift that allows some women and sisters to enter into public dialogue and that makes both terms matter in political debate.

"The Booroom Slave" (Figure 1.3) from the *Forget Me Not* for 1828 resembles but also alters these abolitionist images. In this engraving, a female slave kneels on a beach, clasping her hands and lifting her eyes to an ominous, lightning-streaked heaven. Produced shortly before the official adoption of the female abolitionist medallion, this image differs strikingly from it. Unlike the Wedgwood cameo that shows a slave in profile, this engraving rotates her. The figure kneels

H. Thomson, R.A. del.   *E. Finden sculp.*

THE BOOROOM SLAVE.

Pub. by R. Ackermann, London 1828.

Figure 1.3 "THE BOOROOM SLAVE" *FMN*, 1828
Special Collections, University of Virginia Library

outward, appealing directly to the annual's audience as well as to the heavens for aid. Despite the relatively dynamic pose of "The Booroom Slave," she averts her gaze from the reader, seeking benevolence in a vulnerable, grateful posture.[57] One of many female portraits in the annuals, this passive image of feminine suffering places readers in the roles of benevolent female abolitionist and voyeur simultaneously, demanding their anti-slavery sentiment and making them complicit in the unbalanced exchanges of female abolitionism. Freedom, again, depends not upon slaves' agency but upon readers' generous interest.

A story by Sarah Bowdich[58] accompanies the image of "The Booroom Slave" and highlights many of the tensions underlying such representations of female anti-slavery activism as a gift. The titular slave is Inna, an African chief's daughter who, during the course of the tale, is captured by traders. Before her capture, Inna is part of the Booroom nobility, celebrated for her status and beauty ("Slave," *FMN* [1828]: 38). The story does not open with universal abolitionist claims: in common with many Europeans, Inna's family holds slaves, a practice that is never denounced. But these many slaves vanish quickly from the narrative, dropped in favor of the one upper-class female "Booroom slave" who (like Sophie from "The Planter") more closely resembles her female audience. Along with stereotypically racialized traits (Inna is a wild animal who has to be "tamed") she has other, more traditionally and attractively "feminine" traits. In times of sickness, Inna is a giving woman, gentle, caring, and helpful. Relieving the suffering of others through service and sympathy, her nursing is not unlike the efforts of benevolent abolitionists to confer pleasure through gifts.

Her resistance to male authority similarly aligns her with many abolitionist proponents of women's liberty. Gold changes hands in a betrothal ceremony that makes Inna's first subjection a function of gender, not race; after this transaction, her fiancé joins her father and brother in restricting her movement, "'command[ing her] never again to venture beyond the walls of the quadrangle without a proper escort.' The word *command* did not accord with the free and daring temper of Inna; 'This,' thought she, 'is the good of being betrothed!' and as she silently walked home by the side of Miensa, she resolved, in her own mind, not to heed what he had said" (*FMN* [1828]: 43). Here, Inna's "free and daring temper" ceases to be a trait of racial savagery and instead allies her with the spirit of an emerging women's movement. Yet the text backs quickly away from these interracial affinities. Despite the narrative's brief sympathy with Inna's views, it contains and punishes them: slave traders capture her when she ventures beyond the parameters demarcated by her father, brother, and fiancé. The rest of the story disregards the implicit parallel between this new captivity and her old containment. Faced with slavery, Inna will yearn to return to the kinder bonds of patriarchy.

Only before her capture are Inna's spirited thoughts and feminine service depicted as attractive. After she has been enslaved, the story grows far more ambivalent about women's anger and agency. The pages that follow linger on female victimization; they describe the violence inflicted on the female body and the cruelty of slave traders toward mothers and their children. As the narrative increasingly opposes slavery, however, it also increasingly subdues Inna, espousing interracial benevolence at the expense of (black) feminism. *Now* Inna's spirited manner becomes the source of her suffering: "the proud and thoughtless Inna answered each stroke of the whip by a scowl of defiance, and thus brought double punishment on herself" (48–49). Before Inna can receive the "gift" of independence, she must learn submission. She will escape, but only after she has been reduced to a single suffering female victim—not the type to incite rebellion among women or slaves.

English readers of the annual who have identified with Inna's status, compassion, independence, or courage so far are asked to shift that identification rather abruptly when Inna, having escaped the slave traders but not yet found her way home, encounters an English couple. As she tells her story, kneeling before them, they assure her that "English people never made slaves" and offer to assist her by training her as a servant (64, 66). Inna's subservient posture parallels that of the kneeling slave in the images I have described. No longer in a position to give, she supplicates the Englishman and Englishwoman who, as givers, are now aligned with both the female abolitionist medallion's standing figure and the reader gazing at the annual's engraving. Conferring the status of a waiting maid on a chief's daughter, they complete the diminishment begun by Inna's captivity. In the move from independence to servitude, Inna is infantilized, forced to relearn both language and religion. Once a fluent native speaker she is reduced to broken English; once the chief's favored daughter, she becomes a "savage" who must learn to forgive the slave traders. The story casts aside its earlier gesture toward women's interracial similarities and confirms the Englishwoman's higher status by making her Inna's mistress. Despite the iconography of the engraving's kneeling slave ("am I not a woman and a sister?"), Inna remains outside a "sisterhood" established instead between the annual's readers and the generous benefactress of the narrative.

The hierarchy bends, albeit briefly and partially, as Inna once more steps into the privileged role of giver. Reciprocating her mistress's generosity by tending to her in sickness, Inna asks:

> "Missy, [. . .] Why for you no cry?" "Because, Inna," answered her mistress, "I think the great and good God will take care of me, and I hope he will let me live to see my husband again." "Ah, look, lady! you want to see your husband—you no think I want to see my brother, my father, my mother;—can great God take me back to Booroom?" "Certainly, Inna [. . .]" "Oh then Missy, teach me to pray to God, that I may ask him." (69)

Inna's conversion to Christianity occurs at the moment in which the story again gestures toward the possibility that black and white women might enter into more balanced exchange.[59] Repaying her mistress's aid to her, Inna emphasizes their shared feeling and insists that her mistress recognize her equally powerful family ties. The contrast in grammatical as well as religious authority overpowers this fleeting recognition of likeness, however. Uncertain what to do with a free black woman other than make her a servant and convert her, the narrative returns Inna to her own people. While "The Gipsy Mother" merely rids itself of Ayeshe by sending her to the colonies, this story capitalizes on Inna's departure; she continues to repay English benevolence by acting as a native missionary, converting her family to Christianity. She regains her status as a benevolent, compassionate giver, but only at a distance from her benefactress. In the annuals, the "gift" of freedom is an unbalanced exchange, one that limits the degree of intimacy between recipient and benefactor in favor of the network of implied readers who will recognize themselves as the givers they are being asked to become.

The abolition of slavery in the British colonies shifted the attention of English annuals to other transactions, but in the United States, where annuals became popular almost immediately after their British inception, Maria Weston Chapman's *The Liberty Bell* accompanied an anti-slavery bazaar from 1839–1857. If images such as the frontispiece in Figure 1.4 proclaimed that "Truth shall make you free," "truth" was generally understood to be bestowed by benevolent white women and men distributing books, bibles, and pamphlets. Here, as in its production, marketing, and distribution, *The Liberty Bell* echoed earlier annuals' alignment of gift practices with abolition. Modeled on other popular annuals,[60] it extended the genre's claims to generosity through its sale in a charitable bazaar, which operated according to non-commercial practices and claimed non-commercial benefit.[61] It was made possible by the gifts of well-known writers sympathetic to the cause; British contributors included Harriet Martineau, Lady Byron, and Elizabeth Barrett Browning.[62]

Barrett Browning's "The Runaway Slave at Pilgrim's Point," written for the 1848 volume of *The Liberty Bell*, illustrates the increasingly vexed relationship between abolitionist women's generous gift-giving and the female slaves who incite but are ultimately excluded from these exchanges. Her protagonist repeats the posture of Bowdich's "Booroom Slave"; kneeling at Pilgrim's Point, she imitates "the first white pilgrim's bended knee."[63] This slave, however, refuses to thank "God [. . .] for liberty" that will never be hers (4): "About our souls [. . .] / Our blackness shuts like prison-bars" (38–39). In Barrett Browning's poem, God cannot liberate a soul imprisoned in a slave's body; nor can the slave expect help from the "white [. . .] ladies who scorned to pray / Beside me at church but yesterday, / Though my tears had washed a place for my knee" (110–112). Removing the options of heavenly succor and white sympathy that we saw in Bowdich's tale, Barrett Browning eschews any gesture toward the "sisterhood" offered by

Figure 1.4 "TRUTH SHALL MAKE YOU FREE"   *The Liberty Bell,* 1839 Frontispiece
The Newberry Library, Chicago. Call # Case Y 244.5, Vol. 1.

abolitionist benevolence and refuses to whitewash the woman who insists "I am
black, I am black!" (22, 99).

   This poem, even more explicitly than the earlier British tales, divorces abolitionist action from its possible benefit to slaves. The protagonist proudly distances
herself from the "White men" whose "hunter sons" surround her and from whom
she begs no favors—"Keep off! I brave you all at once" (245, 197, 199). Her
speech, which addresses these hostile slave catchers and the absent "pilgrim-
souls" of her earlier apostrophe (8), ignores her other audience, readers of the
poem and annual who are left to overhear her poignant tale of rape, infanticide,
and recapture. Even as Barrett Browning's dramatic monologue insists upon
distance between slave and reader, the speaker, vividly "tethered to circumstances," forces those readers to confront the specific, political condition of slavery among themselves.[64] Her lack of direct appeal to the reader in favor of her
auditors (imagined pilgrims, present slave catchers) is consistent with the
annuals' increasing emphasis on the transactions within an abolitionist community over any personal exchange between slave and benefactress.[65] Readers of the

poem are unable to aid this particular slave, whose "countless wounds [...] pay no debt" in return (231) and who demands that her immediate auditors "Stand off!" (236). They may feel pity or guilt, yet unlike the readers who receive the specific supplication of the "The Booroom Slave," or the English couple who responds to it, they must ultimately look outside the slave/benefactress relationship to a larger network of giving women if they seek to advance broader abolitionist sentiment or policy.[66] *The Liberty Bell* shared in the tradition of circulation we have seen. As one of this annual's female admirers wrote in 1843, "I am tempted to put it carefully by with my other valuables; but it has rung so many touching appeals... that I think I must circulate it, [... so that it] may awaken [the community's] sympathy and interest, for the poor slave."[67] Like Amelia in "The Souvenir" and the clergyman's daughter of "The Gipsy Mother," recipients of *The Liberty Bell* learned to use their annuals for public benefit in part by keeping the gift moving.

III. Alliance and Exchange

Although *The Liberty Bell* was produced for an American audience in a distinct political climate and published after the British volumes I have considered, Barrett Browning's contribution to it suggests that the interracial "sisterhood" established out of abolitionist gifts—only ever ambivalently expressed in earlier British fiction—remained problematic even for an anti-slavery English author by the 1840s, well after the abolition of slavery in British colonies. During the 1820s and '30s, however, when emancipation was still a pressing question in England, the preference for balanced transactions among white female givers over interracial exchanges prompted two types of revisionist tales in the annuals. One, which I address briefly, removed women entirely from the discourse of abolition-as-gift. The other, which would have a lasting effect on women's mid-century fiction, removed "sisterhood" from the public realm of abolitionism and placed it firmly within a sphere of white women's more intimate gift exchanges. Using gifts to consolidate tightly knit communities, the women in the final pages of this chapter make their own families the recipients of their most significant transactions.

An anonymous example of the first mode of response, "Daddy Davy, The Negro: A True Tale by the Old Sailor," appears in the *Forget Me Not* for 1831. In this emphatically masculinized narrative, the "old sailor" who relates the story opens with the words of his "worthy grandfather, a veteran captain in his majesty's navy" (35). Women's gifts and women themselves disappear from this story, which re-inscribes English anti-slavery activities and English gifts within the structure of patriarchy. A former slave, having received gifts of both freedom and land from the speaker's grandfather, proves unable to maintain himself and comes begging for food. After concealing his own identity and cruelly subjecting "Daddy Davy" to prolonged questioning, the grandfather finally acknowledges and welcomes him. Though (or perhaps because) both "The Planter" and "The Booroom Slave" are invested in defining England as free and freedom loving, neither story is set in England. Closer to home, "Daddy Davy" reveals how anxieties about alliance and exchange come together around the figure of the freed black slave in England who is blamed rather than pitied for his poverty: "we have beggars enough of our own nation [. . .] without having a swarm of black beetles to eat up the produce of our industry" (39). Ignoring the importance of black labor to the "industry" the grandfather claims as his own, the story uses the former slave's mendicant status to justify paternalist racial ideology: slaves, it suggests, will never be the worthy recipients of abolitionist gifts. The familiar title "Daddy" (which a footnote assures readers is a "term of kindness used by the male negroes") is a mockery of familial relations for a former slave and future servant whose place in the "family" will always be an unequal one of dependence and servitude to the man who turns out to be his long-lost "massa" (41) and benefactor.[68] Signs of wasted kindness, not kinship, gifts seem incapable here of establishing either the "sisterhood" that female abolitionists invoked or any other kind of intimate tie.

Authors in annuals also addressed their ambivalence toward (or lack of interest in) interracial gifts of sisterhood by redirecting readers to exchanges within white women's community. In the 1828 *Forget Me Not*, the first pages of the same volume that printed "The Booroom Slave" focus on sisterly exchanges within the family. Felicia Hemans's "The Sister's Dream" portrays a woman visited by her sisters' ghosts while she sleeps. The poem tells of solemn exchanges between sisters: the departed "bequeath'd a mournful home" to the remaining one, whose tender feelings requite this unhappy bequest (*FMN* [1828]: 1). Visually differentiated from images of the "Gipsy Mother" or "Booroom Slave" in the engraving that accompanies the poem, these pale, sororal spirits are depicted in the more elongated style typically reserved for white, bourgeois femininity (Figure 1.5), and their cluster of bent heads attempts to narrow their distance from the living, dreaming sister. Sisterhood is endogamous here. Poems and pictures such as this emphasize the importance of kinship within the immediate family, privileging the private realms of home and sleep over more public action or alliances.

Even romance seems unable to surpass the intimacy reinforced by sympathetic exchanges between sisters. "The Black Seal," a poem by Letitia Elizabeth Landon, substitutes the mutual affection of two orphan sisters for parental or marital relations. These sisters, who anxiously await news of a lover at sea, finally receive a scroll that announces the sailor's death (*FO* [1836]: 362, 364). In the associated illustration (Figure 1.6), sympathy again closes the physical distance between suffering and standing sister. The seated figure receives a comforting embrace and support from the other, who bows her head and holds the black-bordered paper. While one mourns the loss of her love, the other wears a cross that hints at a sororal alternative to male protection, suggesting that the gifts of God and sisters will ultimately suffice. As in the previous poem, this immediate, horizontal tie obviates

Figure 1.5 "Sister's Dream" *FMN,* 1828
Special Collections, University of Virginia Library

any need for relationships constructed out of public benevolence. Depictions such as these no longer attempt to create equal relationships out of fundamentally unequal social relations. Instead, they reroute sympathy back to familiar, even familial, relationships.

Figure 1.6 "THE BLACK SEAL" *FO*, 1836
Special Collections, University of Virginia Library

The final two stories I discuss here similarly and strictly contract communities of "giving women" by making their gifts of greatest benefit to their own sisters. In "The Sisters of Albano," one of two tales Mary Shelley contributed to the *Keepsake* for 1829,[69] Maria leaves her younger sister for a larger religious sisterhood after nursing their ailing mother:

> The nuns thought her an angel, she [Maria] deemed them saints: her mother died [...] and she became one of the Sisters of Charity, the nun-nurses of Santa Chiara. Once or twice a year she visited her home, gave sage and kind advice to Anina, and sometimes wept to part from her; but her piety and her active employments for the sick reconciled her to her fate. (*Keepsake* [1829]: 83–84)

Despite Maria's almost supernatural caregiving abilities, the narrative privileges family ties—hence its ambivalence toward Maria's parting and "fate." Ultimately, however, it approves of the choice that she makes. Santa Chiara's nuns are not merely pious but also active; they are "Sisters of Charity" and "nurses" as well as nuns.[70] Maria's gift practices within this Order come to seem more effective than those generated by worldly passions (84), as her sister Anina is captured and sentenced to death for aiding her hidden lover, an outlaw.

Maria and Anina initially choose to devote their energy to different communities, but the key action of the story returns them to the familial relationship of sisterhood, focusing on these women rather than on the other nuns, the ineffectual lover, or their father, who quickly "yield[s] to [Maria's] superior courage and energy" (91). Persuading Anina to exchange places with her, Maria gives her sister clothing and an identity that she (mistakenly) hopes Anina's French captors will respect: "'[D]earest sister,' she cried, 'I will—I can save you—quick—we must change dresses—there is no time to be lost!—you must escape in my habit'" (93). The sisters, dressed in each other's clothing and bowing their heads in grief, are interchangeable—as is their fate. Maria is killed in Anina's stead, and Anina resolves to reciprocate her sacrifice by entering the Sisterhood: "'God has saved me in this dress; it were sacrilege to change it'" (97).

Shelley's tale unites Maria and Anina as sisters first by blood and then by religious choice, conditions which enable and also emerge out of the story's gifts. Although the religious order of Santa Chiara presumably engages in service, Shelley elides these charitable acts in favor of Maria's more personal gift to her sister, just as Anina's desire to reciprocate her sister's gift supersedes her subsequent acts of service as a nun. Benevolence is thus reserved for and contained within the sororal relationship. The story's solution to exogamous giving is to valorize it (the nuns are "saints") and erase it at the same time through the sisterhood relationship that rhetorically ennobles such giving but restricts it to those sisters already "dearest." Shelley imagines and constructs reciprocal transactions among women who are interchangeable. Set against a backdrop of anti-French sentiment (87, 88, 92, 94), these intimate exchanges constitute sisterhood in its most narrow sense and ask readers to invest in their own closest connections rather than extend them past lines of class, race, or even blood.

Gifts similarly stay in the family in Barbara Hofland's 1830 tale, "The Orphan Family." After fever kills their parents, Elizabeth, Alice, and James are left to fend for themselves—a state which again allows this story to emphasize lateral relationships. Immediately after the family tragedy, their community comes together to offer help: "The awful circumstances [. . .] touched every heart, and opened every hand" (*FMN* [1830]: 135). Despite its efforts, however, this community has limited aid to offer: as is the case for so many women in nineteenth-century fiction and fact, their material gifts cannot match the sympathetic feelings that generate them. When the children's rich but estranged aunt agrees to take in one "clever [. . .] and tolerably pretty" girl under the condition that she "'on no account hold intercourse with the relatives she was leaving,'" the orphans are desperate (136). The aunt's cruel offer, which uses the power of gifting to dictate her niece's affections, throws into relief the less calculated generosity of the eldest orphan, Elizabeth, who persuades her more "delicate" sister Alice to accept the offer.[71]

Initially, Elizabeth's generosity seems to bring her good fortune. She provides for her brother, James, and then marries a kind man who "offered to take both for better and worse" (138). But the story passes quickly over the happiness that brothers and husbands can give. She is a poor, sick widow by the time her sister (now a wealthy lady, unknown to her) and husband come to town. Elizabeth finally "determined to [. . .] throw herself before this charitable pair as an object of pity. Still desiring to claim help though any medium rather than that of downright beggary, she collected her humble merchandise into a basket" (142). (See Figure 1.7.) Elizabeth's desire to work establishes her as one of the "deserving" poor; she does not attempt to raise her "station," like Jewsbury's Boor of Brocken, or rely on handouts, like Daddy Davy.

Her virtue and work ethic would make her a fitting recipient for a wealthy couple's patronage by most nineteenth-century standards, but the giving that this story endorses is more particular than that: it depends upon pre-existing kinship and previous exchanges. Recognizing her own siblings in a scene that treats this recognition as virtuous, Alice acknowledges the connection and "confesse[s] her alliance with poverty" (143). Her husband shows "mercy" toward that confession by taking James as his heir and transferring Alice's dowry to Elizabeth. Elizabeth goes before Alice as a supplicant, and Alice's "confession" is depicted as benevolence rather than balanced exchange; yet the dowry is a gesture of reciprocity, repaying the sister who had once "resigned the goods of fortune for her sake" (144). The transaction thus takes the form of charity while simultaneously limiting its reach by revealing that the would-be donor and recipient are already closely related and mutually indebted.

Figure 1.7 "THE ORPHAN FAMILY" *FMN*, 1830
Special Collections, University of Virginia Library

The story privileges gifts between women and attempts to distinguish between their gifts and those given by Alice's aged husband. (The recognition and money Elizabeth receives are from Alice, while their brother alone becomes his heir.) Nevertheless, this husband plays an important role in the sisters' transaction by approving it and transferring the funds. It is unclear to what extent their new relationship depends upon his approval, but the money, which allows Elizabeth to become a "suitable sister for the elegant Mrs. [Alice] Delville," is crucial (144). By making the sororal relationship at least partly contingent upon patriarchal structures of giving, "The Orphan Family" reminds us that "sisterhood" is not a freestanding construct but—as my discussion of *Jane Eyre* and *Aurora Leigh* will explore in further detail—one that often depended upon and responded to larger financial systems as well as gifts and good will.

For annual readers, however, even these limited exchanges could be enabling. Stories such as "The Orphan Family" suggest that gifts among "suitable sister[s]" can establish intimacy without requiring that women be in control of the purse strings. At a time when coverture made husbands legally responsible for their wives' money and financial acts, the gifts that the annuals propose allow some women to imagine and begin to construct their own alliances out of mutual, reciprocal exchanges, even before popular women's writing challenged property law more directly. Throughout the proliferation of capable nurses, charitable givers, and benevolent abolitionists in their pages, annuals promote women's giving but limit it at the same time, advocating gift practices that engage their readers in current events but finally do so to create semi-closed circuits of balanced, sisterly exchange. In the decades that follow, writers build on these transactions and the benevolent books that showcase them as they work to establish, sustain, and eventually mobilize larger networks of giving women.

Fictions of Reciprocity
in *Jane Eyre* and *Aurora Leigh*

"[D]id you expect a present, Miss Eyre? Are you fond of presents?" [. . .]

"I should be obliged to take time, sir, before I could give you an answer worthy of your acceptance: a present has many faces to it, has it not? and one should consider all before pronouncing an opinion as to its nature."[1]

During an early interview at Thornfield, Jane resists Rochester's "cadeau," preferring to fully assess the implications of the presents that his young ward, Adèle, ecstatically welcomes. This caution reflects Jane's experiences with gifts thus far and is emblematic of the novel's approach to gift practices throughout. From the beginning to the end of Jane's narrative, gifts variously aid and curtail her ability to establish intimate connections. Charlotte Brontë's novel is in many ways a large-scale attempt at taking time to consider the gift and its power to shape relationships. This approach puts *Jane Eyre* (1847) in good company; other mid-century tales of female development, such as Elizabeth Barrett Browning's verse novel *Aurora Leigh* (1857), follow its lead. Although these two works have been united in critical conversation since the latter's publication, the often-cited independence of their heroines and the humbling of their heroes obscure the centrality of gifts to both works. Barrett Browning, as we have seen, contributed to annuals, and Brontë took "detailed notes" on volumes of *Friendship's Offering*, the *Forget Me Not*, and the *Literary Souvenir*.[2] Their narratives continue where the literary annuals of the earlier nineteenth century left off, constructing women's gift practices in a more sustained manner and on an expanded scale. By focusing on the long-term importance of gifts to female development, they ultimately show how the right kind of presents can establish ideal kin relations and also create viable economic means for their subsistence, subverting both economic custom and property law.

Critics typically cast these familiar progress narratives of young, friendless orphans in terms of Jane's and Aurora's personal growth. Whether they attend to the ambiguous social positions of a governess and a laboring artist, respectively, or test these protagonists' affinities to and appropriation of racial and working-class suffering, they focus primarily on the unique development of independent women and their relatively privileged status.[3] Despite its significance for influential psychoanalytical, Marxist, and postcolonial readings of the works, this critical emphasis on individualism elides an equally important strand of interpersonal exchange. Individual development depends upon and also makes possible the networks of giving that will define these works. I argue that plain Jane's progress and Aurora's poetic advancement are also stories about social interaction, about the economic relationships that each forms or discards. Far more committed to community than the individualist approach acknowledges, *Jane Eyre* and *Aurora Leigh* chart the development of "giving women" and reveal how gift exchange and kinship formation are fundamental parts of the trajectory of each heroine's subject position. Making sense of gifts in these seminal feminist texts helps us to better understand the socio-economic visions of *Jane Eyre* and *Aurora Leigh* themselves and how Victorian discourses of giving enabled women to re-imagine their closest alliances.

Attention to gifts also helps us to see how Victorian narratives re-imagined women's relationships to legal theory and practice. At the close of the eighteenth century, when *Jane Eyre* begins,[4] gift exchange was a particularly important economic maneuver for women, who frequently acquired financial agency in spite of, rather than under, the explicit protections or assistance of British common law. At least in theory, if not always in practice, the legal doctrine of coverture undermined women's individual rights to property, making it impossible for wives to earn separate income or enter into contracts without their husbands' consent.[5] Meanwhile, land or "real" property was increasingly bequeathed to male heirs. *Jane Eyre* and *Aurora Leigh* explicitly invoke the common law practices of coverture and primogeniture, but they do so to show how women were not entirely constrained by them. The disinheritance of Jane's mother upon her marriage to a poor clergyman seems to mirror, on a small, personal scale, the pattern of female disinheritance that Ruth Perry traces from the mid-eighteenth through the early nineteenth centuries.[6] Brontë's novel makes Jane's economic dispossession a particularly female condition, even as it uses her rebellious anger at her young "master" and her pointed privation at the Lowood charity school to gesture toward the broader economic and political turmoil of the "hungry forties" that preceded *Jane Eyre*'s publication.[7] Later, in *Aurora Leigh*, women's economic rights and roles come similarly under scrutiny as the poet begins her career through a parallel legacy of disinheritance. Yet in the gift practices of Jane and Aurora, we see other, more optimistic visions of women's economic position and power, reminding us that the common law doctrines of coverture and primogeniture are only two of the most well-known ways through which nineteenth-century women's economic standing was defined. Even before they submitted petitions to challenge the common law, women were working around it to assert forms of economic agency.[8] These narratives are part of that project.

Against this legal landscape, and in contrast to male-dominated publishing conditions that saw *Jane Eyre* pseudonymously authored by Currer Bell and the financial profits of Barrett Browning's poem negotiated by her husband,[9] gifts offered women opportunities to imagine and acquire alternative forms of social and economic authority. As Jane Eyre makes clear from the beginning, however, and as Aurora Leigh will discover, not all gifts are equally beneficial. In their autobiographical narratives, gifts take the guise of welcome, reciprocal overtures that produce close relations or poisonously unilateral, hierarchical gestures that stipulate dominance and dependence. Through these opposing economies, the novel and epic alert us to the doubleness of gifts even as they authorize their protagonists' progress from object to subject of gift transactions. They use that progress to reconstruct both gift exchange and family ties, replacing unequal gifts with reciprocal gestures that constitute affective and seemingly egalitarian forms of kinship. Jane and Aurora will use gifts to search out and create better alliances, developing and reconstituting mutually beneficial relationships as much as their own independent self-worth.

I. Jane's Inheritance

The gifts that characterize Jane's early years and that her narrative subsequently attempts to supplant are unequal exchanges, typified by the "cold charity" she receives from the Reeds and Mr. Brocklehurst and that she still dreads reverting to many years later (276). At the novel's opening, orphan Jane lives "under obligations" to her relatives (10), the poor object of one-sided gifts she can never repay.[10] Demanding returns of gratitude and subservience, her aunt places Jane in a position of perpetual dependence while passing herself off as an "excellent benefactress" among her acquaintance (27).[11] Years later, at Thornfield, Jane will reject Rochester's gifts when they appear similarly tainted.[12] Shopping for her trousseau, she distrusts the "unnatural and strange" clothing he offers her (220) and the degraded sexual status it implies because the purchases would again leave her "crushed by crowded obligations" (230).[13] In place of unequal gifts, Jane desires balanced exchange: "you shall give me nothing but [...] [y]our regard: and if I give you mine in return, that debt will be quit" (230). For Rochester, however, who smiles like a "sultan" at Jane and claims that he "would not exchange this one little English girl for the grand Turk's whole seraglio" (229), gifts are a form of domination. As much as he despises the foreign women he has formerly purchased with "satin and jewels" (123), he has not yet learned to embrace alternative models of exchange. The gifts Jane receives from Rochester and Aunt Reed are dangerous, material counterparts to the etymological slippage that Mauss and others have noticed between the meanings of present and poison in German.[14] Brontë explicitly gestures toward this slippage in Rochester's remarks.[15] Fearing that Jane, to

whom he has promised an unspecified gift, will inquire too closely into his clos-
eted personal affairs, Rochester exclaims, "'Don't long for poison [. . .]!'" (223)
When Jane describes opening the "costly" wedding present that he has sent her
against her wishes, he asks, "'Did you find poison, or a dagger, that you look so
mournful now?'" (239, 240)

If gifts are frequently poisonous in the first chapters of her life, however, Jane
will find an antidote in the open hearts and hands of the Rivers sisters.[16] Penniless
and hungry after her arduous flight from Thornfield, she receives room and board
from these new friends but proclaims herself "no beggar," affirming that she has
"kept myself; and, I trust, shall keep myself again" (290). Shabbily but respectably
genteel, she resembles the women who take her in. "I liked to read what they liked
to read: what they enjoyed, delighted me [. . .]. Thought fitted thought, opinion
met opinion: we coincided, in short, perfectly" (298).[17] Matching her new bene-
factresses in temperament and taste, Jane conforms to the standards set out by the
literary annuals for receiving gifts;[18] she feels akin to Mary and Diana Rivers long
before she learns that they are her blood relations. An example of the popularly
depicted *cri du sang* which privileged blood relations in fiction, these cousins "are
drawn to" each other, despite being "ignorant of their connection."[19]

The perfect union they share is more than a function of kinship. Jane's earlier
benefactors included cousins who were hateful to Jane and to each other.[20] Part
of what allows the women to experience such affinity to one another is that the
Riverses' assistance does not demand subservience. Diana calls Jane a "visitor"
and, treating her as such, quickly forbids Jane's attempts to help in the kitchen
(293). In contrast to her earlier days of dependence, Jane is no longer expected to
work "for [her] keep" (9, 24). Mary and Diana offer a different kind of gift here,
one that constructs a more sympathetic connection by treating Jane as a peer.[21]
Even before they are revealed to be kin, their gifts constitute grounds for alliance. St. John Rivers offers yet another foil to his sisters' caregiving. In place of
the "spontaneous, genuine, genial compassion" that secures the women's affectionate bonds, he practices a more distant, impersonal "evangelical charity" (296).
Their opposing versions of exchange derive from and produce different relationships. St. John "[can] not sympathise" in his sisters' feelings (299, 335) and considers kinship "a matter of no moment" (328). His demands, like Mr. Rochester's
gifts, require Jane to "disown half [her] nature" (339). Reclaiming herself among
the Riverses, Jane finally establishes her own version of giving. More calculated
than that of Mary and Diana but also more invested than St. John's in constructing social relationships, her gifts will allow her to establish both independence
and kinship.[22]

When Jane inherits £20,000 and immediately decides to share that inheritance
evenly with her cousins, her gift acquires legal as well as social and financial significance by allowing her to bypass a number of nineteenth-century restrictions
on women's property rights. Most critics have focused on how Jane's newfound

wealth enables her to marry Rochester on equal or superior footing.[23] She is an independent woman when Thornfield is in ruins. Her refusal to keep the entire sum (326) is typically read as the suggestion that her riches will not make her selfish; she offers a moral contrast with Eliza Reed's hoarding (24) and Rochester's association with Eastern excess.[24] More recently, Mary Jean Corbett has shown how Jane's redistribution of wealth resolves family conflict set in motion by a previous generation.[25] None of these readings, however, addresses the mechanisms by which she receives and redistributes such an immense gift, the motivations for her generosity, and the nature of the newly reconstituted family that she so richly endows. By exploring these aspects of her gift transaction, we can see how Jane transforms a patriarchal inheritance into a means of establishing and sustaining kinship outside conventional marriage and closer than bloodlines or common law would otherwise dictate.

Despite the initial silence with which she greets it, her inheritance is hardly a surprise. Jane first meditates on the possibility of being her uncle's "legatee" when, "annoy[ed] and degrade[ed]" by Rochester's insistence that she choose silks for her trousseau, she thinks that if she "had but a prospect of one day bringing Mr. Rochester an accession of fortune, [she] could better endure to be kept by him now" (229). Writing to Madeira that very day, she sets in motion the chain of events that will interrupt her wedding and eventually make her an heir. This point has interested scholars for its hint that Jane's anger plays a role in disrupting the bridal ceremony,[26] but it is largely forgotten in discussions of the inheritance. Yet by informing her uncle of her welfare and whereabouts, she essentially lays claim to the legacy he once hoped to bequeath to her. Safely away from Thornfield and a bigamous marriage, she again makes herself known when, in "some moment of abstraction" (325), she writes her full name, rather than her alias, on a portrait-cover. Signing *Eyre*, she also reasserts herself as *heir*.[27]

Jane temporarily loses both her legacy and her groom when she learns about Bertha and flees Thornfield. The delayed gratification is significant, as is the order in which she reassumes both property and husband. Only by inheriting her fortune between weddings, when the prospect of marriage is dim, is Jane able to distribute her uncle's wealth. Coming into her money as a married woman would merely grant her initial wish of bringing fortune to Rochester, by making the £20,000 his alone. As Mrs. Rochester, Jane would have no right to possess separate property.[28] Of even greater importance here, Jane would have no right to divide that property, either during her life or after her death. During the eighteenth century and most of the nineteenth, legal transfers of property, either by gift or by will, required a husband's consent, unless that property had previously been secured as a wife's separate estate.[29] Even engaged women could not give away property because, in the words of the *Westminster Review*, such a transaction "would be a fraud practised upon her intended husband."[30] The revelation of Jane's identity only in her "moment of abstraction" hints at the difficulty that women faced in attempting to inherit or bequeath property independently. In common law, if not always in practice, wives notoriously lacked economic agency until the Married Women's Property Act of 1882;[31] Jane is able to act as a "*feme sole*" with respect to her inheritance only because her engagement and marriage are temporarily aborted.[32] Thus the deferment of her wedding makes possible her fleeting possession of £20,000 and her immediate gift of £15,000. It allows her to benefit her cousins and, simultaneously, to limit the wealth that her (future) husband will acquire.

These transactions are all emphatically couched in legal terms. Jane's signature, "written down, fairly committed to black and white" and the words "Legacy, Bequest" that she broods over as she begins to "ponder business" (325) frame the gift as an expression of her legal agency even as she is acting against common legal practice. That Jane thinks of her gift as "equity" toward her cousins and shares it through the official "instruments of transfer" which her judge and lawyer draw out show her ability and willingness to operate within this presumably masculine sphere (331). By separating Jane from Rochester, Brontë gives her temporary but sufficient access to the legal maneuvers, documents, and property rights that her marriage will officially take from her. These documents are obscured in the larger context of Jane's more privileged, autobiographical authorship, just as the novel's commercial circulation is obscured through the story's emphasis on gift transactions and "dear" readers. But even as the novel deflects attention away from its own financial know-how, it enables Jane to turn her uncle's property—the tainted legacy of colonialism and of his bitter quarrel with the Riverses' father[33]—into an intimate transaction that allows her to determine her own alliances while single and maintain those relations when married.

By redistributing her fortune, Jane challenges the primacy of her uncle's legal document and also acts against the predominant inheritance laws of her time.[34] When Gateshead's John Reed evokes primogeniture by declaring to Jane that "all the house belongs to me, or will do in a few years" (8), he gestures toward his own sisters' relative disinheritance, in addition to Jane's. Blanche Ingram's despicable fortune-hunting signals a similar dispossession; she pursues Rochester's wealth because her father's estates are entailed on her eldest brother (136).[35] Primogeniture even shapes the tragic life of Bertha Mason Rochester, whose marriage brings Rochester the wealth otherwise denied to him by his father's refusal to divide his property. As the insane Mrs. Rochester, Bertha is trapped by inheritance—both financial and hereditary—that she cannot control. The former serves to "secure" her husband and then, when he inherits his brother's estate and finds her wealth unnecessary and her habits distasteful, the latter justifies her imprisonment (260–261). Bertha acts out against this "inheritance," but her violent methods lack the subtlety of Jane's legal maneuvers, and she serves more as a cautionary tale of women's legal difficulties than as a viable model for challenging them.

However, primogeniture, like coverture, was never the only option for women, even if it was the one overwhelmingly featured in fiction and prescribed by common law. Eliza Reed's ability to "secure" her own fortune (200) against her brother's gambling losses suggest that she, too, has separate and sufficient provisions, despite the consolidation of land in her brother's hands.[36] By similarly grounding Jane's new wealth "in the English funds" (325) rather than in land, the novel supports Amanda Vickery's observation that even women without "real" property might comfortably receive other, moveable goods instead.[37] But by dispersing this wealth during her own life, instead of after death, Jane not only reverses her uncle's decision to amass family property for one specific heir but also challenges the general cultural imperative to accumulate, rather than share, fortune during one's life; "it is contrary to all custom," notes a startled St. John (330).

Through Jane's gift, the novel also reverses the prevailing kinship patterns that Perry has observed throughout the early nineteenth century: the distribution of Jane's inheritance to her cousins emphasizes blood ties over conjugal bonds. Husbands are at least momentarily absent from her financial plan. "'Marry! I don't want to marry'" (330). This reprioritization of kinship is something of a convenient fiction, of course. As recently as the previous chapter, Jane has dreamt of Rochester's love and "the hope of passing a lifetime at his side" (312). By disavowing these lingering desires at the moment of inheritance, however, she keeps the focus squarely on blood. Through the inheritance Jane receives and the gifts she then makes of it, the novel creates an alternative to the marriage plot, one that privileges "kindred" over heterosexual union (330). When it turns out that she can have both relationships, and on her own terms, it is notable that she neglects to mention her division of fortune to Rochester.[38] Telling him of her "accession of fortune, the discovery of [her] relations" (375), she condenses and even conceals this episode, simply informing him that her dead uncle "'left [her] five thousand pounds'" (370). She cultivates his romantic jealousy of St. John but, perhaps wisely, avoids stirring up the feelings that a man in reduced circumstances might experience upon learning that 75 percent of his potential income has been irrevocably signed away.

Jane invests in three possible domestic arrangements before returning to the one she will share with Rochester. Instead of endowing her (future) husband with a fortune, she secures a "competency" for her cousins, allowing Mary and Diana to quit their positions as governesses and subsidizing St. John's future missionary work. The transaction makes amends for her uncle's antagonism toward the Rivers family, as Corbett observes,[39] but it also transforms the nature of their kinship. Rather than simply replace one set of "bad" cousins with a better one at the end,[40] the novel substitutes a closer connection.

As soon as she learns what their blood relationship is, Jane changes it, clapping her hands for joy that she has "found a brother [...] and two sisters" (328). "'You [...] cannot at all imagine the craving I have for fraternal and sisterly love,'" Jane insists, against St. John's protest that she might regret dividing her wealth. "'I never had brothers or sisters; I must and will have them now'" (330). And even though (for various reasons) St. John does not live up to his promise to treat her as a sister,[41] Mary and Diana are willing and eager to embrace the new relationship. The rhetorical shift from cousin to sibling, though sudden, would not have been as surprising to a Victorian audience (or to Jane's turn-of-the-century companions) as it may be today. Naomi Tadmor has shown how kinship names defied rigid classification in eighteenth-century England, and throughout the nineteenth century, *sister* served as a flexible shorthand for affective, religious, professional, and erotic alliances, as well as for biological kinship.[42] That this shift to a closer affiliation has, for Jane, everything to do with her ability to give them an inheritance, is yet more striking. A woman's gifts—here, and elsewhere in Victorian literature—are instrumental in altering the nature of kinship. Jane scoffs at St. John's promise to "'be your brother— my sisters will be your sisters'" without sharing her fortune (330). "'Brother? Yes; at the distance of a thousand leagues! Sisters? Yes, slaving amongst strangers! [. . .] Close union! Intimate attachment!'" In her view, and in the relations between women that the novel bears out, the most intimate connections depend upon gift transactions that operate contrary to legal customs or social traditions.

Hearing that the Riverses are her "near kinswomen," Jane instantly starts thinking about her money. No longer a "ponderous gift of gold" (328) or a "mere bequest of coin,—it [becomes] a legacy of life" (329) as soon as she can share it, as soon as it allows her to (re)construct kinship ties. Jane's transaction does more than simply purchase the closer connection. It allows her to reciprocate and keeps them in the same class bracket, much as their refusal to let her help with kitchen work once did. On the one hand, she thinks of this gift in terms of equality, calling it "justice." On the other, though, and more emphatically in her subsequent arguments, it is part of a larger pattern of exchange that recalls her earlier experiences being under obligations and reminds us that she is not overwhelmingly eager to form close alliances with women in general—with Bertha, for instance, or with Adèle—if they have not previously benefited her. Until she has the power to provide for her cousins with this "ponderous gift," she remains the indebted object of their apparently weighty gifts. "Those who had saved my life, whom till this hour I had loved barrenly, I could now benefit" (328). "Barren," not a commentary on the quality of her feelings or the degree of her love, speaks rather to her inability to give back material assistance to the friends who have offered her a home and livelihood. (While Jane finds love without issue or reciprocal benefits uncomfortable, "barren" attachments and fertility itself acquire even greater significance by the end of the century, as we will see in Chapter 6 of this volume, when female reproduction itself takes on new meaning in terms of gifts.)

Jane is explicit about the importance of reciprocity: even more valuable to her than the immense fortune of £20,000 is "the delicious pleasure [. . .] of repaying, in part, a mighty obligation, and winning to myself life-long friends" (330). In this representation of the case, the "justice" of having equal shares in their uncle's wealth loses out to the more pressing imperative that Jane balance her accounts. Redistribution becomes, first and foremost, repayment for her own "mighty" debts. By receiving an inheritance, Jane becomes a giving subject, capable of matching or exceeding her sponsors' largesse. Her transaction even earns interest. More than simple reimbursement, it settles her debt and then goes further, "winning" lifelong friends or "sisters," as she will continue to describe her relationship with Diana and Mary. The kind of kinship that Jane hopes to secure here requires reciprocity in gift-giving, and suggests that if there *is* to be any slight imbalance, it should favor the new giving subject. Indeed, Jane's newly endowed pocketbook allows her to become the benefactor in less intimate relationships, "taking care that the parting should not be barren on my side" when she closes her rustic village school (331). Once she has become the comfortable, money-owning subject, capable of paying and repaying through gifts, she welcomes the position of donor in the one-sided, cross-class transactions she shrank from as a powerless recipient. Like the literary annuals I have discussed, and from which Brontë may have drawn inspiration,[43] the novel is more interested in the gift practices of middling women than in the results of those gifts for the poor.

Through Jane's shared inheritance, as we have seen, the novel renegotiates the terms of women's property and kinship formation. Jane's gift also allows the novel to stage a debate about other contemporary economic laws. By privatizing the dispersal of wealth, *Jane Eyre* takes a stand on nineteenth-century questions of taxation and the relative responsibilities of individual agents and public policies. Jane's refusal to keep her full inheritance, her compulsion to use it to repay services and benefit a larger community, initially appears to conform to and even implicitly endorse the system of duties imposed upon legacies and transfers of property at that time. Between 1796–1815, dates which mirror the approximate action and retrospective narration of *Jane Eyre*, the need for greater wartime revenue changed the British government's approach to property rights.[44] Inheritance taxes in particular came under scrutiny, as economic theorists and budget-pinched politicians increasingly sought to ensure that, legally speaking, there could be no free gifts.[45] Although inheritance taxes were nothing new to England or to Europe, they had been studiously evaded for centuries, making them unreliable sources of income for a war-strapped nation.[46] A more rigorous system was implemented in 1796.[47]

The new inheritance laws privileged direct, lineal descendants of the deceased, taxing distant connections at higher rates. Legally speaking, the Riverses would be under greater tax obligations as Jane's cousins than they would be as her siblings, offering yet another possible reason for her kinship conversion, and another clue that *Jane Eyre* does not simply abide by nineteenth-century legal codes.[48] In 1795, as these laws were being revised, philosopher and legal theorist Jeremy Bentham proposed an even more dramatic way to regulate the inheritance that distant relations could receive. Arguing to "*limit*[. . .] the power of *bequest*," he advised that, in the absence of "near relations," all property should revert to the state, and suggested that in the case of any relations not in direct line of descent from the deceased, including nieces and nephews, the public should be entitled to half of a testator's property.[49]

Later, agreeing with Bentham's proposal, his disciple John Stuart Mill also reasoned that large taxes should be levied upon inheritance. "It is not the fortunes which are earned, but those which are unearned, that it is for the public good to place under limitation."[50] Despite the different audiences and aims of theorist and fictional character, Mill's proposal echoes Jane's partial repudiation of "gold I never earned and do not merit!" (330) and her sentiment that fortune should promote the "public good" as well as one's own private interest. Eager to "benefit" the kin community "who had saved [her] life" (328), and asserting that she is "not brutally selfish, blindly unjust, or fiendishly ungrateful" (329), she seems as ready as Bentham and Mill to limit her own bequest and thus fulfill an acknowledged duty toward a common good. Viewed in this way, Jane is hardly reveling in sacrifice when she redistributes her fortune, despite suggestions by both St. John and Rochester that this is her preferred mode of giving (344, 379).[51] Not only does she ultimately receive as much as she has ever "calculat[ed] on" (326) but the division of wealth becomes her part of the "equal sacrifice" that, according to Mill, was "demanded from all" to ensure the public good, not a one-sided offering but a reciprocal act of civic or social exchange.[52]

Despite the commitments it seems to share with Bentham and Mill, however, Brontë's novel ensures that its heroine, not political theorists, will determine what constitutes the "public good" or "near" relations. "Public" has different meaning for them. Mill endorses Adam Smith's notion that "[t]he subjects of every state ought to contribute to the support of the government" insofar as they receive its benefits.[53] Jane, in contrast, credits her own local family network with the "protection" that Smith, Bentham, and Mill assign to the state.[54] Whether or not the law was truly a "bachelor," as Charles Dickens once quipped,[55] Jane Eyre makes it clear that the law privileged men over women, whose condition, single or married, depended greatly upon the kindness of their kin. But by making Jane's division of wealth a function of personal choice rather than legal imperative, the novel allows private feelings of affection and reciprocal obligations to govern her prevailing sense of duty. It suggests that intimate alliances offer women greater benefits than those they receive through legal systems. And it gives those private relationships larger social significance by allowing a single, personal gift to reshape a woman's experience of property, inheritance, and family.

II. "An[other] Undowered Orphan"

Aurora Leigh, like Jane Eyre, is raised in the cold comfort of an aunt's measured "duty" (Book I: line 361).[56] Observing this aunt's charitable work—"knitting stockings, stitching petticoats, / Because we are of one flesh after all / And need

one flannel (with a proper sense / Of difference in the quality)–" (I: 298–211)—
Aurora learns how unequal gifts can enforce hierarchies of difference and power
within the façade of "one flesh." Their early experiences sensitize both Jane and
Aurora to the complexities of giving. Whereas Jane must acquire the ability to
give, Aurora's developmental trajectory takes another direction. She must learn
how to receive.[57]

"An undowered orphan" from Italy (II: 606), Aurora is the poor offspring of a
wealthy line because her English father's foreign marriage violated a legal clause in
the estate's ancestral provision. "'Child,'" her aunt informs her, "'your father's
choice / Of that said mother, disinherited / His daughter, his and hers'"
(II: 606–608). Barrett Browning follows Brontë's lead, presenting women's legal
economic disabilities as a private affair in order to suggest how matters of women's
property had everything to do with marriage but might be renegotiated through a
shifting of intimate alliances.[58] Again, as in *Jane Eyre*, only one "generous cousin"
(II: 631), the philanthropist Romney Leigh, will inherit the family wealth. He, too,
feels the weight of an unequal legacy and wishes to benefit the cousin he loves. In
this case, however, his sex changes the methods and meaning of redistribution.
Gifts come less easily from men than from women in these mid-Victorian tales of
women's development. Aurora's inheritance, though it differs from Jane's, will similarly enable her to give, but she has not yet learned that reciprocal gifts can prove
as mutually beneficial as personal income in combating Victorian property laws.

Proposing marriage to Aurora without mention of these financial matters,
Romney initially seeks to share his inheritance not through division but through
union, covertly taking advantage of coverture to make his wealth hers. Aurora
rejects his offer before learning of its financial underpinnings, but once she understands his intention, she refuses him even more adamantly. "Do we keep / Our
love to pay our debts with?" (II: 716–717), she muses.

> Romney now was turned
> To a benefactor, to a generous man,
> [. . .] If I married him,
> I should not dare to call my soul my own
> Which so he had bought and paid for [. . .]. (II: 773–774; 785–787)

Speaking of gifts as a "danger" averted (II: 655), Aurora Leigh treats a financially
advantageous marriage in much the way that Jane Eyre treated the jewels Rochester attempted to buy for her, as an unequal sexual contract, generosity that her
independent soul can "ill afford" (II: 802). Both women know that—even with
love (II: 801)—marriage is a hazardous playing field for gifts.[59] In Aurora's case,
remaining single keeps her free of a benefactor and allows her to pursue and profit
from her own poetic labor. For Barrett Browning, who had signed the unsuccessful
petition for Married Women's Property reform earlier in 1856, Aurora's rights to
her art, income, and "soul" alike depend upon her publishing that art while single.[60]

Romney accepts his cousin's rejection of his heart but finds it more difficult to accept her repudiation of his wealth. He is uncomfortable with laws that force him to "make [her] poor by getting rich" (II: 1028). Marital union failing him as a method for sharing his riches with Aurora, he next attempts to divide the money itself, by making a gift of £30,000 to their aunt. Borrowing Jane's legal savvy, but less open in his dealings, he then cites this deceased aunt's will to Aurora in order to legalize his gift:

> "You're richer than you fancy. The will says
> *Three hundred pounds,*[61] *and any other sum*
> *Of which the said testatrix died possessed.*
> I say she died possessed of other sums." (II: 987–990)

Aurora is skeptical of his word and still unwilling to be the object of his or any gifts. "'I, who share your blood, / Am rather made for giving, like yourself, / Than taking, like your pensioners'" (I: 1005–1007). If Romney presumes to use the law to assist his giving, moreover, his cousin proves his match in legal debate. "'My aunt possessed this "sum,—inherited/" From whom, and when? bring documents, prove dates'" (II: 1018–1019). As they battle out "'claim[s]'"—of "'woman's etiquette'" as well as those "'of nature, law, and right'" (II: 1038–1039)—they find that in this case gifts cannot unilaterally remake inheritance.

Romney's admission that their aunt "died possessed of" but did not inherit the money is a significant detail. Any sum, any "pittance" she had received through "heritage" would revert to Romney (II: 639, 1067), according to legal arrangements that would effectively consolidate Leigh property for the benefit of its single male heir. Their aunt's most impassioned statement to Aurora comes in her explanation that her hands are tied, equally in life as in death:

> "For when I die and leave you, out you go,
> (Unless I make room for you in my grave)
> Unhoused, unfed, my dear poor brother's lamb,
> (Ah, heaven,—that pains!)—without a right to crop
> A single blade of grass beneath these trees,
> Or cast a lamb's small shadow on the lawn,
> Unfed, unfolded!" (II: 595–601)

Unable to bequeath her "handful" to her niece (II: 591), she is aware of the great importance of landed property and understands what the loss of this synechdo-chic "grass" and "lawn" will mean for Aurora's survival as well as her status. Never as tender as when she explains her own inability to give, the aunt serves here as a tragic reminder of the vital importance and difficulty of women's financial gift transactions in the legal landscape of the nineteenth century. Jane saves her cousins from "slaving amongst strangers" through her own reworking of bequests (330). Charitable Aunt Leigh, in contrast, has no personal wealth to dispose of. Even if she, like the nephew and niece who share her blood, is "made for giving," she lacks the means to do so; enjoying family riches in her own lifetime but incapable of either possessing this property in her own name or sharing it with her female kin, she dies a victim of property laws that privileged male ownership.[62]

Romney attempts to bypass these laws and his aunt's impotence by making her a "deed of gift" (II: 1083). Drawn up properly through a court of equity, this substantial transfer could potentially make Romney's £30,000 his aunt's "separate estate," not subject to the reversions of her other life-ownerships and consequently able to be bequeathed as she wishes.[63] Aurora astutely understands this difference between "heritage" and "gift," acknowledging that if her aunt has indeed accepted "[a] gift intended plainly for her heirs" (II: 1091) it will bind her legally, forcing her to accept as her own rightful legacy the cousin's gift that she had determined to reject.

Ultimately, however, to her own delight and his dismay, Aurora is not "snared" by this gift (II: 1093). Contrary to Derrida's twentieth-century philosophical assertion that the recognition of a gift dissolves it,[64] for Aurora as for other nineteenth-century women in fiction and practice, gifts require some kind of acknowledgement. Victorian literature and subsequent gift theories diverge here, primarily with respect to the practical implications of gift-giving for women. The intensity with which Aurora debates and discusses Romney's offer points to its insolubility in the life of a mid-Victorian woman; neither the gift itself nor its affective aftermath will vanish as quickly for Aurora as Derrida seems to suggest.

Legally speaking, then, gifts require delivery and acceptance, as our protagonist is quick to point out.[65] "'This gift of yours / Was tendered . . . when? accepted . . . when?' I asked. / A month . . . a fortnight since?'" (II: 1103–1105) Although Romney asks "'What matters when?'" (II: 1108), Aurora's precision gives her the legal edge—another suggestion that women were not entirely the passive victims of economic laws. She realizes that gifts are not simple, unilateral gestures but multifaceted transactions. Showing him the letter "'(unread, mark, still sealed) / [. . .]' found enfolded in the poor dead hand'" (II: 1130–1131), she opens and then tears it up, finally dispelling his attempts to share his wealth through joint inheritance or equitable gift:

> "Here's a proof of gift,
> But here's no proof, sir, of acceptancy,
> But rather, disproof. Death's black dust, being blown,
> . . . .
> Dried up for ever the fresh-written ink,
> Annulled the gift, disutilised the grace,
> And left these fragments." (II: 1155–1162)

In this final repudiation of Romney's generosity, Aurora anticipates Mauss and other theorists by insisting that acceptance, as much as giving and reciprocating, is central to the structure of the gift.[66] But unlike the giving most frequently discussed in anthropological accounts, the gift loses its power in Aurora's case because she is willing and able to reject it, suggesting another way in which Victorian authors imagined even portionless women engaging with gifts as agents, through negation. The sealed letter seals the case; had their aunt read it, her acceptance might be presumed, but, as Aurora insists and as Romney accedes, her ignorance amounts to refusal, annulment. The dead cannot accept gifts.

Aurora appears to triumph over Romney, whose eyes well up in "despondent and surprised reproach" (II: 1173). Her deeply individualist triumph, which many critics have appropriately praised for its establishment of Aurora as an autonomous artist-worker not subject to marital laws of coverture, has a steep opportunity cost, as she will come to realize later. It takes her further from the interpersonal relations that this autobiographical progress narrative, like *Jane Eyre*, will ultimately privilege—a fact more easily discernible here because of Romney's key role in the early and final chapters of Aurora's narrated life. Through Aurora's subsequent regrets, we see that even as this triumph over the gift allows her to embrace her own independence, her vocation, and eventually her income, she loses out through her inability to recognize other people's capacities to give or to consider the kind of alliances that mutual gifts can establish. Thus despite her achievements, she misses the mark with respect to the gifts that dominate this protracted episode and pervade the *Künstlerroman*. Using gifts as more than a placeholder for marital ownership or a way to distance the artist from financial concerns, this verse novel suggests that they can solidify or foreclose the intimate relationships on which *Aurora Leigh*'s social narrative (if not necessarily her professional development) depends.

When Aurora learns of Romney's next one-sided attempt to arrange kinship through gifts, she reveals that her earlier concern centers not on the fear that marital property laws might make women in general the indebted objects of exchange but simply on the fact that she herself, certainly in her poetic production and possibly through a generosity we have not yet seen, is "made for giving." As Aurora pursues her art, Romney takes up social work and engages himself to the working-class Marian Erle, whom he intends as his bride in a revolutionary—if misguided—marriage of classes. Endorsing Romney's new proposal, Aurora is implicated in the kind of unequal transaction she avoids for herself. Indeed, she takes on the traditionally patriarchal role reminiscent of *Bleak House*'s Mr. Jarndyce by coolly considering another woman as a gift. In the presence of the silent and passive Marian they outrank, Aurora and Romney use his engagement to attempt an exchange of their own. Romney's response to Aurora's rather condescending thanks for the "doglike" working-class cousin she will receive through his marriage is to ask if "'[y]ou accept at last / A gift from me, Aurora, without scorn? / At last I please you?'" (IV: 281, 286–287, 287–289) Turning Marian into their gift object in a transaction that would establish their own power rather than mutual benefit, Aurora and Romney together repeat Romney's earlier mistake by substituting a kind of "arrogan[ce]" for egalitarian alliance (IV: 300) and thereby contributing to the chain of events that will direct Marian away from Romney and into even greater danger.

The proposed transaction, like Romney's earlier proposal to Aurora, offers a pointed contrast to the gift exchanges that will follow in the second half of the narrative. This mid-century heroine must learn Jane's epic lesson that "a present has many faces." Even as the narrative reveals how a woman in Marian's position may be marginalized by the gifts of her social superiors, the gifts of *Aurora Leigh* are not necessarily a danger, not necessarily a snare for their more privileged heroine. Just as they allow Jane to form an independent home with a family she redefines, they will eventually allow Aurora to reestablish kinship on her own terms—but only after she discovers that gift exchange can produce mutual benefit. Years later, in Paris, Aurora will finally come to understand this when she encounters Romney's former fiancée and learns that Marian was deceived, led away from the altar, and raped.[67] Determining to share her own home and livelihood with Marian and her son, Aurora declares that she will provide for them, thereby transforming her relation to both:

> "Come with me, sweetest sister," I returned,
> "And sit within my house and do me good
> From henceforth, thou and thine! ye are my own
> From henceforth. [. . .] Come,—and henceforth thou and I
> Being still together will not miss a friend,
> Nor he a father, since two mothers shall
> Make that up to him." (VII: 117–120, 122–125)

Like Jane, Aurora radically, if rather imperiously, reconstructs family ties through sharing her money. In this famously provocative scene, she takes the woman who might have been her cousin-in-law and makes her a sister, takes her illegitimate child and makes him her son, and establishes a domestic unit of female partners, two mothers who stand in place of the absent father and husband.

There are a few crucial differences between Aurora's kinship-earning transactions and Jane's, however. Aurora's ability to give is not a function of any monetary legacy. Her primary "inheritance" is poetic, born jointly of her English father's books (I: 710–711, 727–728) and her Italian mother's "spark" (I: 31–33). This inheritance is profitable, too, but in a different way. Through the sale of her father's books, she clears the shelves to replace his literary inheritance with her own literary income. Arranging for her manuscript to be published before she leaves England, she subsequently receives critical acclaim for having "written a good book" (V: 1263–1265; VII: 563).[68] The book's financial success enables Aurora to live on her literary proceeds (VII: 548–549) and use them to support a family on her own terms.[69] Income, rather than inheritance, becomes her most direct financial means of giving. And this means that Aurora's ability to give depends upon her own exertions, rather than patriarchal legacies—an important reminder, at mid-century, that single women's employment could create opportunities for gifts that enabled independent lives, female alliances, and alternative living arrangements.

Furthermore, while Jane gives in direct reciprocation, ecstatic to finally "repay" her debts to her cousins, Aurora shies away from any implication that her own initial condescension might have helped to convince Marian that "a man like Romney Leigh / Required a wife more level to himself" (VI: 1026–1027). Instead of acknowledging Aurora's shared responsibility for Marian's plight, the narrative uses this moment to extend the circle of obligation and suggest that gifts can connect a larger network of giving subjects: "Oh, Romney Leigh, I have your debts to pay" (VII: 143). Eager to show that she, like Romney, is "made for giving," Aurora thus uses her encounter with Marian in part to reverse her own earlier standing with her cousin. No longer the object of his gifts, she is instead able to give on his behalf.

Aurora's gifts have larger legal and economic significance. Just as *Jane Eyre* stages a debate about inheritance through Jane's recognition of a common duty, *Aurora Leigh* invokes a similar ethos when Aurora uses her own means of subsistence to benefit the larger community she claims as her "own." It also invokes a similar law. Income, like inheritance, was increasingly taxed throughout the nineteenth century. Whereas inheritance tax was accepted as the lesser of the two evils and even praised for its relative "unburthensomeness,"[70] income tax, lifted after 1816 but reinstated by Peel in 1842 and increased in 1854 during the Crimean War, was extremely unpopular,[71] seen by political theorists and *Household Words* editorials alike as an "objectionable" measure.[72] Despite the tax's general unpopularity, it was framed as "necessary for the public interest."[73] It seems plausible that this is the subject of Aurora's father's speculations, when, wandering through Florence before meeting her mother, "[h]e mus[es] somewhat absently perhaps / Some English question .. whether men should pay / The unpopular but necessary tax / With left or right hand" (I: 73–76).[74] Aurora's decision to share her home and her wealth echoes but also exceeds the income tax's "unpopular but necessary" duty to benefit the "public interest."[75] Yet "duty" itself, a term for payments to the public revenue but also associated with the narrative's cold aunt and the "not [. . .] ungenerous" visit Aurora first pays to her cousin's working-class bride (I: 361, 363; IV: 446), is a word that *Aurora Leigh* despises and that its heroine must learn to surpass in favor of a less measured but more fully reciprocated generosity.

Aurora benefits herself at least as much as she benefits Romney, Marian, and Marian's infant through her decision to share her income. "[D]o me good," she tells Marian, claiming her peremptorily and possessively as her "own." The same narrative that celebrates Aurora's ability to reject a gift seems unable to imagine the same agency afforded to a working-class, "fallen" woman, whose child offers a more privileged Aurora the opportunity to forge new kinship relations; there is no suggestion that Marian, like a younger Aurora, might begin to battle out the "nature, law, and right" of Aurora's gift or of the surrogate parenting it will entail. Again, as we saw in the annuals, *Aurora Leigh* is more interested in the gift practices of its middling heroine than in the status or agency of her recipients. Yet despite the poem's many blind spots with respect to Marian and cross-class exchange, it attempts to stage this transaction as far more balanced than the one earlier attempted by Romney. Unlike his gifts, which leave Aurora feeling a mere "pensioner," Aurora's offers, like Jane's, propose reciprocity. And they appear to obtain it. Through Marian, she learns for the first time not only how to give but also how to receive a gift, accepting an equal part of a communal good and realizing that the "interest" of her community is also her own.

> She looked me in the face and answered not,
> Nor signed she was unworthy, nor gave thanks,
> But took the sleeping child and held it out
> To meet my kiss, as if requiting me
> And trusting me at once. (VII: 133–137)

In thus accepting Aurora's offer, Marian reaffirms Jane Eyre's earlier stance after saving Rochester's life, by acknowledging "'no debt, benefit, burden, obligation, in the case'" (129).[76] In a move that replaces gratitude with mutual benefit, she proffers her own gift, using the child to "requit[e]" Aurora's generosity and to make a further claim on her, demanding a physical sign of affection in her kiss.

This first moment of reciprocity, which shakes the tense of Aurora's very narrative from retrospective recollection to the "now" of present observation (VII: 139), also signals a shift in Aurora's ability to admit aid. Arriving in Italy with her newly reconstituted family, she welcomes and expresses gratitude for the support of her new "sister."[77] "Sweet the help / Of one we have helped! Thanks, Marian, for such help" (VII: 513–514). The verbal overflow in these lines, which recognize Marian's "help" not once but thrice, echoes the idea of gratuity that they profess, suggesting that Aurora's new recognition of reciprocity has made its way into the form of her narrative as well as its content.[78] Finding pleasure in an exchange that the narrative stages as balanced and recognizing the reciprocal advantages of their separate gifts, Aurora learns Jane's lesson—that gifts can be a benefit as well as a burden—from the recipient's side.

This lesson will be instrumental for establishing Aurora's heterosexual union, too, when Romney, learning of Marian's trials, seeks out the new family in Italy. Sharon Marcus, arguing persuasively that female intimacy is an important precursor to the male-female romances of many Victorian marriage plots, claims that "the [verse-narrative's] final marriage is the result of an exchange between women that asserts the generative energies of friendship."[79] Certainly, in the moment she describes, when Aurora advises Marian to "'Accept the gift'" of Romney's legitimating marriage (IX: 255), and Marian gives him back, asking Aurora to "'Come down to Romney—pay my debt'" (IX: 444), Romney becomes the gift "between women" that inverts both his earlier attempts to make Marian his gift to Aurora and the patriarchal kinship transactions described by Eve Sedgwick and a long line of other theorists. But even though the telos of the developmental narrative leads Aurora back to Romney, we shortchange *Aurora Leigh's* extended meditation on giving if we isolate this transaction from the ones that precede it or too quickly subsume women's gifts in the marriage plot. The power of this transaction derives from its reciprocity, from the mutual offers that Aurora and Marian make to and for each other. It derives, too, from Aurora's gradual understanding that gift exchange can open up same-sex egalitarian kinship opportunities, rather than trapping women in marital (or other forms of) debt. It reverses Romney's two earlier offers through a different vision of the gift. Even as it rather too neatly removes Marian from the problematic romantic triangle, Marian's desire that Aurora pay *her* debt again extends the circle of gifts and of family, allowing Marian to cancel her own obligations to both Leighs by directing Aurora's action and by acknowledging that Marian's earlier, aborted engagement was founded on unequal gifts. "'I gave you love? / I think I did not give you anything'" (IX: 372–373). With or without Romney, Aurora's relationship with Marian has proven that gifts offer new opportunities for female alliances.

Aurora's marriage depends upon Marian not merely because Marian so willingly transfers Romney's hand—indeed, Marian, like the "fallen" Jenny of Dante Gabriel Rossetti's poem, quickly "fades from view" (line 277)—but also because, through Marian, Aurora has learned to receive and reciprocate gifts in the interest of kinship. She admits as much when, declaring her love to Romney, she denies that she is merely feeling pity for the blindness with which he (like *Jane Eyre's* Rochester) has been afflicted.

> "Obviously
> I'm not a generous woman, never was,
> Or else, of old, I had not looked so near
> To weights and measures, grudging you the power
> To give [. . .]. I would have no gifts
> Forsooth, but God's,—and I would use *them* too
> According to my pleasure and my choice,
> As He and I were equals, you below,
> Excluded from that level of interchange
> Admitting benefaction." (IX: 626–630; 631–636)

Many critics have taken issue with the poem's resolution, which forces Aurora to admit being "'wrong in most. / Oh, most!'" (IX: 637–638) and subordinates her poetic prowess to proving that she is "'So mere a woman!'" (IX: 713).[80] But this passage, while it assuredly humbles Aurora, also grants her forms of gift-giving that are less "danger[ous]" than those she has previously encountered, proving that she does not depend upon Romney to keep her "'Safe and inviolate from gifts'" (II: 1053). It concedes that human connections depend upon equal "interchange" and that generosity means accepting other people's "power / To give" as well as giving. And, against Jane Eyre's careful repayment of debt, it also signals that reciprocity in gift-giving, unlike commercial transactions, cannot simply be measured or weighed in advance but will work itself out in relations of intimacy.[81] Even though Marian exits the scene after sanctioning her friends' marriage, Aurora's new use of gifts to construct, if not ultimately to sustain, family ties with her has radical potential to alter the nature of kinship for the more privileged woman, suggesting that Aurora's union with Romney, like the one she forges with Marian, will not be conventional. Furthermore, since Aurora's authorial income is not at odds with but actually enables her gifts, these final scenes undo the earlier binary between Romney's desire to provide for Aurora through giving and Aurora's determination to earn her own way. Instead, they intimate that financial independence (here as in Jane's case, but to the ultimate exclusion of Marian) might help to facilitate the kind of mutual gift exchange and revisionary relationships idealized by mid-century narratives of female development.

III. Blind Economies

No discussion of *Aurora Leigh* and *Jane Eyre* would be complete without addressing the final episodes that, even more than the protagonists' fierce rejections of St. John and Romney, united the works for so many contemporary authors and continue to do so today: the blazing halls of both Rochester's and Romney's homes; their heroic attempts to rescue the arsonists; and their subsequent injuries—blindness, in both cases, along with the destruction of Rochester's hand and Romney's social handiwork.[82] Typically seen in terms of the heroes' humbling through symbolic castration, these dramatic conclusions, with their self-sufficient women and their self-doubting men, have suggested to many critics the difficulties that Charlotte Brontë and Elizabeth Barrett Browning faced when trying to imagine female independence within marriage.[83] But even this parallel mutilation has greater meaning in the context of the gift-giving I have discussed. Through it, these marriages show the lingering appeal of the reciprocal transactions ultimately favored by Jane and Aurora.

The common loss experienced by Romney and Rochester appears to offer a startling contrast to Jane's carefully balanced exchange. In the extreme, gratuitous, and unilateral destruction of their health and homes, they present spectacles of sacrifice, while Jane and Aurora utterly reject traditional notions of feminine self-lessness in their pursuit of independence. Even the more empowering economies of sacrifice that the women in Part II of this study will take up in the service of social activism are ultimately foreign to them. In answer to Rochester's comment that she "delight[s] in sacrifice" (379), Jane protests that there is nothing unequal about their exchange. Aurora reaches a similar declaration when she refuses to compromise art or love: "'I will not [...] cease to love high, though I live thus low'" (V: 968, 971).[84] Sacrifice is not their preferred mode. Nor is it Romney's or Rochester's. Romney's charitable social efforts at "hospitals, almshouses, infant schools, / And other practical stuff of partial good" (II: 1224–1225) initially seem more sacrificial than Rochester's self-serving deceit, but even Romney pursues only what he feels is his "reasonable duty" (II: 1200) and learns to regret the "tyrannous constraint" that his mistaken efforts force upon the poor (VIII: 893).

Despite acknowledging their significant losses—Rochester compares himself to an "old lighting-struck chestnut tree" (378) and Romney declares that he is "mulcted as a man" (V: 564)—neither man is willing to sacrifice the love of the woman whom he claims would be better off without him. And neither tale asks it of him. In each case, despite the heroism of the action that precipitates it, sacrifice ("struck," "mulcted") is not the active choice of the character but passive loss, part of the narrative plot set in motion by its author. This is an important distinction. Sacrifice, according to the Maussian tradition, "is an act of giving that is necessarily reciprocated."[85] Intentional acts of destruction become, in this view, powerful gestures that highlight a sacrificial agent's status and construct relationships of obligation even more extreme than those demanded by Jane's Aunt Reed. In Jane Eyre and Aurora Leigh, in place of Mauss's willing and even heroic sacrifice, we have something more akin to sacrificial slaughter, to the involuntary condition that René Girard describes as a community's violent scapegoating, or to the violent consumption that, according to Georges Bataille, severs a sacrificial object from "the world of profitable activity," from "the *real* order."[86] Neither Romney nor Rochester gouges out his own eyes in an Oedipus-like act of penitential self-destruction. Their lost vision and charred ancestral homes remove them from the activity they consider profitable and separate them from the "real" of their former social worlds.

Whereas sacrifice for Girard and Bataille serves primarily to purge or to dissipate an unwelcome element, sacrifice in these narratives violently counters the unbalanced patriarchal economies that have previously dominated each text and offers an economic substitute for them. Formerly threatening Aurora and Jane with presents that inched uncomfortably close to purchase, Romney and Rochester are accustomed to the positions of power that unequal gift transactions can yield. By the narratives' end, however, they are grateful for blessings they no longer feel they deserve. This debt offsets their earlier prestige. Retributive though it may be, their loss also provides the narratives with economic equilibrium, a way not simply to emasculate their heroes but, more positively, to allow them to enter into the more balanced economies that Aurora and Jane have learned to embrace. Rather than reading Brontë and Barrett Browning as unable to imagine healthy men in egalitarian, companionate marriages,[87] it is important that we read against physical loss here[88] in order to again see how they imagine balanced gift exchanges as the mechanism for creating new, diverse, and even ideal(ized) forms of kinship.

Like Aurora, Romney and Rochester must both learn to be recipients as well as givers. Jane, now able to requite the gifts he had earlier pressed upon her, informs Rochester that she prefers his current state to his "proud independence, when you disdained every part but that of the giver and protector" (379). Converted to her model of reciprocity, Rochester admits that although "[h]itherto I have hated to be helped [. . .] henceforth, I feel, I shall hate it no more." (379). Accepting her offers and recognizing that it is no longer always his prerogative to grant a return, he asks that "God bless and reward you" (379). Both men look upward and outward for the first time, attributing their losses and their gains alike to divine intervention and reminding us yet again that individualism is not the final word in these narratives. "My heart swells with gratitude to the beneficent God of this earth just now," exclaims Rochester, noting also that "*His* chastisements are mighty" (380). Romney echoes this sentiment: "Thank God, who made me blind, to make me see!" (IX: 308).

Recalling classical traditions that associate the loss of worldly vision with the acquisition of new, prophetic insights,[89] Romney's remark also demonstrates how, after the economic world of the narrative has reached equilibrium, neither man is left utterly debased or deprived. Invoking gifts from their creator, they learn, as Aurora and Marian have also learned, that gift economies can open out to involve more than the people immediately party to exchange. If their losses serve to pay a larger debt, then their gains might also be predicated on the larger system of economic balance favored by a more omniscient design—by God or, as it happens, by narrative plot. Such is the sacrificial economy discussed by Derrida, in which extreme offerings seemingly "beyond recompense" are re-inscribed within the realm of economic calculation through the Judeo-Christian promise of heavenly rewards.[90] Unlike the precisely balanced exchanges favored by Jane, sacrifice ruptures the symmetry of gift transactions, "breaking with exchange as a simple form of reciprocity" by substituting, on one end, "infinite, heavenly, incalculable, interior" returns.[91] If, along these lines, we consider the narratives' sacrifice as enacted not by Romney and Rochester but by authorial intervention, with writer and God included in the balance sheets of each text, then despite the passivity of their losses, our heroes' invocation of and gratitude for divine gifts that will benefit both themselves and the women they love reinstates them within a larger gift economy that begins to resemble Jane's and Aurora's more closely than it does their earlier, one-sided exchanges. The gift economies so crucial to nineteenth-century women's recon-figuration of female opportunities consequently afford us new ways of reading the men in their texts, as well.[92]

Romney embraces the thought of this larger economy even before Aurora declares her passion for him, noting that:

> From his personal loss
> He has come to hope for others when they lose,
> And wear a gladder faith in what we gain.
> Through bitter experience, compensation sweet,
> Like that tear, sweetest. (IX: 590–594)

Similar to Tennyson's lyrical desire to "find in loss a gain to match,"[93] but seeking something more generous than personal compensation, he emphasizes his hope for others and his blind faith in incalculable returns. Romney and Rochester learn to appreciate and recognize the larger systems implicated in and shaped by their own personal losses and gains.[94] As chapter three will further demonstrate, the balancing acts of mid-century gift exchanges are increasingly expansive, eschew-ing direct repayment and immediate reciprocity in favor of the indirect but bal-anced returns of wider circulation, again privileging community over individual (and individualist) selves.

The nature of subjecthood itself—critics' common focus within both narratives—is altered by these final interpersonal exchanges. Again Victorian lit-erature offers a vision of gifts that ultimately diverges from theorists' accounts. In contrast to Derrida's assertion that gifts are annulled "as soon as the donor and donee are constituted as [. . .] identifiable subjects," we have seen that Jane and Aurora can only become givers once they have asserted their roles as subjects, not objects, of exchange—a more fraught process for nineteenth-century women, perhaps, than for some of the subjects Derrida contemplated, which may explain why women's writing from that earlier period took greater pains to emphasize it.[95] However, it is not finally subjecthood or even married subjects that conclude each narrative. Aurora and Romney, despite their two, separate hearts, appear to merge together in their embrace: "were my cheeks / Hot, overflooded, with my tears, or his? / And which of our two large explosive hearts / So shook me?" (IX: 716–719). And although Jane's vision will more explicitly dominate in her rela-tionship with Rochester, they, too, share sight and more. "No woman was ever nearer to her mate than I am; ever more absolutely bone of his bone and flesh of his flesh. [. . .] I was then his vision, as I am still his right hand" (384).[96] Com-bining separate hearts with shared experiences, blurring the bodily boundaries between his and hers, these moments privilege unity over self. At the same time, though, they again offer a counter to coverture's legal submersion of a wife in her husband, by allowing the wives' gifts to create the union, by making husbands equally dependent upon their wives, and by showing how husband and wife alike are reshaped by the union. In this way, they mimic each narrative's earlier structures of alliance. Just as Jane and Aurora used gift transactions to rewrite their connections with female friends and partners, even their marriages create nonconventional kinship out of balanced gift exchange.

Though the mid-nineteenth century *Bildungsroman* propels these heroines away from female kin toward marriage, the alliances they forge with cousins and "sisters" have lasting appeal both for companionate marriage and for communities of giving women. If Marian Erle is frustratingly absent from the final 277 lines of Aurora's poem, and Bertha killed off without any hope of redeeming her inheritance or constructing her own alliances, Mary and Diana Rivers remain a lingering source of pleasure and companionship for Jane and a suggestion that reciprocity among women can be more than a fiction. As we will see, the gift transactions of relatively privileged female communities take on further significance in other and subsequent nineteenth-century fiction, poetry, and prose. Only a few years after the publication of *Jane Eyre*, and shortly before the publication of *Aurora Leigh*, Elizabeth Gaskell (friend to Brontë and, like Barrett Browning, a petitioner for women's property rights) replaces their narratives of progress with one of circulation and conservation. Pushing beyond the driving force of the Victorian marriage plot, she envisions a system of gift exchange capable of constructing and more fully sustaining a larger network of single women.

CHAPTER 3

Conservation in *Cranford*

SYMPATHY, SECRETS, AND THE FIRST LAW OF THERMODYNAMICS

In *Jane Eyre* and *Aurora Leigh*, reciprocal gift-giving sets the terms for both "sisterhood" and egalitarian marriage; as we have seen, each protagonist's growing ability to give back allows her to create and define her most valued relationships, in defiance of common law. For the vast majority of Victorian women who were neither earning nor receiving wealth, however, the inheritance or income that enabled such gifts remained no more than a fiction. At mid-century, property laws continued to deprive most married women of personal capital[1] while new statistics revealed a "surplus" of unmarried middle-class women who lacked both employment and the education necessary to procure it.[2] Most women had no property of their own, much less any extra to give.

Elizabeth Gaskell, whose letters indicate her interest in the condition of unmarried women, addresses some of their financial challenges in *Cranford* (1851–1853). There, she meditates on how reciprocal gifts might not only establish but also maintain intimate relationships. *Bildungsroman* gives way as Gaskell's novella explores a network of women whose gift transactions and stories offer a cyclic and corporate alternative to the individual, upwardly mobile givers we saw in Chapter 2 of this volume. *Cranford* features an entire town of shabby-genteel ladies who support each other, in the virtual absence of men and marriage, by giving and conserving resources. Gaskell's system of gift exchange thus reworks material limitations, turning these women's lack of extensive private property to their advantage.

As this chapter shows, *Cranford* uses principles of conservation to establish community and narrative outside of traditional kinship practices and storylines. Many readers express frustration with the novella's meandering design, but in *Cranford*, gifts among women secure both plots and female relationships that do not follow the imperatives of heterosexual romance. By writing women's economic practices in terms of sympathetic gifts and the balanced, peer relationships they support, Gaskell sidesteps the questions of cross-class philanthropy that her other "social-problem" fiction takes up, keeping her focus on Cranford's own impoverished "ladies" as both the donors and recipients of its gifts. Substituting middle-class women's egalitarian caregiving for condescending gifts of unfeeling, upper-class wealth,[3] she also defines her sympathetic gift economy in opposition to the masculinized marketplace essential to such models of charitable giving as that of Dickens's turkey-buying Scrooge.[4]

To say that Cranford offers a counterpoint to a more masculine market is, in itself, nothing new. Noting Cranford's resemblance to Knutsford, where Gaskell spent much of her youth,[5] critics overwhelmingly read this fictional town as its author's quaint and old-fashioned feminine utopia. In contrast, the story's other fictional town is an acknowledged site of modern industry and finance. Drumble, whose very name echoes the dreary rumble of machinery, stands in for Manchester, home of Gaskell's adult life and source of her "industrial" novels *Mary Barton* and *North and South*.[6] According to this distinction, Cranford may very well seem like the wrong place to posit economic power. Nonetheless, even if we insist on the literary importance of these biographical geographies, Manchester offered more to Gaskell's literary imagination than industry and factories. Home to the theories of political economist Friedrich Engels and scientific engineer James Prescott Joule, Gaskell's Manchester was, in the 1840s, fertile ground for two important intellectual pursuits, one detailing the circulation of capital and commodities, the other exploring the conversion and conservation of energy. *Cranford* brings together these contemporary interests in finance and physics to offer a practical counterpart to Drumble's industrial development. Its alternative economy corresponds to new scientific theories that were popularized in *Household Words*, site of *Cranford*'s serial publication and, for this reason, perhaps an even more important space than Knutsford for ascertaining the place of Gaskell's fictional town in mid-Victorian culture. Lacking factory engines but not nearly as old-fashioned as most accounts describe it to be,[7] the female and feminized Cranford community is itself a tightly knit system of sympathetic energy. In Cranford, where materials are scarce, streamlined processes of conservation and circulation replace consumption and growth. These new processes then serve, in part, as a model and defense for realist fiction that rejects the conventional trajectory of the mid-nineteenth-century marriage plot.

I. The Science of Giving

Sympathy—like money—is a limited commodity in Cranford. This is not to say that the ladies are incapable of great love, exertion, and gift-giving. Rather, their primary stores of sympathy are reserved for each other, to the exclusion of outsiders.[8] Their "tender good offices to each other whenever they are in distress" contrast starkly with their "kindness (somewhat dictatorial) to the poor" (1).[9] Indeed, when opportunities for charity arise, the women of Cranford often view them with suspicion. They reserve their sympathetic gifts for the would-be donors of charity rather than their recipients, treating poor elderly women, Irish beggars, and starving children as impositions or impostors.[10] The mention of (dictatorial) kindness to the poor gestures toward the hierarchical, "cold charity" we saw from Aunt Reed and Aunt Leigh. Charity fares poorly here, too. Rather than condemn the ladies' insularity, however, Gaskell's gentle mocking emphasizes the importance of intimacy to this small, egalitarian gift community and suggests that cross-class interaction is beyond its scope. From the first page, readers learn that the story will focus almost entirely on the empowering lateral relationships of the town's principal residents, a group narrowly defined by gender, birth, and nationality.

Rather than forming new affiliations, women in the town use sympathy to underwrite and police a tightly knit and fairly closed community. Their gift-giving is never a static, completed operation but one that requires continual, cyclical motion. Despite her apparent disregard for a neighbor's present of a homemade wooden fire-shovel (11), Miss Deborah Jenkyns nevertheless responds to it by preparing a scented apple for his invalid daughter's room (15); that invalid's sister will later send her own daughter to visit and read to the aging Jenkyns sisters (22). These gift practices operate according to a principle of conservation. What goes around comes around: the sum of sympathy never diminishes.

Even when gifts seem to benefit those beyond the women's intimate circle, they ultimately cycle back to them. When the traveling conjurer Signor Brunoni comes to town, the ladies conclude that his foreignness, his broken English, and even his turban make him "a French spy, come to discover the weak and undefended places of England" (90). They soon work themselves into a panic by attributing to him "all manner of evil"—robberies, dog murder, and even ghosts (102). After they discover that Brunoni has been injured and that his real name is Samuel Brown, however, the women rally together to help him.

Learning that he is one of their own and not a magical foreigner relieves the women of their anxiety. They are then able to give back some of that relief, attending to his medical needs, and even giving him Mrs. Forrester's highly coveted bread-jelly:

> It was wonderful to see what kind feelings were called out by this poor man's coming amongst us. And also wonderful to see how the great Cranford panic, which had been occasioned by his first coming in his Turkish dress, melted away into thin air on his second coming—pale and feeble, and with his heavy filmy eyes, that only brightened a very little when they fell upon the countenance of his faithful wife, or their pale and sorrowful little girl.
>
> Somehow, we all forgot to be afraid. (104)

In this passage, knowledge of sameness dissolves ethnic fear; that dissolution in turn gives rise to sympathetic energy. The "great panic" that has been circulating subsides but is immediately converted into "kind feelings," which have as much to do with the women's relief from panic as with Signor Brunoni's relief from pain. Indeed, their help—they "did as much as if there was great cause for anxiety" (103)—is in proportion to their former anxiety, not to Signor Brunoni's case. We might say that his medical needs serve as the catalyst for converting nervous energy into sympathy.[11] The narrator goes on to attribute the ladies' communal relief to "finding out that he, who had first excited our love of the marvellous by his unprecedented arts, had not sufficient every-day gifts to manage a shying horse" (104). This exchange of the exotic for the local, the "marvellous" for the mundane—in short, of romance for realism—is also a conservation of sympathetic feeling predicated on the exchange of the angry, bearded, "magnificent gentleman" (86) for a "pale and feeble" man. Feminized in this way, he bears more resemblance to the ladies themselves and becomes a more sympathetic subject to them. The unveiling at once celebrates the novella's generic interest in the "everyday" and shows how that everyday depends upon its contrast with the masked figure at the margins. Realism, here, requires a degree of insularity. But insularity should not be confused with stasis. Unlike Nina Auerbach, who claims that Cranford denies motion through "its protective resistance to the rhythms of the universe,"[12] I am arguing that endogenous sympathy is key to the novella's sense of cyclical motion and sympathetic circuitry. We can contrast this episode with a similar unveiling in *Jane Eyre*: there, the unmasking of Rochester's performance as gypsy woman ruptures exchange by revealing his gendered sympathy to be nothing more than manipulative performance (172).[13] Here, however, the unmasking demasculinizes Signor Brunoni in a way that permits sympathy to flow toward him.

The expressions of sympathy in the women's gifts to the Brunoni family seem generous, but the donors, here as in most gift economies, get something back.[14] Along these lines, I join Amanpal Garcha in understanding *Cranford* as "*resistan[t]* to selflessness," though, unlike him, I believe that self-interest can play out in communal as well as individualistic forms.[15] Through the conservation of sympathy, every act of generosity becomes the focus of reciprocal acts and gifts. Miss Matty Jenkyns, for example, benefits considerably through her own kindness to the conjurer; his wife connects her name with that of the "good, kind Aga Jenkyns" who aided them in India (110), setting in motion the chain of events that will restore Miss Matty's brother, the "lost Peter," to her.

Gaskell's conservation of sympathetic feeling in a (nearly) closed community is analogous to the conservation of energy that was being theorized by her contemporaries. In the 1840s, several scientists scattered throughout Europe simultaneously hypothesized energy conservation in both general formulation and concrete quantitative application, while an additional eight scientists derived either the general idea or a concrete application of energy conservation between 1830 and 1850.[16] That is, in varying ways, and at about the same time, scientists began to articulate the first law of what would later be called thermodynamics: they noted how heat, work, and other forces—eventually known as "energy"[17]— were "quantitatively interchangeable" and "could never . . . be created or destroyed."[18] William B. Carpenter, Michael Faraday, William Robert Grove, Hermann von Helmholtz, James Prescott Joule, William Thomson (later Lord Kelvin), and others tested versions of hypotheses determining that "wherever mechanical force is expended, an exact equivalent of heat is *always* obtained."[19] Popular journals circulated these theories widely, *Punch* through cartoons, songs, and other references to "Professor Faraday," and *Household Words* through more serious attempts to inform readers that "[t]he progress of Science has already shown [. . .] that heat may be concentrated into electricity, and this electricity reconverted into heat; that electric force may be converted into magnetic force [. . .] and *vice versa* [. . .]."[20] Charles Dickens admired Michael Faraday's scientific lectures and even borrowed his notes in order to disseminate them to a broader audience in his journal.[21] The articles that followed—"The Chemistry of a Candle," "A Shilling's Worth of Science," and "The Mysteries of a Tea-Kettle," among them—appeared during the autumn of 1850 and helped to popularize scientific principles including conservation just over a year before *Cranford*'s serial debut in *Household Words*.[22] Gaskell, of course, was already familiar with Dickens's journal and at least some of its contents; she had published her short story "Lizzie Leigh" in its pages earlier that spring.

The mixture of chemistry and fiction within *Household Words* reminds us that "scientific" and "literary" minds shared interests at mid-century, a time when such disciplinary boundaries had not yet solidified and writers were "absorb[ing] and testing" various scientific paradigms.[23] Displays such as the Great Exhibition of 1851—which Gaskell and her family attended[24]—popularized technological and scientific innovations, and observers there and elsewhere were eager to draw analogies between natural and social law.[25] Theories of conservation shared, with new and developing economic discourses, an interest in exchange. Thermodynamic principles were significant to the evolving ideas of Karl Marx[26] in part because "thermodynamics," as Nicholas Georgescu-Roegen notes, "is at bottom a physics of economic value."[27] Gaskell's formulation of conservation in *Cranford* is one literary expression of a larger cultural interest in joining economic and scientific theories.

Theories of conservation also shared, with earlier Romantic doctrines, a desire to see nature as a unity of forces.[28] George Levine reminds us that "thermodynamics was, like evolution, in the air."[29] Unlike evolution, however, conservation appeared, at least initially, to be more compatible with religious belief.[30] Joule used his experiments to argue "that the grand agents of nature are, by the Creator's fiat, *indestructible*."[31] Grove, acknowledging in his similar work that "humanly speaking, neither matter nor force can be created," concludes that their "Creation [is] the act, of GOD" alone.[32] At mid-century, religion both inspired and justified scientific work on the conservation of pre-existing forces. It is not a huge leap to consider that Gaskell, the wife of a Unitarian minister who was himself "absorbed in the new scientific studies,"[33] may have found interest in research popularized by her editor and theorized in part by Joule, a fellow Manchester thinker. More importantly, *Cranford* reflects these contemporary discourses, sharing with scientific theories an interest in discerning a single and conservable force.

Interest in conservation not only shaped various theoretical models for contemplating life but also produced systems, both fanciful and practical, for studying it. In *Cranford*, a seemingly out-of-place anecdote about the preservation of Mrs. Forrester's "fine old lace" (78) becomes a humorous case study for the indestructibility of matter, despite its circulation and its changes in form. Drinking tea with a peeress, Mrs. Forrester describes how her cat gulped down her treasured lace, which had been soaking in milk to achieve the appropriate stiffness and color. Determined not to lose this lace, Mrs. Forrester concocted an emetic for her pet, who "returned the lace to sight, very much as it had gone down" (79). Despite the boiling and soaking required to return the lace to its former state, "now," she notes triumphantly, "your ladyship would never guess that it had been in pussy's inside" (79). Even this rather awkward tale of a "naughty cat" (79) showcases the importance and visibility of conservation at the most everyday and apparently insignificant level of Gaskell's novella.

On a larger scale, fiction writing itself was being implicated in systems of conservation. In 1860, Nathaniel Hawthorne famously compared Anthony Trollope's writing to "a great lump [hewn] out of the earth and put . . . under a glass case," a comparison Trollope welcomed, and that Walter Kendrick has since described as a metonymic account of realist fiction's relationship to the world, on account of the enclosure it presumes.[34] Surely Gaskell's earlier novella stands even more clearly as a "world under glass," circumscribing a town whose inhabitants are almost entirely secluded from the outside world except at points of such violent contact—a train accident, a bank failure—that the community might be expected to shatter under their impact. More materially, Victorian science during this period offered popular examples of life sustained and examined in "almost but not quite completely closed" systems under glass.[35] Nathaniel Bagshaw Ward's fashionable fern-growing bottles (also called Wardian cases) were on display at the Great Exhibition that Gaskell frequented.[36] The Crystal Palace that housed the Great Exhibition itself, influenced by gardener-architect Joseph Paxton's earlier horticultural efforts, was an even more dramatic attempt to enclose, preserve, and display life.[37] Just as Ward had to reiterate that his cases did not actually stop time,[38] Gaskell balances her reflection that "the last gigot, the last tight and scanty petticoat in wear in England, was seen in Cranford" (2) with an acknowledgment of the inexorable passage of time that brings the railroad to Cranford (16) and makes pearls and muslin age-inappropriate gifts for a no longer "youthful" Miss Matty (151).

In these cases, as in the case of energy conservation, popularized science and its social implementation offered Gaskell models for *Cranford*. Her realist fiction renders the minute details of women's lives as if they were observed and also preserved under glass. A *Punch* essay, reflecting on the vast number of international visitors "throng[ing]" to the Great Exhibition, suggests that Paxton and Faraday might work together to create ideal climates for them in similar "glasshouses"; "Why," it quips, "[. . .] should we not rear young ladies under glass, and see if we cannot grow Circassian beauties?"[39] If *Punch* found humor in the idea of using closed systems to farm beautiful slave girls,[40] however, Elizabeth Gaskell preferred using them to rear up "Amazons" (1). *Cranford* eschews both beauty and heterosexual exchange as the governing ideals for her own bounded system of conservation.

Gaskell's desire to establish fictionally a hermetic community of women may thus have drawn on, and certainly resembles, contemporary ideas of other closed systems. Her story offers the possibility of a cyclical system in which sympathetic energy remains an equivalent force throughout frequent and varying exchanges.[41] This sympathetic economy makes a virtue out of the ladies' material limitations and gives them a way to maintain their community in the absence of men, consumption, or procreation. Conservation presents both a sustainable economy for the "surplus women" of Cranford and a structure for a realist novella that rejects the conventions of marriage plots or other teleologies in favor of circulation.[42]

Gift exchanges function largely to open up economies, according to Marcel Mauss's influential anthropological study and the many critical accounts that have followed it, expanding communities by helping groups to form alliances. In contrast, Cranford's virtually closed economy limits the pool of potential recipients, super-charging the bonds between each member of the community by keeping gifts close, at the expense of traditional kinship structures.[43] The town's sympathy, like its material wealth, is always already straitened, its gift-giving deliberately restrained. Rather than form new affiliations, the town uses its obligations to underwrite a tightly knit society. Peter Jenkyns's history of cross-dressing, like Sam Brown's feebleness, makes Miss Matty's brother an easy addition to the feminized circuit of sympathy when he returns home. His generosity to the Brunoni family in India also suggests the possibility that he has never truly left Cranford's economy.[44] This economy seems to account for and contain such reappearances. In her opening sentences, the narrator remarks that when a married couple settles in Cranford "somehow the gentleman disappears" (1). Like scientific systems of conservation in which energy is indestructible but changes form, Gaskell's novella maintains its own sympathetic energy by allowing gentlemen, too, to come back in their own or other forms. Indeed, men never simply appear but only reappear in *Cranford*, Sam Brown/Brunoni replacing the deceased and similarly surnamed Captain Brown, Major Gordon returning to Captain Brown's daughter after her invalid sister's death frees her to marry him. At home, after Peter has returned to his sister, he will perpetuate the conservation of kindness: "In short no one was forgotten; and what was more, every one, however insignificant, who had shown kindness to Miss Matty at any time, was sure of Mr. Peter's cordial regard" (153). Peter's return to Cranford after a long, self-imposed exile occurs at precisely the right moment for him to assist Miss Matty. When Peter arrives and helps to pay his sister's debts, he also helps to resolve a series of exchanges begun (if, in this conservation of sympathy, we can ever point to a "beginning" of exchanges[45]) by the failure of Miss Matty's bank.

The bank failure and the personal accountability that Miss Matty feels for it as a shareholder have attracted much critical attention to mid-century financial systems.[46] This episode is of particular interest here because Miss Matty's reaction to bankruptcy and the town's reaction to her loss show the conservation of sympathy at work. Despite the protests of a shopman and her companion, Miss Matty offers five sovereigns for a farmer's now useless bank note:

> "I don't pretend to understand business; I only know, that if it is going to fail, and if honest people are to lose their money because they have taken our notes—I can't explain myself . . . only I would rather exchange my gold for the note, if you please," turning to the farmer, "and then you can take your wife the shawl. . . . Then, I have no doubt, everything will be cleared up."
>
> "But if it is cleared up the wrong way?" said I.
>
> "Why! then it will only have been common honesty in me, as a shareholder, to have given this good man the money." (124)

Miss Matty directs her "common honesty" toward an "honest-looking" man (121) whose desires are not for himself but for his family, his largest expense a shawl for his wife which, in turn, recalls the shawl Peter once sent to his own mother from India. This farmer quickly puts his family's wants before his own, giving up his tobacco but choosing "yon figs for the little ones—I promised them to 'em" (123). His seemingly transparent honesty, his ability to moderate his own desires, and his concern for his family would all mark him as a deserving recipient of Miss Matty's gold by nineteenth-century standards for giving charity, but conservation has a different set of standards, and this is a different kind of story. The farmer's purchase of luxury items shows that he does not actually require her aid. In this case, what makes him deserving of help is that, like the ladies of Cranford, he exists outside of a charitable economy. Poorer than before, but not needing charity, he proves himself a true member of Cranford's community because of, not in spite of, his loss of wealth. His similarities to Miss Matty, with respect to his limited resources, his honesty, and his prioritization of others' desires, allow sympathy, instead of charity, to flow toward him. And this sympathy will therefore find its way back to Miss Matty.

The episode marks Miss Matty (unlike the bank) as fit to judge gift recipients. Consequently, this apparent sacrifice (Miss Matty met the farmer when she was shopping for silks that this exchange prevented her from buying) is figured as noble in spite of our narrator Mary Smith's caustic (and quickly regretted) question to Miss Matty, "if she would think it her duty to offer sovereigns for all the notes of the Town and County Bank she met with?" (125). Miss Matty's ostensibly generous exchange operates according to an economy utterly divorced from the system to which Mary is accustomed; Mary's father, in Drumble, is a "capital man of business" (140). Miss Matty, of course, cannot afford to reimburse all of the bank notes. After the bank fails, she will have only £13 a year (less than half of the salary that Jane Eyre earns as a governess, and without the board that Jane additionally receives). It appears to be an economy of sacrifice, a one-sided gift transaction from a person who cannot afford such an exchange. And yet the novella insists that such gift transactions are never truly one-sided.[47] In Cranford, bank notes can lose value, but true currency—that of Miss Matty's kindness, for example—is stable. She will get her return.[48] The narrative rewards her to such a degree that, if we consider the act solely in terms of its return, the decision could not have been better calculated. But Miss Matty is no capitalist, nor does she have the advantage of narrative omniscience. Part of what distinguishes gift circulation from a two-person reciprocal trade transaction is that the giver has limited knowledge about the source and timing of the return, which in Miss Matty's case does not come directly from the farmer who receives her gift.[49] After the act, we see Miss Matty (unknowingly) collect on it and countless others, reinforcing community through balanced but in some ways blind acts of gift exchange. The moral and motive of these "just deserts" assuredly owe much to Gaskell's Christian sensibility, but Cranford, like much closed-system realist fiction, rewards its good Samaritans on earth rather than in heaven.

The plot structure of Cranford rewards Miss Matty by returning her long-lost brother to her; the community structure of Cranford also rewards her through individual acts and gifts. Indeed, the two structures merge, as the narrative circulates and returns brother Peter to mirror the community's conservational economy. As soon as Miss Matty's reduced circumstances are known, everyone to whom she has shown generosity returns it. (They, in turn, will not have to wait long for Peter to repay them.) Miss Matty's maid, Martha, repays her former kind treatment with affection, unpaid service, and the offer of a home.[50] Similarly, the Cranford women who secretly come together to "give what we can to assist her" (137) tearfully remember the many good deeds that Miss Matty has done for them, when they resolve to provide her with a supplemental income.[51] Mrs. Fitz-Adam, for example, affectionately recalls Miss Matty, many years ago, "[running] after me to ask—oh so kindly—after my poor mother, who lay on her death-bed; and when I cried, she took hold of my hand to comfort me; and the gentleman waiting for her all the time; and her poor heart very full of something, I am sure" (139). Mrs. Fitz-Adams values Miss Matty's former kindness all the more since it came at a cost, and Mrs. Fitz-Adams takes that cost into consideration as she prepares to repay it by giving "a little more" (139).

Returns come in more concretely financial terms as well. When Miss Matty decides to sell tea but "had some scruples of conscience at selling tea when there was already Mr. Johnson in the town, who included it among his numerous commodities," she approaches him to "tell him of the project that was entertained, and to inquire if it was likely to injure his business" (144). Her financial advisor— Mary's father—fears that this "'great nonsense [. . .] would put a stop to all competition directly,'" but our narrator no longer disapproves of Miss Matty's transactions. Shifting her allegiance from father to friend, she concludes now that "perhaps, it would not have done in Drumble, but in Cranford it answered very well; for not only did Mr. Johnson kindly put at rest all Miss Matty's scruples, and fear of injuring his business, but I have reason to know, he repeatedly sent customers to her" (144). Critics such as Hilary M. Schor and James Mulvihill use this quote to distinguish between "male" and "female" economies and to show that Miss Matty's economy, comprising both the "moral" and the "material," surpasses those that only serve the latter.[52] This is true—but "female" economy in *Cranford* is not merely "moral." Compassion, sympathy, and even generosity have an economic value, returning to the woman whose expenditure began the cycle. Miss Matty's gold allowed the farmer to spend his money at Mr. Johnson's store; Mr. Johnson, in turn, sends customers to Miss Matty's tea shop.

This recycling of *Cranford*'s sympathetic energy within a nearly closed system, like scientists' "indestructible" force, contrasts with capitalism's putative drive toward accumulation and expansion.[53] As "a rather stingy theory," thermodynamics, along with Cranford's system of gift exchange, ensures that energy "does not increase and is only redistributed."[54] The transactions of Cranford, whose business it is to conserve rather than consume, will always differ from those of Drumble, the money-making town. Mary's father would be quite right to encourage competition in Drumble, but Cranford's gift practices make conservation the more profitable practice.

The economies of the two towns produce different forms of narrative as well as different financial accounts. Drumble showcases competition and the accumulation of value over time. The development that we saw in *Jane Eyre* and *Aurora Leigh* follows this accumulative model; in the economic trajectories of their linear progress narratives, our heroines' gifts increase over time, from their initial lack of wealth and sympathetic transactions to the vast store they acquire of each. In *Cranford*, however, exchange and storytelling work differently.[55] With no room for the upward movement of marriage, inheritance, or self-help, the women of

Cranford reconcile themselves to limited commodities, operating on a horizontal plane of equivalences that substitutes conservation for accumulation and circularity of action for forward motion.

In its communal approach, Cranford reflects the changing emphasis from individual to corporate liability that Andrew Miller has observed in the emergence of joint stock companies.[56] But the models differ along an axis of gender. That is, despite their similar movement to communal systems, such mid-century ventures are deliberately opposed to Cranford's alternative, feminized gift exchanges. Even as banks fail, gifts present other economic opportunities for the women to assemble, pool their resources, and implement plans for the well-being of community members. As one part of a new collective system whose aim is to conserve rather than increase sympathy, Miss Matty's sense of personal accountability is not merely old-fashioned, nor is it limited to sympathetic expenditures that involve money. This system of conservation allows Miss Matty and the other "ladies" of Cranford to maintain their social status as givers without requiring the individual wealth that such giving usually entails. It thereby imagines some sense of economic control for them within a culture that denied this control to its "surplus" women, and shows how this agency can benefit an entire community.

II. Secrets in Circulation

Lacking material commodities, the women in this community circulate symbolic capital instead. Secrets, too, are central to their system of communal conservation and narration. Through secrets as through sympathy, Cranford proposes a system of gift exchange that is in tension with both marketplace capitalism and the ideology of separate spheres. While Cranford's community of women is generally understood as the quintessential private sphere—a feminized world set apart from the public, masculine concerns of business and politics—I am interested here in how this women's community creates its own alternative definitions of "public" and "private."[57] The ladies of Cranford pretend that the knowledge they share belongs instead to individuals in secret. Through this public fiction of secrecy, the community creates a sense of privacy for women who have relatively few other claims to private property, private interest, or private lives. In short, secrets function as forms of what anthropologist and gift theorist Annette B. Weiner has called "inalienable possessions," objects withheld from regular exchange, conferring status through their irrevocable association with a person or family.[58] Both as nonmonetary, nonmaterial gift and as a structure of knowledge, secrets help to weave individuals into a community and serve as a form of ownership for that community, giving it property rights, the possibility of inheritance, and perpetuation through nonprocreative means.[59]

In the nearly closed circuit of Cranford, sympathy cycles back to the same women who generate it, circumscribing community participation. This system of conservation relies on secrets to further demarcate insiders and perpetuate the community. In contrast with the other works discussed in this study so far, where gifts and community follow from the recognition of women's similarities, in *Cranford* likeness is not discovered but cultivated, through common codes and shared secrets. In Cranford, the public fiction of private secrets forges a communal identity and narrative which are maintained through those sympathetic transactions already discussed.[60] Mrs. Forrester's unconcealable poverty and Miss Matty's romantic history are two secrets, scrupulously kept by every member of the community, that give those two women the fiction of privacy and also help the community maintain its collectivity. This paradox of a secret that is also "the best-shared thing in the world" depends upon common knowledge, as Jacques Derrida has noted.[61] But while for Derrida people share only the knowledge that the secret cannot be known, that it is "*tout autre*," in Cranford secrets are precisely what the women both know and commonly deny.[62] In place of the "responsible self" constituted by Derridean secrets, *Cranford*'s secrets construct interdependence.[63] And unlike the "open secrets" which, according to D. A. Miller, similarly constitute subjects, *Cranford*'s secrets are "rigorously maintained" by—and on behalf of—the community.[64] Shared knowledge and shared concealment of these secrets allow the ladies to erase (or ignore) difference, and to validate the (public) community that shares in the secret-keeping.

In Cranford, secrets are the shared business of the poor but genteel "ladies." The narrator treats the women's communal knowledge as an established fact, information so taken for granted that it can be glossed in dependent clauses: "for obtaining clear and correct knowledge of everybody's affairs in the parish . . . the ladies of Cranford are quite sufficient" (1). Each lady's personal daily management is information commonly known and suppressed: "We none of us spoke of money," recalls the narrator (3). At the home of Mrs. Forrester, however, they play along with their host, "pretending not to know what cakes were sent up; though she knew, and we knew, and she knew that we knew, and we knew that she knew that we knew, she had been busy all the morning making tea-bread and sponge-cakes" (3). The circumlocution necessary to maintain the fiction of servants whose existence would secure Mrs. Forrester's gentility suggest that there is much at stake in that fiction, which is maintained equally by the "private" secret holder and the other members of her community: "We had tacitly agreed to ignore that any with whom we associated on terms of visiting equality could ever be prevented by poverty from doing anything that they wished" (4).

As we have seen in Miss Matty's case, material gifts in Cranford's circuit of sympathy conservation are sometimes able to ameliorate the poverty of women who have "come down in the world" (126). But the full license to do or wish "anything," to keep up the "terms of visiting equality," and even to speak in the communal "we" requires their tacit public agreement to ignore and suppress private knowledge. Cranford's *collective* pretense is something more than etiquette or self-preservation, two of the functions that Patricia Meyer Spacks considers important to eighteenth-century ideas of privacy.[65] It is also distinct from Jane Eyre's pretense at Marsh End, where Jane conceals her name to protect herself and reveals the concealment right away in order to create a community of trust with the Rivers sisters. And it is finally distinct from D. A. Miller's notion of "the subjective practice in which the oppositions of private/public, inside/outside, subject/object are established, and the sanctity of their first term kept inviolate,"[66] because it is an intersubjective practice. In Cranford, the fiction of privacy preserves a whole public community, not just a self. Privacy is, of course, a class marker, "the ultimate generalized privilege."[67] A fiction of privacy serves the women of Cranford in much the same way that their fiction of financial stability serves them: to preserve (or create) their ties to a class beyond their present means, through unspoken etiquette. By loudly and openly acknowledging his poverty, newcomer Captain Brown breaches this sense of etiquette—poverty "was a word not to be mentioned to ears polite" (4)—and ruptures the public fiction of private secrets, thereby threatening the very basis of their community.

Secrets are among the few possessions to which the women of Cranford can lay claim.[68] It is not surprising that Captain Brown gains greater status among the ladies—and becomes more sympathetic to them—when they learn that he, too, has a secret. The illness of one daughter and the efforts that he and his other daughter make to keep the invalid comfortable are known to all of Cranford, though the family "never spoke about it" (14). Ownership, in Cranford, depends upon silent public knowledge. Secrets are shared and then deliberately suppressed in order to secure collective interest, the very definition of community in Cranford. Just as the community's sympathy operates according to principles of conservation rather than accumulation, here too it favors shared property over private ownership. The resulting system of ownership is at odds with Drumble's competitive economy.[69] In the ladies' opposing gift system, the only way to "have" something is to share it, and possession gains value through suppression.[70]

Secrets, then, have symbolic value in gift exchange, and they help to define the boundaries of the Cranford community. They also ensure the community's continuity. Any community, even one so adept at conserving its own sympathetic energy, requires the addition of new community members to maintain equilibrium when it loses the old. The nonprocreative membership of the Cranford community—not unlike that of many religious orders both Victorian and contemporary—renders biological reproduction unlikely,[71] and not until later in the century (as I discuss in Chapter 6 of this volume) will conservation be associated with fertility. Miss Matty may dream of having a little girl (107), but in the absence of children, the ladies' primary relationships occur along the horizontal lines of friendship rather than the vertical axis of motherhood.[72] In place of generational models of mothers and births, the town reaches out laterally to perpetuate itself. Through its membership recruitment, *Cranford* reveals that its limited economy cannot actually succeed merely by continuing its fantasy of self-containment. Even Miss Matty's slight venture into tea implicates her in a global economy, despite her preference for intimate gift transactions over public sales. In this sense, Cranford again resembles those glass cases which also sought to conserve life in nearly but not quite closed environments. Margaret Darby reminds us that these terraria "could not have been 'hermetically sealed'; if airtight, the plants would [. . .] die[. . .]."[73] Gaskell's town, too, must remain somewhat open to external conditions if its inhabitants wish to maintain their communal life.

This idea that a fully closed system cannot survive—that even a system which presumably conserves energy must suffer loss—also foreshadows the second, and, as Barri J. Gold and others have shown, notably less optimistic law of thermodynamics.[74] Formulated after *Cranford* had begun to appear in print, and popularized after the novella's publication, this law emphasizes the "dissipation" of energy.[75] It asserts that "'[t]he entropy of the universe tends towards a maximum,'" or, in other words, that even though energy is never destroyed, its conversions are to a certain extent irreversible; it "always changes to increasingly less orderly, less usable forms."[76] Conservation in a closed system can or even must yield to chaos, according to this law.[77] Along these lines, the ladies of Cranford require, even as they resist, exogenous supplies of material goods and sympathetic energy. However, *Cranford* transforms loss itself into an opportunity for recruitment and conversion through its shared secrets.[78] Carefully and optimistically balancing its books, *Cranford* is aligned more closely with first-law conservation than with either second-law dissipation or the other economies of loss that I explore in the following three chapters.

Cranford compensates for the passing of Deborah Jenkyns by initiating Mary Smith, the narrator, into the community's secrets. If, as Weiner's anthropological studies show, the transmission of "inalienable possessions" legitimates kinship ties, the transmission of communal secrets here works in a similar way.[79] Mary's lessons in Cranford's personal affairs allow her to advance from the perimeter to the center of community life. Through hints and guesses, she learns the town's secrets, particularly one about Miss Matty's former romance, thwarted by her disapproving sister and father: "It seems that Miss Pole had a cousin, once or twice removed, who had offered to Miss Matty long ago" (28). Neither Mary nor Miss Pole professes direct knowledge, but their reluctance to be open and forthcoming does not prevent them from confidently speculating on the subject. Miss Pole disavows her knowledge even as she shares it: "Nay, now, I don't know anything more than that he offered and was refused . . . it is only a guess of mine" (29). Yet this "guess" is based on Miss Pole's first-hand observations and borne out by the succeeding narrative. It is also corroborated by Mrs. Fitz-Adam's recollection about the gentleman and a younger Miss Matty (139). Without ever confronting Miss Matty about her feelings for Mr. Holbrook, Mrs. Fitz-Adam and Miss Pole know them. And they also know when not to keep her secret, letting a calculated leak draw Mary into their circle by teaching her how and what to observe. Mary's eye-witness accounts of these feelings soon after Miss Pole's (tacit) disclosure help to ensure the fiction of Miss Matty's "secret" while also reinforcing Mary's developing insider status in the community.

When Miss Matty's erstwhile lover appears, Mary actively commits herself to the personal observation and speculation necessary for public knowledge: "I saw Miss Matilda start, and then suddenly sit down; and instantly I guessed who it was" (30). Until this point she has included herself in the communal "we" only because the ladies have impressed their rules upon her. But if "[i]t was impossible to live a month at Cranford, and not know the daily habits of each resident" (10), it is more difficult to know their daily feelings. Rules alone cannot create intimacy. Mary must work to verify the secrets she has discovered. Her new project, upon learning of the love affair, is to study and conserve the secrets of Miss Matty's heart. After this first reunion between the former lovers, Mary notes that Miss Matty "looked as if she had been crying" (30), and after the ladies pay a visit to Mr. Holbrook's house, Mary observes that "[Miss Matty] had probably met with so little sympathy in her early love, that she had shut it up close in her heart; and it was only by a sort of watching, which I could hardly avoid, since Miss Pole's confidence, that I saw how faithful her poor heart had been in its sorrow and its silence" (36). Mary chooses to take the hint, but Miss Pole's "confidence," which entails both the secret she shares and her trust that Mary will respond appropriately, also exerts pressure for actions "which [she] could hardly avoid."

Confidence here mandates watching. The lateral bonds of Cranford's closely knit community require a (silent) delving into the secrets of other members' hearts—a sympathetic invasion of privacy that knits each member still closer. Surveillance has been shown to be the medium of modern power and individualism in capitalist societies,[80] but in *Cranford* surveillance serves a different economy. Rather than grant power to the viewer at the expense of the observed object, it commits the group more firmly to shared communal codes and sympathetic circulation. When Mr. Holbrook is ill and Miss Matty silently distressed, both Miss Matty's reticence on the subject and Miss Pole's own decision to tell her immediately about the illness confirm suspicions of romance. Miss Pole remarks that it is "odd" that Miss Matty has not told Mary of this illness, but Mary's (silent) response acknowledges their communal fiction of ignorance: "Not at all, I thought; but I did not say anything. I felt almost guilty of having spied too curiously into that tender heart, and I was not going to speak of its secrets,—hidden, Miss Matty believed, from all the world" (38). Mary's sense of guilt and her (voluntary) refusal to tell Miss Matty's secrets underscores the power that her surveillance has indeed granted her. Yet this is less the power to tell than the power to refuse telling—the power to hold on to information, conserving it rather than spending it.[81] The refusal is thus part of the town's larger gift economy. Despite her silence, Mary does not actually hoard her knowledge. Instead, she circulates it selectively, with care. Just as Miss Pole has passed it along to her, Mary passes it and other secrets along to the reader. In this way, the fictional narrative is *Cranford's* secret-sharing writ large. The narrative's emphasis on Mary's feelings of guilt rather than power again serves to acknowledge Miss Matty's inalienable rights to her own "secret." Mary's power to observe, withhold, and inform a sympathetic reader of this secret is predicated on her drive to preserve the private property—and propriety—of the community.

Both Mary's knowledge and the women's shared silence intensify after Mr. Holbrook's death:

> Miss Matty made a strong effort to conceal her feelings—a concealment she practiced even with me, for she has never alluded to Mr. Holbrook again, although the book he gave her lies with her Bible on the little table by her bedside; she did not think I heard her when she asked the little milliner of Cranford to make her caps something like the Honourable Mrs. Jamieson's, or that I noticed the reply—
> "But she wears widows' caps, ma'am?" [. . . .]
> This effort at concealment was the beginning of the tremulous motion of head and hands which I have seen ever since in Miss Matty. (39)

In accordance with *Cranford's* system of conservation, Miss Matty's secrets are converted from strong feelings and spoken language into equally legible bodily signs. Her constantly quivering frame reflects contemporary scientific interest, by William Carpenter and others, in the physiological ramifications of energy conservation: extreme emotional force is transformed into physical movement.[82] And again we see the fiction of privacy ("she knew, and we knew, and she knew that we knew, and we knew that she knew that we knew") that reinforces a sense of community, revealing information to its members through visible signs (a widow's hat, a tremulous motion), even as it conceals their knowledge of that information through silence—"practiced even with me."

As Mary watches and learns to keep silent about Cranford's common secrets, she too becomes an active member of the community, remaining there and helping Miss Matty. The shift in tense in the passage quoted above ("the book he gave her lies with her Bible") indicates her present stance in Cranford. In the very next chapter, Mary shares secrets of her own with us in the context of revealing her observations of others. She notes, "I have often noticed that almost every one has his own individual small economies [. . .] any disturbance of which annoys him more than spending shillings or pounds on some real extravagance" (40), while also revealing her own private "human weakness" that makes her part of this collective: "String is my foible" (41). Her narrative movement from "they" (1) to an "I" that un-self-consciously considers itself part of a larger "we" (41) shows her successive movement from outsider to insider. Without recourse to biological means of reproducing their community, the ladies of Cranford, like the mid-century Anglican Sisterhoods which the next chapter of this study discusses, have to recruit their membership instead. As Rae Rosenthal notes about the narrator's initiation, Mary is "the clearest evidence of Cranford's strength and its capacity for self-perpetuation."[83]

Equally indicative of Cranford's success and ability to perpetuate itself is the way the text initiates the reader, as well as the narrator. Along these lines, Hilary Schor has valuably pointed out similarities between Mary's role in Cranford and the reader's role outside that community, calling the novella a "commentary on the ways women are taught to read cultural signs."[84] While Schor suggests that Mary's "narrative has meaning only in that community" (117), I prefer to extend her reading here. If the reader learns to observe with Mary; to hold, with Mary, the common unspoken knowledge of the Cranford community; and to speculate, with Mary, on some of her own personal economic "foibles," then the relationship between text and reader is more than analogical. Meaning extends beyond the single fictive midlands community to embrace an even wider circle of "con-scripted" readers.[85] Public knowledge and the fiction of private secrets create membership in the Cranford community and also contribute to a model for an (imagined) women's community beyond the textual borders of the novel. Eliza-beth Gaskell's 1851 letter to Eliza Fox famously shows the slippage between the novel's community and her own: "I've the comfort of sitting down to write to you in a new gown, and blue ribbons all spick and span for Xmas—and cheap in the bargain, 'Elegant economy' as *we* say in Cranford." She refers to her novel affec-tionately in other letters—to John Forster in 1854, "Shall I tell you a Cranford-ism"; and again, to John Ruskin in 1865, "It is the only one of my own books that I can read again; [. . . .] And it is true too, for I have seen the cow that wore the grey flannel jacket."[86] From the informer stance that Gaskell takes in relation to these publishing men to the inclusive, communal "*we*" of her letter to Fox, Cranford's meaning and community reach beyond the text.[87]

Cranford thus creates a women's community capable of self-perpetuation, able to harness its store of secrets to establish an intimate social network and to pre-serve, by conserving within the community, the sympathetic energy that keeps the town moving. Cranford's conservation of sympathy asks us to think more broadly about what's at stake in the idea of conservation for women.[88] Later in the century, as we see in Chapter 6 of this volume, scientific discourses will link con-servation even more firmly to the female sex, but even here the concept is decid-edly gendered. Conservation offers a way to conceive of alternative economies of generous giving for women without money, reconciling liberality of sympathy with the conservation of social structure. It is, in a large sense, reactionary, a (conservative) contrast to the forward-pressing mind-set of the mid-nineteenth century. Cranford's conservation draws imaginatively on cyclical time, rather than the future-tending progressivism of the 1851 Great Exhibition, pseudo-evolutionary theories, or, narratively speaking, the *Bildungsroman*. But the conservation of sympathetic energy is also remarkably progressive.[89] By avoiding the primacy of the marriage plot, it insists that "surplus" women have their own stories. By echoing contemporary scientific theories, it suggests that the mid-century project of forging communities for these women borrows from and contributes to additional contemporary discoveries and concerns. It also shows the centrality of sympathetic gifts to the blending of communal, economic, and industrial ideals. In its merger of old and new, conservation offers a useful language for thinking about the shape of gift economies and their place in a century-long, proto-feminist attempt to imagine elective communities of active women. And female community itself, as we will continue to see, was anything but a socially conservative idea in the mid-nineteenth century.

PART

II

MUCH OBLIGED

The Price of Redemption in "Goblin Market"

Christina Rossetti's short story "A Safe Investment" (1867)[1] begins one "utterly starless" night with a series of uncanny fiscal calamities: merchants toss treasures from their ships into the boiling sea that threatens their lives and their livelihoods; the old county bank fails, provoking a panicked run on every last penny; and the national bank itself goes under, leaving members of a stricken community overwhelmed by the private grief of personal ruin. This tale, first published following the banking crisis of 1866, joins *Cranford* in indicting traditional models of investment and exchange.[2] Rossetti shares Gaskell's interest in alternative economic options for single women and similarly suggests that gifts can secure higher dividends than banks. Here, however, gift economies are resolutely religious. Rossetti's emphasis on spiritual salvation alters the terms of the gift and the kind of community it creates.

This parable leaves one woman uninjured by financial disaster because her "investments" are in God's hands. Her frequent gifts trade on prospects of interest "everlasting" (251–252). Preparing for an eternal home that will arise from and safeguard her "treasure," she sends weekly "deposits" to an interest-bearing "account" and "give[s . . .] freely" to unknown "collectors," taking it on faith that these strangers, widows, and children "would carry all entrusted to them safely to [her] account" (252). Confident and comfortable on this night of reckoning, she "look[s] for the recompense of the reward" (253). The allegory of heavenly rewards uses commercial language to link gifts with religious redemption and to substitute these transactions for market dealings. Rossetti's heroine "gladly spend[s] and [is] spent" (253), offering up her resources and life in a spiritual economy that conflates consumption (spending) with sacrifice (being spent). Promising salvation through a triangulation of giver, recipient, and heavenly reward, this model of giving defers payment beyond the temporal bounds of life or narrative; it expands the circuit of exchange beyond human kin and community; it underscores the difficulty of extracting "gifts" from the "markets" they are used to critique; and it also signals a shift away from the balanced exchanges I discussed in Part I of this study. As this and subsequent chapters show, during the latter half of the century women "spend" and are "spent" in extreme measures. They eschew *Cranford*'s "elegant economy" to enter new scenes of consumption, attempting to reap spiritual as well as material rewards through spectacular gifts.[3]

Redemptive gift economies take different shapes in Rossetti's fiction and poetry, as she experiments with the practices and rewards of religious exchange. In the model proposed by "A Safe Investment," spiritual transactions are a solitary affair. Despite the collective reach of a crisis that emerges from every side and threatens "persons of all ranks and ages" (247), this bank failure brings about none of the communal pooling or sympathetic returns that feature so prominently in Gaskell's novella. While Miss Matty's loss, as we have seen, prompts general generosity, the one that Rossetti describes stirs self-interest: "none stretched a helping hand to his neighbour [. . .] or cared who sank or who swam" (249–250). The religious woman's traffic in salvation elevates her above the greedy populace but also isolates her; the light that uniquely brightens her home draws attention to its solitary state (250). Although she responds to travelers with warmth and cheer, her "reward" appears to come at the expense of the sustained lateral ties so important to *Cranford, Jane Eyre,* and *Aurora Leigh.*

Elsewhere, however, Rossetti takes a more social approach to redemptive economy, indicating that spiritual exchange might emerge from and benefit more than one single woman. Female intimacy remains crucial to the saving force of other gift economies by Rossetti and social activist Anna Jameson, as I show in this chapter. Salvation itself depends upon these social gifts, which will be the preferred model for religious and social crusaders in the remaining decades of the nineteenth century. Yet "A Safe Investment" offers more than a didactic diversion from their project. It significantly emphasizes the economic nature of religious practice and the redemptive purchase of gifts that take commercial form. By demonstrating how currency can function simultaneously within commercial and religious discourses, the story urges a careful reconsideration of the kind of exchange that female communities transact and suggests precisely how scholarship has shortchanged Rossetti's most popular work, "Goblin Market" (1859/1862).

This chapter accounts for diverse images of Victorian women's religious community by highlighting their common economic structure. Examining Rossetti's poem alongside Jameson's well-received lectures on Anglican Sisterhoods (1855, 1856), I show how, together, they create systems of female intimacy and religious investment that explain the price of redemption in "Goblin Market" by making sense of a noncommercial coin. In critical readings of the poem, the titular and titillating market has increasingly taken center stage as a site of coercive practices and a symbol of gendered trade.[4] "Sweet-tooth" but penniless Laura buys goblin fruit with a lock of hair, representing the perils of female consumerism by becoming the very object consumed.[5] This market research teaches Lizzie to use coin instead. Refusing to taste, she locates exchange value in a silver penny to safeguard her own body and restore her sister's. Lizzie's penny, described as the "central mystery" of the poem,[6] has been a challenge for critics who question how she obtained it and why, if it is key to her successful consumer practices, the goblins fling it back at her. Only sisterhood appears to have any real saving power in this market—but it remains frustratingly unclear why this is so.[7] Sisterhood, however, is central to the poem's economic discourses, in which coins are more than small change. The penny's interpretive payoff comes in understanding that it is not part of the market economy associated with the goblins' male brotherhood but part of a gift economy tied to both religious salvation and sisterhood.

Initially, both sisters are suspicious of trade. When the goblins' call and the sight of "luscious grapes" attract Laura, her sister reminds her that "Their offers should not charm us, / Their evil gifts would harm us" (65–66). This seductive market, Lizzie notes warily, has adopted the language of hospitality. The goblins attempt to conflate sale with gift practice, offering a "taste" and later inviting Lizzie to be their "guest," but Lizzie recognizes (in anticipation of theorists from Mauss onward) that even "gifts" come at a hefty cost.[8] This is an offer she can refuse.

Laura, less wary than her sister, and less wealthy, makes a hasty disclaimer to the goblin vendors.

> "Good folk, I have no coin;
> To take were to purloin:
> I have no copper in my purse,
> I have no silver either,
> And all my gold is on the furze
> That shakes in windy weather
> Above the rusty heather." (116–122)

Like many other women of her time, Laura has no liquid assets. Instead, the goblins appraise her "golden curl[s]" (125). Clipping a "precious" lock of hair from her head, she pays a symbolic price, a representative, physical exchange for the value of fruit and gold. Laura's "gold," a mere token of the nineteenth-century English gold standard, lacks the metal's intrinsic value. Too late she learns that the goblins will not be satisfied with this gesture; they want the real thing, the material value backing Laura's symbolic currency. Thus Laura deals unwittingly in synecdoche. Literary descendant of Pope's Belinda and other women whose sexuality is seized through a curl of hair, Laura trades a lock but ultimately surrenders her body.[9]

This market proves hostile to first-time shoppers. Without understanding the goblins' insistence on physical value, Laura buys on credit. She clips one lock but pays the balance later, her prematurely graying hair a sign of deferred costs

(126, 277). The goblins take much more than a single curl: Laura loses her hair, her health, her happiness. The narrative makes literal her "interest" payment by depicting her loss of interest in life. Of more material impact to the girls' domestic economy, Laura can no longer keep house (293–298). The sisters' private, self-sufficient household management, presumably differentiated from the goblins' market economy, suffers from contact with that market.[10] After entering it, Laura becomes alienated from her work; she labors "in an absent dream," "sick in part," "longing for the night" (211, 212, 214). Indeed, the poem gives more space to Laura's changing perspective toward work than it does to her failing body. Her sexual "fall" is also economic, a fall from her gendered sphere of work and household management, *oikonomos*, into the insatiable desires of consumerism.[11]

Redeeming Laura's fall requires that the goblins' economic system be supplanted. While Lizzie's rescue mission seems to rely on the market, her system of exchange differs from the economic system indicted by Laura's fall. I propose that Lizzie's transaction has origins, distinct from commercial exchange, that align it with forms of religious service described by Rossetti's contemporaries. Moreover, Lizzie's financial dealings explain why her rescue mission must be accomplished by a sister. Her dealings with the goblin men parallel the economic structure of those other mid-Victorian sisterhoods, Anglican women's communities.

I. Sisterhood "Beyond the Reach of Any Remuneration"

In order to square Lizzie's financial savvy with her status as religious savior, it is useful first to remember that nineteenth-century sisterhood, more than a biological relationship, was also an elective affiliation, "an achieved and achievable state of relationship to others,"[12] one that frequently came with an economic structure. Both Christina Rossetti and the sister to whom she dedicated the manuscript of "Goblin Market" were active in the communal lives and social services of Anglican sisterhoods.[13] Maria Rossetti joined the Sisterhood of All Saints at Margaret Street. Christina volunteered, with her aunt, to join Florence Nightingale's team of nurses in the Crimea. Although this application was rejected (she was too young), she later became an Associate or "lay sister" of the St. Mary Magdalene's Penitentiary in Highgate, participating in that sisterhood's work to rescue women from the margins of Victorian sexual propriety.[14] Rossetti's relationship to the Anglican sisterhood movement has influenced many interpretations of "Goblin Market" that rightly draw analogies between the poem's devoted duo and contemporary religious sisters who reclaimed and rescued the "fallen." Such interpretations trace the literary sources of "Goblin Market" to the textual materials of these religious institutions and locate not only the poem's themes but its narrative mode in the Anglican sisterhood movement.[15] Yet the poem owes Anglican sisterhoods more than its images of women's solidarity, activism, and rescue. Not only the redemptive subject and strategy of the poem's sisterhood but also the structure of its economic systems draw on contemporary debates about Anglican sisterhoods.

In the eighteenth and early nineteenth centuries, the "sister of charity" was a model for benevolence, piety, and duty.[16] As we saw in Mary Shelley's tale for *The Keepsake*, fiction in the 1820s and '30s used foreign, Catholic "sisterhoods" to signify women's sacrifice and devotion,[17] but by the mid-nineteenth century writers became more explicit about the educational and professional value of such institutions for English Protestant women.[18] The establishment of those institutions in fact as well as in fiction, through the rapid formation of Anglican women's religious communities following the Oxford Movement and the rise of Anglo-Catholicism, shifted their focus to nursing, administration, and the rescue of the fallen, homeless, or orphaned.[19] As these Anglican women's religious communities proliferated, writers who took up the theme of sisterhood in the 1850s and '60s expanded their conception of women's communities to give their work new, professional status. Anglican sisterhoods appealed to and influenced a number of progressive female writers. Elizabeth Gaskell, for instance, corresponded enthusiastically with such advocates of religious sisterhoods as Anna Jameson and Florence Nightingale, and *Cranford*'s collective structure speaks, although in secular terms, to the popularity of the female communities that those women endorsed and organized.[20]

These Anglican sisterhoods were extremely controversial.[21] They challenged British anti-Catholic sentiment of the sort voiced by Jane Eyre, who disapproved of Eliza Reed's desire for permanent "retirement" from a "frivolous world" (200).[22] They also challenged traditional attitudes toward gender roles, family structure, and Church hierarchy.[23] Defending themselves against accusations that the sisterhoods led to Rome, advocates attempted to differentiate their sisterhoods from their cloistered, Catholic counterparts, emphasizing their unpaid social services over contemplative behavior.[24] In answer to complaints that Anglican sisterhoods caused women to abandon family duties, advocates reminded audiences that the 1851 census reported an "excess" of half a million women; they argued that these single women should be permitted to extend domestic tasks into a wider sphere.[25] In response to suggestions that these "surplus" women be transported, sisterhoods created domestic colonies at home and co-opted colonial spaces, claiming empire as the site of action by Florence Nightingale and Caroline Chisholm rather than as a refuge for the redundant.[26] More significantly for our understanding of redemptive economies, supporters of Anglican sisterhoods also legitimated the status of their gendered work by calling into question the equation of professional activity with payment. They argued for a sphere of highly trained and disciplined work "beyond the reach of any remuneration,"[27] pitting their communities against market forces both to stave off criticism that they were entering into men's sphere and to argue for an alternative model of women's religious and professional social activism.

One popular advocate of Anglican Sisterhoods who took up the issue of remuneration was writer, art historian, and activist Anna Jameson, mentor of the early feminist Langham Place Group.[28] In *Sisters of Charity, Catholic and Protestant, Abroad and at Home* and *The Communion of Labour*, two lectures delivered to private audiences and then published, to popular acclaim, in 1855 and 1856, Jameson sets out a non-profit stance for professional women.[29] She justifies Anglican women's communities as a spiritual obligation by calling their work a "divinely appointed" vocation. Insisting on the equality of men and women's religious responsibility, she highlights the importance of vocational training and deplores the fact that "[no] provision is made to enable the woman to do *her* work well and efficiently." Jameson dissolves gendered hierarchies of work to set out a professional model for women's religious labor: "why should not charity be a profession in our sex, just in so far (*and no farther*) as religion is a profession in yours! If a man [. . .] publicly preaches religion, are we, therefore, to suppose that his religious profession is merely a profession, instead of a holy, heartfelt vocation?"[30]

Jameson invokes the ideology of separate spheres to establish male and female labors as complementary. Calling for a "communion of labor," she suggests that "an enlarged sphere of social work" for women would lead not only to better public institutions but also to "a finer harmony between men and women." Despite Jameson's rhetorical efforts to make male and female labor compatible, however, men in the medical and clerical professions saw the sisters' work as unwelcome competition: the efforts of "surplus" women threatened to make male labor redundant. Accordingly, medical students and apothecary workers in Piedmont drew up a petition against sister-run infirmaries there. And even though Jameson "laugh[s] at this short-sighted folly and cruelty, which supposes that the interests of the two sexes can possibly be antagonistic," she, like Rossetti, pits her "sisters" against the cruel "brothers" of competitive markets. Her response to their petition aligns the sisters' non-profit professional model with generosity and expertise: "The plea was, *not* that their infirmaries were ill-served or that the medicines were ill compounded, or that any mistakes had occurred from ignorance or unskilfulness, but that this small medical practice, unpaid and beneficent, 'took the bread out of the men's mouths.'" Distinguishing between male and female professionalism, Jameson privileges the latter by implying that "unpaid" practices are necessarily "beneficent" and operate entirely outside competitive market principles.[31]

But such a complete separation of gift and market requires the degree of fantasy that we see in the apocalyptic night of Rossetti's "A Safe Investment" or in the "merchant men" of "Goblin Market." Even in the poem's supernatural scenes, Lizzie and Laura's domestic economy cannot avoid contact with the market.[32] The Anglican sisters' work did compete, of course; they offered an alternative to male medical models, and what they performed for free or for collective pay removed other opportunities for profit taking.[33] Sisterhoods and many other female philanthropists justified their work in part by claiming this unpaid status. Dorice Williams Elliott further argues that sisterhoods' advocates stressed "vocation" as a strategy to justify professional wages.[34] Certainly, Jameson's emphasis on women's vocational aptitude opens up the possibility that women, as "professionals," might be entitled to the salaries that men received. And the implicit rationale for payment in Jameson's description of vocation has particular appeal for a twenty-first-century audience that equates women's professionalization with equal pay. Yet such an equation does not project backward easily. Sisters such as those described in "The Unseen Charities of London" gained public admiration in part by refusing compensation,[35] and Jameson's lecture is similarly more interested in getting women recognition than remuneration. Her description of "unpaid" service as "beneficent" should remind us that middle-class Victorian women workers had a significant counter discourse, one that separated professionalism from pay. As Alison Booth has noted, "[m]any placed a value on the privilege of choosing a vocation regardless of pay."[36] Some of this value surely comes from making a virtue out of necessity. Many women, as we saw in Part I of this study, lacked discretionary income. However, the image of the unpaid, beneficent female worker was, to my mind, more than merely a "ploy [. . .] to deflect male professionals' anxieties about competition from paid female professionals."[37]

Jameson actually disparages the idea of payment and the workers who receive it. Describing the medical students as "dissipated, thoughtless boys," and noting their "great laxity of morals," Jameson equates men's "paid" status with youth, inexperience, and immoral expenditure, which she then juxtaposes with the beneficent service of the (unpaid and experienced) sisters. Unlike self-indulgent male professionals, the sisters spend wisely: capable of doing good with a small sum, "'they are admirable accountants and economists.'" Also unlike male professionals, sisters receive no personal financial profit from their work. Jameson eschews individual profit to elevate a communal model of women's professional service. Anglican sisterhoods, by Jameson's account, reject the so-called cash nexus of relationships in favor of non-profit service motivated by sympathy and religious obligation. "The idea in this country that every thing has a money value, to be calculated to a farthing, according to the state of the market, is so ingrained into us, that the softest sympathies and highest duties, and dearest privileges of Christians, are never supposed to be attainable unless sold and paid for."[38] According to Jameson, religious sisterhoods cast off market calculations and considerations; their economy is modeled on religious service rather than salary. In contrast to the lax morals of "dissipated, thoughtless boys," mid-nineteenth-century sisters have the power to heal the sick and redeem the fallen precisely because they are not concerned with counting their farthings.

This non-profit approach—the ability for a woman to give both "her whole property" and "herself besides"[39] without pay—requires a privileged position, however. Varying degrees of wealth and status gave upper- and middle-class women the prerogative to offer their services as unpaid work. Here as elsewhere, the horizontal character of "sisterhood" limits the extension of sympathetic gifts down the social ladder. *The Lady's Newspaper*, which in 1849 urges "those women, who are rich and zealous enough" to devote themselves to the sisterhoods' work, joins other contemporary authors in favoring women with money.[40] Novelist Dinah Mulock Craik, writing "About Sisterhoods" in 1883, is not need-blind: "An institution which absorbed the waifs and strays of gentlewomanhood—ladies of limited income and equally limited capacity, yet excellent women so far as they go, which could take possession of them, income and all, saving and utilising both it and themselves—would be a real boon to society."[41] Craik suggests that Anglican sisterhoods might not only use but actually save both the ladies and their incomes, a conflation of economic and sisterly salvation that relies not on payment but on possession. Jameson similarly limits sisterhood to those "bring[ing] a small sum of money," noting that "if a woman be at all respectable [. . .] she must have friends, or find friends, to subscribe for her this small dowry."[42] The equation of respectability with the ability to procure funds also drives Jameson's distinction between paid and unpaid labor. Explaining that there should be "two classes [of women]; those who receive direct pay, and those who do not," she explicitly places the (working-class) "hired labor [. . .] at the disposal of the voluntary and unpaid labor," and considers this hired laborer "in all respects subordinate": "can we hope to obtain these qualifications [humility, intelligence, enthusiasm, self-command, benevolence, religious spirit] for any pay which our jails, workhouses, or hospitals could afford?—or indeed for any pay whatever? Yet it is precisely an order of women, quite beyond the reach of any remuneration that could be afforded, which is so imperatively required in our institutions."[43] Class, as well as gender, is at stake in Jameson's emphasis that sisters are above hire, as it is in many other contemporary tributes to these gentlewomen, "endowed with those capabilities which an education superior to that of the lowest class imparts."[44]

Within these religious communities themselves, sisters were split along hierarchical lines. Working-class women, who comprised only 10 percent of sisters, joined these religious orders as "lay" sisters who observed a longer novitiate, held fewer offices, performed domestic labor, dressed differently, and were prohibited from voting; the larger portion of sisters came from the middle and upper classes. These "choir" sisters bought privileges with their capital or income.[45] By downplaying the question of pay, sisters, like salaried male professionals, tried to distinguish themselves from the wage-earning working class. Participating in the religious economy of sisterhood was primarily an upper- or middle-class freedom. Jameson even makes religious feeling a function of class: "The two meanest forms of sensuality and selfishness in our lower classes, the love of money and the love of drink, are best combated by the combined religious and feminine influence."[46] This binary leaves no room for working-class women to be religious, professional, or even fully feminine saviors.[47]

The sisterhoods' distinction between moneyed and penniless sister, their privileging of voluntary work over market pressures such as a demand for "bread," and their "unpaid, beneficent" extension of domestic duties such as nursing and rescue work into a larger arena shaped the specific exchange practices of their service economy. These practices will be central to Rossetti's vision of redemptive sisterhood, as well.

II. Lizzie's Silver Penny

Like the Anglican sisters Jameson describes, Laura and Lizzie of "Goblin Market" are "redundant," single and set apart from men whose absence from the poem hints that there may be no market other than the goblins' for the girls. Even the alliterative names and repetitive similes that describe them ("Like two blossoms on one stem, /Like two flakes of new-fall'n snow") suggest redundancy (188–189). The poem explores the limited options available to "superfluous" girls. Without husbands or fathers to care for them, they can turn to sexualized exchange (like Laura) or the transactions of religious sisterhood (like Lizzie). Lizzie participates in a service economy that intersects the marketplace but maintains different strategies for exchange.[48] As I now show, her silver penny, while an object of exchange, is not a commercial one. As a symbol of domestic and religious duty, it resonates with Anglican sisterhoods' similarly noncommercial, gendered exchange.

Lizzie watches her sister's decline and initially has mixed feelings about her market price. She

> Longed to buy fruit to comfort her,
> But feared to pay too dear.
> . . . .
> Till Laura dwindling
> Seemed knocking at Death's door:
> Then Lizzie weighed no more
> Better and worse;
> But put a silver penny in her purse. (310–311; 320–324)

It is important that Lizzie has this penny. Laura's pennilessness meant powerlessness. Lizzie's coin insures her against market forces, protecting her own curls from the goblin merchant men and allowing her to take on the role of rescuer rather than victim. This split of moneyed and penniless sisters into savior and fallen parallels the sisterhoods Jameson and others describe, where wealthier women can afford to be unpaid and beneficent.

In this passage, Lizzie sets aside her cost/benefit analysis, aware of market considerations but rejecting them (or, in Jameson's terms, rejecting the idea "that every thing has a money value, to be calculated to a farthing") in order to rescue her sister. Laura's salvation depends upon Lizzie's rejection of standard commercial practices. Not only does Lizzie make a noncommercial decision to stop weighing her options, but the silver penny that she puts in her purse (324) as she kisses Laura and departs for market (325) is also a rejection of that market: the coin is nonstandard issue.

Critical interpretations of the poem consistently highlight Lizzie's silver penny and the "prudent precaution" she exercises by putting it in her purse, calling her a savvy shopper, diligent saver, and successful consumer. Herbert Tucker further notes that the penny "expose[s] the goblin traffic for what it is—a market."[49] Yet how Lizzie happens to have a silver penny to put in her purse has also been the subject of much speculation. Indeed, Richard Menke muses that "it may ultimately be the central mystery of the poem."[50] To Terrence Holt it presents less of a mystery: "[B]y figuring the sisters' only exchangeable goods as their bodies, the poem makes that penny nothing but a sign of sexual experience."[51] While I disagree that the penny represents prostitution—Lizzie's newly open eyes and ears resist imputations of a prior fall—Holt's emphasis on the poem's bodily exchanges is apt. Lizzie does offer up her body to the goblin men and, even more provocatively, will later give it as a Eucharistic offering to her sister in her oft-quoted imperative: "Eat me, drink me, love me" (471).[52] Laura's feasting on Lizzie may be a form of spiritual communion, yet Lizzie implores her sister not only to "eat" and "drink" her but also to "kiss me, suck my juices" (468), confusing critics who aren't sure how to reconcile the homoerotic frenzy of this scene with the religious economy of a single wafer and sip of wine. Caroline Walker Bynum's study of medieval religious imagery provides a partial explanation; according to her records, the Eucharist did at times provoke the intense cravings that Laura experienced, while the belief that bodily excretions could nourish or save helps to make sense of Lizzie as a juicy sort of Christ-figure.[53] The Christian belief that bodily exchange carries spiritual as well as sexual meaning underscores the importance of extra-commercial value to the poem's exchanges. But the place of the silver penny in those exchanges remains mysterious. Critical conversation is still searching for a way to talk directly about a coin that appears out of nowhere and serves no real purpose in the market: the goblins hold it briefly but do not finally accept it.[54]

Gift theory proves more valuable than market equations for understanding the worth of Lizzie's penny. In gift economies, the items withheld from circulation are as important as those that are traded. Other items are exchanged for the sake of keeping the "inalienable possessions" that Weiner argues are central to the giver's status. For the ladies of Cranford, secrets function as these inalienable possessions. In "Goblin Market," part of Laura's problem is that she doesn't hold anything back. Like other women exploited by both gift and market economies, she becomes the object rather than the agent of exchange. In contrast, Lizzie attempts to keep-while-giving, offering a coin but keeping herself.[55]

Lizzie's penny has two noncommercial sources that further allow us to make sense of its gift function in her rescue mission, one fantastical and one numismatic. The first requires us to remember that "Goblin Market" is, on one of its many levels, a fairy tale. The poem resists realism not only with its talk of goblins, "charms," and "haunted" sites but also through its generic, rural setting and indistinct temporality. Rossetti's original title, "A Peep at the Goblins," references a collection by her cousin, Anna Eliza Bray: *A Peep at the Pixies*. Rossetti was also familiar with Bray's *Traditions, Legends, Superstitions, and Sketches of Devonshire* and Thomas Keightley's *The Fairy Mythology*, an anthology that reprinted some of Bray's tales.[56] In the revised and expanded edition of Keightley's volume, tales of fairies, goblins, elves, pixies, dwarves, and other fantastical beings redound with wealth: silver horns and bells, gold harps, and precious stones.[57] The *Mythology*, along with Bray's *Traditions*, also describes the use of silver pennies in fairyland.

According to Keightley and Bray, goblins used silver pennies as currency. When maidens swept their houses and set out food or water for fantastical visitors, they found money—often silver pennies—in their shoes or water basins. If they failed to please the pixies, hobgoblins, or other guests, they were pinched black and blue instead.[58] Rossetti's description of domestic labor echoes the coin-worthy maiden behavior:

> Laura rose with Lizzie:
> Fetched in honey, milked the cows,
> Aired and set to rights the house,
> Kneaded cakes of whitest wheat
> Cakes for dainty mouths to eat,
> Next churned butter, whipped up cream,
> Fed their poultry, sat and sewed;
> Talked as modest maidens should: (202–209)

In fairyland, Lizzie's penny would be the standard return (economic but not commercial) for the gendered household work that she continues to do even after her sister has ceased to perform it:

> [Laura] no more swept the house,
> . . . .
> Brought water from the brook:
> But sat down listless in the chimney-nook [. . . .] (293, 296–297)

The "chimney-nook" particularly recalls Bray, whose tales of pixie trade include model maidens dutifully placing water basins in such nooks. Lizzie's coin, as fairy currency, would reward her for domestic activities rather than provide payment for commercial dealings.[59] It would also provide another literary source for the physical abuse that the goblins inflict upon Lizzie, whose treatment in the market is, I think rightly, often read as rape or sexual assault. The goblins "pinched" and then "Kicked," "knocked," and "Mauled" her (427–429). This pinching, as we have seen, has precedence in pixie displeasure. (The sexual undertones of Lizzie's assault suggest the darker side of Bray's fairy tales, as of the Grimms' before them.)[60] Of course the goblins resent Lizzie's attempt to return the penny; she turns her reward for "proper" maidenly deference into a sign of her refusal to "Honour" them by eating with them (369).

Lizzie's penny represents deference and domestic duties. It also represents religious labor. In another tale from Keightley's collection, we learn that hobgoblins punish those who fail to observe religious rituals as well as domestic duties. Linking pagan superstition to Christian tradition (and reminding us, in the process, of the pagan roots of Judeo-Christian observances), the tale warns: "'if a Peter-penny or a Housle-egge were behind, or a patch of tythe unpaid—then [be]'ware of bull-beggars, spirits, &c.'" "Peter pence" or "Peter's penny" had religious significance as the pre-Reformation tax paid by English householders to the Pope in Rome.[61] Keightley's editorial note, moreover, speculates that the "Housle-egge" may be "an egg at Easter or on good Friday" and goes on to trace "*Housle* [. . . or] *hunsl*, sacrifice or offering," to the Eucharist.[62] According to this tale, the "bull-beggars" or "spirits" would have been even more angered by the neglect of Christian ritual than by listless housekeeping. And that Christian ritual points to a second source for Lizzie's silver penny.

In the early years of the nineteenth century, silver pennies were legal tender, more highly valued than their copper counterparts because of their intrinsic value.[63] By the 1850s and '60s, however, the silver penny was no longer a regular form of currency, and the country's use of a gold standard meant that silver was then measured by the price of gold.[64] The goblins' refusal to accept it as an equivalent for Laura's hair may simply mean that one silver penny holds insufficient value compared to gold. But this penny is no mere token. In 1859, silver pennies would have had value as "Maundy money." These were coins minted for and given to the "deserving" classes of the poor by royalty, as part of an Anglican ceremony on Holy Thursday, before Easter.[65] (If the "Peter penny" taxed landowners, it seems that the Maundy ceremony redistributed some of this money to the poor.) This Easter service tradition of giving to the poor derives from the New Testament tale of Jesus washing the Disciples' feet at the Last Supper and telling them to follow his example.[66] Maundy money, specially minted after 1822, became the formal, conventionalized substitute for other gift-giving and foot-washing practices.[67] A Victorian audience would have been familiar with these coins, produced in excess of ceremonial requirements and available at the bank.[68]

Maundy money, as the currency of service, clarifies one aspect of Rossetti's religious-economic imagery. Lizzie's Christ-like scourging, her sacrifice, and her bodily delivery of saving fruits—"Eat me, drink, me, love me" (471)—have frequently been taken as references to the Eucharist that Maundy money commemorates. Rossetti's own Holy Thursday observances would likely have entered into her imaginative work for "Goblin Market." The manuscript is dated April 27, 1859,[69] just three days after that year's Easter Sunday. Silver pennies further represent Eucharistic imagery through their association with the penny distributed to each laborer equally in Christ's parable of the vineyard. In medieval texts, this penny was popularly understood to represent Christ's sacrifice, the gift of salvation, the consecrated Host of the Eucharistic Feast.[70] Small wonder, then, that Lizzie rejects the goblins' attempts to host a debilitating feast. Her coin offers Christian service or salvation; the goblins decline the currency.

Lizzie's silver penny jingles with religious resonance as it bounces in her purse (452–453) and also marks her participation in the economic structures of contemporary religious sisterhoods. Like the Anglican sisterhoods Jameson describes, Lizzie enters the market not by looking to buy or sell but by extending her domestic and religious obligations from hearth to heath(en). Lizzie's silver penny is a token of domestic duties and religious sacrifice rather than financial savvy or savings. The penny simultaneously ties Lizzie's currency to correct, modest behavior and links her to religious models of "unpaid and beneficent" exchange, placing her in a symbolically significant gift economy that emphasizes the saving power of sisterhood. More than merely legal tender, Lizzie's silver penny marks her as attending sister, caregiver, Christian miracle worker; her role as a sister pertains to her purse as well as her heart. Like Jesus washing the feet of the Disciples, Lizzie puts Christian service before self.

III. The Safest Investments

And yet, Maundy money—this symbol of service and sacrifice—is impersonal. As a conventionalized substitute for foot-washing, it is also a mass-produced proxy for intimate, physical contact with the poor, hardly the Eucharistic gift of body and blood. Lizzie's enactment of the ritual comes at an even further remove. When Lizzie approaches the goblins and "tosse[s] them her penny" (367), she holds out her apron for fruit and space. Her fearful toss is a distortion of the Christian service practices it imitates. Victor Mendoza has argued that Lizzie takes on the role of a monarch by distributing Maundy money, but eighteenth- and nineteenth-century monarchs were far less active in the ceremony than their forerunners. (During Queen Victoria's reign, the Sub-Almoner distributed the

coins.)[71] Rather than revising this trend by recalling earlier sovereigns' more intimate transfers, Lizzie keeps her own queenly distance from the goblin recipients.
The poem seems to endorse this distance. Lizzie's repeated references to Jeanie
(the goblins' prior victim) suggest that her fears are not unfounded. Hers is a spe-
cialized form of service, an exclusive practice directed toward her sister. As we
have seen throughout this study, women's gifts in nineteenth-century literature
change hands primarily between "sisters," the century's flexible shorthand for
women already affiliated through ties of blood, taste, or status. The goblins get a
token; only Laura can receive the personal gift of a sister's sacrifice.

Here, as in the earlier literary annuals I have discussed, sacrifice-worthy sisterhood is ultimately white—"White and golden," in Lizzie's case (408).[72] The girls
together are "Like two flakes of new-fall'n snow, / Like two wands of ivory"
(189–190). In "Goblin Market," this whiteness stands for innocence, but it also
stands for racialized purity. These descriptions follow Laura's feast, and race provides one answer to the important question of why Laura retains this whiteness
even after her fall. The goblin men, in contrast, are exotic creatures, hybridized
mixtures of wombat, rat, snail, and parrot, racialized, as Krista Lysack similarly
notes, by the sexualized force they exert as well as by their mysterious and indistinct origins.[73] A foreign presence endangering domestic life, these goblins are
marginalized by the girls' suspicions even before their fruit exacts its toll:

> We must not look at goblin men,
> We must not buy their fruits:
> Who knows upon what soil they fed
> Their hungry thirsty roots? (42–45)

The question Laura raises here lingers on line 44, "upon what soil they fed"; the
pronoun's doubled antecedents problematize the source of the goblin men as well
as their fruits. The enjambment carries us to roots which presumably belong to
the fruits but whose adjectives "hungry" and "thirsty" better describe nineteenth-
century stereotypes of rapacious savages sprung from an exotically other family
tree. When Lizzie rejects their hospitable offer to "take a seat with us" (368) and
"Be welcome guest with us" (381), the fact that they fling the penny back to her
suggests that the goblins are beyond the scope of her religious economy of service
and salvation as much as she is outside their market economy.[74] Whether the goblins' origins, Jeanie's precedent, or Laura's decline makes Lizzie keep her distance
from them, the goblins attribute this rejection to her sense of status, angrily
calling her "proud" and "uncivil" (394–395).

Class suspicion enters into the characterization of these "merchant men" (474)
as well. The iterations of "brother" ("Brother with queer brother" and "Brother
with sly brother" [94, 96]) suggest not only the Pre-Raphaelite Brotherhood of
Dante Gabriel Rossetti but also other brotherhoods (Masons, trade unions) that

would have registered as sly or devious to a nineteenth-century audience.[75] Unlike religious sisterhood, which was often criticized as a removal from family ties,[76] brotherhood was seen as an "uncivil" merging of parts—working-class "combinations" as horrifying to some spectators as the menagerie of animal parts that the goblin men represent.

Through Lizzie's refusals to look at and sit with the other-specied, racialized, and classed goblins, "Goblin Market" echoes but revises the barriers presumably constructed by Anglican sisterhoods. As we have seen, popular representations of Anglican sisterhoods showed them struggling over the question of incorporation, using class and financial status to measure a woman's ability to be a sister. These communities were particularly ambivalent with regard to their treatment of "fallen" women. They reclaimed some as "sisters"; Jameson mentions with satisfaction the once "unfortunate girls" who "were no longer objects of pity or dependent on charity; they had become objects of respect [. . .]." But these reclaimed women, she notes, observing their "superior" appearance and conduct, "belonged apparently to a better class" than other "unfortunate" girls.[77] Historical records suggest that those other "fallen sisters" of "inferior" classes were welcomed more equivocally; their ties to the community were shaped by guilt as much as by the reciprocal obligations that surely served to bind the other sisters together.[78]

Rossetti's poem agrees with Jameson and Craik that the moneyed sister is in a better position to rescue the fallen. But the poem's descriptions of Lizzie and Laura barely distinguish between them in any further way, doing so only to show the girls' mutual growth.[79] Not only does "Goblin Market" remove the hierarchy that wealth and sexual difference established within sisterhood,[80] but, because the proscriptive element of the poem's sisterhood is biological and racial, it displaces onto the goblin men the forms of censure and rejection often given to "fallen" women. The goblin men are thrust to the margins of the text while Laura's fall, strikingly, is forgiven. At the goblins' expense, the poem reclaims a fallen woman through the gifts of a sisterhood that removes any lingering sense of obligation.[81] Using goblin men as the scapegoats for simplified community formation, then, "Goblin Market" offers a vision of sisterhood which eliminates hierarchy. This sisterhood is perhaps Rossetti's fantasy, or possibly an account of the real, active sisterhoods she witnessed; most likely, it is a combination of both that sets many women's desires for sisterly unification against the social reality of difference.[82]

The most radical suggestion Rossetti's poem makes is that Laura (or other fallen women) might be completely redeemable. Victorian discourses of fallenness frequently saw women's purity as irrevocably lost; the "fallen" could reenter society only at a distance, as servants or emigrants, as we saw with the "Gipsy Mother" in Chapter 1 of this volume.[83] In contrast, Laura's reclamation borrows both from discourses of spiritual salvation and also from a more commercial form of redemption. As if Laura's hair and innocence had been pawned, rather than irretrievably lost, Lizzie is able to restore them both completely. This transaction thus opens up the possibility that even a woman's sexual purity—bemoaned by the poem as something to be sold on the market—can also be restored through a different kind of market dealing, exchanges "beyond the reach of any remuneration," but profitable nonetheless.

Rossetti's radical revision of sexual purity also rewrites women's community. Laura's "fall" is no bar to sisterhood. Indeed, only after it does the poem refer to Lizzie as "sister." Sisterhood, in this sense, requires and is constituted by a fall.[84] The fall itself becomes a source of satisfaction and long-standing community for the girls. By the poem's end, when Laura's fall becomes an opportunity for her to teach their children the merits of sisterhood, she fondly recalls her experience as "pleasant days long gone" (550). Lizzie, too, benefits from Laura's fall. Acting in accordance to the service economy of sisterhood offers her new experiences, letting her "for the first time in her life / Beg[i]n to listen and look" (327–328). The juice that covers Lizzie as she runs away with her penny is most often seen as her "steal," but her new experiences and her "inward laughter" (463) at "feel[ing] the drip / Of juice that syrupped all her face" (433–434) are also part of her proceeds, the indirect return for the gift she gives her sister. Most discussions locate Lizzie's desire—when they grant her any—in the homoerotic exchange that follows her fruit retrieval. We can also find her desires and their physical gratification in the mixture of pain and pleasure that Lizzie encounters through her mission to the market.[85] Lizzie's bodily glee is new. Before offering herself up for sisterly sacrifice and service, she is merely "content" and "placid," concerned and fearful. Her effort to redeem her sister aligns her service economy with that of the Anglican sisterhoods; her inadvertent but pressing proximity to fallenness—her joy in her "resistance" but also in her brush with marketplace "evil" (438, 437)—suggests that she, too, profits from this redemptive economy.

The profit reaches beyond the poem, both by encouraging its audience to engage in similar service economies and by validating that audience's desires. Rossetti's verses share in the sensory delight that Lizzie takes away with her. Constance Hassett convincingly argues that the lyric strand of the poem "celebrates" the desire that the narrative strand resists and that Rossetti herself "rid[es] the euphoria of language" through spinning syntax and "dazzling" images.[86] The reader takes part, if not in Rossetti's "euphoria," then certainly in her poem's sounds and syllables, its compelling orality, its "frisky metrics [that] practically have to be sounded out."[87] Many other readers and critics have recognized the linguistic pleasures of plump fruits that fill not only Laura's mouth but those of the readers who voice them, infinitely extending the implied author's exuberance to a larger reading community.

The rich, bountiful descriptions signify poetic enjoyment. They are also poetic excess. When Lizzie tells Laura to "make much of" her, the poem responds in equally exaggerated terms (472). Laura doesn't just "kiss" her sister but "kissed and kissed and kissed her" (486). This paratactic, repetitious line replicates the excessive approach of the entire poem, in which sales pitch follows sales pitch and simile chases simile. Like the goblins whose fruit juice covers Lizzie's entire face and neck, the poem feeds its readership much more than the requisite bite. Rossetti's poetic excess, then, proffers not merely pleasure but a sense of gratuity; it, too, becomes a gift, stylistically echoing Lizzie's preferred currency. By approaching it as such, we are better able to reconcile this anomalous, generous, overflowing narrative with the body of Rossetti's other poems more frequently associated with "loss."[88] Both perform and rejoice in giving to excess, in sacrifice. In the verses it coins, as in the coin it subverts, "Goblin Market" shows how gift offerings—of poetry, of religious service, of sisterly sacrifice—can be pleasures for giver and recipient alike, as much a realization of the self as its repudiation.[89]

By 1862, when Rossetti's poem was published, Victorian markets were offering female shoppers new consumer pleasures.[90] But as "Goblin Market" suggests, the financial transactions associated with market capitalism were frequently risky business for women. The "safe[st] investments" diversified this risk through joint ventures that emphasized the importance of gift practices within and alongside the market. Throughout the latter half of the century, as shopkeepers were enticing consumers with plate-glass window displays, colorful advertisements, and catchy jingles, many female writers and reformers celebrated spectacle in a different way by offering up the sounds and sights of women's extreme gifts. Like Lizzie, they would "gladly spend and [be] spent" in sacrificial, religious economies that traded on danger and redeemed "sisters" by bringing gifts to the market. In the following decades, women's sacrificial gifts continued to penetrate the market, securing alliances and professional opportunities for giving women. As we will see in Chapter 5, the extreme offerings of religious women established and consolidated female networks that ultimately enabled them to solicit, spend, and even showcase the very money that earlier authors downplayed. Rather than reject the market outright, the evangelical "Slum Sisters" of the Salvation Army used gift practices to transform the market itself into a sign of salvation, teaching impoverished families to save their souls by saving (and then spending) their coins.

CHAPTER 5

Service and Savings in the Slums

Lizzie's tight-lipped rejection of consumerism, her devotion to a less fortunate sister, and her sacrificial gifts of body and coin align her not only with the Anglican Sisterhoods discussed in Chapter 4 of this volume but also with other female networks of religious reformers who were attempting to navigate a tempting but dangerous marketplace. Evangelical activists in the London slums similarly relied on sacrificial gifts to construct their larger religious "sisterhoods," but unlike Lizzie, who completes her errand after procuring the goblins' juice, the women I describe in this chapter used sacrifice as an empowered strategy to repeatedly enter into and work alongside the market that Rossetti and Jameson reject.

Sacrifice gets short shrift in studies of the early women's movement. Some see sacrifice as little more than a socially conditioned response to nineteenth-century conduct books that defined women as "relative" creatures and advised them to forget their own needs in order to better serve their husbands, fathers, and sons.[1] Others associate it with the term *selfless*, which so often accompanies descriptions of "sacrifice" and literally undercuts the intense subjectivity and self-scrutiny of the critically favored modern individual.[2] Yet sacrifice, as Ilana M. Blumberg and others have argued, is more than a condition of diminished selfhood or a necessary evil of Victorian separate spheres ideology.[3] This chapter explores how a group of early Salvation Army women wrote about and enacted forms of sacrifice in order to build community and indulge safely in their growing consumer desires under the auspices of social service. Sacrifice (of clothing and class, safety and even self-hood) actually enabled these women to consolidate both their own robust subjecthood and a larger, active sisterhood.

The slums of late-Victorian London—home of the impoverished, haunt of the thrill-seeker—provoked widespread consternation among readers and activists. Journalists' exposés, private philanthropy, and public legislation sought to uncover and correct these unsanitary and unsafe spaces where, in the words of the early Salvation Army, the "submerged tenth" of the population lived. In 1884, Toynbee Hall and Oxford House opened as university settlements for men; philanthropic ladies were discovering that London's slums provided sites for "adventure, self-discovery, and meaningful work"[4]; and a group of Salvation Army workers known as "Slum Sisters" began to live and work among London's East End paupers. As members of an evangelical Christian reform organization, Slum Sisters ministered to the poor, stressed conversion of body and soul, and tried to improve sanitary conditions in slum dwellings. Like investigative journalists, too, they often dressed incognito, disguising themselves to enter and shed light on the dark spaces of the slums. Yet Slum Sisters stand out among other institutions and individuals with similar methods because of their discursive strategies for bringing about and reflecting upon this work. In an abundance of print materials, they deploy extreme, sacrificial gifts to create a powerful, fluid network that offered them privileged access to an increasing range of urban spaces and economic roles. Using sacrifice to shift rhetorically among subject positions, Slum Sisters attempt to speak to and for women across class. This "sisterhood" that they create out of sacrifice is more than an effacing of self on behalf of a larger community. Sacrificial sisterhood emerges out of an organization that simultaneously valued individualist action and collectivist spirit, and Slum Sisters benefit from it both individually and collectively, as they use it to raise and spend money, to encourage consumer desire, to reconcile the purchase of material goods with spiritual salvation, and to authorize professional goals including authorship itself.

The Salvation Army, founded as the Christian Mission in 1865 by William Booth, adopted military titles and dress in 1878. Its evangelical fervor, bold costumes, and crowd-gathering music met with mixed reviews, but the organization grew rapidly and widely. Despite its rigid military hierarchy[5]—or perhaps because its system of ranking actually permitted greater social mobility than many other Victorian hierarchies—the Army was more inclusive than other groups of late-nineteenth-century "slummers" and district visitors. Army soldiers stationed in the slums came from diverse socioeconomic backgrounds and had opportunities to rise in rank. The Army self-consciously recruited both men and women, and although it distributed the higher-ranking titles unevenly, welcomed roughly equal numbers of male and female officers in 1883.[6]

Women were in particularly high demand in one Army brigade, which called for healthy, single females between the ages of 20 and 30 to come and serve as angels, saviours, lassies, or sisters of the slums.[7] I refer to them as Slum Sisters partly because they themselves emphasized this name, partly because it was the name increasingly used to describe them, but largely because, as we will see, "sister" was a term that did quite a bit of work for this network of giving women. General Booth's philanthropic treatise, *In Darkest England and the Way Out* (1890), describes the Slum Sisters' work, but, like many histories of the Army, his account passes quickly over both their slum work and their writing.[8] Since Booth, historians and literary critics have also bypassed Slum Sisters' emphases on religion and sacrifice in an effort to produce more secular histories of women's political activism, narrowly defined. In books, pamphlets, weekly papers, and monthly magazines published by the Army between 1884 and 1890, however, slum sisterhood offers Army women an intriguing compromise between serving others and serving themselves. Religious sacrifice, in the service of sisterhood, enabled Army women's increasing economic agency and facilitated their social action.[9]

Salvation Army Slum Sisters, contrary to most historical accounts, have at least two points of origin. The first dates to 1884, when Training Home Cadets led by Emma Booth (later Booth-Tucker) and Maud Charlesworth (later Booth) took a room in London's Seven Dials and began ministering to the inhabitants of the slums. Eva (Evangeline) Booth joined her sister's work soon afterwards. Their effort, known as the "Cellar, Gutter, and Garret Brigade," continued for a few years under the supervision of Blanche B. Cox, the Slum Sister and officer who wrote many of the Brigade's early reports. In 1886, Harriet Webb and Polly Redmead inaugurated the similar but separate "London Slum Work" which eventually merged with and supplanted the earlier Brigade.[10] Staff-Captain (later Major) James J. Cooke, shown with Slum Sisters or "Saviours" in Figure 5.1, supervised this second wave of slum work.[11]

We learn still more about the early slum work from this photograph. Neat rows of nearly indistinguishable women call attention to these military workers' codes and regulations; visible steps provide height adjustments for the group shot while simultaneously recalling the ladder of Salvation Army hierarchy. In the front row, the awkward display of women's hands, flat and prominent against the backdrop of their aprons, emphasizes the manual work that these humbly though uniformly

THE SLUM SAVIOURS.

Figure 5.1 "The Slum Saviours" *AW* (November 1887), 336
The Salvation Army International Heritage Centre

clad women performed. Two figures stand out among rows of identical aprons and hats. Up front and center sits James Cooke, his own hands partially obscured by his military-styled hat. I return, later, to this suggestive synecdoche and to the increasingly central role he played in shaping Army histories of the Slum Sisters. Here, however, I wish to draw attention to another soldier, who stands behind him and toward the right in the fourth row. This woman makes her hands visible by resting them on the shoulders of two women in front of her, a stance part possessive, part affectionate, suggesting an affiliation beyond the photograph's rank-and-file composition. This strange mixture of uniformity and individuality, service and ownership flourishes in Army women's self-presentation of sacrificial sisterhood and highlights the tension of an organization that derives personal and collective strength out of a seemingly selfless corporate mission.

I. "Lower Still": Sacrifice and Sistering in the Slums

For Army women, gifts of service and sacrifice in the slums were a function of, and sometimes synonymous with, sisterhood. *Sister* appears frequently in Army publications as a familiar and universalizing term that attempts to bring reader, officer, and slum dweller together by referring emphatically to women of all ranks both inside and outside the Army, the "fallen" women they seek to help, and the women who read about them.[12] Sisterhood never signifies static relations but instead serves as shorthand for affiliations constructed actively through giving. One article notes that "wherever there was hunger, sorrow, sin or pain, [slum workers] have entered quietly in the spirit of sisterly love and readiness to help. They are universally greeted as 'Sister' by the young and old"; another article records an incident that "blessedly illustrate[s]" their "claim to be regarded as real sisters of the poor women of the streets."[13] Indeed, in Army publications *sister* becomes a verb to describe the way that the slum workers take the poor in hand to offer relief: "we clasped baby close, put an arm round the frowsy-headed girl nearest us, and thanked God for this handful of fifteen or twenty, gathered in that peaceful little room, to be [...] sistered by [Captain Polly's] lassies, and to sing and read and pray the Sunday evening through." "Sisterliness" describes how "Army friends" share freely with a "poor, unfortunate sister" and at the same time asks the reader if she is willing to give help to "'[m]y sister and yours.'"[14]

Although Slum Sisters use the term "sister" to imply an intimate and egalitarian alternative to "visitor," the sisterhood they actually endorse emerges out of unequal gift transactions. Unlike the networks of women who trade equivalent gifts in *Cranford*, *Jane Eyre*, or *Aurora Leigh*, Salvation Army slum workers constitute sisterhood through varied forms of physical, emotional, and financial sacrifice. Styling themselves the "real sisters of the poor" requires that Slum Sisters give something up. The clearest visual markers of this sacrifice appear in the dress code initiated by Blanche B. Cox (shown with Slum Sisters in Figure 5.2),

Figure 5.2   Blanche B. Cox with (clockwise from top left) Cadets Cameron, Smith, Layton, and Morgan, November 1884
(printed in *WC* December 25, 1884, 1) The Salvation Army International Heritage Centre

which stressed deprivation and made even the acts of putting on and removing garments a way to perform the extreme giving that, as we will see, came to characterize these Army women.

> We *dress like the people*—with shabby clothes, shawls, aprons, and often bare heads. This enables us to make ourselves at home in the poorest hovel […]. Our dress, we find, helps us to go as SISTERS—not VISITORS […].[15]

Women's fashion favored the showy and voluminous in the final decades of the nineteenth century, but the simple lines of form-fitting sleeves and hip-skimming skirts modeled in these images were in keeping with the clothing donned by other serious social workers, who "wore their skirts on the short side and chose dark colors, washable fabrics, and simple styles."[16] Many district nurses and women of other religious orders dressed in uniform, thereby making themselves "both more and less visible"[17] than other urban philanthropists. Slum Sisters' dress and its description differed, however, from the "bonnet, collar, [and] dark gown" favored by these other groups.[18] Throwing on aprons and shawls, they took off collars and hats and are frequently pictured in torn and threadbare fabrics (see Figures 5.3 and 5.4).

Articles in the Salvation Army newspaper *The War Cry* (WC) describe the standard Army uniform as a "Public Confession of Christ," but Slum Sisters dressed for private access as well, going "native" in the slums to win converts.[19] Unlike similar Army strategies in India, where prominent Army leaders exoticized themselves for an English audience by dressing in foreign turbans and robes, Slum Sisters in London capitalized on the insubstantial, dirty, and relatively revealing attire to make their own shabbiness at once a mark of femininity and of sacrifice. Cox, credited with initiating "what we learned to call 'Lower Still' dress,"[20] reiterates frequently that Slum Sisters "seek, as far as possible, to put ourselves on a level with the people, entering into their sorrows and cares" by adopting their ragged dress.[21] Literal signs of divestment, this clothing also stood in for the larger sacrifices that would define sisterhood in the slums.

More immediately, the clothing proposed a leveling that, like sisterhood, could at least theoretically collapse distinctions, creating sartorial and rhetorical slippage among workers, readers, and paupers. For Army writers, "sisterhood" itself came to signify an overlapping of speakers, audience, and charitable objects and provided a mode for one woman to speak for another by making them rhetorically interchangeable through a common name.[22] This overlapping discourse of sisterhood afforded one "sister" access to another and gave her the authority to offer perspectives on sights revealed through that access. Slum Sisters' unique position between "sister" readers and "our poor sisters" allowed them to see and claim knowledge of some portion of the slums, ultimately shaping the way their "poor sisters" and the slums themselves were read. Dressing down to be a "Sister" attempted to make visible this rhetorical interchangeability of subject positions, allowing slum-goers to cross socially bounded spaces, and also to claim, through sisterhood, the ability to transcend and traverse class. Slum Sisters attempted to put themselves literally in others' places, speaking to as well as for them, and showing how readers could do so too.

In part, this gesture aligned their efforts with other working-class sources of community support, such as Ellen Ranyard's working-class Bible Women.[23] Many Slum Sisters were themselves workers and the daughters, wives, and sisters of skilled and unskilled laborers. Women who identified themselves with the Salvation Army by the 1891 census came from households headed by relatively comfortable grocers and merchants of the middle or lower middle classes but also by brick layers, carpenters, smiths, farmers, grooms, boot makers, straw hat sewers, wool shearers, coal heaters, and members of other trades likely to suffer from seasonal vagaries or periodic unemployment. For the London poor, employment was often temporary. Even moderately comfortable families might experience cycles of extreme need.[24] As Ellen Ross has shown, impoverished families were often sustained for a time by working-class mutual aid, rather than

Figure 5.3 "Lower Still," 1886 *AW* 2.3 (March, 1886), 50
The Salvation Army International Heritage Centre

Figure 5.4 "WE DRESS LIKE THE PEOPLE" *Called Out* (1886), 43
The Salvation Army International Heritage Centre

top-down gifts of charity. This support reinforced neighborhood networks.[25] It also made the designation of poverty flexible; any family could rise up or fall "lower still" down the social ladder. The Army was "wide awake to the dangers of becoming [...] too respectable to welcome the lowest and the worst"[26]; the "lower still" dress of the largely though not entirely working-class Army attempted to demonstrate that many Slum Sisters had been and saw themselves as neighbors, not just visitors. Unlike the "lady bountifuls" lampooned by Dickens and others, they were as susceptible to changing circumstances as the poor whom they attempted to help.[27]

And yet, the clothing also constructed distance between slum workers and their "poor sisters." Though many Slum Sisters came from working-class and sometimes impoverished backgrounds, this history is visually bypassed by "lower still" dress that indicates a simple, unidirectional descent from their present comfort to their (staged) distress. The use of tattered threads to construct sisterhood, moreover, suggests that this sisterhood is only one-sided. The poor are never shown "dressing up" to be sisters. Army women choose their own rags carefully; despite the Army's interest in reclaiming prostitutes, for instance, Slum Sisters never attempt to dress like *these* "sisters." Dressing down to be a "sister" draws attention to how *un*natural and selective the relationship really is. By emphasizing the very hierarchy that it tries to traverse, cross-dressing calls attention not to slum inhabitants' sisterhood but to the vertical axis of Slum Sisters' "going lower."[28] This sacrifice offers them, first, spiritual rewards: "Let us not forget," Emma and Ballington Booth instruct readers, "what joy the 'cheerful giver' at this Christmas time will receive from the Master's lips at His coming, by hearing the words, 'Inasmuch as ye have done it unto one of the least of these my brethren, ye have done it unto Me.'"[29] Slum Sisters' sacrifices also suggest their material remove from the neighbors they were helping. Mrs. [Lydia Corbett] Cooke informs *War Cry* readers that "all of them have left comfortable homes [...]."[30] When they put on shabby clothing, Slum Sisters construct their own "natural" distance from that dress.

Through their sacrifices, Slum Sisters simultaneously constitute an idealized sisterhood of intimate and interchangeable women and stand in its stead. Army women and their gifts become the focus of slum reform. Drawings of the Slum Sisters predominate over those of the poor, coming to stand metonymically for slums and paupers alike. Frequently shown in pairs, as in Figure 5.3, Slum Sisters represent sisterhood through these doubled images, together, with each other, rather than pairing themselves with the poor whom they claim to sister.[31] When the poor do appear, shriveled bodies and emaciated faces firmly distinguish them from those full-figured Slum Sisters with whom they are purportedly interchangeable. The eroticization of working women was one of the attractions of slum work for middle-class female readers, according to Seth Koven.[32] Along these lines, the Army's readership consumed abundant images of attractive Slum

Sisters in working-class drag. In an important reversal of Koven's findings, however, descriptions of Slum Sisters sexualize the charity workers rather than the recipients of their aid. Figure 5.4 underscores the physical health, stature, beauty, and strength of the Slum Sister shown in a position of prayerful supplication before a woman and child who offer a striking contrast with the gypsy mother depicted in Chapter 1 of this volume. Here, the image of religious *caritas* serves a different purpose; Slum Sister, not pauper, makes the appeal to the Army's readership on behalf of "sisterhood." Gifts of sacrifice thus empower the Army's network of female activists in the slums.

II. Cupboards, Chairs, and Conversion

Slum Sisters are able to solicit and direct their audience's giving because they have already given up so much. This mixture of giving and taking requires constant negotiation in essays and pamphlets by the early Salvation Army. The Army, growing aggressively throughout the 1880s and '90s, needed money to wage its ambitious campaigns.[33] Its papers introduce the slum work by begging working-, middle-, and upper-class readers to "Please Read this, and Help!"[34] Subsequent articles—in the weekly *War Cry*, the monthlies *All the World* and *The Deliverer*, and a number of pamphlets—make similar appeals, offering first-hand descriptions (read this!) in exchange for money, clothing, energy, and prayers. "Will *you* be a worker?" they inevitably demand. "What are *you* going to do? Your heart is stirred, perhaps [. . .] but how are you going to help?"[35] Targeting hearts and pockets alike, the Army passed the hat at public meetings, sold copies of *The War Cry*, and used its vast publications to solicit as much as to inform. But the Army walked a fine line with regard to these revenues. Like Christina Rossetti and Anna Jameson, the Army tried to keep its sisters and other soldiers out of a suspicious and potentially dangerous market. An article's title betrays some of this anxiety: "Can our Soldiers be bought? How much a week?"[36] Fearful that it would be accused of worldly corruption, the Army published its financial accounts and stern injunctions against receiving individual gifts. It also stressed the difference between the communal Christian ethic motivating Army requests and the self-interested worldliness it denounced.[37] Slum Sisterhood was important to this balancing act because it offered the Army the plurality of subject positions that so delicate an institutional condition required, subsuming individual workers and their profits into a larger family of military and civilian "sisters." While Slum Sisters' sacrifices guaranteed the larger Army a net loss to offset any uncomfortable gain, these efforts to go "lower still" also allowed individual workers to explore, express, and pursue material desires, justifying forays into the market even as they disavowed for themselves the consumer activities they encouraged among the poor.

Slum Sisters attempted to purify their share of Army profits, not through "convert[ing] everything to good," as Shaw's *Major Barbara* (1905) and historian Diane Winston's gloss on the play suggest, but by deflecting attention away from their participation in the marketplace.[38] The language of sisterhood in particular offered them a way to defend and disavow their financial interests. Slum Sisters, as we have seen, considered themselves most vividly "sisters" when they made one-sided gifts of sacrifice. But by employing the familial language of sisterhood for themselves, readers, and paupers, the Slum Sisters rhetorically collapse distinctions between recipient and giver. Thus "sisterhood" enabled slum workers to insinuate their appeals without directly asking for money; the request to not forget our sisters implies, but elides, a more direct request for the donation of coins.[39] Appealing to readers ("sister-Soldiers," "wealthier, highly favored sisters," and "my sister") to help their "little," "poor, unfortunate," "dear," and "fallen" sisters transforms class hierarchy into an unfortunate distribution of the family wealth and makes the affective act of sistering consonant with sharing wealth.[40] The Army's calls to aid militarize sympathy and sisterhood alike, sometimes gently ("I want, God helping me, to enlist the sympathy of my sisters for [. . .] our poor fallen sisters") and sometimes grimly ("My sister, how much longer are you going to fight against God?"), but all invoke sisterhood as a surrogate for more "practical sympathy."[41] I examine the Sisters' use of military language in greater detail below; here, it is important to note that in Army fundraising, sisterhood literally pays off. Family feeling conveys Slum Sisters' financial requests, which draw simultaneously on sisterly hearts and philanthropic pockets—both apparently good liquid assets, as this call for help suggests: "Would to God some of those who have abundance would [. . .] look at some of those poor creatures I am sure their hearts would melt with sympathy."[42]

In exchange for readers' sisterly contributions, Slum Sisters offered intimate access to unfamiliar slum dwellings: "Did you ever visit a slum, Reader?" "Will you look at a few of the homes [. . .]?" "Come into this little room, and I shall tell you the story of that poor woman on the bed."[43] Doubly representing the poor by standing for their welfare and presenting their images, Slum Sisters' articles also and repeatedly express their own fascination with the material conditions of the slums. Indeed, the "story" of slum inhabitants often becomes the story of these homes, rooms, and beds. Although the Army proudly announced its interest in both physical and spiritual relief, claiming to feed the body as well as the soul,[44] Slum Sisters' attention to poverty extended beyond alleviating hunger to include other worldly concerns.

At the most basic level of their interest in the slums' physical environments, Slum Sisters recorded the cleanliness of each "dark, dirty, nearly empty little room" they visited.[45] Dirt takes on literal, metaphoric, and metonymic properties, as Slum Sisters confront the practical problems behind the dirt ("they cannot get bread—leaving soap and brushes out of the question altogether"[46]) and attempt to tidy both souls and slums by sweeping it up. *War Cry* songs suggest that they served God by scrubbing slum floors,[47] and Slum Sisters tell many success stories through neat rooms and clean children, the visible signs of salvation.[48] An article entitled "Sisters of the People" is typical in its conflation of hallelujahs with hygiene: "Dropping on their knees to scrub as well as pray [... Slum Sisters ...] pioneered what has now become a recognized and most necessary force in connection with The Army's manifold labours."[49] Slum Sisters' emphasis on being physically as well as spiritually clean is not, in itself, unique. The saying "cleanliness is next to godliness" is of early nineteenth-century Methodist coinage, and social housekeeping (in all of its erotic and imperial dimensions) was popular throughout the nineteenth century.[50] Elizabeth Gaskell presented fictive scenes of ill-kept working-class homes in *Mary Barton* (1848) and *North and South* (1854–1855), and Engels's depictions of laborers' filthy living conditions are infamous.[51] Salvation Army accounts draw on these familiar literary conventions, but use them to different effect: the interchangeable images of scrubbing and praying that routinely show Slum Sisters kneeling (see Figures 5.2, 5.4–5.6) indicate that dirt also gave them another opportunity to go "lower still." Wholeheartedly shaking filthy hands and washing filthy rags, Slum Sisters show more concern for the material conditions of the slums they visit than for

"PUT UP A PRAYER FOR US, SISTER."

Figure 5.5 "Put Up a Prayer for Us, Sister" *Four Years Slumming*, 1891, 36
The Salvation Army International Heritage Centre

their own comfort or appearance, eager to assure readers that the home improve-ments they desire will benefit the slum dwellers, not themselves.[52] *The War Cry* is emphatic on this point: Slum Sisters are there to "scrub floors, and [...] scrub the selfishness and other sins of the world away, without any guarantee of salary and no prospect of presents!"[53]

Scrubbing down is only part of Slum Sisters' response to dirty rooms and their inhabitants. They move quickly past soap to fixate on property ownership. Salva-tion Army workers were expected to renounce personal, worldly interests; the sac-rificial cross-dressing of the Slum Sisters nods to these expectations, even as it constructs an element of choice in their class trappings. But the lack of material objects in the slums becomes a source of anxiety for Slum Sisters. Like the ladies of *Cranford* who obsessively account for remnants of candle or string, Slum Sisters repeatedly and meticulously catalogue scarcity in these rooms: "There was not a scrap of furniture in the room, with the exception of (if such can be so called) a cup without a handle, a little saucepan, a dilapidated oil lamp, and an old soap box."[54] Other slum visitors and social investigators shared Slum Sisters' concerns insofar as they centered on a lack of appropriate bedding. Middle-class proponents of "whole-some home life" were primarily alarmed by the prospect of multiple inhabitants

Figure 5.6 "Cleaning Away Five Weeks' Dirt" *WC* March 19, 1887, 13
The Salvation Army International Heritage Centre. The handwritten date that appears on this *War Cry* image was added after its 1887 publication, but may refer to the date of the original drawing.

sleeping in a single bed, "mixed indiscriminately."[55] Slum Sisters similarly equate decorous behavior with home décor. But property overwhelms propriety in their accounts. The saucepans, lamps, and cups that they catalogue threaten to push beyond the values assigned to them as symbols of dwindling domesticity.

Embracing stark sartorial and domestic sacrifice for themselves, Slum Sisters recoil from the bareness they encounter in the slums. If, as Elaine Freedgood notes of the earlier nineteenth century, the "ownership and display of [. . .] small luxuries" offered the working classes visible "insurance against hard times, when such items could be pawned,"[56] Slum Sisters' records seem intent on demonstrating the utter dearth of redemption (material or otherwise) available to slum dwellers without the Army's aid. Their negative inventories suggest absolute lack, no temporarily lost property that might yet be recovered or redeemed, certainly no luxuries: "there were neither chairs, tables nor beds, nor even the bundle of straw to lie upon—nothing but bare boards."[57] Such vacancies offered the Salvation Army empty spaces to fill up in its ethnographic mapping of "darkest England."[58] Rather than attempt to restrain alcohol consumption alone, which so many other nineteenth-century urban reformers describe as the most considerable drain on working-class finances and families,[59] Army reports attempted to re-train working-class desire, creating demand for consumer goods even as Slum Sisters personally made a show of giving up these goods.[60] Pushing the poor (as well as readers) to seek comfort by engaging in the market, Slum Sisters demonstrated the need for donations and offered the poor the middle-class system of materialism that their own sisterhood appeared to sacrifice.

Slum Sisters urge property acquisition and attempt to turn this acquisition into a sign of spiritual salvation.[61] Furnishing domestic spaces, they convert not only souls and bodies—both standard placeholders in evangelical conversion narratives—but slum spaces themselves.[62] In metonymic substitutions that personify poor neighborhoods and make their spaces interchangeable with their inhabitants, Cooke and others note that "Our poor slums are perishing" and sign their articles "Yours for the Slum's Salvation."[63] By substituting space for souls, the Army rallied people of disparate religious creeds and made its requests for money a sign of salvific materialism for the poor, rather than a symptom of Army self-interest. "Before" and "After" images speak to instances of salvation by showing broken homes and then placing nuclear families in well-stocked rooms with such captions as "'Home' as it used to be before The Army came along. Home as it is now. Are you doing your best to multiply all of this?"[64] Drawings of new homes boast tablecloths, wall ornaments, pictures, and toys in addition to heavily laden tables (see Figure 5.8), while the "before" family shown in Figure 5.7 lacks even the shelter of an indoor space.

One "Cellar, Gutter and Garret Work" writer, describing her movement "through some of these miserable dens," notes parenthetically, "(we cannot call them homes)."[65] Refusing to call these slum rooms "homes" is a choice repeated in

Figures 5.7 and 5.8 Before and After *Four Years Slumming,* 1891, 22–23
The Salvation Army International Heritage Centre

Army literature. Emphasizing their ability to define and move within the domestic sphere justified Slum Sisters' more untraditional work and appealed to a middle-class female readership who might more happily contribute to furnishing homes than to supporting a radical evangelical enterprise.[66] Despite attempts to dress as the neighbors of the poor, Slum Sisters took their cue from middle-class domestic ideology here, equating material possessions with morality. By the 1860s and '70s, as Deborah Cohen has demonstrated, rapid growth in middle-class wealth along with an increasingly forgiving view of the Christian God encouraged middle-class Victorian men and women to assign moral value to their newly affordable furnishings.[67] Clergymen and artists alike came to believe that "things had the power to influence people for good or for ill."[68] Along these lines, attributing righteousness to residence, the first Salvation Army Slum Meeting boasted "two nice little houses erected at the back of the platform—one to represent the home of a drunkard, cheerless and forlorn; the other, suggestive of 'Our sunshine within,' is, need we say? a small Salvationist home!"[69] Figures 5.9 and 5.10 emphasize the physically and spiritually uplifting nature of home improvements by showing how even body posture mimics domestic space, straightening in Figure 5.10 with the vertical lines of walls and curtains in contrast to the sloped ceilings and shoulders of the "before" image. "'How do I know I'm saved?'" one convert was reported to ask, "'—Look at the cupboard!'"[70] Another report notes with satisfaction that "Since [salvation . . .] a bit of furniture and clothing have made their appearance, and there is the prospect of a complete change taking place both in the drunkard's life and his home."[71] Yet another article enthusiastically describes a poor woman asking slum officers "to go and see her three new chairs which she had bought since her salvation."[72] This woman's ability to buy chairs reflects a newfound ability to save money as well as her soul; among records of high unemployment and alcoholism in the slums, chairs represent wages earned through work and not spent in pubs.

By stressing ownership as a sign of salvation, the Slum Sisters make the poor's purchasing power a form of self-help. Even as they broadcast their own ability to give up, they endorse the marketplace as an engine of growth and change, recognizing charitable gifts (and the sisterhood they presumably create) as a short-term solution for the poor who must learn to provide for (and perhaps "sister") themselves. Slum Sisters' focus on domestic space and its furnishings shifts the problematic act of acquisition away from their own fund-raising campaigns onto the poor men and women stockpiling cupboards and chairs; it purifies possession as a symbol of moral prowess; and it domesticates an organization whose military codes and public movement were both liberating and marginalizing for late-Victorian women. Yet the new, positive inventory of "three new chairs" and things like them takes on a luster of its own. Any piety that might be found in property is disrupted and surpassed in the sheer excitement of purchase and display.[73] The enthusiasm of the officers who record these new chairs offers them something of the vicarious consumer pleasure that we see in Lizzie's "inward laughter" as she departs from the goblins' market, and that, in another social sphere, women were

A TYPICAL SLUM HOME.

THE SLUM HOME CHANGED.

Figures 5.9 and 5.10 "A Typical Slum Home" and "The Slum Home Changed" *AW* January 1900 (XXI:I), 44–45. The Salvation Army International Heritage Centre

experiencing from window shopping in London's West End. Slum inhabitants' new property thus disrupts straightforward symbolic readings that would equate household objects with either domesticity or salvation. Slum Sisters call attention to the things themselves, revealing an interest in the purely material goods that the Army women give up in their own lives, and showing that their sacrifices are made not merely in deference to the next life, spiritually speaking, but also in order to help them enjoy, then and there, the consumer impulse that they culti-vate in the slums.

III. "Coming Down" in Order to Rise Up: Risk and Asset

Gift and market economies coexisted throughout the nineteenth century; as Mar-got Finn has demonstrated, the emergence of market capitalism relied on those ear-lier structures of gift exchange that it supposedly marginalized.[74] We see these dual systems here: Slum Sisters engage in an economy of sacrifice by wearing shabby dress that simultaneously unites them with but also distinguishes them from the poor; the poor, in turn, become consumers in an alternative economy of shopping-driven self-help and salvation that affords Slum Sisters some access to their market pleasures. I have argued that Slum Sisters' sacrifices make one "sister" rhetorically and sartorially interchangeable with another. Here, I want to suggest that this sacri-ficial sisterhood also explains the interrelatedness of the Army's competing systems of exchange. Slum Sisters appropriate the authority of Christian sacrifice by going "lower" and use it, in part, to justify and direct their "sisters'" material transactions, some of them more dependent on markets than gifts. These opposing patterns of economic movement complement but also obfuscate each other when Slum Sisters represent their own loss as others' gain, yoking them together as if they were cause and effect, independent of other sources of income for the Army and slum inhabi-tants, such as donations, sales, or labor conceived of in nonsacrificial terms. Thus as slum inhabitants and slum homes acquire chairs, tables, and the material trappings of salvation, as the Army solicits contributions and sells papers and pamphlets, Slum Sisters are shown stripped of everything—fine clothing, as we have seen, but also homes, sleep, and meals. The Army believed that Jesus's sacrifice was an unlimited spiritual resource, potentially making salvation available to everyone. However, un-like salvation (or the sacrifice that saves both sisters in Rossetti's poem), Slum Sis-ters' economy of sacrifice is bounded; it stresses material scarcity, treating physical comfort as a limited resource in a self-sustained, zero-sum economy. Cultivating an image of sisterly sacrifice enables Slum Sisters to differentiate their work from and take precedence among other charities because, according to this equation, *only* Slum Sisters can perform the sacrificial balancing act necessary to help the poor.

Slum Sisters sacrifice not only hats and houses but also safety. Insults and threats from "rough" men and boys lurking on stairways contribute to the daily challenges Slum Sisters confront and indicate that, despite the Army's inclusive language, not all of the slum dwellers welcome these women as sisters.[75] The dangers that Slum Sisters face draw attention to their special access to the slums. "We used the word 'safe' [. . .] relatively," Suzie Swift explains in the article accompanying Figure 5.11:[76]

> "If you will go down that street," said a Whitechapel policeman, "I'll watch you down. But I daren't go myself alone."
> "You don't know what you're doing," said a rent-collector, who met two of them in a passage, "There's not a house in this street where its [sic] safe for you to go. *Men* daren't. [. . .]"
> The girls thanked him, "but we finished the house," says one of them, "tranquilly."

Figure 5.11 "We Used the Word 'Safe' [. . .] Relatively" *AW* August 1885, 188
The Salvation Army International Heritage Centre

Report after report undermines local male governance by reiterating the ease of Slum Sisters' movements in spaces men dread.[77] Even as the Army applauds the ability of these "lassies" to move freely through urban space, though, it also details their risks.

The spectacle of women in danger is an important part of Slum Sisters' appeal, as we saw it to be in Lizzie's perilous but ultimately profitable encounter in the goblins' market. Dark, rickety, broken lodging-house stairs are conventional images in slum reports, repeatedly illustrating the danger of the Sisters' entrance into the slums as if the poor could only benefit in proportion to Slum Sisters' own social descent, as if only that descent could justify the prosperity (and property) they sought on behalf of slum inhabitants (see Figure 5.12). The vertical axis of climbing calls attention to the unstable stages of urban poverty, to the possibility that a comfortable family might fall to harder times or that the circumstances of a poor person might improve.[78] It also gives sacrifice a place in the hierarchical organization that this military unit envisioned for the slums. Even as the Army tried to ignore conventional class distinctions by conferring positions of authority on working-class converts, publishing reports by mere "lasses," and dressing "lower still," Slum Sisters' emphasis on salvation and sin nevertheless creates its own rank. Their merit depends upon the dangers of class crossing, or, in the words of the Army Commissioner George Railton, the Army's "coming down to the level of those who suffer [. . .] has been one of the great secrets of the Army's rising up."[79]

So risk becomes an asset. Danger grants Slum Sisters a privileged position between reader and slum, reinforced by the plurality of subject positions that "sisterhood" offered. They promise readers intimate access to poor "sisters" and sites through direct, present-tense, second-person address. They also guarantee "sister" readers protection from the dangers their encounters reputedly entail. Slum Sisters make spectacles of their own vulnerable bodies to compel the reader to give up something material too, financial contributions which, triangulated around Slum Sisters' sacrifice and the shopping of the reformed poor, manifest as the chairs and cupboards of self-help. Tour-guide narratives create intimate, shared experience while warning the reader which way to step: "I would like you to come with me down these broken stairs—take care, for it is very dark."[80] This would be a serious warning if those readers were actually following them into the slums; many people perished in accidents and violent encounters on the unstable stairs of tenements (see Figure 5.13). As it is, though, the warning asks readers to imagine themselves in their "sister's" place and implicitly demands a reciprocal gesture, compensation for the protective exchange, for *not* having to go there. By making a show of giving and risking everything, Slum Sisters' sacrifice of safety— like other extreme gifts—seems one-sided, demanding nothing. According to the spectrum of reciprocities sketched by Marshall Sahlins, this is the most generous, intimate kind of giving, one that suggests a closer because less calculated bond than the series of equivalent transactions that create community in *Cranford* or

Figure 5.12 "Come With Me Down These Broken Stairs"
WC December 25, 1889, 19. The Salvation Army International Heritage Centre

Jane Eyre. But this intimacy comes at a price. As we learn from a long line of other gift theorists, and as we see in the demands that Slum Sisters' sacrifices make on readers' hearts and pockets, such total expenditure obligates a significant return.

Slum Sisters capitalized on danger most explicitly during the Jack the Ripper scare of 1888, claiming that the episode proved their "right to be regarded as real sisters of the poor women of the street."[81] Noting their own proximity to these

Figure 5.13 A VIOLENT ENCOUNTER *WC* November 29 1890, 13
The Salvation Army International Heritage Centre

Whitechapel murders they "tak[e] advantage of this terror [. . .] to bring the people to repentance" and appeal for readers' assistance.[82] The sexualized nature of the Ripper attacks eroticizes the risks that the "young, healthy" Slum Sisters were taking and broadcasts their difference from their "murdered sisters," those "poor women of the street" who faced the most danger.[83] Unlike the victims of the mysterious serial killer, Slum Sisters walk the streets "pure," as philanthropists. Public attention centered on the streets and alleys where most of the victims were found, but what emerges in Army reports are images of "slumdom" at home and Slum Sisters in transit. Emphasizing their own "tranquil" progress through alleys that policemen feared, Slum Sisters become confident urban spectators, street-walking woman.[84] In contrast, the poor people they describe are enclosed within domestic space. Thus descriptions of the Ripper terror afford agency to women walking the streets but assign this agency solely to the Sisters.[85] This striking elision of the prostitutes targeted by these attacks again disavows the possibility that a "sister" might need to solicit money (from licentious men, from readers, from *War Cry* sales). It also allows Slum Sisters to extend their own labor beyond the gendered sphere that justifies cleaning, feeding, and nursing the slums. Threatened by mutilation and murder, in the case of the Ripper scare, and, on a more regular basis, by assault, insult, vermin, and unsafe housing conditions, Slum Sisters gained license to do much more than scrub floors. Facing threats head on, they climb stairs, duck down alleys, enter private spaces, and confront men and women in public areas. An army on the march, they win popular support through an unparalleled display of sacrifices on the front line.

Slum Sisters "take advantage of" other, less overtly violent terrors, too, raising their own value by emphasizing the dangers that even charitable readers face and showing how in these cases, too, only Slum Sisters have the wherewithal to manage these risks. When Army articles warn of the "danger of forgetting that these are *our* sisters,"[86] they stress the danger of not giving. But charity emerges as a hazard nearly as great to donors as poverty or sin is to the poor, or physical assault is to the Sisters. Booth refers to the "danger" of "mistaken kindness"; the third annual slum report calls it "a difficult matter to give without injuring."[87] The threat implicit in gifts (a variation on Jane Eyre's earlier recognition that "a present has many faces") underscores the Army's anxiety about monetary exchange but also highlights its unique ability to contain and defuse the danger for readers. Turning charity into a risky enterprise gives Slum Sisters—well-schooled in danger—the position of savior to would-be philanthropists as well as to the people they seek to convert. One of the greatest dangers of charitable giving, according to the Army and other groups including the Charity Organisation Society (COS), is that top-down approaches might make people dependent. Thus Slum Sisters repeatedly distinguish between the "soup kitchen system" that creates paupers through handouts and their own work to distribute "glad tidings" and even encourage consumerism.[88] Suzie Swift recounts a tale of a cold, starving man standing in sleet to sell miniature ships. After a lady in furs haggles with him to reduce his already scant profit, a "Slum lassie," recognizing that it would be "little use to preach love and charity just then," attempts to make sales on his behalf at a meeting: "Help given like that does not pauperize."[89]

Just as Slum Sisters overcome the dangers of the streets, they master the dangers presented by giving. In each case, the confrontation pays. Their ability to go where "*men* daren't" gives them privileged access and privileged knowledge, as slum workers and writers are quick to point out. This advantage allows them to determine how and what to give. In contrast with "Newspaperlings" and "easy-chair philanthropists," and in competition with other contemporary social reformers such as the COS and the Fabian Society, the Army refers to its unique position to see, to understand, to write, and to give correctly:[90] "Our officers have an advantage here over most Slum visitors, in the fact that they live amongst the people, know their habits of life and needs."[91] Again, Army Slum Sisters are more than just visitors; their sacrifices, having made them "sisters" rather than workers, also make them better able to serve a larger community. While the familial language of sisterhood gives Slum Sisters the affective authority to work in the slums and solicit funds, the Army's military language and front-line stance offers Slum Sisters experience, knowledge, and the exclusive ability to recruit and report.[92] Along these lines the Army claims an authority similar to what James Campbell, in a different context, has called "combat gnosticism": direct access to knowledge through a privileged position in the fight.[93] Not only does the spectacle of risking everything demand a greater return from its reader, but the Army shows itself to be the only force capable of knowing or managing that danger. Access—with its entailing dangers—underwrites the Army's authority and incurs the reader's debt, vast reserves of guilt on which Army authors avidly draw. Its economy of sisterly sacrifice depends upon exchange, the promise (however implicit) of a return for Slum Sisters' gifts. Sacrifice offers Slum Sisters the kind of spiritual rewards we saw in Rossetti's "Safe Investment" (a place in heaven, or, as they described the conversions in increasingly market-inflected terms, a "share" in the "harvest" of souls[94]), but it also transforms material conditions in the slums, elevates the professional status of the women who worked in and wrote about them, and heightens the obligations (both emotional and financial) of readers increasingly invested in the networks of Slum Sisters' social activism.

IV. Writing the Slums

Sacrificial displays in newspapers, magazines, and pamphlets urged readers to make substantial donations, but this was only one of the ways in which the press furthered Slum Sisters' campaigns. In their first decade, Army publications increased in production and sales dramatically, a growth that corresponded with the new prominence of women's journalism. Although women had been publishing actively throughout the century, they achieved more importance in the 1880s, when, as Seth Koven notes, the British press gained political power "by providing news to an increasingly democratized and literate electorate."[95] Many women contributed to the *War Cry*, *All the World*, and *The Deliverer*. Proceeds from sales of these and other books, pamphlets, magazines, and songbooks comprised a significant portion of early Salvation Army earnings.[96] As we have seen, the Army assigned meaning to these profits in terms of community rather than money; the growth of *War Cry* distribution meant that its "war in print" would more successfully "arouse everybody to fight against sin."[97] While military metaphors of books sent out "with overwhelming force against the fortresses of the enemy" transform the Army's pen into a sword, other publications follow the patterns of sacrificial affiliation that advanced Slum Sisters' work; for example, an advertisement introducing *The Deliverer* refers to the new monthly magazine as *All the World*'s "new sister."[98] The Army's publications, like its soldiers, formed a military family, sisters and fighters alike, and both their military function and their sororal networks legitimized their sales by rhetorically removing them from the realm of more profit-driven commercial transactions.

In print journalism as in slum exploration and philanthropy, sacrificial sisterhood provides a representational strategy for Slum Sisters to shore up both individual and collective professional authority. Sistering shapes the very structure of Army articles and authorship, mediating between the corporate "Cry" of this military organization and the personal agency of its recruits. In Army periodicals, subject matter, nation, and author all appear to be subsumed under a single "cry" directed at "you," the reader, the "sister." Sisterhood in these articles signifies *many*, representing women in need of aid, women who give it, women who read about it. In this sense it is a term for the typical, the collective, interchangeable women going "lower still." It also means *one* in the most direct way possible: you, the individual worker, the individual reader, the case study in the slums. In this sense it is deeply personal and individualized. Slum Sisters' narrative modes capture the tension between these two ideas. Almost compulsively providing first-hand impressions of their slum visits, Slum Sisters claim to eschew the statistics they also print in favor of case studies. *War Cry* "biographers" trace "the genesis of one slum-sister at a time," narrating the histories of Army workers as well as slum inhabitants because "Salvationists love to deal with the individual."[99] However much one is *like* another—a slippage borne out through the constant repetition of stock phrases, tropes, images, conversion patterns, statistics, and even case studies that are representative rather than exceptional—Army publications also make room for individual cases and writers.[100]

Through their common "cry," Army periodicals construct a fiction of unity among various contributors; in this, they resemble the "Old Journalism" of earlier nineteenth-century publications that used anonymous writers in part to make claims to monolithic, corporate authority.[101] By the end of the century, according to the dominant critical narrative, authors and editors of the periodical press were debating the merits of attaching signatures to their writing,[102] and mainstream periodicals were increasingly disrupting the earlier journals' corporate authority by including individual bylines that strengthened the separate author position of each contributor.[103] However, as Rachel Sagner Buurma argues, and as Army articles confirm, print culture at the fin-de-siècle continuously "offered viable models of collective authority that were as much a part of readers' and writers' everyday understanding of authorship as was the idea of the individual author."[104] Army articles bridge the journalistic divide of the late-century signature debates by interspersing signatures with anonymous reports. In and alongside its named articles, the Army draws on unnamed and pseudonymous contributions. This combination admittedly highlights certain well-known bylines at the expense of others, but at the same time it puts each in service of the other, as some individual authors may have "sacrificed signature in order to produce the illusion of an omniscient corporate authority" while others assembled recognizable, individual Army characters out of more voices than their own.[105] Although the balance is inconsistent, what emerges throughout the papers is a collective mission and corporate "Cry" resting not necessarily on uniform style, tone, or pseudonymity but, paradoxically, on the general fragmentation of journalistic authority within and among the unique personalities that present themselves. The Army takes pride in showcasing correspondents of all experiences, juxtaposing reports by unnamed cadets or "lasses" with articles by officers.[106] But it does so to disperse, rather than to consolidate, individual authority.

Army articles were usually coauthored, pieced together at central locations out of news from increasingly distant districts and countries. Slum writers regularly include other officers' reports in their articles, and those reports, in turn, often contain quotes from slum dwellers—sometimes entire conversations cited from memory or shorthand.[107] This inclusion of diverse ranks and voices from the Army and slums alike—a broader and less clearly demarcated strategy than the interviews favored by New Journalism[108]—makes the Army enterprise collective and appears to render its contributors interchangeable. Writers speak with (and for) others. They consequently become the narrative equivalent of Cox's "dressing like a sister": even as voices repeatedly call attention to their own individual perspectives and experiences, their authorship is leveled and put in service of communal gain, of sacrificing personal profit or identity in order to identify and elevate descriptions of needy sisters at hand.

Many articles deny any authorial agency at all, claiming that the facts speak for themselves. "We do not propose to 'write an article' on the slum work this month—only to give a brief statement of some facts which came out in this most unconventional officers' meeting."[109] In these cases, the "facts" typically provide the praise for Army work that the Army refuses to claim for itself, as in an article on girls from the "Midnight Rescue Brigade":

> The following are two or three letters from the girls. They were not intended for publication when written, but to those friends who have watched with such affectionate interest the reports which have appeared in the "War Cry" from time to time [...] how that [sic] poor girls drunk, all in rags, with bare and bleeding feet, black eyes and blood-stained faces, and broken hearts, have been gathered in and led to Jesus [...] these letters will not be without interest [...].[110]

The vagueness of "two or three" letters suggests a selection process as cavalier as the letters' preparation for publication. But the appeal to "friends" in this preamble, like Army appeals for "sisters" elsewhere, forwards the work of the anonymous and self-effacing Army writers by rhetorically leveling the readers and converts who might both fit this description. If the casual tone and passive voice make the girls' conversion agentless, furthermore, the letters that follow the preamble give the Army its due: "May God bless you [. . .] and may you be the means, in His hands, of rescuing many more of these poor sisters of mine." They also contribute to the Army's appeals by making titillating promises of first-hand knowledge. A hesitant postscript to one letter, introducing the author's verses on a girl's salvation, increases the individual value of this "poor sister's" intimate verses: "You will wonder at my writing to you, but I cannot sleep, so I just thought I would write to you what I was thinking, but don't laugh at me." Far from being a casual matter, letters such as these are skillfully deployed by their editors, who gather voices on behalf of Army authority in letters, interviews, and conversation. The third annual slum report references slum inhabitants in sup-port of the Army's work: "An infidel woman [. . .] hearing some unkind things about The Salvation Army, said, 'I know different to that. I have seen two Salva-tion Sisters come day after day to nurse a sick neighbor of mine.'" Another con-vert testifies to salvation brought about "'all through these Salvation Sisters in the lodging-house. [. . .]'"[111] Unnamed, the "infidel woman" passes into print only long enough to vouch for the Slum Sisters. The publications' careful use of such personal materials, as well as other respected references such as the Chris-tian bible,[112] publications from London and New York,[113] and the comments of fellow slum worker and COS founder Octavia Hill,[114] suggests rhetorical prowess in the construction of a centralized but not monolithic authority, of dif-ference within unity.

The compilation of notes and reports into the collective "cry" so proudly acknowledged in many Army papers gives rise to a remarkable diversity of voices. At the same time, however, joint authorship is often not so much partnership as rewriting, as "C." notes in "The 'War Cry.' A Peep Behind the Scenes":[115]

> The work done by the Editorial Staff is much heavier than with an ordinary newspaper. Many of their correspondents have not had the advantage of a collegiate education, and their writing is often not of the best [. . .]. A con-siderable quantity of the matter, or to use the technical term, 'copy,' has to be revised and rewritten.[116]

The broad range of correspondents with respect to both class standing and lit-erary training augurs well for a democratic journalism, calling attention here to the uneven resources and talents that fill its pages, but the slippage of voices in revision simultaneously threatens to erase individual writers, not merely equalize them. Nineteenth-century traditions in publishing offer both possibilities for these anonymous Army contributors: that they are overwritten in favor of better "copy," and that they share profitably in the larger collective that puts their insights on paper. Both dynamics—one favoring the individual, one sacrificing her in favor of the collective—operate at every level of the Army's sacrificial sisterhood.

The many voices of these anonymous contributors are frequently amassed into the singular voices of Army characters, the individual writers whose bylines introduce the reports. For these women, Army publications offered a wide readership, name recognition, and authority in the growing fields of journalism and philanthropy. Some would be well known to readers of slum writing. Most prominent among them are Blanche B. Cox, Suzie F. Swift, and Mrs. (Lydia Corbett) Cooke, though other names (Jessie McClellan, Isa Cartner, Mrs. Carleton, Helen Hudson) become familiar as well. We have seen examples of Staff-Captain Blanche Cox's writing in connection to the "Lower Still" dress. On the occasion of her departure for work in India, a farewell tribute's illustration emphasizes her importance to the *War Cry* by depicting that publication atop a ladder that recalls the Slum Sisters' frequent climbing (see Figure 5.14). This drawing figures Cox jointly (counterclockwise from the left) as Army officer, Slum Sister, and Indian missionary. The fragmentation of one "sister's" identity into three separate persons mimics the Trinitarian nature of the Army's Christian God as well as the structure of sisterhood itself, as it appears in Army literature and as it shapes Army authorship. Cox's tripartite portrait highlights one woman's fluidity of purpose and identity but also emphasizes the varied faces behind individual Army characters, the collective that coexists with every attempt at personal tribute.

Staff-Captain Suzie Swift (Figure 5.15) was another noteworthy officer, editor, and prolific writer before eventually leaving the Army for a different sisterhood under the auspices of Roman Catholicism. In Swift's distinctive hands, the collective authority amassed by Army reports and interviews takes a more literary turn than most, as she puts works by Percy Bysshe Shelley, Barrett Browning, and Tennyson to service for the slums.[117] Quoting Shelley in an epigraph to one "Cellar, Gutter, and Garret" report—"Hell is a city very much like London"— Swift continues:

> As this rescue work has gone lower and lower, as its workers have seen deeper and deeper into the very heart of sin and misery, such as can only be understood by those who live in its midst, they have been tempted sometimes to question how long they should find each day blacker sin, deeper misery than they had known of before, to ask whether Shelley was not right, and whether our social strata, if one dug deep enough, would not lead straight to the very pavement of hell![118]

Swift takes some literary license, here. The diversity of Army backgrounds makes it unlikely that Slum Sisters in general would have much experience with Shelley; some were illiterate, and, as the *War Cry* editorial quoted above makes clear, the

STAFF-CAPTAIN BLANCHE B. COX.

Figure 5.14 STAFF-CAPTAIN BLANCHE B. COX
WC July 30, 1887, 3. The Salvation Army International Heritage Centre

literary experiences of the others varied. Workers' reports, moreover, contemplate the sturdiness of a stairway or the state of a soul far more often than they
speculate on the poet's accuracy (or Swift's).[119] This literary license is beside the
point, to a certain extent; her article targets a reading audience familiar with his
name, if not with the line. And that literary license is also precisely the point. In
the slums, colonized through ethnographic treatments such as Booth's *In Darkest
England*, Swift's quotes act as the "portable property" described by John Plotz, a
way to carry "Englishness" into foreign territory, an "immunization" against this
alien culture.[120] Yet Swift does not bow deferentially to the poet as a revered authority. Subjecting him to question, she claims the "combat gnosticism" I mentioned earlier. Misery "can only be understood by those who live in its midst";
accordingly, it is the prerogative of Slum Sisters, of Swift—not of Romantic poets,

Figure 5.15 Photograph of Staff-Captain Suzie F. Swift
The Salvation Army International Heritage Centre

literary critics, men of leisure, or ladies bountiful—to gauge the value of Shelley's description. Encompassing poverty and poetry alike, Swift's journalism establishes authority over more than the philanthropy that motivates it.

Swift gains renown as an individual; hers is a name commonly referenced as an authority by other Army writers. But even as her signature and style implicitly set her apart from the others, she speaks of and casts her lot with the collective "they" of her free indirect discourse. Like other Army writers, Swift draws on other Army workers' reports to supplement her own articles and authorship. We might easily read her introduction to slum testimony as simply downplaying the other writer's authorial agency in favor of her own: "Read this scrap of a letter stolen by us from a girl officer who never dreamed of 'seeing herself in print [. . .].'"[121] The diminutive language (scrap and girl) and the distinction between this "raw" or "natural" writing and Swift's journalistic craft underplay this officer's professional authority, resulting in a literary hierarchy within the alleged equality of sisterhood. Swift, as the Army officer literally signing off on the piece, is both senior officer and senior journalist here. But this anecdote gives the "girl officer" more agency, and Swift somewhat less, than this reading suggests. The presumed sincerity of not writing for print aligns this "girl officer" with the gendered work that many other Army "sisters" were doing, reminding us that sacrifices (of clothing, of authorial identity) were not necessarily passive and certainly not without purchase. Swift's "stolen" letter speaks to larger Army concerns about writing for and then claiming profits, substituting cautious informality for her more effective editorial system. Finally, Swift's accomplices in the crime (the theft is committed by "us") reiterate to readers that Army women, working in or writing on the slums, are never alone. Dressing, walking, and writing together, they construct alliances that simultaneously advance individual and collective professional goals.

Sacrificial sisterhood offered Salvation Army workers a way to bridge personal and institutional aims, but most of the individual "sisters" and even the "sisterhood" itself have largely dropped out of histories of Army (and other) slum work. In part, this is because not only literary rank but also gender creates a hierarchy that disrupts and erases some of the Army's collective "cry." We can trace this erasure in Army bylines; inconsistently mixing anonymity with initials, names, and titles, they nevertheless reveal a pattern that favors male leadership over a larger sisterhood. Slum District Officer James J. Cooke, for example, is credited with enough articles that it is possible to identify the very week of his promotion from "Staff-Captain" to "Major" simply by scanning his signature.[122] Cooke, the central figure of the group photograph that began this chapter, is made central to Army writing as well. Like Swift, Cox, and other Army women writing about the slums, he draws upon or "steals" reports from other soldiers, officers, and slum inhabitants in his articles. Like them, too, his voice occasionally effaces others, as we see in his treatment of Harriet Webb and Polly Redmead,[123] pioneers of the London Slum Work. Reprinting entries from their first slum diary, he subordinates their military intelligence to his own.

> *Sunday, October 17th.* Held an open-air meeting. (Their first open airs were extremely rough. Captain Webb was knocked down by a public-house pewter pot. But they got the victory; and from then till now, on every Sunday morning for nearly two hours, a large crowd is dealt with. Many souls have been saved through these open-airs.)
> *October 28th.* Sold the first "War Cry." (We now sell in our London Slums, 1,000 copies of the "War Cry" and "Young Soldier" every week.) [. . .][124]

Cooke's parenthetical additions contextualize but also take over their recollections, making them secondary to his own, more up-to-date knowledge of the slums. Although he, too, speaks in the plural voice of a collective "we," the alliance has shifted. The Army and its Slum Work, not Slum Sisters, get the final word. The reporting strategies of Army women, when employed by those outside the "sister-hood," bolster others instead.

Cooke was, by all accounts, a devout Army convert, a hard-working supervisor, and an extremely prolific writer, who earnestly attempted to transform (or, in his words, save) the slums. Yet, as Figure 5.16 vividly shows, images of Cooke and his wife eclipse other agents of the slums. Their portraits, presented in dignified, halo-like roundels, sit directly under a banner "For Jesus." They visually push the Slum Sister (right) and her "poor sister" (left) to the margins of a drawing that seems barely to have room for the crowded scenes serving as a backdrop for the Cookes. Flagpoles leading diagonally inward from the central banner bring to focus the symbols of sin that sit between the portraits but distract readers from the two seemingly passive figures on either side. The original "Cellar, Gutter, and Garret Brigade," we may recall, merged with and was subsumed by Cooke's London Slum Work. James Cooke wrote admiringly of the Slum Sisters' work but took it over in service to the Army. Cooke devoted his life to saving the slums, but he is also one reason why Slum Sisters have all but vanished from cultural histories of late-Victorian slum work.

STAFF-CAPTAIN AND MRS. COOKE, OF THE LONDON SLUM WORK.

Figure 5.16 "STAFF-CAPTAIN AND MRS. COOKE, OF THE LONDON SLUM WORK"
WC August 27, 1887, 1. The Salvation Army International Heritage Centre

But before we assign too much blame to one man, we should remember that Cooke, like Swift, speaks for more than himself. His construction as a model Army officer owes as much to Suzie Swift's glowing endorsements as to his own writing. Introducing an interview with Cooke, Swift declares that

> No one better appreciates the value of the press as a mode of communication with the public than does Major Cooke [. . .].
> "It's because he gives so many little cases that the 'Cry' readers support Cooke's work so largely," said a literary man the other day.[125]

The "many little cases" attributed entirely to Cooke by one of Swift's favored "literary" sources elide other labor and other voices; "Cooke's work" refers primarily to his reports of the slum work being performed and written about by a number of other Army officers and soldiers. Thus Slum Sisters' sacrifices themselves are folded within Cooke's work. Readers' donations, meanwhile, become the direct responses to Cooke's communications, reciprocal gestures for his "giv[ing] so many little cases" rather than remaining the problematic profits of Army sales or of Slum Sisters' solicitations.

Pushed aside or actively stepping aside, Slum Sisters sacrifice themselves for the slums, their readers, and their commanding officers. Cooke's fame is not the only reason that Slum Sisters' works have been so generally eclipsed. Their emphasis on sisterly sacrifice and their enactment of that sacrifice in the very structure of their writing offer another explanation for why they have been overlooked ever since. Histories of Victorian feminism have largely taken such women at their word when they underplay their agency through the language of sacrifice and selflessness or describe their achievements as work done "all unknowingly."[126] Slum Sisters justified and advanced their actions through their claims to sacrifice, but in Army literature as in the poetry and fiction of the late nineteenth century, "sacrifice" emerges as a gift transaction that allows single women to shore up spiritual, material, and professional returns. Through public displays of giving up, Slum Sisters also took much in. Sacrificial sisterhood offered slum workers a safe way to talk about, solicit, and spend money, to create markets for volunteerism, journalism, and domestic furnishing, to establish shared and personal authority. Like the other communities of real and imagined women that this project has explored so far, Salvation Army Slum Sisters used extreme gifts to turn their alliance to profit.

CHAPTER 6

The Give and Take
of "New-Woman" Eugenics

Women's gift exchanges, as we have seen, were instrumental in redefining kinship and community to galvanize social action among Victorian women. While the Salvation Army Slum Sisters used gifts to alleviate poverty by changing the urban landscape, stressing environmental measures such as housekeeping and consumerism, other fin-de-siècle writers shifted the emphasis of reform toward the biological. This final chapter turns to what many of these writers, well into the twentieth century, depicted as the ultimate gift: eugenic motherhood. Sir Francis Galton's 1869 *Hereditary Genius*, through its promotion of "good" births, initiated the work that, in the following decades, would attract reformers across a broad political spectrum. By the time Galton coined the term *eugenics* in 1883, the idea that people (particularly mothers) could take control of evolution had already begun to shape popular Anglo-American scientific discourse.[1] Eugenics appealed to a number of late-century English and American women not merely because, as Angelique Richardson argues, it granted women intellectual prowess in the "rational selection" of a proper mate (*passim*), or even because it drew on women's "socially conditioned propensity to self-sacrifice" in that selection.[2] Eugenic discourses, mapped onto nineteenth-century traditions of women's giving, amplified the scale and social significance of their gifts; they redirected women's intimate, private exchanges toward frankly national ends.

Eugenics appeared in women's novels, science fiction, and economic treatises in part as their solution to what popular culture was representing as an economic problem. By the turn of the century, according to some accounts, women seemed to be taking too much. The donations that Salvation Army women took in throughout the 1870s and '80s and the purchasing power that their charitable appeals gave them for the homes of the East End poor were mirrored in more affluent communities by dramatic increases in women's consumerism. West End department stores, clubs, and public transportation catered to shopping women. Encouraging consumption, they also sparked anxiety about "gluttonous" women with insatiable appetites.[3] Efforts to accommodate middle- and upper-class women's urban leisure through the establishment of restaurants and lavatories presented women as "ingesting and digesting bodies."[4] Women were increasingly depicted as extravagant economic consumers; the framing of economic desire in physical terms meant that women's bodies, as well as the shopping bags they carried, appeared excessive. Swelling to new proportions economically and physically, women in the last third of the century loomed large in the popular imagination. As this chapter shows, literature of the period attempted to confront and resolve anxieties about women's economic intake through attention to their reproductive output. Women's bodies would compensate for gain through gifts that tied eugenic sacrifice to personal loss.

In Sir Edward Bulwer-Lytton's commercially successful evolutionary tale *The Coming Race* (1871),[5] an American man of English descent and education stumbles upon an advanced subterranean society where the women (Gy-ei) "are usually superior to the Ana [men] in physical strength." These underground women also excel intellectually, mastering the "abstruse and mystical branches of reasoning, for which [. . .] the Ana are unfitted" (62). With both brains and brawn, they outstrip the narrator, who uneasily explains that "woman loses [. . .] her special charm of woman if [man] feels her to be in all things eminently superior to himself" (145). Echoing the sentiments that many of Bulwer-Lytton's contemporaries felt toward members of the women's movement boldly emerging above ground, he notes that a beautiful Gy "rather awe[s him] as angel than move[s him] as woman" (185). For the daunted narrator, Gy-ei lack feminine "charm"— rather like those late-century women who distressed contemporary observers by roaming the streets of London unchaperoned to publicly protest the Contagious Diseases Acts and advocate both women's suffrage and married women's property rights.[6]

Women's advancement, here as in other anxious responses to the mid-Victorian women's movement, produces females who are not only unsexed but also sexually hostile. Comparing them to various female insects and fish whose size also exceeds that of their mates,[7] the narrator observes that those "females are generally large enough to make a meal of their consorts if they so desire" (63). The superior strength of females threatens male society: "[T]hey can not only defend themselves against all aggressions from the males, but could, at any moment when he least suspected his danger, terminate the existence of an offending spouse" (63). Without speculating on those male aggressions (a relevant concern at a time before wife abuse was grounds for legal separation[8]), the narrator finds the women monstrous in their ability to eat, terminate, or "brain" men (104). This race, he predicts, will "emerge into sunlight our inevitable destroyers" (208). Contributing to his fears is the Gy-ei's superior ability to wield "vril"—a single force that can destroy, heal, or aid in communication. "[I]n vril they have arrived at the unity in natural energetic agencies, which has been conjectured by many philosophers above ground," he reports, citing the English chemist and physicist Michael Faraday's theory that "'the forces of matter [. . .] are convertible, as it were, into one another'" (45–46). "Vril" draws on the scientific ideas of conservation that I highlighted in Chapter 3, again placing a single, powerful energy, conserved through its conversion, in the hands of women (63). Now, however, it signals the race's evolutionarily advanced state and ties that advancement to women.[9] It suggests, moreover, that women, in advancing the race, must be aggressively selective: "after the uses of vril became familiar to us, all creatures inimical to us were soon annihilated" (133). Control of this precious resource—an economic prerogative—is also a racial, evolutionary prerogative, giving women power over life and death.

This striking tale, drawing on mid-century discourses of evolution, thermodynamics, eugenics, and feminism, speaks to widespread perceptions of women's growing powers. First, women appear uncomfortably larger than life. Second, their physical, intellectual, and economic advancement directly threatens men's powers; in this zero-sum game, their gain entails men's loss. Third, women's advancement is linked to biology and racial supremacy, suggesting that gendered gains have hereditary consequences. Not merely the inventions of science fiction, these perceptions would shape the scientific "facts" behind marriage-plot novels, economic treatises, and even biology textbooks in the decades following Bulwer-Lytton's work. Between the 1880s and 1915, even writers who welcomed bourgeois women's advancement were anxious about the perceived economic imbalance of their gains. Female advocates of eugenics attempted to resolve these anxieties by demonstrating how much they gave back. Directing the language of exchange away from the individual and toward "the race," these women attempted to settle accounts through a growing emphasis on childbearing as a gift. Through a discourse of eugenic motherhood, derived from contemporary discussions of heredity, they tried to revise perceptions of their excessive gain by stressing the sacrifices women made, not for themselves or for men but on behalf of the nation. These "sacrifices"—more than the simple or self-effacing signs of women's "propensity to self-sacrifice"[10]—resemble the conspicuous expenditure seen in gift exchanges that purport to be one-sided, such as those described by the Salvation Army Slum Sisters. In its similarly spectacular display of giving, eugenic "loss" becomes a way for certain women to restore economic equilibrium while also redefining both the private meaning and public stakes of motherhood's martyrdom.

For such writers as Ménie Muriel Dowie, Sarah Grand (Frances Elizabeth Bellenden Clarke), Olive Schreiner, and Charlotte Perkins Gilman,[11] sexual reproduction thus takes on economic, religious, and political significance. While the history of women's advancement is often told through the discourse of rights, highlighting women's slow but steady gains in education, employment, and suffrage, these women's focus on biological difference from men tells a different story.[12] It ties women's eugenist[13] beliefs and actions to a long tradition of gift practices that gave a selective group of women the means to imagine themselves uniting in action to serve and save not only each other but the entire Anglo-Saxon race.

I. Consuming Women, Selfish Mothers

Throughout the first half of the century, as previous chapters have shown, women turned their relative economic disenfranchisement into the opportunity to imagine alternative practices of exchange, using gifts to redefine, protect, and promote their nearest interests. By the end of the century, however, women's activism was being rewarded with increasing socio-economic roles and rights. Opportunities for education were on the rise; Girton and Newnham Colleges for women were established in 1869 and 1871, and by 1881 women were admitted to university examinations at Cambridge. In 1882, married women were granted legal identities apart from their husbands in the common law,[14] and the repeal of the Contagious Diseases Acts in 1886 acknowledged the public power of women's political voices. Literary emphasis on strong, sturdy women underscored both pleasure and anxiety about these gendered gains; their physical bodies stood in, metonymically, for their expanding economic and social stature. For some, however, the "new woman" was growing too big for the britches that defenders of "rational dress" wanted her to wear.[15] Bulwer-Lytton's tall, muscular, fearless Gy-ei are cut from the same cloth as the powerfully "athletic" women of Charlotte Perkins Gilman's 1915 utopian novella *Herland* (19).[16] If, earlier in the century, *Cranford*'s female rent-holders were "Amazons" in their fierce spirit of independence, these new, muscular leading ladies offer the physical counterpart of the type. Their healthy bodies reject the self-negating implications of traditionally feminine "selflessness." Unlike Brontë's Jane Eyre, Gaskell's Miss Matty, and Rossetti's Laura, they have no need to breakfast on burnt porridge, skimp on tea cake, or pine away for fruit. As we will see, fin-de-siècle eugenic discourses will transform these healthy bodies into new kinds of gifts.

Late-century fears about male decadence and "effeminacy" exacerbated the perceived problem of muscular women.[17] Bulwer-Lytton's narrator is not alone in fearing that men will pay the price for women's advances; the dire consequences often assigned to women's actions in fiction suggest anxiety about the real or perceived toll that women's achievements were taking. Men's relative risks are borne out dramatically in Sarah Grand's transatlantic bestseller, *The Heavenly Twins* (*THT*) (1893).[18] Angelica, like the Gy-ei of Bulwer-Lytton's tale, is "taller, stronger, and wickeder" than her twin brother from an early age (*THT* 1:28), and later rebels against the customs of her married, upper-class life by cross-dressing as a boy. Disguised by costume, the night, and the fiction of her brother's identity, she befriends a man known simply as the "Tenor." Her male role grants her freedom of intimacy, expression, and movement, but these benefits have a steep price.

After a boating mishap reveals her true identity, that knowledge—along with the chilly water he enters to save her life—kills the Tenor, who dies broken-hearted and alone.[19] Grand's novel takes radical stances (against sexual double standards, in favor of women's education), but even here, women's independence proves fatal for men.[20]

While Grand uneasily implies that women's liberation can threaten men, others suggest that women's profit-seeking will threaten the entire Anglo-Saxon race. In her internationally acclaimed *Women and Economics* (*WE*) (1898),[21] Charlotte Perkins Gilman criticizes women's economic dependence on men by denouncing the one-sided, "'unearned increment' of masculine gifts'" that women receive. Women, according to Gilman, are "forbidden to make, but encouraged to take" (59).

> To consume food, to consume clothes, to consume houses and furniture and decorations and ornaments and amusements, to take and take and take forever [. . .] always to take and never to think of giving anything in return except their womanhood,—this is the enforced condition of the mothers of the race. What wonder that their sons go into business "for what there is in it"! (59)

Gilman frames women's taking as a "perverted condition of female energy" (60), as an *un*natural economic state for women. The rhetorical force of her statement derives from a century of writing that, as we have seen, established giving as natural as well as beneficial for women. But the problem Gilman identifies is not simply that economic dependence makes women selfish; worse, here, is that *mothers* are selfish, and that sons (according to a Lamarckian view of acquired traits) inherit this selfishness. Women's economic condition has reproductive consequences for "the race"—a phrase which, for Gilman, collapsed the human race in general with the white, Anglo-Saxon race in particular.

Women's economics are thus figured in and made significant through biological terms. Gilman explicitly draws on the work of Patrick Geddes, botanist, social evolutionist, and urban planner. Best known today for his organic approach to urban life and his influential work *Cities in Evolution* (1915), he was in 1889 the renowned coauthor, with former student J. Arthur Thomson, of the *Evolution of Sex*.[22] This popular study measures sexual difference in economic language. It characterizes women's "anabolic" or "constructive" metabolic processes in terms of "credit," "income," and "gain" (v–vi). In contrast, men's "katabolic" changes are "disruptive," entailing "outlay," and debt. Females "live at a profit"; male energy favors expenditure and loss. In "the fundamental, the physiological, the constitutional difference between the sexes," the science of the day found that women were taking too much. Even the ovum was over-fed, "large, passive, [and] highly nourished" in comparison with "small, active [. . .] sperm"

(125). If at mid-century, theories of conservation posited genteel women as the preservers of existing states of life (offering *Cranford* sustainable community, as we saw in Chapter 3 of this volume), here they show women of the leisure classes profiting personally.[23] While those profits support life (women "can afford to bear the larger share") they also designate women as passive, parasitical creatures.[24]

Olive Schreiner, in *Women and Labour* (*WL*) (which she published in 1911 but dates to 1888–1889), joined Gilman in identifying greedy women as the cause of racial degeneration. Arguing that industrial society has reduced bourgeois woman "to the passive exercise of her sex functions alone" (44), Schreiner characterizes middle- and upper-class women as "sex-parasites," economically dependent on men, taking without giving anything except their bodies in return.[25] The consequence, for Schreiner, is not only that women become less active and intelligent but also that they produce degenerate men. "No man ever yet entered life farther than the length of one navel-cord from the body of the woman who bore him," Schreiner declares. "It is the woman who is the final standard of the race" (60). Attributing the decline of Rome to parasitic women who "at last [gave] birth to a manhood as effete as itself" (51), Schreiner insists that "Everywhere [. . .] the parasitism of the female heralds the decay of a nation or class" (54). The hereditary consequences of women as economic parasites threaten to destroy the British Empire.

Schreiner and Gilman hold parasitic mothers responsible for race degeneration. Others saw motherhood itself as proof of women's insatiable taking.[26] Geddes and Thomson argue that the mammary gland pressure prompting lactation shows how "even maternal care has its selfish side" (291). Similarly, in internationally known writer Ménie Muriel Dowie's 1895 novel *Gallia*, which met with sufficient success to justify a second edition within the year despite mixed reviews,[27] the title character initially sees childbearing as "the most subtle kind of selfishness in the world. Motherhood is selfish after all. [. . .] A woman gets a good deal out of motherhood; more than she does out of marriage" (91). Gilman, too, rejects the idea that there is anything innately sacrificial or giving about motherhood. "Simply to love the child does not serve him unless specific acts of service express this love" (97). Across fiction, economic treatises, and biological textbooks, women are depicted as taking too much and failing to give. Even motherhood bears the taint of selfishness, which it risks passing along to weaken the Anglo-Saxon race.

The fin-de-siècle discourse described here measures women against the standard of "giving women" that I have traced throughout the century, only to find these late-century specimens unfit. While for Bulwer-Lytton, Geddes, and Thomson, women's gain, however problematic, was "natural," Gilman, Schreiner, Grand, and Dowie drew on the rhetoric of selfishness in order to pose a social solution. If selfish, "parasitic" women were "bad" for the race, then it followed that women might help the race (and themselves) by giving. For Gilman and Schreiner in particular, this binary offered a way to claim new economic roles for women; they demanded new forms of labor for women and justified these gains by reframing them as generosity: "not for ourselves alone, but for the race" (*WL* 21).

By stressing the links between women, forged through generations and traditions of exchange, Gilman and Schreiner attempt to mitigate the perception of women as selfish individuals. They rebut economic accounts of women's selfishness to remind their audiences that giving (rather than taking) offers women a larger, political sphere of collective action. Praising and promoting women's combined efforts, Gilman carries forward earlier writers' appeals to "sisterhood." She asserts that "[t]he women's movement rests not alone on her larger personality [. . .] but on the wide, deep sympathy of women for one another" (*WE* 69). Sympathetic exchanges among women presumably stem from literature; they have been "kindl[ed]," she claims, by such fiction as Harriet Beecher Stowe's *Uncle Tom's Cabin* (*WE* 80). Acknowledging that fiction has also ridiculed women's activism "through such characters as [*Bleak House's*] Mrs. Jellyby or Mrs. Pardiggle" she responds that now nearly every "intelligent" woman will "recognize some duty besides those incident to her own blood relationship" (*WE* 81). Pushing beyond kinship to stress women's public interests, Gilman suggests a broader sphere for their desires and duties. Women have fought and made sacrifices, she declares, "not for themselves alone, but for one another" (*WE* 83). Schreiner, too, emphasizes the link between sacrifice and women's solidarity. "[T]he women taking their share in the Woman's Movement of our age" she asserts, are conscious "that their efforts are not, and cannot be, of immediate advantage to themselves, but that they almost of necessity and immediately lead to loss and renunciation [. . .]" (*WL* 68). Loss, not gain, renunciation, not selfishness, characterizes women's communal efforts. These, too, are "not for herself, nor even for fellow-women alone, but for the benefit of humanity at large" (*WL* 68). Drawing on traditions that created intimacy out of gifts, Schreiner and Gilman derive benefits from women's sacrifices that emerge from and reach beyond those alliances.

Other writers take a more skeptical view. When Dowie's Gallia rejects the idea of women's individual freedoms, she does so ambivalently. "Women are like members of an Alpine party—looped each to one long rope" (*Gallia* 187). Her metaphor knots women together passively; their communal trek seems less a function of choice than of bondage. Elsewhere in this novel, women's connections are equally problematic. Early on, Gallia speaks of her "indebtedness" to prostitutes and later reiterates her gratitude (*Gallia* 115) for the gift of "immunity" that "that class of society" offers her own (*Gallia* 34). Joining contemporary assessments of vicarious suffering by acknowledging that her own sexually privileged position as a respected upper-class lady depends upon the economic dependence and sexual denigration of the prostitute,[28] Gallia figures her connection to the prostitute in terms of unequal exchange. Her understanding that prostitution implicates women in common with each other echoes contemporary protests against the

Contagious Diseases Acts. Reformers such as Ellice Hopkins campaigned for and popularized the "Social Purity" movement of the 1870s–1890s (often seen as an important precursor to the eugenics movement) by seeking to change male sexual activity and calling on a "vast, silent woman's movement" that would join middle-class and working-class interests against sexual double standards.[29] In Dowie's novel, however, Gallia's words also distance her from the prostitute by keeping them in distinct classes. By stressing the seemingly insurmountable inequalities among women, *Gallia* assigns a clear, class-based limit to women's capacity for generous, collective action.

Inequalities between women and men diminish women's solidarity as well, as Grand's *The Heavenly Twins* observes bleakly. Evadne, who makes the first of the novel's disastrous marriages to men with tarnished pasts, tries but fails to prevent Edith's similar marriage. Edith subsequently contracts her husband's syphilis, gives birth to a diseased child, and goes insane. When Evadne's friends then urge her to join with them to take a public stance against such marriages (*THT* 2:32), a promise to her husband restricts her social-purity activism. Collective action, the novel suggests, will occur only when women listen to each other, rather than to unfit husbands, and put the needs of the nation's children before both.

II. Bio-Altruism

Responding to late-century backlashes against women's gains through a tradition of gendered gifts enabled these writers to develop a discourse of biological altruism. Through eugenics, they appropriated the traditional feminine role of motherhood for radical feminist politics, addressing popular fears about race degeneration[30] and reframing women's communal economic and social gain as sacrifice.[31] During the last decades of the nineteenth century and the early decades of the twentieth, eugenics became a new and improved philanthropic method, "the truest charity" for those who worried that indiscriminate gifts of money would simply help to keep "unfit" populations alive.[32] In this, eugenics followed other neo-Malthusian discourses, which emphasized the evolutionary mandate for incessant struggle. Sir Francis Galton's disciple Karl Pearson, for example, believed that misdirected charity kept natural selection from acting as a racial purifier.[33] Eugenic visions of philanthropic work privileged "nature" over "nurture," finding biological selection a more valuable social remedy than handouts or environmental reforms, even as they continued to promote the latter.[34] The Malthusian League sought to mitigate "the sufferings of the poor" by "spreading the law of population among the people, and recommending scientific checks to replace the cruel natural ones."[35] In 1877, Annie Besant published the popular but highly controversial *Law of Population*, which explicitly detailed such "preventive checks" or methods of birth control; withdrawal, solutions of zinc or alum, "a covering," and vaginal sponges would offer "salvation to the poor" by limiting birth rates in general as well as ensuring that "those who suffer from hereditary diseases [. . .] would preserve the race from the deterioration which results from propagating disease."[36] Along similar lines, Mrs. Mary Sowden agreed that widespread knowledge about limiting births "would do much to limit the misery and wretchedness at present existing in society," while Dr. Alice Vickery, then president of the Malthusian League, argued by 1909 that "the declining birth-rate" had done more to "promote human welfare" than the "millions of pounds wasted on the Church and on charities [. . .]."[37]

Men and women alike responded to eugenic calls for more scientifically based "human sympathy,"[38] but, as critics such as Allison Berg and Angelique Richardson have demonstrated, women in particular found a role reclaiming "the race." They donated money and energy to eugenic research, but their greatest contribution was seen in terms of reproduction or "civic motherhood."[39] As Alice Ravenhill put it in a 1909 pamphlet for the Eugenics Education Society, "[w]oman's great and incomparable gift of motherhood must be set in the new light of racial responsibility" (15). Through eugenics, novelists re-envisioned this "gift of motherhood" as women's personal loss, translating maternity into a sacrifice for the nation.

The eugenics movement and its English and American proponents believed that "eugenics [wa]s going to save the world," regenerating the Anglo-Saxon race, as Caleb Williams Saleeby put it in 1909, by "get[ting] the right people born and the wrong people not born."[40] The movement had two branches, "negative" eugenics (to which I return shortly) and (so-called) "positive" eugenics. "Positive" eugenics referred to acts of encouragement; in contrast with the emphasis on prevention in "negative" eugenics, "positive" eugenics actively promoted "good" births by offering financial incentives[41] and by making sexual education more widely available.[42] This branch of eugenics, in common with the late-century social purity movement, tried to make members of the working classes and women and girls in general aware of potential health problems arising from men's sexual practices. "'Educate, educate, educate!' should be our cry," maintained one paper, as Edward and Eleanor Marx Aveling declared that "the reproductive organs ought to be discussed as frankly, as freely, between parents and children as the digestive."[43]

Reversing popular perceptions of consuming women and selfish mothers, advocates of positive eugenics considered sex education a "generous" practice that would eventually "emancipat[e]" women from men's "selfish and unnatural laws."[44] Indeed, sex education for females was intended to counteract "the selfishness of the husband," which "in the overwhelming majority of cases [leads to] the deterioration of the wife" in addition to overpopulation and race degeneration.[45] Educational pamphlets, advertisements for birth control, and fiction alike reflect these efforts to educate women about "the duty to avert conception."[46] Like the

literary annuals of the 1820s and '30s, which became "benevolent" books by virtue of their production, consumption, and circulation as gifts, and Salvation Army
periodicals, which made Slum Sisters' writing a form of sacrifice, literature at the
fin-de-siècle claimed to serve altruistic ends. Even as female authors benefited
professionally from this new cultural mandate to publish, they could assert the
generosity of their work through its transmission of purportedly life-saving eugenic principles. One popular example of such a novel, Grand's *Heavenly Twins*
traces the tragic lives of three women, Angelica (whose cross-dressing kills the
Tenor), Evadne, and Edith. Showing how the sexual pasts of their dissolute husbands present physical and moral dangers to Evadne and Edith, as well as to their
children, the novel joins contemporary essayists who deplore their "lifelong martyrdom": since "marriageable girls" seldom receive "any information as to sexual
relations [. . . .] their knowledge [. . .] often comes too late to prevent unhappy
results."[47] Evadne radically refuses to consummate her marriage when she learns
of her bridegroom's past,[48] while, as noted above, Edith's syphilitic child ("of an
unmistakable type") provides a cautionary lesson for other characters and for an
increasingly well-educated readership fearful of racial decline.[49] Positive eugenics
advocated frank discussions of sex and pregnancy to hold men responsible for the
spread of venereal diseases (reversing contemporary sexual double standards evident in such laws as the Contagious Diseases Acts), to educate women about their
sexual choices, to make women the authors of that education, and to encourage
women to select "fit" fathers for their babies.

While the emphasis on women's sexual education offered progressive ways for
women to take reproductive health into their own hands, fitness and fatherhood
depended upon more than health and moral choices, as Gilman suggests:

> Suppose the female of some other species, ignoring her racial duty of
> right selection, should mate with mangy, toothless cripples,—if there
> were such among her kind,—and so produce weak, malformed young,
> and help exterminate her race. Should she then blame him for the result?
> (*WE* 100)

A duty, not merely a choice, "right selection," for Gilman, depends on and also
collapses the categories of "species," "kind," and "race." Her slippage from human
fathers to the mangy, toothless cripples of another species classifies the physically
unfit as subhuman. By making women responsible for keeping categories distinct,
Gilman offers them the chance to save the human race from "extermination" but
limits this saving eugenic role to women who fit her racial parameters. She pathol-
ogizes those who do not. "Marry an Anglo-Saxon to an African or Oriental," she
explains, "and their child has a dual nature" (164).[50] While some scholars have
suggested that eugenic ideology took national forms (for instance, an American
emphasis on race in contrast to England's preoccupation with class), and while

eugenic practices certainly varied among nations, Richardson notes that British eugenic thought merged class with race in a "*biologization of* [...] class."[51] Through depictions of positive eugenic selection, women drew the biological boundaries of their national communities.

These depictions of positive eugenic selection allowed late-century fiction to replace women's purportedly "selfish" desires with the saving gifts of sacrificial motherhood and martyrdom, "subordinat[ing] the individual to the race."[52] Along these lines, Dowie substitutes eugenics for romance in her novel's marriage plot. Gallia, who once saw motherhood as pure profit, learns about loss in the process of selecting the "right" mate. Rejected by the man she loves, she begins to endorse good breeding instead, appreciating her future husband's physical features "rather as a dealer might notice the points in a horse" (121). As Richardson notes, Gallia, like Grand's Evadne, has read Galton and Spencer.[53] She turns her previous romantic disappointment into an opportunity to proselytize for eugenics in a scene that merges economic and spiritual sensibilities.

> I could spend myself and lose myself in my child, if I had one, and ask for no return; for everything else *I* come first; but I shouldn't come first there. When I marry, I shall, of course, marry without love. For that is used up. [...] On the whole, it may be an advantage. If I were to fall in love again, it might be with someone quite unsuitable to be the father of my child—someone who would not be fine and strong and healthy, and of a healthy stock. As it is [...] I shall marry solely with a view to the child I am going to live for. (129)

Ready, now, to "spend' and "lose" herself with "no return," Gallia reverses her earlier conception of motherhood as necessarily selfish. Sacrificing her chance of heterosexual romance through a selection process that leaves love out of the question, her "spiritual feeling" lights "strange fires" (129) in the man she once cherished, who is (belatedly) impassioned by the sacrificial sentiments she expresses and also horrified at the prospect of her martyrdom in marrying without love.[54] "I look at it like the women who marry for position and money—as a price," Gallia states (131)—though later she reflects that "one may over-do one's sacrifices" (180).[55] From a eugenic standpoint, she is indeed better able to choose a "fit" mate once she has shed love's blinders; the novel's conclusion dramatically reveals that her first choice had hereditary heart disease (200). Gallia sacrifices romantic desire to eugenic reproduction. Here again, the positive eugenic emphasis is on the choice of a partner as much as on the future child itself. By framing eugenic selection as romantic sacrifice, the novel inserts its heroine in a tradition of extreme giving.[56]

Gallia's eugenic sacrifice provides a model for a woman's private sexual decisions to contribute to a larger political project of racial salvation. This project assumes a sufficient supply of "fine and strong and healthy" men (coded variously as Anglo-Saxon, professional, robustly heterosexual, and also free of venereal disease). But what if there were no such men? As we saw earlier with Bulwer-Lytton, some writers feared that women's development would inevitably diminish men, from physical as well as political standpoints. At a time when Oscar Wilde's 1895 trial was making homosexuality a household word and when writers such as Schreiner feared that men were growing "effete" or "decadent," male degeneration was becoming cause for national concern. Other writers attempted to sidestep the problem entirely, proposing new possibilities for women's eugenic sacrifice without mates. Shifting generically to science fiction allowed Gilman to offer parthenogenesis, or asexual birth, as an alternative to both romantic and eugenic marriage plots. Her fictional parthenogenesis even had some backing in scientific fact. Geddes and Thomson provide a detailed history of female animals producing offspring on their own in cases of "occasional" "partial," and "total" parthenogenesis.[57] In *Women and Economics*, Gilman enthusiastically takes note of "[r]aces [. . .] which reproduce themselves without the masculine organism."[58] Her later fiction combines this scientific premise with traditions of women's gift offerings to create a utopian community that fundamentally redefines the nature of kinship.

In Gilman's *Herland* (1915), three male explorers learn, to their shock, that the rich country they discover has existed without men for two thousand years, since war and natural disaster eliminated them (39). Years ago, a woman bore a child— "a direct gift from the gods" (48)—who gave rise to a race of parthenogenetic women, "a holy sisterhood" (49) merging "mother-love" with "sister-love" (49). Producing a peaceful, intelligent, healthy population of cooperative workers who specialize in everything from childrearing to astronomy, the inhabitants of *Herland* advance their race through their eugenic resolve to produce only as many people as their geographical limits allow (58).

> You see, they were Mothers [. . .] in the sense of Conscious Makers of People. Mother-love with them was not a brute passion, a mere 'instinct,' a wholly personal feeling; it was—a religion.
>   It included that limitless feeling of sisterhood, that wide unity in service which was so difficult for us to grasp. (58)

The "gift" of motherhood yields a "sisterhood" of women who sideline personal or selfish aims to serve the race as the conscientious devotees of a spiritual movement.

Choosing whether to bear children or to simply "put the whole thing out of her mind" (61), each woman's childbearing is a fully conscious act, a unique function of mental energy. Gilman's motherhood makes biological reproduction dependent on intellectual production, tying childbearing to women's creative labor. Eugenic parenting thus offers Gilman a way to talk about and justify other intellectual efforts, such as authorship. Although the conflation of women's artistic production with biological reproduction is familiar from Alexander Pope's eighteenth-century jibes at prolific writer Eliza Haywood's promiscuous output and Mary Shelley's early nineteenth-century references to the "hideous progeny" she sends forth,[59] the far more exalted nature of childbearing in *Herland* and other fin-de-siècle texts suggests a more confident approach to acts of intellectual birth and reminds us that for many women writers, discussions of motherhood also figured (and enabled) statements about the political force of writing itself.[60] Whether offering analogies between the two forms of (re)production or using eugenics as a mandate to educate women about sex and motherhood through fiction, works by Gilman and others fold literature into traditions of women's gifts by implying that the combination of women's mental energy and eugenic sacrifice has the potential to save the race.

Childbirth and racial selection are sanctified by religious feeling in this utopian society, as in *Gallia*. Gilman's vision of "limitless" sisterhood initially appears to exceed *Gallia*'s ambivalent image of women looped together on a long rope. As we will see, however, its vague strategies for "consciously" shaping the population undercut its avowals of "wide unity" by linking this community more particularly to the "negative" eugenics that sought to limit birth than to the "positive" eugenics that encouraged it.[61]

III. The Sacrifice of Motherhood

Today we are more familiar with the negative branch of eugenics than with its positive complement, primarily through its associations with twentieth-century racial politics and practices ranging from enforced sterilization to mass extermination. We are less aware of the wide range of social reformers, female and male, feminist and others, who supported and developed negative eugenics as a progressive agenda between 1880 and 1920 in England and America.[62] (The early birth control movement itself emerged out of eugenic concerns as much as out of women's desire for sexual "liberation."[63]) While positive eugenics promoted "good births" through educated choice, the negative eugenics that the rest of this chapter discusses aimed to actively prevent less suitable breeding. Olive Schreiner, who joined with Galton's disciple Karl Pearson to discuss such matters in the Men and Women's Club,[64] stressed the importance of negative eugenics in the name of "the race":

> It is certain that the time is now rapidly approaching when child-bearing
> will be regarded rather as a lofty privilege, permissible only to those who
> have shown their power rightly to train and provide for their offspring,
> than a labour which in itself, and under whatever conditions performed,
> is beneficial to society. (*WL* 36)

Schreiner opposes "excessive and reckless child-bearing" in part to protect and improve the lives of undereducated and starving children. A similar desire to guarantee children food and education led other charitable activists to employ negative eugenics on behalf of child welfare; in this sense, it mirrors the biological altruism claimed by positive eugenics. It looks less benevolent, however, when we see that the "lofty privilege" of bearing children requires permission. Schreiner's statement elides the methods and agents of this permission. (Who will evaluate parenthood? And by what standards?) Many writers found it easier to locate eugenic standards for forbidding reproduction than for encouraging it.[65] According to eugenic principles, "provid[ing] for" one's offspring properly meant not only selecting the right parent but also preventing the wrong birth. Only under eugenic conditions, advocates argued, could childbearing be "beneficial." Through this logic, negative eugenics made even enforced sterility a gift to the race.

Negative eugenics thus afforded women additional ways to sanctify motherhood. Beyond sacrificing romantic desire in the choice of a fit mate, as Dowie's Gallia chooses to do, women could sacrifice motherhood itself in order to be the saviors of their race. Despite their emphasis on the national significance of childbearing, these discourses on negative eugenics implicitly exempt women from the mandate to be mothers—a potentially liberating option for women without the means or desire to bear children. No longer simply "redundant," "surplus," or "odd," women without children might be martyrs instead—but only if the choice were theirs and did not irrevocably mark them as unfit.

In *Herland*, the country's parthenogenetic inhabitants, like the Gy-ei of Bulwer-Lytton's *The Coming Race*, limit the population through "a period of 'negative eugenics'" which, the narrator realizes, "must have been an appalling sacrifice. [. . .] they had to forego motherhood for their country—and it was precisely the hardest thing for them to do" (59). Parthenogenesis removing the urgency for fit fatherhood, Gilman's novella places racial duty, sacrifice, and salvation solely in the hands (and reproductive organs) of its "sisterhood." But the methods behind this holy sacrifice bewilder *Herland*'s male explorer.

> I understand that you make Motherhood your highest social service—a sacrament, really; that it is only undertaken once, by the majority of the population; that those held unfit are not allowed even that; [. . .]. But what I do not understand [. . .] is how you prevent it. (59)

His Herlander guide essentially deflects the question for the time, noting simply that young women "often [. . .] voluntarily defer" motherhood (60), making a willing sacrifice in the service of the race. Only later do we learn that the country's negative eugenic practices rely on involuntary selection. The Herlanders work "to train out, to breed out, when possible, the lowest types." They attempt to "appeal" to these unfit women "to renounce motherhood," but if this fails they forbid them to raise their own children. Happily, the Herlanders observe, "fortune" makes "some of the few worst types [. . .] unable to reproduce" (70).[66] Birth control, here, is not a woman's choice. By making "fortune" (in this case, convenient infertility) aid their eugenic efforts, Gilman naturalizes sterilization. Her Herlanders never have to prevent births; they appear shocked by a query as to whether they "destroy the unborn" (59). The slippage here between "natural" and socially imposed restrictions, however, suggests that "forego[ing] motherhood for the country" may be compulsory service. Fortune, voluntary sacrifice, and spirituality allow Gilman to veil the dirty work of selection. Whether they like it or not, the women of *Herland* cede their reproductive choices to the national imperative for negative eugenics.

Eugenics offered women a wide range of options for giving. It justified productive labor and sanctified reproductive practices, from educating women about healthy sexual decisions to sacrificing desire for a "fit" marriage, from bearing "fit" children for the race to giving up childbearing itself. At stake in all of this was the depiction of sexual choice as the prerogative of women (albeit a select group). In the 1890s, a woman's right to say "no" was still very much under contention. Activist Elizabeth Wolstenholme Elmy, fighting against the legalized sexual submission of wives to their husbands, pointed out that marital rape essentially "enforced maternity."[67] In contrast, eugenics seemed to offer women choice regarding their sexual and maternal functions. And it made those choices matter. Writers such as Dowie and Gilman sanctified these choices, depicting women's childbearing as mystical acts of service in ways that obscure the varying degrees of power and choice among women.

While "fortune" rids Gilman's Herlanders of their "lowest types" and keeps them appalled by the prospect of abortion, Grand's *The Heavenly Twins* takes a more extreme, fundamentalist approach to the sanctity of eugenic feminism. Edith dies of syphilis after condemning the social order that allowed her marriage to take place, but Evadne, who safely outlives the marriage she never consummates, remarries to Dr. Galbraith, a "charming" and "distinguished" medical man known for "the confidence he inspires" (*THT* 1:68). The narrative encourages readers to admire Galbraith, his kindness, and even his prescient and progressive first impression that Evadne will suffer somehow from women's marginal social status (*THT* 1:131). Like Evadne, he is appalled by Edith's sad fate, and, in a discussion of "the heredity of vice," concurs with her positive eugenic stance that "'[i]t is criminal to withhold knowledge from any woman who has the capacity to acquire it'" (375).

Galbraith gets the unique privilege in Grand's two-volume novel of narrating its sixth and final book, a privilege which seems to endorse his perspective and align it with that of the novel's previous, omniscient narrator. As doctor and then husband, he reviews Evadne's case, her sad first marriage and the "unhealthy state of mind" it has produced (2:343). Like the doctor-husband who preceded him in

Gilman's short story "The Yellow Wall-Paper" (1892), Galbraith's caregiving combines professional and patriarchal prerogatives to limit his wife's autonomy. His prescriptions offer different restrictions, however. In a reversal of Gilman's notorious rest cure, Galbraith stipulates activity (and less time to think) for Evadne. "I kept her constantly out of doors, and never let her sit and sew alone [. . .]. I made her ride, too, and rise regularly in the morning [. . .]" (2:371). Rather unsurprisingly, she remains depressed.

A crisis point in their marriage comes when, pregnant, she attempts suicide. Fearing that their child too might someday suffer from a dysgenic marriage, she decides to prevent its birth by killing herself. The suicide note that she leaves for her husband reads: "'I am haunted by a terrible fear [. . .] I have tried again and again to tell you, but I never could. You would not see that it is prophetic, as I do— in case of our death—nothing to save my daughters from Edith's fate—better both die at once'" (2:377). Although Galbraith intercepts both note and poison in time, he fails to alter her mind-set, despite concerted efforts. Her prediction that he will not share her vision is correct. Infantilizing her as a "Poor little innocent sinner" (2:378), he remains troubled that she lacks the "saving suffering of an agony of remorse" (2:379). For Evadne, however—and, I want to argue, for the novel—the real "saving suffering" is this suicide attempt, which she defends as eugenic martyrdom, a divine gift which will promote the welfare both of her private family and of humanity at large. Galbraith later asks her to admit that her suicide attempt was "a mistaken notion" (2:383):

> "I do not feel any regret," she said at last. "I would not do the same thing now, but it is only because I am not now occupied with the same thoughts. [. . .] I no longer perceive the utility of self-sacrifice."
> "But do you not perceive the sin of suicide?"
> "Not of that kind of suicide," she answered. "You see, we have the divine example. Christ committed suicide to all intents and purposes by deliberately putting himself into the hands of his executioners; but his motive makes *them* responsible for the crime; and my motive would place society in a similar position." (2: 383–384)

Galbraith, horrified, rejects Evadne's troubled (and potentially insulting) "prophecy" that their children will face the problems of hereditary illness, either through birth or through marriage. He quickly condemns her eugenic solution (to "save" her unborn children through suicide-cum-abortion) as murder. He gets the last word. Refusing to acknowledge the striking comparison Evadne makes to Christian martyrdom, Galbraith closes the final volume of the novel sadly hoping to "make her life endurable" (392). He attributes her actions to depression and infirmity rather than to a radical feminist vision entailing a principled commitment to eugenic sacrifice.

And yet, if Evadne's suicide attempt offers a rare example of how "new women" were approaching negative eugenics, her radical effort to use this suicide to abort her pregnancy nevertheless strikes a chord with other late-century female writers. Lady Cook [Tennessee C. Claflin] provocatively asserts that, in many cases, "legalized infanticide [. . . .] would be the truest humanity." Calling for publicly appointed doctors to inspect infants and spare the "unfit" from "[t]he dreary years of painful existence and watchful cares," she defends her proposal of a "painless death to the unfortunate new-born infant" against the "daily horrors" of their lives.[68] Galbraith's assumption that Evadne is simply sick and depressed cannot account for the way that other proponents of negative eugenics rationalized similar trade-offs.

Grand's novel as a whole is far more ambivalent about Evadne's suicide attempt than Galbraith. The narrator of its first five books notably absents herself from his conclusion after uniquely prefacing this final book with an author's note that undermines his authority, despite his privileged professional and narrative positions.[69]

> NOTE.—The fact that Dr. Galbraith had not the advantage of knowing Evadne's early history when they first became acquainted adds a certain piquancy to the flavour of his impressions, and the reader, better informed than himself with regard to the antecedents of his "subject," will find it interesting to note both the accuracy of his insight and the curious mistakes which it is possible even for a trained observer like himself to make by the half light of such imperfect knowledge as he was able to collect under the circumstances. [. . .] But more interesting still, perhaps, are the glimpses we get of Dr. Galbraith himself in the narrative, throughout which it is easy to decipher the simple earnestness of the man, the cautious professionalism and integrity, the touches of tender sentiment held in check, the dash of egotism [. . .]. (2:253)

The note (forgotten by many critical discussions of the novel) reminds us that the doctor is at a disadvantage here, less informed than the reader, observing in "half light." Just as Evadne believes that Galbraith won't hear her prophecy or "see" her vision, Grand's narrator is skeptical of his verdicts. She impresses upon the reader Galbraith's own "curious" mistakenness as well as his egotism. Privileging reader over doctor, and stressing the importance of "early history" to a "subject," Grand emphasizes the role of character development—a task better suited to the novelist than to the male medical expert.[70] This note, in its explicit endorsement of literary interpretation and its implicit suggestion that a female writer might have more accurate perception than a scientific man, echoes *Herland*'s opposition of male scientific explorers against the mystical women who teach them, as well as Bulwer-Lytton's nervous prediction that women

might soon be superior "in all those abstruse and mystical branches of reasoning, for which [. . . men] are unfitted" (62). The "mystical" reasoning that
Evadne uses to trace out the "divine example" of martyrdom certainly mystifies
Galbraith; but then, his judgment of her in general is far from secure. His
opening sentence is, after all "'Evadne puzzled me'" (2:255). Rather than indicating that marriage clears his judgment, the author's note on his "curious
mistake[nness]" asks readers to evaluate even Evadne's radical position on suicide in terms of their earlier knowledge of her sound moral judgment, intellectual ability, and emotional conviction.

Raising but refusing to explicitly answer the question of whether eugenic suicide might be justifiable, *The Heavenly Twins* leaves readers somewhat uncomfortable with the patronizing attitude of Evadne's second husband, who shares
his Christian name (George) with her first, morally degenerate spouse.[71] The
novel's larger focus on the tragedy of unfit marriages also lends support to her
startling version of negative eugenics. Earlier books, for instance, bear out
Evadne's account of Edith's extreme suffering and even trace it, indirectly, to
Galbraith. As a physician, he is one of three representative men, along with her
diseased husband and bishop father, whom Edith bitterly indicts as the "arrangement of society which has made it possible for me and my child to be sacrificed in this way" (1: 351). When her syphilitic child seems to "ask[. . .] dumbly,
why had he ever been born?" (1: 339) the novel suggests, as Beth Sutton-
Ramspeck notes, that his mother should have known enough to prevent his conception.[72] When Evadne, after seeing him, exclaims "the awful needless
suffering!" (2:390) and wonders how her children will escape a similar fate, the
novel suggests that more drastic solutions might be necessary. It makes of her
sacrifice an aggressive gift that demands accountability. Galbraith's inability to
"reason with her" and his fear that she has become unstable come across as
grossly inadequate responses to her reasoned, if disturbing comments (2:390),
displacing responsibility away from male sexuality and onto female hysteria. At
a time when women still lacked equal rights to custody of their children,[73]
mothers might well search for extralegal means of assuring that their children
avoid the suffering seemingly brought about by the patriarchal triad of medi-
cine, clergy, and fatherhood.

Through its two narrators as well as the narrative distance between the final
book's prefatory note and concluding words, the novel takes a cautious stance,
refusing, as Gilman's *Herland* also does, to explicitly endorse either abortion or
suicide in the name of eugenics. But *The Heavenly Twins* implicitly validates
Evadne's position by giving voice to her idea that this death comprises a form of
Christian "self-sacrifice" and by placing in the mouth of a fallible man the novel's
lone condemnation of a woman who sees such extreme measures as the only way
to save her children. Though it deplores the fact that "women have practised
self-sacrifice, when they should have been teaching men self-control" (1:125),

the novel transforms the possible meaning of this self-sacrifice.[74] Evadne's eugenic martyrdom—like those of Dowie's Gallia and Gilman's Herlanders—follows the tradition of "giving women" who take on active, Christ-like roles to serve and save the nation. Recalling literary types, such as Rossetti's Lizzie and the heroine posited by Florence Nightingale's prophetic *Cassandra*, as well as historical women such as the Anglican and Salvation Army Sisters I have discussed, Grand links Evadne's scientific "philanthropy" and sexual choices back to women's gift practices and their role in allowing women to rework the meaning of both religious observation and kinship. She reminds us, further, that the female writer is an important mediator of these gifts. Evadne carries to its uncomfortable extreme the logic of women giving life for the nation, with her desire to give *up* life when such a sacrifice might be of still greater value for the race. As she implies, this gift creates a powerful obligation. In Grand's vision of giving women, men like Galbraith will pay the price for "crime[s]" against women's health and happiness.

Feminist eugenics, promising to unite racially "fit" women through their common maternal sacrifices, sanctified women's gifts and reinforced a gendered economy in the early women's movement. As givers, rather than takers, women could assuage fin-de-siècle fears of their dangerous profits while simultaneously benefiting from the greater sexual choices, maternal rights, and civic roles attributed to them as giving women. They made explicit what the past century of writing had suggested: that women and the nation had much to gain through offerings that were both gendered and also sexed. The social costs were equally high, however. Distinctions between the agents and objects of eugenic selection underscore the wide-ranging and often troubling conclusions reached in the name of women's gifts. In the years before suffrage, women used traditions of giving to form civic alliances and justify their political interventions. But, as we have seen throughout this book, nineteenth-century women's activism was simultaneously progressive and problematic. Even as gift practices helped to consolidate certain national communities, they limited others. Eugenic discourses at the end of the century, like earlier images of kinship, remind us of the inequality of "sisterhood."[75] In the most forward-thinking movements of the day, many women were deemed "unfit" to be the givers or recipients of exchange. Closer attention to the give and take of women's transactions provides a richer, more complicated vision of the early women's movement. It suggests some of the ways in which the emphasis on sexual "difference" helped women to achieve greater egalitarian rights, and it allows us to balance our celebration of nineteenth-century women's growing social and civic authority with the realization that the "sisterhood" who first benefited from such advances never was and never aimed to be the all-inclusive, utopian society that many "second-wave" feminist critics took as the given of women's civic exchanges.[76]

Homemade Jams & Militant Martyrs

POLITICS OF GENEROSITY IN CAMPAIGNS
FOR WOMEN'S SUFFRAGE

The traditions of gendered gifts and sacrifices that this book has traced finally promoted women's fight for the vote. As this brief epilogue argues, the suffrage movement—a side of women's social activism more readily written into histories of the early women's movement than eugenics—also benefits from this legacy of Victorian women's giving. The connection may not be immediately evident today, because women's suffrage is now typically understood as the result of feminist discourses on equal "rights." Along these lines, many early suffragists insisted on their "recognition as citizens possessing the same responsibilities and rights as men."[1] Capitalizing on the passage of the Married Women's Property Act, advocates pointed out that "with property goes taxation, and with taxation must and shall go representation."[2] They declared it to be "manifestly unjust" "[t]hat female householders, who possess the same property qualifications which entitles male householders to the franchise, should be denied the same civil rights [...],"[3] and proposed "'[t]o grant the parliamentary franchise to women on the same terms as it is or may be granted to men' [.... with] no appeal for privilege."[4]

Such arguments, grounded in conventional ideas of economic privilege, tend to garner more critical attention than movements that attempted to take advantage of women's biological and gendered "difference." But another, vocal strain of suffrage activism asked, with Olive Schreiner and the other women discussed in Chapter 6 of this volume, "Has the soldier's mother no stake in the country?"[5] Drawing on "separate spheres" ideology to justify the vote for female householders and working-class women alike, this side urged women to demand respect for "*the distinctive qualities of heart and mind, the special aptitudes, intelligence, and aspirations of our sex.*"[6] And it profited from women's gendered reputation for giving. By establishing shops that sought and sold women's gifts, by militantly offering themselves up as martyrs for the cause, and by eventually offering to sacrifice suffrage itself in the interests of Britain's larger war efforts, suffragettes drew on varied gift strategies to gain popular support and ultimately achieve the victory that egalitarian political arguments and more openly aggressive techniques had failed to win. Yet these strategies, which were sometimes perceived as detrimental to other women's efforts, provoked dissent and remind us that sacrifice comes at a high cost. Women's extreme giving, politically efficacious though it was, did not necessarily entail and frequently came at the expense of political solidarity.

Scholars often dismiss feminine sacrifice as "sentimentality and domestic feeling" and pit it against more "rational political calculus."[7] Although Laura Nym Mayhall rightly points out that suffragettes "sought to represent themselves politically, not merely visually" and that these processes should not be conflated,[8] her argument obscures important connections between suffragettes' bodily spectacles of giving and their more "rational" economic maneuvers, including commercial ventures based on gifts. Campaigns for the vote shared a number of the strategies we have seen in sacrificial depictions of eugenic reform, urban slum work, and religious service, as well as in earlier fictions of reciprocity.[9] Suffragettes, too, calculated the returns on their gifts, and benefited accordingly. Giving ultimately allowed women to make egalitarian arguments through discourses of difference. It thus demands that we consider depictions of sacrificial bodies alongside other forms of politically motivated gift exchange and offers a new paradigm for reading narrative traditions of women's social activism and political engagement.

I. Appealing for the Vote

Like Salvation Army efforts in the slums, campaigns for women's suffrage relied, first and foremost, on volunteer labor and donations. Newspapers such as *Votes for Women* and *The Suffragette*—each, in its turn, the official organ of the militant Women's Social and Political Union (W.S.P.U.)—regularly appeal to readers to contribute time and energy to the cause. Calling for newspaper sellers[10] and membership pledges, they also profit from the profusion of gifts provided for campaign shops, jumble sales, and holiday bazaars. Krista Lysack has recently argued that W.S.P.U. members in particular "shop[ped] for the vote," deploying "tactics of consumption" to achieve suffrage.[11] Certainly this organization encouraged politically savvy shopping, both in the many retail venues it created and in department stores such as Selfridges, which advertised in its pages.[12] If female consumers were a force to be reckoned with, however, women had even more striking roles as the producers and organizers of these suffrage sales. Not only were the shops and bazaars non-profit ventures, with sales benefiting the campaign for the vote, rather than individual businesswomen, but they depended primarily upon the gift practices of their members for supplies.

The retail spaces that the W.S.P.U. began opening in 1908 carried suffrage literature and banners, as well as scarves and ribbons in the purple, green, and white colors of the organization. Lysack observes that the shops were to "resemble established commercial enterprises,"[13] but their rooms were rented by subscription, staffed by volunteers, and, for the most part, stocked with donations.[14] The shops were furnished through members' contributions; one local chapter of the W.S.P.U. informed readers that "members [. . .] anxious to make us presents" might provide its office with "long winter curtains to divide small and larger office, one table cover, waste-paper basket; still more chairs."[15] Others requested stoves to warm their shops. "Will friends either give these or pay for them?"[16] Items for sale were similarly supplied by members. "The shop supply of home-made marmalade is just exhausted. Who will replenish from their stock? Jams also very welcome."[17] Acknowledging a list of women who had already donated Jumble Sale parcels, one notice reminds readers of the upcoming "Christmas display [. . .] being planned for our shop; anyone disposed to add to our stock in the way of mincemeat, Christmas puddings, jam, or sweets will receive our warmest thanks."[18] The profit of £30 raised by the 1909 Kensington W.S.P.U. Jumble Sale "is due to much generosity,"[19] not simply to savvy commercialism, wide profit margins, and economic demand.

The W.S.P.U. shops, like their Jumble Sales and large-scale Christmas exhibits, benefited from traditions of charitable ladies' bazaars as much as from the world of department stores populated by increasingly mobile female consumers at the turn of the century.[20] Supporters of women's suffrage were asked to first donate goods, often home-made, and then to go and purchase more from the organization, giving doubly on behalf of their cause. Thus the papers seek a series of gifts. First, contributions:

> [B]efore there is any talk of buying and selling, there is a great deal of work to be done! [. . .] The articles for the Sale must be useful and dainty—suitable for presents. They can be made in white or in the colours, and there is a wide choice in needlework, leather work, carving, painting, and all the other arts and crafts. Others who have less leisure may prefer to *give* beautiful or useful things [. . .]. Decide what you will give, and set about it quickly![21]

Naming donations of Christmas puddings, dolls, mince pies, and blouse trimmings, and reminding readers that "Cakes, home-made sweets, jams, marmalade, new-laid eggs always find a ready sale," the W.S.P.U. insists that "goods must pour in 'thick and fast'" before the sale.[22] In all these accounts, the women's work of creating the items they can then give precedes and makes possible any subsequent "buying and selling."

After sending in their gifts for shops or holiday sales to benefit the W.S.P.U., readers were implored to purchase "Xmas Presents! Xmas Presents! Come and buy at the W.S.P.U. Stall."[23] (See Figure 7.1.) Articles praising the "attractive exhibitions of charming goods suitable for Christmas presents" remind members to

Figure 7.1 "W.S.P.U. BAZAAR, 1911." The Women's Library, London Metropolitan University

"see the great variety offered before they purchase the many things required at this time of the year."[24] Making purchases on behalf of women's suffrage meant paying money for the goods that had been donated by fellow members, shopping at the very displays to which they had already contributed stock. And these displays were, at least according to the articles that inundated the papers, worthy of members' custom. "The jewellery, of which there is an ample amount, is surprisingly lovely, and, with the good lace, Irish crochet, china, antiques, charming basket-work, Chinese costumes, fancy needlework articles, supply all comers with a fine choice of gifts for all tastes and all ages."[25] With such items to choose from, readers might not only delight in shopping these sales but also select holiday presents for friends and family. The W.S.P.U. urged members to commit to continuous giving in the name of women's suffrage, and the organization even stood in as an intermediary for presents between women. Rather than offer a present of homemade jam or needlework directly to a friend, the multistage structure of membership contributions meant that women would give to the Union and then select holiday presents from the pooled resources of members' handicrafts. These gift practices require objects to change hands multiple times, following the holiday pattern set by literary annuals nearly a century before. They also echo Gaskell's description of how individual gifts can sustain a larger community, even as they require the more lopsided offerings we have seen in subsequent emphases on the extreme gifts of sacrifice, by asking women to give, buy, and give again before seeing any sort of return.

Indeed, with women's suffrage as the communal, long-term goal, givers' most coveted return was one that could only be deferred, creating the appearance of one-sided gestures. Suffrage entailed sacrifice, as many members were quick to point out. The W.S.P.U.'s annual Self-Denial Week explicitly aligned women's personal sacrifices with gifts to the movement that might achieve political success in the long run but would have to settle for financial success until then.[26] "It is a week of self-discipline. It is a week of sacrifice that will be expressed in the precise and definite terms of silver and gold," wrote *Votes for Women* editor Emmeline Pethick Lawrence.[27] During these weeks, the organization raised funds through members' direct gifts of money or goods, but, as W.S.P.U. founder Emmeline Pankhurst was quick to point out, "Every week in the year is a Self-Denial Week for the women in our Union."[28]

Although they understood and framed their contributions to the cause as temporarily one-sided, members received other rewards in advance of suffrage: acknowledgment in the papers and a sufficient degree of celebrity status to warrant the sale of postcards depicting various members, from the working-class Annie Kenney to Emmeline Pankhurst. Giving allowed suffragettes to show leadership and strength as well as generosity. As Emmeline Pankhurst's daughter and co-leader of the W.S.P.U. Christabel Pankhurst recalls in her memoir, "Our honorary treasurer was unrivalled in her rare courage to ask others to give, as well as to give herself [. . .]."[29] The "courage" required for appeals and gift-giving recalls earlier descriptions we have seen of risky service among Salvation Army women and in "Goblin Market" and suggests that among suffragettes, as among Slum Sisters, gaining a reputation might be a good thing. Praising a treasurer's "courage" emphasizes her willingness to sacrifice rather than her financial acumen, despite the fact that the W.S.P.U. had the largest annual income of any suffrage society: £36,535 by 1914.[30]

In addition to celebrity and a wide range of leadership opportunities, W.S.P.U. members experienced what one letter published in *The Suffragette* called "The splendid joy of fighting." Noting that "Self-Denial Week is a special opportunity for showing gratitude that such joy should be ours," the letter asked "Comrades" to "make it unique in thank-offerings [. . .]."[31] According to this formulation, the week's "sacrifice" was less a token of generosity than a marker of gratitude for joy, a reminder that here, as in Lizzie's glee as she departs the goblins' market, gift offerings are never one-sided. Nonetheless, even as the W.S.P.U. papers emphasized the financial contributions of its members and delighted in describing the material gifts they gave, remarks about the "joy of fighting" focused equally on suffragettes' physical sacrifices. Drawing on vocabularies of empowered gift-giving that would have been familiar from fictional narratives and political newspapers alike, these militants mimicked the martyrdom that Lizzie risked and that *The Heavenly Twins'* Evadne calculated on, depicting themselves as ready and willing to die for their cause.

II. Dying for the Vote

Listed among the needlework, jams, mincemeats, and other homemade artifacts of W.S.P.U. shops are more startling objects, less likely to be found in traditional, charitable ladies' bazaars. Postcards for sale show militant suffragettes arrested for demonstrations or window-smashing (see Figure 7.2), inhabiting prison cells, and suffering from the hunger strikes they used to protest their imprisonment.[32] One Exhibition included displays of suffragette prison cells ("Real ex-prisoners go through the prison routine at stated times"[33]) (see Figure 7.3) alongside stalls filled with "china, pottery, and foreign embroideries" for sale.[34] Another ambitious shop hoped to pair its Christmas gifts with a display of "instruments similar to those used in forcible feeding"[35]—the government's infamous response to hunger strikes. And a few months later, the W.S.P.U. advertised "[a] coloured poster, representing a Suffragette being forcibly fed" for six or one pence, depending on size.[36] (See, for example, Figure 7.4.) Their willingness to suffer for the vote was a significant part of suffragettes' appeal to readers. Militant members of the W.S.P.U. in particular made their campaign for suffrage an exercise in personal martyrdom between 1905 and 1914.[37] Descriptions of their protests note that militants "faced abuse, insult, ridicule" and bodily harm; risking themselves in demonstrations and imprisonment, they presented a spectacle of women physically endangered, even "tortur[ed]."[38]

MRS. PANKHURST ARRESTED IN VICTORIA STREET, FEB. 13, 1908.

Figure 7.2 "Mrs. Pankhurst Arrested in Victoria Street, Feb. 13, 1908"
The Women's Library, London Metropolitan University

Figure 7.3 "2ND DIVISION CELL ALLOTTED TO SUFFRAGETTES"
The Women's Library, London Metropolitan University

In a 1908 article "Prison Experiences of a Suffragette," actress and W.S.P.U. member Winifred Mayo recalls her desire to take part in presenting a resolution to the House of Commons "at whatever hazards."[39] The women she describes— ranging from "gentlewomen" to members of the working class—are also ready to make sacrifices for the movement: one declares herself "ready, if the need came, to die for her sex's freedom!"[40] The women in her account are "pushed" and "struck,"

Figure 7.4 "FORCIBLE FEEDING." The Women's Library, London Metropolitan University

"seized," and "knocked" about by police who arrest and imprison them.[41] The conditions of the small, sparsely furnished jail cells Mayo describes recall those slum dwellings we saw in Chapter 5 of this volume; crowded, infested, and dirty, they are "a disgrace to any civilised community"—at once evidence of women's willingness to suffer for the nation and a sign that women's civic action is necessary for the literal and figurative work of tidying up that nation.[42] Mayo's companions bide their time in prison by reciting works by Olive Schreiner and "Mrs. Stetson" (Charlotte Perkins Gilman)—choices which gesture toward the perceived connection between the aims of eugenist writers and suffragettes, in particular, and the shared discourses and strategies of literary authors and political activists more generally.[43] These women keep up their humor and (like the similarly battered

Lizzie in "Goblin Market") even find reason to laugh.[44] As we will see, however, imprisonment quickly became less of a laughing matter.

Militant methods leading to imprisonment included demonstrations, "disorderly conduct,"[45] and vandalism. They were highly contentious. Within the W.S.P.U. itself, internal resistance to these strategies contributed to Sylvia Pankhurst's break from the organization led by her mother and sister.[46] *Votes for Women* editors Emmeline and Frederick Pethick Lawrence also split with the W.S.P.U. over militancy; as of October, 1912, *The Suffragette*, edited by Christabel Pankhurst, would be the militant suffrage Union's official paper.[47] Other suffrage organizations were still more explicit in their criticism of these practices. Millicent Garrett Fawcett, president of the nonviolent National Union of Women's Suffrage Societies (N.U.W.S.S.), publicly condemned the "law-break[ing]" tactics of the "stone-throwing" W.S.P.U.[48] and wrote frequent letters to the *Times* expressing her opposition to "the use of violence as political propaganda, holding it to be wrong in itself and injurious to the cause it is intended to serve."[49] (See Figure 7.5.) Along with two dozen other prominent figures, including activist Elizabeth Wolstenholme Elmy and future M.P. Eleanor Rathbone, Fawcett signed a public letter against the "provocative and bellicose" approach of the W.S.P.U., arguing that the "one thing that can now imperil our position [. . .] is the renewal of militancy."[50]

The responses of even pro-suffrage women to the W.S.P.U.'s strategies ranged from devout emulation to bitter opposition and remind us that, despite its forceful

Figure 7.5 "National Union of Women's Suffrage Societies, President Mrs. Fawcett: Law-Abiding Suffragists"
The Women's Library, London Metropolitan University

presence on the national and international stages, the W.S.P.U. was only one of many organizations fighting for women's suffrage. This epilogue seeks to describe some of its gift tactics, rather than represent women's suffrage or any one group *in toto*. It is instructive to see, however, that even as certain vocal and respected campaigners for women's suffrage sought other methods of political activism and resisted any association with the W.S.P.U.'s penchant for destroying property, they frequently expressed sympathy for the organization's *self*-destructive, sacrificial practices. Fawcett explicitly notes that she "supported the militant suffragists [. . . when] they had suffered violence but had used none" and writes on behalf of arrested members of the W.S.P.U. who had been "actuated by 'undoubtedly pure motives.'"[51] Emmeline Pethick Lawrence, in a policy statement for the newly independent *Votes for Women*, insists that "[w]ith criticism of vigorous and self-sacrificing action we have nothing whatever to do."[52] Notwithstanding the paper's break from the W.S.P.U., she expresses her support for its "self-sacrificing" tendencies. Declaring that "whatever tragedy may ensue [. . . .] the Government are responsible," she speaks in defense of the "martyrs of liberty" who have been "maimed" and "tortured [. . .] to the point of death."[53] Militant energy, turned back on the militants themselves, offered opponents of stone-throwing a more familiar image of giving women; against the glass-shattering force of women aggressively demanding the vote, they could approve of women sacrificing *themselves* for suffrage.

Beyond the brutal treatment they received at the hands of the police, these "martyrs of liberty" subjected their bodies to additional suffering behind bars, protesting their time in jail by going on hunger strikes and, like Evadne from *The Heavenly Twins*, hoping to make society responsible for their losses.[54] To encourage the spectacularly sacrificial symptoms brought about by hunger strikes, these periods of starvation frequently persisted long enough that prison authorities would attempt to feed them forcibly—holding prisoners down, inserting rubber tubes through their mouths or nostrils into their stomachs, and then pouring or pumping food into these tubes.[55] *Votes for Women* and *The Suffragette* spill a great deal of ink over women's voluntary starvation and these involuntary feedings, describing each in graphic detail. Sylvia Pankhurst's personal account of "The Hunger and Thirst Strike and Its Effects," for example, lingers over the specific bodily experiences of strikers:

> One's tongue is dry, hot and rough, and thickly coated. The saliva becomes more and more thick and yellow, and a bitter tasting phlegm keeps coming up into one's mouth. It is so nasty that it makes one retch violently, as though one were going to be sick, but sick one cannot be. [. . . .][56]

Sacrifice here is not simply a symbolic gesture but a physical condition with medical consequences, duplicated by repetitive narratives that, as Barbara Green argues, "allowed the activist to envision herself as a martyr" before the event and then "provided a story of collective experience that made sense of individual action."[57] The diminished frames of weakened strikers, aligned with the other economic sacrifices they celebrated, allowed suffragettes to embody the spectacular loss they endorsed. Whereas the sturdy Angelica of *The Heavenly Twins* and the Gy-ei of Bulwer-Lytton's *The Coming Race* threatened male supremacy through their healthy, physical forms, hunger strikers presented their debilitation—their sacrifice—as an even more powerful threat.

Although starvation itself was depicted as a clear danger to suffragettes, those who persisted in their martyrdom were subjected to even greater horrors. Citing medical opinions about the dangers of forced feeding, which included nausea, laceration of throat or stomach, and compromise of lungs or heart,[58] suffrage papers commemorate the personal experiences of women fed by force. Fruit dribbling down Lizzie's clenched jaw and chin in a similar scene of violence from "Goblin Market" is precedent for, but also child's play compared to, accounts of "the women whose bodies are being violated in prison."[59] Prisoners' statements consistently highlight the pain and physical effects of the feeding, along with the vomiting that generally follows and in many cases occurs simultaneously: "the drums of the ears seem to be bursting and there is a horrible pain in the throat and the breast"; "the sensation is of being strangled, suffocated by the thrust down of the large rubber tube"; "I was startled to see my face quite white and my eyes horrible, like cups of blood."[60] Using vivid descriptions of suffering to accuse the government of violence, in contrast with their own voluntary "weapon of self-hurt," they reiterate that they "are prepared to die rather than acquiesce [. . .]."[61]

Critical discussions of hunger strikers and forcible feeding tend to foreground the risks of this "perilous spectacularity," suggesting that suffragettes in these prison scenarios may come across as "sado-masochistic," "helpless victims" rather than "active and rational."[62] Mayhall understands the "embodiment of resistance" to be "more complicated and more contentious" than this, but she focuses primarily on how debates about physical force allow suffragettes to make an argument about where the "state's legitimate authority" resides.[63] In contrast, I am interested in the calculated purchase of pain. The W.S.P.U. awarded a medal for hunger striking (see Figure 7.6). This badge of honor underscores the fact that suffragettes viewed strikers as "active" fighters, not "helpless victims." Moreover, it suggests the organization's sense that these giving women deserved some compensation. Like all of the sacrificial gestures we have seen so far, suffragettes' much-touted willingness to die comes at a specific price, as an exchange for short-term contributions to the Union and the long-term goal of enfranchisement. "We must all die," Christabel Pankhurst reminded followers, "and the belief of the Suffragette is that as we have got to die, happy are those among us [. . .] who can buy something as they die; who can exchange their life for something more precious."[64] According to this representation, parched lips

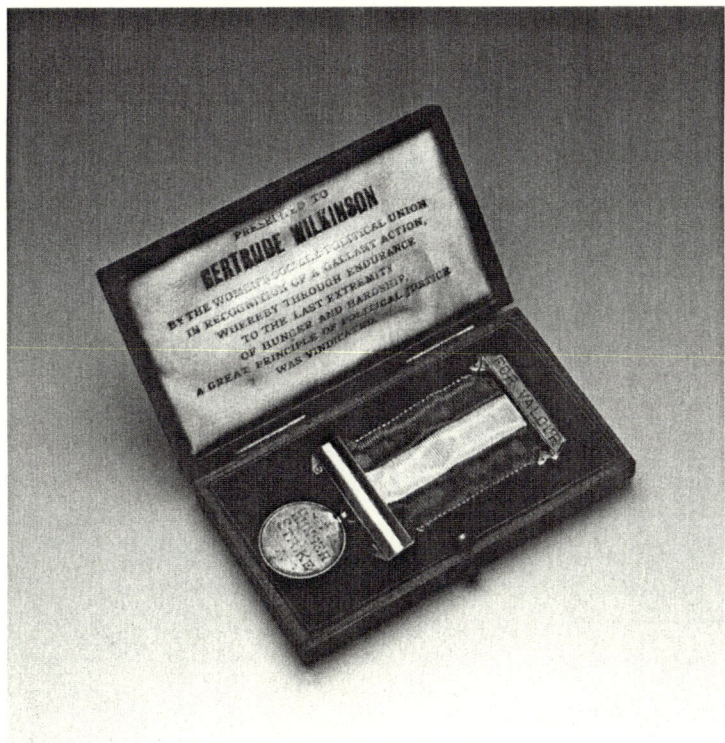

Figure 7.6 "Medal Awarded for Hunger Strike" c. 1910
The Women's Library, London Metropolitan University

and sensations of suffocation are part of a transaction in which bodily sacrifice ensures a "more precious" return.

Spectacles of suffragette suffering—mass-produced in postcards, posters, and the first-hand narrative accounts that often helped to sell newspapers—encouraged members and supporters to give to the cause, either by purchasing items directly from the W.S.P.U. or by making the sort of compensatory gesture of volunteerism or donation that we have seen as responses to Slum Sisters' sacrifices. In many cases, *Votes for Women* and *The Suffragette* represented readers' monetary and physical contributions as the appropriate answer to other women's suffering. Discussions of imprisoned suffragettes declare that "[t]heir noble example inspires us to greater efforts than we have ever made before" and ask readers to "turn their sacrifice to the best account."[65] Sacrifice is a force that, here as in reports of Salvation Army slum work, demands an equal counterforce. "Women never feel more ready to sacrifice themselves utterly [than] when they hear of the untold tortures other women have endured."[66] No doubt some women were simply eager to emulate heroes of a popular movement or enjoy the vicarious drama of their prison stories, but this urge for reciprocal suffering also speaks to the way that sacrifice becomes a political transaction for many women of the W.S.P.U. Holding readers accountable for the sacrifices that militant members have made, the papers insinuate that "[t]hose who cannot go to prison must be anxious to do all they can for the cause" and urge members who lack financial means to "give ourselves, if need be [. . .] as women by the hundred in this Union have given themselves, body and soul."[67] Letters similarly endorse the substitution of body for coin: "'I have not much to give in money,' writes a Lancashire woman" whose daughter had protested imprisonment through a hunger strike, "'but I shall be very pleased to give myself and my life.'"[68] For those members of greater means, the papers explicitly demand that "[w]omen and men who cannot actively serve must give quit-money."[69] Insisting upon material returns for the bodily suffering of its suffragettes in either case, the W.S.P.U. frames other organizational activity—selling newspapers, volunteering time to operate shops or booths, giving mincemeat and money, or taking a place in a protest or prison cell—as "gratitude for what others are doing and sacrificing for the Cause."[70]

Some women had more "quit-money" than others, of course. Readers must have felt the pressure to return bodily sacrifice with physical pain in varying degrees, although the presence of many middle- and upper-class strikers alongside those of the working classes prevents any easy division by class. It is certain, however, that the police did not treat all hunger strikers equally. One recounted her very different experiences imprisoned first as herself (Lady Constance Lytton) and then under the assumed name of Jane Warton. Whereas the "Lady" was given a reduced sentence, medical examinations, and an early release from prison after fifty-six hours of striking, the unknown and powerless Jane Warton was sentenced to hard labor and then subjected to forcible feeding after eighty-nine hours without food or water. Lytton writes of "the gross partiality with which I was treated compared with other Suffrage prisoners."[71] Along similar lines, Annie P. Budgett writes of the working-class W.S.P.U. heroine Annie Kenney, who "came [. . .] with two pounds in her pocket, to rouse London."[72] Waging war with her body instead of money, she spent two months in prison: "it is no mere matter of speech when I say [Kenney] may die in her fight for freedom." In Budgett's account, her subsequent arrest occurred because the police thought "they were safe [. . .] in taking a young work-girl, who had no friends and no power at her back," whereas Mrs. Despard, a more prominent suffrage figure also present at the scene, "had powerful friends all over London."[73] Budgett's interpretation of the event, like Lytton's, suggests that the W.S.P.U. saw itself as an advocate for women of all classes equally: "The woman who has endured imprisonment [. . .], the worker who has contributed her substance, the society queen who has guided the conversation at the dinner-table to this subject."[74] In practice, notwithstanding its origins in the Independent Labour Party, the relationship of W.S.P.U. leadership to both women of the

working classes and socialist politics appears to have been far more complicated.[75] In suffrage politics, as we have seen in eugenic pamphlets and *Aurora
Leigh* alike, gendered gifts rely on an idea of "woman" that inspires both a "Lady
Lytton" and a "Jane Warton" (or an Annie Kenney) but glosses over substantial
differences between them.

Nevertheless, these gendered gifts and their material and symbolic returns
were a vital part of the campaign for female suffrage. They existed alongside
egalitarian demands for "the recognition of [women's] equal rights and duties of
citizenship."[76] Contrary to criticism that explains feminism and the women's
movement primarily through increasing arguments for equal rights and civic
engagement, however, the activists whose sacrifices I am describing "demand
this vote for women not because of her manly capacities, but because of her
womanly capacities."[77] Despite critical distaste for older models of gendered
"capacities," which seem both to endorse the separate spheres whose borders
have long appeared blurry to us and to elide the inequalities among women that
Lytton and Budgett observe, a fuller understanding of the women's movement
and its relationship to a history of nineteenth-century authorship and activism
requires that we take them seriously even as we continue to question their
structures and stakes. Drawing on traditions of giving that had long allowed
some women to form alliances and engage in social and political activity, gift
offerings of health and homemade jams contributed to militant strategies to
achieve the vote.

III. A Politics of Generosity

As the campaign for women's suffrage continued, militants grew to depend
even more upon what many described as a politics of generosity. At the out-
break of World War I in 1914, when English military action abroad made internal strife seem unpatriotic, strategies such as window-smashing became
untenable.[78] Women's collective sacrifices of bodies, money, and time on behalf
of the vote were then amplified by the sacrifice of militant suffragette activities
themselves in a political "truce."[79] Shortly after war was declared, *Votes for
Women* enthusiastically reported both the "Wise Decision" of the government
to "release [. . .] all suffragist prisoners" and the temporary suspension of "all
political work" and "all forms of active militancy" by a number of suffrage organizations, including the N.U.W.S.S., the W.S.P.U., and the Women's Freedom
League (W.F.L.).[80]

Despite the seeming *quid pro quo* of this arrangement, both sides stress the
"unconditional[ity]" of the decision and attribute it to liberality.[81] "Generosity has
a curious place of its own in politics," observes the *Manchester Guardian*, as cited
in *Votes for Women*. "The prisoners had not asked for the amnesty, and the

Government has not asked them for any promise to obey the law. That is the way to do it. Acts of grace must be gracious; they must not be bargains."[82] Other writers pick up on this sense of unilateral sacrifice or "pure" gift, stressing women's particular role in curbing militant actions and government hostilities: "all suffragists declared truce, and offered themselves to the common service of the country at the first sign of external danger. We call their generosity reckless because they made no bargain [.... But] reckless or not, wise or unwise, the uncalculating spirit of generosity was there."[83] Although sacrifice itself is generally presented as risky business, this sacrifice of militant martyrdom strikes many as particularly dangerous. By assuming that a less "reckless" generosity should be compatible with "bargain[ing]," such an assessment reminds us that an important tradition of women's giving explicitly aligns gifts with countergifts, expecting returns on outlays of jams and needlework, hunger and pain. The apparent disregard for calculation that this "generosity" entailed suggested to some observers an even more extreme form of sacrifice than the kind that attempted to pragmatically "buy something" in exchange.

Just as they answered the earlier eugenic call to sacrifice bodies and lives for "the race," women again pledged their service to the country, giving up one set of desires for the more urgently perceived common good of the nation.[84] "[W]omen are just as ready as men to do what is needed for the sake of their country," declared Christabel Pankhurst. "The Suffragettes have always put country first, and self second."[85] While others provided medical care and supplies, Pankhurst went on to rally for war efforts and the defeat of Germany.[86] In part, her emphasis on an Allied victory tapped into the very eugenic concerns that were motivating other forms of sacrifice among women: in a speech in Washington, D.C., she cautions "Unhyphenated Americans" about the "presence of many German electors" in their country, warning that "Prussia [...] seeks now to Prussianise the whole world" but insisting that only a population's "quality" can justify expansion."[87] While Pankhurst suggests that America has reason to fear German invasion,[88] she also implies that countries can reclaim their strength by fighting: war, she avows, has given "new proof of Britain's vitality." By similarly devoting their services to the war, women can protect their nation, help to reinvigorate its "degenerate" men, and show how highly they prize the British citizenship for which they fight.[89] Pankhurst treats suffrage and eugenics as compatible campaigns, both linked to traditions of women's sacrifices. She is not alone in joining the two missions.[90] Others similarly stress the racial importance of women and motherhood during wartime and use it to further claims for the vote. Assigning to women the "preservation of the race," they argue that "the claim of motherhood" is "reason enough" to recognize women's "political equality with men."[91]

If motherhood is one more way in which women serve the country, it is also one more way in which the war asks them to make extreme sacrifices. As many suffragettes point out, women's "generous" suspension of militancy on behalf of the nation does not alleviate their physical or emotional suffering. On the contrary, Pankhurst notes that "women are, indeed, the greatest sufferers in time of war."[92] Echoing Olive Schreiner in *Woman and Labour*, she contends that women "pay the first cost on all human life [by] supplying the men for the carnage of a battlefield."[93] Describing the pangs of childbirth as the "price [paid by women] to bring life into the world," other writers similarly suggest that wartime losses tax women most highly, compelling them to "give[. . .] husbands and sons for the sake of the country."[94]

But again, women's "agony of anxiety"[95] during wartime and suffragettes' willingness to temporarily sacrifice their political activism for the war may be seen as something of a calculated risk. (Sacrifice is never one-sided.) Even as editorials praise women's "uncalculating spirit of generosity" in halting their militancy and actively serving the country's medical, maternal, and other wartime needs, they call on the government to "answer generosity by justice."[96] Insisting that "militants [. . .] will profit later," they suggest that "those very sacrifices [. . .] are enormously forwarding their own cause.[97] Despite protests from both pro-and anti-suffrage camps that the vote should not be seen as a "reward" or "an order of merit,"[98] the idea that women's sacrifices and services for the nation would eventually be repaid with suffrage is prevalent in the publications and speeches of the W.S.P.U. and other suffrage organizations. In 1914, Pankhurst predicted that women's sacrifices would secure suffrage. "[W]hen the war is ended and the women are helping to build up the world again they will not deny us. They must see how the women have suffered through the war, giving up their homes and those they love, starving [. . .], and they will celebrate the end of the war by enfranchising us."[99] Identifying women's war efforts—physical pain, the loss of material possessions, emotional suffering—as sacrificial gifts, she expects that they will be reciprocated. Her vision draws on a long tradition of giving women getting returns. And history confirms this tradition.

In 1918, as World War I was coming to a close, the British government granted the vote to women of thirty or more years.[100] While many factors contributed to this victory,[101] I want to suggest here that it was shaped by discourses of women's *gifts* as well as women's *rights*, benefiting from the very images of exchange that this book has traced. Offering up handkerchiefs and health to the cause, suffragettes joined a long line of female friends, authors, and activists who achieved personal successes by also thinking about women and the nation at large, giving gifts and making sacrifices not only for themselves but, as many declared, "for *us*."[102] By acknowledging the rich, nuanced, and often troubling political legacy of "giving women," we gain broader insight into how models of feminine sacrifice and egalitarian citizenship alike are intertwined in the discursive history of the early women's movement.

NOTES

Introduction

1. Walter Scott, *Ivanhoe* (London: Penguin Books, 2000): 400; Charlotte Brontë, *Jane Eyre* (New York and London: W. W. Norton, 2001): 103; Anthony Trollope, *The Eustace Diamonds* (Oxford: Oxford University Press, 2008): Vol. I: 141.

2. Parenthetical numbers refer to Charles Dickens, *Bleak House* (1853), ed. Nicola Bradbury (London: Penguin Books, 1996).

3. Marcel Mauss, *The Gift: The Form and Reason for Exchange in Archaic Societies*, trans. W. D. Halls (London: Routledge, 1990): e.g., 5; Claude Lévi-Strauss, "The Principle of Reciprocity," in Aafke E. Komter, ed., *The Gift: An Interdisciplinary Perspective* (Amsterdam: Amsterdam University Press, 1996): 18–25: 24; Eve Kosofsky Sedgwick, *Between Men: English Literature and Male Homosocial Desire* (New York: Columbia University Press, 1985): 21, 25–26, 167–168.

4. Mrs. [Sarah Stickney] Ellis, *The Women of England, Their Social Duties, and Domestic Habits* (London: Fisher, Son, & Co., 1839): 155. Ellis's was no naïve stance. See Karen Chase and Michael Levenson's nuanced reading of women's "relative" status in *The Spectacle of Intimacy: A Public Life for the Victorian Family* (Princeton: Princeton University Press, 2000): 82, 67. For Victorian perceptions of women's giving as a risky business, see Nancy Folbre and Heidi Hartman, "The Rhetoric of Self-Interest: Ideology and Gender in Economic Theory," *The Consequences of Economic Rhetoric*, ed. Arjo Klamer, Donald N. McCloskey, Robert M. Solow (Cambridge University Press, 1988): 184–203, 194. Ilana M. Blumberg discusses the mid-century as "a moment when some few Victorian moral thinkers had begun to see danger in the claims of an altruism to extreme it necessitated behavior verging on masochism, especially for women." See "'Love Yourself as Your Neighbor': The Limits of Altruism and the Ethics of Personal Benefit in *Adam Bede*," *Victorian Literature and Culture* (*VLC*) 37 (2009): 543–560, 545. Feminist theologians have attributed sacrifice to "self-lack" (87) or "the sin of hiding"; see, respectively, Judith Plaskow, *Sex, Sin and Grace: Women's Experience and the Theologies of Reinhold Niebuhr and Paul Tillich* (Boston: University Press of America, 1980): 87, 92; Susan Nelson Dunfee, "The Sin of Hiding: A Feminist Critique of Reinhold Niebuhr's Account of the Sin of Pride," *Soundings* 65:3 (1982): 316–327, esp. 319, 322.

5. Aafke E. Komter, *Social Solidarity and the Gift* (Cambridge: Cambridge University Press, 2005): 8, 96; *The Question of the Gift: Essays Across Disciplines*, ed. Mark Osteen (London: Routledge, 2002): 19–20. Martha Woodmansee and Mark Osteen's question of "whether [gifts'] female gendering is an unwanted result of exclusionary historical practices or a source of power" is very much at the heart of this book, which does not see the two possibilities as mutually exclusive. *The New Economic Criticism: Studies at the Intersection of Literature and Economics*, ed. Martha Woodmansee and Mark Osteen (London: Routledge, 1999): 32.

6. Blumberg, for example, points out that while the topic of sacrifice is "burdened [. . .] with our quick associations to the mid-nineteenth-century stereotype of the angel in the house" it also "described economic relations" ("'Unnatural Self-Sacrifice': Trollope's Ethic of Mutual Benefit," *Nineteenth-Century Literature (NCL)*, 58:4 [March, 2004], 506–546, 509, 512).

7. Under the common law doctrine of coverture, married women did not have property rights until 1882, and women were denied university education until the final third of the nineteenth century, despite earlier efforts to secure professional training for nurses and social workers. However, women never lacked economic agency to the extent that these laws and regulations or assumptions about "separate spheres" may suggest. Women of independent means frequently worked in voluntary capacities, and those of the laboring classes worked for pay throughout the period. See Amanda Vickery, "Golden Age to Separate Spheres? A Review of the Categories and Chronology of English Women's History," *The Historical Journal* 36:2 (June, 1993): 388, 399, 405; Vickery, *The Gentleman's Daughter: Women's Lives in Georgian England* (New Haven: Yale University Press, 1998): 3–4. Moreover, as historians of the period point out, despite the real "overarching oppression of the common law for married women," coverture was not the end of the story (see Margot Finn, "Women, Consumption and Coverture in England, c. 1760–1860," *The Historical Journal* 39:3 [September 1996]: 707). "[O]ften ignored or bypassed" in practice, it was also supplemented by laws of equity and "[o]ther, less familiar legal practices that expanded women's economic agency [. . .]." Joanne Bailey, "Favoured or Oppressed? Married Women, Property, and 'Coverture' in England, 1660–1800," *Continuity and Change* 17:3 (2002): 353 (see also 359, 363); Finn "Women" 706.

8. Stefan Collini, *Public Moralists: Political Thought and Intellectual Life in Britain, 1850–1930* (Oxford: Oxford University Press, 1991): 62.

9. Collini notes that the Victorian obsession with altruism "fed into the sentimentalized rhapsodies to the role of feminine influence as an antidote to 'selfishness'" but does not address the possibility that other, more self-interested tendencies existed within women's purported "special gifts for 'feeling' and 'concern for others'" (87). In Blumberg's reading of *Adam Bede*, however, "self-interest proves to be the very source of [. . .] generosity." "'Love Yourself'" 553.

10. Collini 65.

11. Women did not gain the right to vote until 1918. The Married Women's Property Acts of 1870 and 1882, which expanded women's economic rights, also aimed to protect male interests and in some cases made women appear "less creditworthy" because they were not held to the same responsibilities. See Erika Diane Rappaport, *Shopping for Pleasure: Women in the Making of London's West End* (Princeton: Princeton University Press, 2000): 51, 64, 57; Mary Lyndon Shanley, *Feminism, Marriage, and the Law in Victorian England* (Princeton: Princeton University Press, 1989): 8, 71, 127; Ruth Perry, *Novel Relations: The Transformation of Kinship in English Literature and Culture 1748–1818* (Cambridge: Cambridge University Press, 2004): e.g., 34, 40. Among those who explore women's alternative methods of seeking economic agency are Bailey, "Favoured" 353–357; Finn, "Women" 705–709.

12. David Cheal, "Moral Economy," *The Gift: An Interdisciplinary Perspective*, ed. Aafke E. Komter (Amsterdam: Amsterdam University Press, 1996): 81–94, 83. According to Lewis Hyde, "gift exchange is an economy of small groups" precisely because small numbers permit interpersonal ties of affection (*The Gift: Imagination and the Erotic Life of Property* [New York: Random House, 1983]: 89). See also Osteen 17.

13. Deborah Cohen, *Household Gods: The British and Their Possessions* (New Haven: Yale University Press, 2006): x–xvii, 3, 30; Elaine Freedgood, *The Ideas in Things: Fugitive Meaning in the Victorian Novel* (Chicago: University of Chicago Press, 2006): 1–8; John Plotz, *Portable Property: Victorian Culture on the Move* (Princeton: Princeton University Press, 2008): 2, 17–20.

14. Nineteenth-century charity was a contested field for middle-class authority, particularly for women, whose public activities and ambitions it sanctioned. Beth Tobin, *Superintending the*

Poor: Charitable Ladies and Paternal Landlords in British Fiction, 1770–1860 (New Haven: Yale University Press, 1993); Audrey Jaffe, *Scenes of Sympathy: Identity and Representation in Victorian Fiction* (Ithaca: Cornell University Press, 2000); F. K. Prochaska, *Women and Philanthropy in Nineteenth-Century England* (Oxford: Clarendon Press, 1980); Dorice Williams Elliott, *The Angel out of the House: Philanthropy and Gender in Nineteenth-Century England* (Charlottesville: University of Virginia Press, 2002); Judith Walkowitz, *City of Dreadful Delight: Narratives of Sexual Danger in Late-Victorian London* (Chicago: University of Chicago Press, 1992): 18, 53; Seth Koven, *Slumming: Sexual and Social Politics in Victorian London* (Princeton: Princeton University Press, 2004): 183–227; Vickery, "Golden" 399.

15. For the characterization of eighteenth-century giving as "transactions [. . .] between the propertied classes and the lower ranks [. . .] most obviously embodied in paternalism," see Linda Zionkowski, "The Nation, the Gift, and the Market in *The Wanderer*," *The Culture of the Gift in Eighteenth-Century England*, ed. Linda Zionkowski and Cynthia Klekar (New York and Houndmills: Palgrave Macmillan, 2009): 177–194, 179. See also "Introduction" 3. Zionkowski notes, however, that hierarchical gift systems are called into question by the 1790s (181, 192–193). Jennie Batchelor's essay from the same collection ("Fictions of the Gift in Sarah Scott's *Millenium Hall*," 159–175) also observes the potential for gifts to create intimacy when they "are exchanged between equals and friends" in eighteenth-century literature (165).

16. Scholars have established the inadequacy of rational, self-interested *homo economicus* to account for economic woman (or more than the fiction of an "economic man"). See Folbre and Hartman 185–197; Michèle Pujol, "Into the Margin!" *Out of the Margins: Feminist Perspectives on Economics*, ed. Edith Kuiper and Jolande Sap (London: Routledge, 1995): 17–34, 18; Susan F. Feiner, "Reading Neoclassical Economics: Toward an Erotic Economy of Sharing," *Out of the Margins: Feminist Perspectives on Economics*, ed. Edith Kuiper and Jolande Sap (London: Routledge, 1995): 151–166, 155; Paula England, "The Separative Self: Andocentric Bias in Neoclassical Assumptions," *Beyond Economic Man: Feminist Theory and Economics*, ed. Marianne A. Ferber and Julie A. Nelson (Chicago: University of Chicago Press, 1993): 37–53, 37, 40; Diana Strassmann, "Not a Free Market: The Rhetoric of Disciplinary Authority in Economics," *Beyond Economic Man: Feminist Theory and Economics*, ed. Marianne A. Ferber and Julie A. Nelson. (Chicago: University of Chicago Press, 1993): 54–68, 58–59, 61; Martha Woodmansee and Mark Osteen, ed. *The New Economic Criticism: Studies at the Intersection of Literature and Economics* (London: Routledge, 1999): 32, 41 n.2; Finn, "Women" 720; Bailey, "Favoured" 368. Catherine Gallagher reminds us that nineteenth-century economics was sensational as well as rational. *The Body Economic: Life, Death, and Sensation in Political Economy and the Victorian Novel* (Princeton: Princeton University Press, 2006): 50. Although women were frequently excluded from or exploited by many aspects of capitalist systems, they also contributed to it as producers and consumers. See Erika Diane Rappaport, *Shopping for Pleasure: Women in the Making of London's West End* (Princeton: Princeton University Press, 2000); Krista Lysack, *Come Buy, Come Buy: Shopping and the Culture of Consumption in Victorian Women's Writing* (Athens: Ohio University Press, 2008).

17. Victorianists have been somewhat slower than literary critics of the early modern and modernist periods to capitalize on gift theories in any sustained way, but notable exceptions include Blumberg, Finn, Sharon Marcus, *Between Women: Friendship, Desire, and Marriage in Victorian England* (Princeton: Princeton University Press, 2007); and Psomiades. Shorter studies include Margueritte Murphy, "The Ethic of the Gift in George Eliot's *Daniel Deronda*," *VLC* 34:1 (2006): 187–207 and Kathleen Blake, "Between Economies in *The Mill on the Floss*: Loans Versus Gifts, Or, Auditing Mr. Tulliver's Accounts," *VLC* 33:1 (2005): 219–237.

18. Studying systems of exchange in Polynesia, Melanesia, and the American Northwest, Mauss saw the gift as part of larger economic and religious patterns, a "total social fact." See Lévi-Strauss 18; Mauss 5–6, 12. Theorists from Seneca through Hobbes and Emerson to Derrida have remarked upon the equivocal nature of gifts. See, for instance, Ralph Waldo Emerson,

"Gifts," in Alan D. Schrift, ed., *The Logic of the Gift: Toward an Ethic of Generosity* (London: Routledge, 1997): 26; Alison V. Scott, *Selfish Gifts: The Politics of Exchange and English Court-ly Literature, 1580–1628* (Madison: Fairleigh Dickinson University Press, 2006): 236 n.11; Marshall Sahlins, *Stone Age Economics* (Chicago: Aldine Atherton, 1972): 178; Jean-Joseph Goux, "Seneca Against Derrida: Gift and Alterity," *The Enigma of Gift and Sacrifice*, ed. Edith Wyschogrod, Jean-Joseph Goux, and Eric Boynton (New York: Fordham University Press, 2002):148–160, 155–160. Hyde (30) and Sahlins (181) note some of the misperceptions that Mauss, as an early twentieth-century European outsider, disillusioned by capitalism, may have had in his observations of tribal cultures. For anthropological theories of the gift that take women into account, see note 34.

19. Pierre Bourdieu, *The Logic of Practice*, trans. Richard Nice (Cambridge: Polity Press, 1990): 105; Jacques Derrida, *Given Time: 1. Counterfeit Money*, trans. Peggy Kamuf (Chicago: University of Chicago Press, 1992): 13; John Milbank, "Can a Gift Be Given? Prolegomena to a Future Trinitarian Metaphysic," *Modern Theology* 11:1 (January 1995): 119–161, 123–124. See also Woodmansee and Osteen for the question of "whether gift exchanges lie outside of economics" (32).

20. Trollope, *Eustace* II: 235. The way that this "reciprocity system" appears to work differently for different degrees of relation mirrors other nineteenth-century economic and political systems, such as inheritance tax laws which privileged daughters over nieces and sisters over cousins. See Chapter 2 of this volume.

21. See Jacques Derrida, *Given* 7: "Now the gift, *if there is any*, would no doubt be related to economy. [. . .] But is not the gift, if there is any, also that which interrupts economy? That which, in suspending economic calculation, no longer gives rise to exchange? [. . . .] If there is gift, the *given* of the gift [. . .] must not come back to the giving [. . .]. It must not circulate [. . .]. It is perhaps in this sense that the gift is the impossible. [. . .] Not impossible but *the* impossible. The very figure of the impossible." Blumberg has argued that Trollope else-where "scrutinizes what we might call a 'purist' view of sacrifice: the notion common among Victorians that sacrificing oneself on someone else's behalf must not generate any personal reward." See "'Unnatural Self-Sacrifice'" 507.

22. In *The Character of Credit: Personal Debt in English Culture, 1740–1914* (Cambridge: Cambridge University Press, 2003), Margot C. Finn argues that traditions of gifts and credit shaped emerging market activity e.g. 7–8, 44–45, 88, 245.

23. Trollope, *Eustace* II: 235.

24. Sahlins (160, 165) and Hyde (xvi, 16) stress the third-party mediation of gift circulation.

25. For credit as the imperative to reciprocate a gift over time, see Mauss 36 and Finn, *Character* 7–8, 51, 88.

26. Thomas Carlyle, *Chartism* (London: James Fraser, 1840, 61), *The Making of the Modern World. Cengage Learning* collection, <http://galenet.galegroup.com.ezp1.villanova.edu/servlet/MOME?af=RN&ae=U106023541&srchtp=a&;ste=14>. Karl Marx and Friedrich Engels similarly note in 1848 that there is "no other nexus between man and man than naked self-interest, than callous 'cash payment.'" See *The Communist Manifesto* (London: Penguin Books, 1967): 82. Arjun Appadurai notes that this distinction between gifts and commodi-ties has been exaggerated, since gift exchange may entail "calculation" and objects move in and out of gift and commodity states. "Introduction: Commodities and the Politics of Value," in Appadurai, ed., *The Social Life of Things: Commodities in Cultural Perspective* (Cambridge: Cambridge University Press, 1986): 3–63, esp. 10–13. Plotz offers "portable property" as a third term between these two states (17). James G. Carrier, who also observes that "com-modity relations [. . .] are not in any sense unsocial," distinguishes between gift and com-modity relations by arguing that "in commodity relationships the link between the parties is based on alienable attributes, while in gift relationships it is based on inalienable iden-tities." See *Gifts and Commodities: Exchange and Western Capitalism Since 1700* (London: Routledge, 1995): 19, 33.

27. In an important parallel project, Freedgood argues that "social relations hide in things" (53). By ignoring gift exchanges in her search for "a culture that may have preceded commodity culture" (142), however, her focus on "thing culture" fails to account for the broad range of material and symbolic transactions that not only preceded but coexisted with Victorian commodity culture.

28. Mauss 19, 20. Gift giving is a form of what Lee Anne Fennell calls "empathetic dialogue" ("Unpacking the Gift: Illiquid Goods and Empathetic Dialogue," *The Question of the Gift: Essays Across Disciplines*, ed. Mark Osteen [London: Routledge, 2002]: 85–101, 86).

29. For the ceremony of *potlatch* which prompted Mauss's reflections on competitive expenditure, see Mauss 37–46; Georges Bataille notes that, in potlatch or other conditions of extreme expenditure, giving confers rank. See *The Accursed Share: An Essay on General Economy Vol. 1: Consumption*, trans. Robert Hurley (New York: Zone Books, 1991): 68–76. Potlatch was not itself a Victorian practice, though its tendencies toward extreme or competitive gift-giving find analogies in nineteenth-century culture (see Part II of this volume).

30. See Daniel Siegel, "The Failure of Condescension," *VLC* 33:2 (September 2005): 395–414, esp. 396.

31. Finn reads Jarndyce as unable to accept the "two-sidedness of gift transactions" (*Character* 40).

32. Mauss 5.

33. For marriage as the law of reciprocity, institutionalized, see Lévi-Strauss 24. Analogies drawn between the gift and male libidinal economies of expenditure have further masculinized gift theory. See Mark Osteen 19; Andrew Cowell, "The Pleasures and Pains of the Gift," *The Question of the Gift: Essays Across Disciplines*, ed. Mark Osteen (London: Routledge, 2002): 280–297, 286–288. Classic feminist responses to Lévi-Strauss include Gayle Rubin, "The Traffic in Women: Notes on the 'Political Economy' of Sex," *Toward an Anthology of Women*, ed. Rayna R. Reiter (New York: Monthly Review Press, 1975): 157–210, esp. 174, 183; Hélène Cixous, "The Laugh of the Medusa," *Feminisms: An Anthology of Literary Theory and Criticism*, ed. Robyn R. Warhol and Diane Price Herndl (New Brunswick: Rutgers University Press, 1997): 347–362, 357, 352; and Luce Irigaray, "Women on the Market," *The Logic of the Gift: Toward an Ethic of Generosity*, ed. Alan D. Schrift (New York: Routledge, 1997): 174–189, 175. More recently, Maurice Godelier has noted that Lévi-Strauss's understanding of kinship limits the possible configurations of exchange (*The Enigma of the Gift*, trans. Nora Scott [Chicago: University of Chicago Press, 1999]: 35), and Kathy Psomiades has argued that concepts of heterosexual exchange emerged, paradoxically, as women were achieving greater economic autonomy ("Heterosexual Exchange and Other Victorian Fictions: *The Eustace Diamonds* and Victorian Anthropology," *NOVEL: A Forum on Fiction* 33:1 [Autumn 1999]: 93–118, 94, 112, 116).

34. Richard Dellamora notes the reduction of female agency in Sedgwick's model in "Book Review Forum: Friendship, Marriage, and *Between Women*," *Victorian Studies* (*VS*) 50:1 (Autumn 2007): 67. See also Komter, "Women, Gifts, and Power," in *The Gift* 120–124, 231 n.1. Demonstrating women's more active roles within gift economies are: Komter, *Social* 77, 91–92; Marilyn Strathern, *The Gender of the Gift: Problems with Women and Problems with Society in Melanesia* (Berkeley: University of California Press, 1988): 165, 187; Annette B. Weiner, *Inalienable Possessions: The Paradox of Keeping-While-Giving* (Berkeley: University of California Press, 1992): 12–13, 18, 67. See also Psomiades 98, 106–108.

35. For Marcus, female "amity" frequently leads to and is normalized by heterosexual marriage (3–4, 41, 76, 88, 94–99, 108). Caddy Jellyby dates her romance with Prince Turveydrop to when Ada and Esther's first came to her house (220), and Esther stands by her as she breaks the news of her engagement to her parents (375–377, 381–383).

36. Notable recent efforts along these lines include work by Marcus; Mary Jean Corbett, *Family Likeness: Sex, Marriage, and Incest from Jane Austen to Virginia Woolf* (Ithaca: Cornell University Press, 2008); Martha Vicinus, *Intimate Friends: Women who Loved Women, 1778–1928*

(Chicago: University of Chicago Press, 2004); Psomiades; and Elsie B. Michie, "Rich Woman, Poor Woman: Toward an Anthropology of the Nineteenth-Century Marriage Plot," *Publications of the Modern Language Association* (*PMLA*) 124.2, 421–436.

37. Naomi Tadmor importantly suggests the wide range of meanings assigned to familial terms. See *Family and Friends in Eighteenth-Century England: Household, Kinship, and Patronage* (Cambridge: Cambridge University Press, 2001): e.g., 158–159. Carroll Smith-Rosenberg's classic work on female affective bonds stresses women's "emotional centrality in each others' lives" (13) and the fact that "[e]xpressions of hostility" among women were "uncommon indeed" (15). See "The Female World of Love and Ritual: Relations Between Women in Nineteenth-Century America," *Signs* 1:1 (Autumn, 1975): 1–29. In contrast, Helena Michie's *Sororophobia: Differences Among Women in Literature and Culture* (Oxford: Oxford University Press, 1992) traces Victorian patterns of both rivalry and cooperation among siblings or surrogate siblings, attending to the relationship's political use in twentieth-century movements (8) though with little attention to how the relationship was appropriated by the Victorians for social uses. Leila Silvana May also explores broader literary representations of the *brother*-sister relationship in *Disorderly Sisters: Sibling Relations and Sororal Resistance in Nineteenth-Century British Literature* (Lewisburg: Bucknell University Press, 2001). The Deceased Wife's Sister Bill of 1835, which aimed to prevent widowers from marrying their sisters-in-law, underscored the political stakes of sisterhood; see Susan Annes Brown, *Devoted Sisters: Representations of the Sister Relationship in Nineteenth-Century British and American Literature* (Burlington: Ashgate Publishing Company, 2003): 105–121 and Corbett ch. 3, 57–85. Feminism has never had a unified approach (Susan Gubar, "What Ails Feminist Criticism?" *Critical Inquiry* 24:4 [Summer, 1998]: 878–902, 881 n.4). Nevertheless, many "second-wavers" used "sisterhood" to express women's unity (e.g., Elizabeth Fox-Genovese, "The Personal Is Not Political Enough." *Marxist Perspectives* 8 [Winter 1979/80]: 94–113, 103), ignoring their differing needs and positions of power; see bell hooks, *Ain't I a Woman: Black Women and Feminism* (Boston: South End Press, 1981):121; Margaret A. Simons, "Racism and Feminism: A Schism in the Sisterhood," *Feminist Studies* 5:2 (Summer 1979): 384–401, 387–388, 391; Bonnie Thornton Dill, "Race, Class, and Gender: Prospects for an All-Inclusive Sisterhood," *Feminist Studies* 9:1 (Spring 1983): 131–150, 131; Hazel V. Carby, *Reconstructing Womanhood: The Emergence of the Afro-American Woman Novelist* (Oxford: Oxford University Press, 1987): esp. 6, 18, 51, 53, 55; Jean Fagan Yellin, *Women and Sisters: The Antislavery Feminists in American Culture* (New Haven: Yale University Press, 1989): 24. Susan Fraiman regrettably compares this (presumably) utopian use of "sisterhood" by "second-wavers" to that of Victorian feminists ("Review of *Devoted Sisters: Representations of the Sister Relationship in Nineteenth-Century British and American Literature* by Sarah Annes Brown," *Victorian Studies* 48:1 [Autumn 2005]: 177–179, 177).

38. Women's life-writing figured friendship in spiritual terms (Marcus 62–66), and the language of sisterhood was used broadly by Quaker, Methodist, Catholic, and Anglican Communities. For the erotics of sisterhood see Vicinus, *Intimate* xxvi and 195. For the exchange of gifts within "romantic friendships," see Vicinus 7, 41; Marcus 57.

39. We might even say that they "queer" traditional models of exchange. See Marcus for an important discussion of how exchanges between women shaped even heterosexual marriage (e.g., 102).

40. For the limits of female friendship by class, see Vicinus, "Book Review Forum: Normalizing Female Friendship," *Victorian Studies* 50:1 (Autumn, 2007): 81–86, 82, 85. Anne McClintock, Antoinette Burton, and Louise Michele Newman provide models for thinking about the ways in which bourgeois feminism was forged at the expense of racial hierarchy. See Burton, *Burdens of History: British Feminists, Indian Women, and Imperial Culture, 1865–1915* (Chapel Hill: University of North Carolina Press, 1994); McClintock, *Imperial Leather: Race, Gender and Sexuality in the Colonial Contest* (New York: Routledge, 1995); and

Newman, *White Women's Rights: The Racial Origins of Feminism in the United States* (Oxford: Oxford University Press, 1999).

41. For another look at writing as sacrifice, see Blumberg, "Collins's *Moonstone*: The Victorian Novel as Sacrifice, Theft, Gift and Debt," *Studies in the Novel* 37:2 (Summer 2005): 162–186, 168.

42. Gayatri Chakravorty Spivak comments on the shared "recipient function" of fictional character and reader in "Three Women's Texts and a Critique of Imperialism," *Critical Inquiry* 12:1 (Autumn 1985): 243–261, 259. Whereas Spivak discusses a fictional recipient who "does not respond," the texts I examine posit a reader who must.

43. I am not suggesting that men were silent on the subject of giving. As we see even from this brief introduction, Dickens and Trollope alone filled many pages with it. Nor am I suggesting that women's writing differs from men's in some essential way. I am interested here in the historical ways that certain economically marginalized women created agency out of gendered traditions of giving that tend to be critically shortchanged—and writing is part of those traditions.

44. Garrett Stewart's discussion of extrapolation (how you "read yourself in parable") is relevant here. *Dear Reader: The Conscripted Audience in Nineteenth-Century British Fiction* (Baltimore: The Johns Hopkins University Press, 1996): 19.

45. My sense of what constituted social action for giving women does not privilege the "nonliterary" over the "literary," nor does it imply a progression from one to the other. The significant presence of archival material in the second half of the book reflects the growth in women's journalism by the fin de siècle, but there, as in my opening chapter on (equally noncanonical) literary annuals, my focus is on popular forms of women's writing and the way that they both reflect and work to shape women's giving.

46. [Eliot], "The Natural History of German Life," *The Westminster Review* 10 (July 1856): 51–79, 54. For Victorians' belief in "the moral consequences of novel reading," see Suzanne Keen, *Empathy and the Novel* (Oxford: Oxford University Press, 2007): 51.

47. Rachel Ablow, *The Marriage of Minds: Reading Sympathy in the Victorian Marriage Plot* (Stanford: Stanford University Press, 2007): 29.

48. Ablow 42.

49. This phrase is Benedict Anderson's, from *Imagined Communities: Reflections on the Origin and Spread of Nationalism*, revised ed. (London: Verso, 1991). More recently, Lynn Hunt has explored how reading practices create and foreclose communities: *Inventing Human Rights: A History* (New York: W. W. Norton, 2007): 32, 40. See also Kate Flint, *The Woman Reader 1837–1914* (Oxford: Oxford University Press, 1993): 42–43.

50. Audrey Jaffe understands sympathy as "inseparable from representations" (*Scenes of Sympathy: Identity and Representation in Victorian Fiction* [Ithaca: Cornell University Press, 2000]: 9).

51. Keen *passim* (e.g., vii, xv, xx, 16, 107, 140). Keen evokes gift theories when she attributes readers' reluctance to respond actively to the "impossibility of reciprocation"; readers do not have "obligations toward [characters]" (16). As she notes, "joining a crowd of readers" may also diffuse the responsibility individual readers feel (117).

52. See also Keen 142. Her insight ("reading by itself may be insufficient to extend the empathetic circle beyond its predictable reach [...]" [108]) indicates less the failure of a literary project than its redefinition.

53. Sahlins 191–196.

54. Of course, since "mutual exchanges" are not always immediately evident as such, many initially appear as "unilateral acts"; reading beyond the individual transaction allows us to assess the way each is implicated in a larger economy and also reminds us that in gift-giving, "mutual" and "unilateral" are never easy oppositions.

55. Sympathy has a privileged place in nineteenth-century accounts of giving because sympathy is itself often treated as a transaction: David Marshall, for instance, has characterized sympathy "as a transport [...] allowing an exchange between parts, characters, and persons." See

The Surprising Effects of Sympathy: Marivaux, Diderot, Rousseau, and Mary Shelley (Chicago: University of Chicago Press, 1988): 5; like Jaffe's more recent study, this book is most interested in the visual structures of sympathy. As Marshall and others have noted, literature frequently presents the exchanges entailed by sympathy as problematic (e.g., Marshall 5, 48).

56. Susan L. Mizruchi similarly sees sacrifice as "uniquely suited" for "Anglo-Americans in the late nineteenth century." See *The Science of Sacrifice: American Literature and Modern Social Theory* (Princeton: Princeton University Press, 1998): 368.

Chapter 1

1. Literary annuals "for" a year were generally published toward the end of the preceding one—1822, in this case.
2. The predominance of image over text reputedly diminished annuals' literary merit, and though men and women wrote for, edited, and read the annuals, the books themselves were often dismissed as feminine in taste and style. See Kathryn Ruth Ledbetter, "'White Vellum and Gilt Edges': Imaging *The Keepsake*," *Studies in the Literary Imagination* 30:1 (Spring 1997): 35–47, 37, 40. William Makepeace Thackeray's "A Word on the Annuals" attributes the volumes' "sham sentiment" and "sham art" to their female authors and readers. See *Fraser's Magazine* 16 (December 1837): 758. For debate on the quality of gift books' written and engraved contributions, see Gregory O'Dea "'Perhaps a Tale You'll Make It': Mary Shelley's Tales for *The Keepsake*," in *Iconoclastic Departures: Mary Shelley After Frankenstein: Essays in Honor of the Bicentenary of Mary Shelley's Birth*, ed. Syndy M. Conger, Frederick S. Frank, and Gregory O'Dea (London: Associated University Presses, 1997): 62–78, 62; Anne Renier, *Friendship's Offering: An Essay on the Annuals and Gift Books of the 19th Century* (London: Private Libraries Association, 1964): 15; and Bradford Allen Booth, ed. *A Cabinet of Gems: Short Stories from the English Annuals* (Berkeley: University of California Press, 1938): 7.
3. For the price of print materials, including annuals, see Katherine D. Harris, "Feminizing the Textual Body: Female Readers Consuming the Literary Annual," *The Papers of the Bibliographical Society of America* 99:4 (2005): 573–622, 579. Kathryn Ledbetter cites S. C. Hall's estimate of the annuals' extensive earnings; see *British Victorian Women's Periodicals: Beauty, Civilization, and Poetry* (New York and Houndmills: Palgrave Macmillan, 2009): 162; Ledbetter, "'BeGemmed and beAmuletted': Tennyson and Those 'Vapid' Gift Books," *Victorian Poetry* 34:2 (Summer 1996): 235–245, 235; and also Harris, "Borrowing, Altering and Perfecting the Literary Annual Form—or What It Is Not: Emblems, Almanacs, Pocket-books, Albums, Scrapbooks and Gift Books," *Poetess Archive Journal* 1.1 (April 12, 2007): 3. One early volume notes that its disadvantaged predecessor sold 6,000 copies (*LS* 1826 v); others sold as many as 15,000 to 20,000 (Paula R. Feldman, "Introduction," *The Keepsake for 1829*, ed. Frederic Mansel Reynolds [Orchard Park: Broadview Press, 2006]: 7–32, 23). For Wordsworth's and Tennyson's contributions, see Peter J. Manning, "Wordsworth in the *Keepsake*, 1829," in *Literature in the Marketplace: Nineteenth-Century British Publishing and Reading Practices*, ed. John O. Jordan and Robert L. Patten (Cambridge: Cambridge University Press, 1995): 44–73, 49–51; Ledbetter, "BeGemmed" 244; and Ledbetter, *Tennyson and Victorian Periodicals: Commodities in Context* (Aldershot: Ashgate Publishing Limited, 2007): 8–9. Felicia Hemans "would have been able to support her household of seven comfortably on her literary annual income alone" between 1827 and 1830 (Feldman, "The Poet and the Profits: Felicia Hemans and the Literary Marketplace," in *Women's Poetry, Late Romantic to Late Victorian: Gender and Genre, 1830–1900*, ed. Isobel Armstrong and Virginia Blain [New York: St. Martin's Press, 1999]: 71–101, 81), and Letitia Elizabeth Landon earned at least £250.00 per annum from publications that included the annuals. See Anne K. Mellor, *Romanticism and Gender* (New York and London: Routledge, 1993): 113. See also Harris, "Feminizing" 576.
4. Feldman, "The Poet" 80–81; Judith Pascoe, "Poetry as Souvenir: Mary Shelley in the Annuals," in *Mary Shelley in Her Times*, ed. Betty T. Bennett and Stuart Curran (Baltimore: The

Johns Hopkins University Press, 2000): 173–184; and Beverly Taylor, "Elizabeth Barrett Browning's Subversion of the Gift Book Model," *Studies in Browning and His Circle* 20 (1993): 62–69, 62.

5. The first *Forget Me Not* includes the subtitle: *A Christmas and New Year's Present*, but the subsequent volume simply lists the main title and year. By then, the annual's holiday significance was sufficiently well known to warrant the abbreviation; its status as a Christmas and New Year's present would have been understood.

6. Cindy Dickinson, "Creating a World of Books, Friends, and Flowers: Gift Books and Inscriptions, 1825–1860," *Winterthur Portfolio* 31:1 (Spring 1996): 53–66, 54 n.3: "Unlike annuals, true 'gift books,' which developed out of the annuals genre, were published only once. However, these 2 genres seem to have been indistinguishable for gift-giving purposes, and the 2 terms were usually used interchangeably." See also Harris, "Borrowing" 20; Harris, "Feminizing" 580–581.

7. Feldman, "Women, Literary Annuals, and the Evidence of Inscriptions," *Keats-Shelley Journal* 55 (2006): 54–62. Women owned 73 percent of the volumes Feldman analyzed (57). Dickinson similarly bases her assertion that "the overwhelming majority of recipients were female" on an analysis of inscriptions (58). Contemporaries observed that they were "the only books bought for presents to young ladies" (quoted in Feldman, "Introduction" 16).

8. Feldman, "Women" 57. Feldman also notes the surprisingly "large number of uninscribed volumes—sixty percent" (58). Some of the annuals' female readers may have purchased the volumes as gifts to themselves.

9. Feldman's study newly suggests that women were given annuals by family members much more frequently than by suitors ("Women" 57–58). In contrast, popular depictions often belittled the annuals by relegating them to courtship objects. Ned Plymdale, "one of the good matches in Middlemarch, though not one of its leading minds," attempts to court Rosamond Vincy over the latest *Keepsake*. See George Eliot, *Middlemarch* (London: Penguin Classics, 1988): 302.

10. That we talk about literature's "reception" suggests that it can on some level always be considered *given*—see, for instance, Hyde's note: "[a]s is the case with any other circulation of gifts, the commerce of art draws each of its participants into a wider self" (152)—but the material form that proclaims itself to be gift heightens this effect.

11. For the "recipient-function" of readers, see Gayatri Chakravorty Spivak, "Three Women's Texts and a Critique of Imperialism," *Critical Inquiry* 12:1 (Autumn 1985): 243–261, 259. To her account, I would add that the reader-recipients of literary annuals are obligated to reciprocate, not just receive.

12. Steel plates had recently made this liberal sharing of images possible. See Heather Glen, *Charlotte Brontë: The Imagination in History* (Oxford and New York: Oxford University Press, 2002): 107 n.39.

13. See also, for instance, *FMN* 1831, iv. J. Paul Hunter notes that prefatory materials "that in fact stand between reader and text pretend instead to be connecters, things that bring together writer and reader in a more personal way" (*Before Novels: The Cultural Contexts of Eighteenth-Century English Fiction* [New York: W. W. Norton, 1990]: 237). These materials further set the conditions for connection, dictating the terms of a reader's engagement. According to Gérard Genette, a preface has two objectives, "*to get the book read* and *to get the book read properly*" (197, emphasis in original). This matter of "*proper*" reading often entails "attribut[ing] high value to a subject by demonstrating its importance and [...] usefulness," which, in the case of works such as annuals might include "moral usefulness" (199). Genette categorizes the expression of thanks in prefaces as "information for the reader, and perhaps also, obliquely, [...] value-enhancement" (211–212). See *Paratexts: Thresholds of Interpretation*, trans. Jane E. Lewin, trans. (Cambridge: Cambridge University Press, 1997). For the annuals, reading "properly" entails understanding that editors' expressions of thanks are part of the books' larger constructions as gifts.

14. Montgomery, who coauthored *Poems on the Abolition of the Slave Trade* (1809), appears frequently in the annuals.

15. See also Dickinson 57. According to Genette, "Inscribing a copy is not only a symbolic act but also a real act, accompanied in principle by a real gift, or at the very least by a past or present sale. Accompanied, that is, by an ownership that the inscription in fact stamps and ratifies" (139–140). He distinguishes between this "symbolic" but also "real" gift of specific inscription and the solely "symbolic" act of the work's dedication (140).

16. See also Introduction (in this volume). If, as Anderson has argued, print material draws readers together into an "imagined community," then print material as gift does something more, drawing readers together into an imagined community with the obligations of gift recipients.

17. See also Harris for the books' emphasis on "the female recipient who will pass it on to others rather than keeping it forever" ("Feminizing" 612).

18. *The Pearl; or, Affection's Gift. A Christmas and New Year's Present* (Philadelphia: Thomas T. Ash, 1830). Annuals were a transatlantic phenomenon, and despite regional and national differences, frequently shared audiences and strategies. Credited by "The Souvenir" as "The Author of the Young Americans" and "E. L.," Eliza Leslie (1787–1858) was best known for her popular cookbooks but also wrote for and edited annuals. After passing most of her childhood in England, she lived and published in the United States.

19. In this story, Amelia's brother assists with her gift-giving, but it also serves his own friend. When this scrupulous friend returns the volume, because it was given without the knowledge of her father, her father commends Amelia's "kindness and benevolence" (121) and then bestows it on the artist once again, from Amelia but with his sanction (122). Like the female writers whose annual "contributions" were frequently mediated by male publishing hierarchies, Amelia may assert her right to bestow her own property as she wishes, but the direction of her gift and its delivery are also heavily mediated.

20. Barbara Wreaks Hoole/Hofland (1770–1844) was a popular and prolific author of children's books as well as a contributor to the annuals (Dennis Butts, *Mistress of Our Tears: A Literary and Bibliographical Study of Barbara Hofland* [Aldershot: Scolar Press, 1992]: 19).

21. The 1830s and '40s saw surging interest in fallenness. See Amanda Anderson, *Tainted Souls and Painted Faces: The Rhetoric of Fallenness in Victorian Culture* (Ithaca: Cornell University Press, 1993): 50, and Chapter 4 of this volume. For the criminal and sexual status of gypsies, see Deborah Epstein Nord, *Gypsies and the British Imagination, 1807–1930* (New York: Columbia University Press, 2006): 3, 20, 12–13, 40. See also Robert Knox, *The Races of Men: A Fragment* (Philadelphia: Lea & Blanchard, 1850): 300, quoted in Susan Meyer, *Imperialism at Home: Race and Victorian Women's Fiction* (Ithaca: Cornell University Press, 1996): 15–16.

22. Extrapolation ("choosing to read yourself in parable") occurs both within the scene and between the reader and story. See Garrett Stewart, *Dear Reader: The Conscripted Audience in Nineteenth-Century British Fiction* (Baltimore: The Johns Hopkins University Press, 1996): 19. See also Robyn R. Warhol, "Toward a Theory of the Engaging Narrator: Earnest Interventions in Gaskell, Stowe, and Eliot," *Publications of the Modern Language Association of America (PMLA)* 101:5 (October 1986): 811–818; although the passage does not directly address the reader as "you," it functions, like Warhol's "engaging narrator," to "encourage[...] the reader to apply to nonfictional, real life the feelings the fiction may have inspired" (816). For reading practices and social responses to sentimental literature, see John Mullan, *Sentiment and Sociability: The Language of Feeling in the Eighteenth Century* (Oxford: Clarendon Press, 1988): 25, 29; Janet Todd, *Sensibility: An Introduction* (London: Methuen, 1986): 4. William's concern for his child's welfare emerges out of his reading experience, but some recent strands of criticism resist efforts to recover actual nineteenth-century readers' experiences. See, for instance, Rachel Ablow, *The Marriage of Minds: Reading Sympathy in the Victorian Marriage Plot* (Stanford: Stanford University Press, 2007): 9.

23. The reference to "Grace Huntley" reminded the book's regular readers that they were already part of a reading community and offered the promise of such a community to newer readers.

It was also a particularly politic gesture by the author, since "Grace Huntley" was written by Mrs. S. C. Hall, the wife of the *Amulet*'s editor.

24. See Hyde 4.

25. Marshall Sahlins notes the importance of passing along the gift's "issue" or profit (*Stone Age Economics* [Chicago: Aldine Atherton, 1972]: 160).

26. According to Rachel Ablow, novels attempt to create the same sort of "female influence" and attachment that domestic ideology afforded to wives (29, 42–43). Like her, I stress the significance of relationships for defining selfhood (46), but by looking beyond heterosexual marriage plots (and their fictional homologies), I suggest that "female influence" had greater meaning. In the *Amulet*'s tale, William's feelings seem to arise for and toward a future wife, but their derivation in another woman's tale of a female character and the direct influence that the clergyman's daughter has upon Ayeshe point to the importance of "female influence" on women, too.

27. Offering pity or condescension (sympathy *for* rather than *with* another), imbalanced exchange maintains social distance, even as it reaches temporarily across class. See Daniel Jeremy Siegel, "The Failure of Condescension," *Victorian Literature and Culture* 33:2 (September 2005): 395–414, e.g., 395, 403–404, 410 and Audrey Jaffe, *Scenes of Sympathy: Identity and Representation in Victorian Fiction* (Ithaca: Cornell University Press, 2000): 5, 12–13.

28. See R. Freyhan's analysis of Caritas iconography for commentary regarding reproductions of classically garbed Caritas figures suckling children ("The Evolution of the Caritas Figure in the Thirteenth and Fourteenth Centuries," *Journal of the Warburg and Courtauld Institutes* 11 (1948): 68–86, 81–85).

29. See also Sharon Marcus, *Between Women: Friendship, Desire, and Marriage in Victorian England* (Princeton: Princeton University Press, 2007): 114–115.

30. The woman's rough slouch, her seeming disregard for physical exposure, and the lack of apparent affection for the child at her breast all conform to nineteenth-century attitudes about the domestic failures of working-class families. Friedrich Engels offers one prominent example of how nineteenth-century writing conflated class with race when he describes members of the working-class as a "race apart" and offers childrearing as an example (*The Condition of the Working Class in England* [Oxford: Oxford University Press, 1993]: 135, 138).

31. Urania Cottage—the joint venture of Charles Dickens and heiress-philanthropist Angela Burdett Coutts—sought to reform "fallen" women and then send them to the colonies, where their chances of marriage were thought to be greater than in England.

32. For other depictions of gypsies' generational "upward mobility through the denial of an ethnic past," see Nord 47.

33. As Nord points out, gypsies were a "symbol for dispossession and homelessness" in nineteenth-century England (67). Colonial emigration was a common "solution" for undesirable populations. This story's emigration project is run by a benevolent Earl, but the aristocratic largesse occurs off stage, keeping the story's focus on the gifts of the middle classes instead.

34. By privileging consanguineal kin over marital ties, the story initially seems to offer an alternative to the historical narrative of women's kinship traced by Ruth Perry, an alternative I return to in Chapter 2 of this volume (see Ch. 2, n.6). However, in this tale, blood and marriage alike are strained by ineffective gift-giving.

35. See Beth Fowkes Tobin, *Superintending the Poor: Charitable Ladies and Paternal Landlords in British Fiction, 1770–1860* (New Haven: Yale University Press, 1993), and Jaffe for charity as a contested ground for middle-class authority. The New Poor Law (1834) rejected paternalism by discouraging handouts. But movements that claimed to merge middle- and working-class interests frequently served primarily middle-class interests, instead. The Reform Bill of 1832 extended voting rights to a limited and elite segment of the population; see Harold Perkin, *The Origins of Modern English Society*, 2nd ed. (London: Routledge, 1969, 2002): 313. Alternate solutions to working-class poverty, such as working-class trade unions

and Chartism, were often associated with violence. The revolution-wary middle classes were reluctant to promote confederations of workers.

36. See Peter Mandler, "Poverty and Charity in the Nineteenth-Century Metropolis: An Introduction," *The Uses of Charity: The Poor on Relief in the Nineteenth-Century Metropolis*, ed. Peter Mandler (Philadelphia: University of Pennsylvania Press, 1990): 1–37, 13, and Gertrude Himmelfarb, *Poverty and Compassion: The Moral Imagination of the Late Victorians* (New York: Random House, 1991): 12.

37. This is a variation on the *cri du sang*, which I address in my subsequent discussion of *Jane Eyre*. See Chapter 2 of this volume.

38. Along these lines, Anne McClintock discusses similarities between the urban and imperial reforms initiated by activists; see *Imperial Leather: Race, Gender and Sexuality in the Colonial Contest* (New York: Routledge, 1995): 118–122. For feminism's relationship to slavery and British imperialism, see Louise Michele Newman, *White Women's Rights: The Racial Origins of Feminism in the United States* (Oxford: Oxford University Press, 1999): 1–21 and Antoinette Burton, *Burdens of History: British Feminists, Indian Women, and Imperial Culture, 1865–1915* (Chapel Hill: The University of North Carolina Press, 1994): e.g., 7–13, 17, 32.

39. Rachel Ablow reads the sympathetic workings of nineteenth-century fiction through the lens of female "influence," made popular through separate spheres ideology. Although she notes that women's "influence" operates "less as a counter to [men's] ambition than its alibi" (29), gift practices reveal women's influence as both ally and alternative to male ambition, providing an outlet for women's own ambitious practices.

40. See Harris, "Feminizing" 575; Ledbetter, *Tennyson* 15.

41. Glen remarks upon "the energy with which [annuals] point away from 'women's sphere'" and notes that "there is much in the annuals that invites one to read them in a different spirit: as offering powerful alternative images to those of female subordination and passivity, and affirming the central importance of that which the culture of early nineteenth-century England relegated to 'woman's sphere'" (110, 116). See also Glen 136.

42. Women's emancipatory activities were often based on and continuous with other charitable work. See, for instance, James Walvin, *England, Slaves and Freedom, 1776–1838* (Houndmills: Macmillan, 1986): 100, 158; Clare Midgley, *Women Against Slavery: The British Campaigns, 1780–1870* (London: Routledge, 1992): 82; and Kate Davies, "A Moral Purchase: Femininity, Commerce, and Abolition, 1788–1792," *Women, Writing and the Public Sphere, 1770–1830*, ed. Elizabeth Eger, Charlotte Grant, et. al. (Cambridge: Cambridge University Press, 2001): 133–159, 133. For discursive continuities between charitable work and colonialist discourse, see Alison Twells, "'Happy English Children': Class, Ethnicity, and the Making of Missionary Women in the Early Nineteenth Century," *Women's Studies International Forum* 21:3 (1998): 235–245, 241. Historians of women's abolitionist work frequently exaggerate the distinctions between philanthropic and abolitionist discourses, which relied on similar strategies for extending women's political roles. See, for instance, Moira Ferguson, *Subject to Others: British Women Writers and Colonial Slavery, 1670–1834* (New York: Routledge, 1992): 299 and Midgley 5, 154–155. As Leonore Davidoff and Catherine Hall have demonstrated about religious movements in the first half of the nineteenth century, political change did not necessarily occur through conventionally political means. See Davidoff and Hall, *Family Fortunes: Men and Women of the English Middle Class 1780–1850*, 2nd ed. (London: Routledge, 2002): 95.

43. Thomas Pringle (1789–1834), secretary of the Anti-Slavery Society, was the editor of *The History of Mary Prince, a West Indian Slave. Related by Herself* (1831). Unlike the poem he wrote for *Friendship's Offering*, in which a slave's liberation is a gift, Mary Prince's narrative depicts a more assertive slave, who attempts to and finally does leave her masters, speaks boldly to them, and even works to earn the money to buy her own freedom. Whether or not publishing in the annuals contributed to the choices authors made, it seems that treating a slave's freedom as a benevolent gift was a strategy better suited to some genres than others.

See Moira Ferguson, "Introduction to the Revised Edition," *The History of Mary Prince, a West Indian Slave. Related by Herself*, Revised ed., ed. Moira Ferguson (Ann Arbor: The University of Michigan Press, 1997): 1–51, 5, 9, 11, 29.

44. After the *Somerset* decision in 1772 it became illegal for slaves to be forcibly deported to the colonies from England, but the slave trade wasn't abolished until 1807, and ambiguity about slavery in England itself remained until 1827. Not until the end of slavery in the British colonies (legally in 1833, enacted in 1834) were blacks in England granted legal protection. See James Walvin, *England, Slaves and Freedom, 1776–1838* (Houndmills: Macmillan, 1986): 67; Walvin, *Britain's Slave Empire* (Stroud: Tempus, 2000): 64–66; also George Boulukos, *The Grateful Slave: The Emergence of Race in Eighteenth-Century British and American Culture* (Cambridge: Cambridge University Press, 2008): 7. The colonial apprenticeship system did not end until 1838 (Midgley 121).

45. As Ian Baucom has noted, the emphasis on freedom in *England* conceals England's colonial interests and splits the nation (England) from its (British) empire in order to "simultaneously avow and disavow its empire" (*Out of Place: Englishness, Empire, and the Locations of Identity* [Princeton: Princeton University Press, 1999]: 6).

46. Violent slave rebellions of 1819 and 1823 added fuel to English anti-slavery activism.

47. By marrying John, Sophie will immediately lose her rights to body and property again, in accordance with the laws of coverture, which I discuss further in Chapter 2 of this volume. By securing her land, the story actually protects Sophie's future husband's property rights as much as or more than her own.

48. After he marries Sophie, however, John opts for immediate emancipation.

49. A powerful strategy, this emphasis on "gift" over "right" will shape campaigns for women's suffrage as well. See this book's epilogue, for example.

50. In 1823, The Society for the Mitigation and Gradual Abolition of Slavery, more popularly the Anti-Slavery Society, was established. This all-male Society affected women's abolitionism largely by prompting women to form their own independent anti-slavery organizations. Many women, most notably Elizabeth Heyrick, took issue with the Society's ameliorative plan. Heyrick argued in a number of pamphlets for immediate, rather than "gradual" abolition (Ferguson 250, 233–234). Shortly after her first pamphlets (1824) and two years after the establishment of the Anti-Slavery Society, Lucy Townsend and Mary Lloyd established the first British women's anti-slavery society, the Ladies Society for the Relief of Negro Slaves, later called the Female Society for Birmingham. Clare Midgley characterizes women's earlier efforts to end the slave trade as marking "an individual woman's commitment"; the new network of ladies' associations, on the other hand, made "anti-slavery [...] a collective female endeavour" (44).

51. See Midgley 108. Along these lines, in "The Planter," John Vivian's marriage to Sophie might be responsible for the change of heart that makes him grant the slaves freedom immediately instead of gradually, as he first intends.

52. See Newman 60–62; Hazel V. Carby, *Reconstructing Womanhood: The Emergence of the Afro-American Woman Novelist* (Oxford: Oxford University Press, 1987): 17–18; Twells 243; Midgley 102, 203; Burton 4; and bell hooks, *Ain't I a Woman: Black Women and Feminism* (Boston: South End Press, 1981): 144.

53. Boulukos's history of grateful slaves contends that abolitionist images such as Wedgwood's have their roots in fiction that aimed to defend or at most ameliorate slavery, while also suggesting essential racial difference (e.g., 3, 14, 16–17).

54. Susan B. Egenolf, "Josiah Wedgwood's Goodwill Marketing," in *The Culture of the Gift in Eighteenth-Century England*, ed. Linda Zionkowski and Cynthia Klekar (New York and Houndmills: Palgrave Macmillan, 2009): 197–213; 202, 203.

55. The Ladies Negro's Friend Society of Birmingham, England, used the figure of a single female supplicant slave as early as 1826. Jean Fagan Yellin, *Women and Sisters: The Antislavery Feminists in American Culture* (New Haven: Yale University Press, 1989): 10–12. For images, see Yellin 4, 6, 11, 16, 18 and Midgley 99–101.

56. Yellin 16–26, esp. 24–25; Mellor 318; Midgley 204.

57. Boulukos notes that late-eighteenth-century depictions of slaves' "gratitude," set in op-position to Enlightenment ideas of independence, feminized slaves while simultaneously denying them the "deeper, more genuine feelings, the much more complex psychic interior-ity, [attributed to] white women" (25–26). Although many of the annuals' engraved women avert their gaze, not all do so; see Figure 1.1 as well as Harris, "Feminizing" 600–601.

58. Sarah Eglonton Wallis Bowdich/Lee (1791–1856) was well-known for writing about natural history and African exploration; her works ranged from the illustrated *Fresh Water Fishes of Great Britain* (1828–1838) to the stories she published in the annuals. See Donald deB. Beaver for her publication history. The annuals, apparently an important source of income, gave her the opportunity to produce very different material from her scientific essays and drawings ("Writing Natural History for Survival, 1820–1856: the case of Sarah Bowdich, later Sarah Lee," *Archives of Natural History* 26:1 [1999]: 19–31, esp. 21–24).

59. Newman also notes, though in the context of later nineteenth-century America, that black women had to profess Christianity "in order to gain access to the sisterhood" (8).

60. This activists' annual resembled others that had preceded it, if somewhat shorter and less embellished than they. Though relatively unadorned, most volumes had at least one or two engravings, and the bindings varied from paper to tooled leather and silk (Ralph Thomp-son, "The Liberty Bell and Other Anti-Slavery Gift-Books," *The New England Quarterly* 7:1 [March 1934]: 154–168, 154, 159–160). Karen Sánchez-Eppler remarks that the *Liberty Bell* "fit without apparent incongruity into any household library." See "Bodily Bonds: The Inter-secting Rhetorics of Feminism and Abolition," in *Interracialism: Black-White Intermarriage in American History, Literature, and Law,* ed. Werner Sollors (Oxford: Oxford University Press, 2000): 408–437, 418. See also Lee Chambers-Schiller's treatment of this abolitionist annual ("'A Good Work Among the People': The Political Culture of the Boston Antislavery Fair," in *The Abolitionist Sisterhood: Women's Political Culture in Antebellum America,* ed. Jean Fagan Yellin and John C. Van Horne [Ithaca: Cornell University Press, 1994]: 249–274, 258–259, 265–266) and Yellin 59–61.

61. For the gendered implications of charity bazaars, see Leslee Thorne-Murphy, "Women, Free Trade, and Harriet Martineau's *Dawn Island* at the 1845 Anti-Corn Law League Bazaar," in *Economic Women: Essays on Desire and Dispossession in Nineteenth-Century British Culture,* ed. Lana Dalley and Jill Rappoport (unpublished manuscript). Unlike other annuals, the *Liberty Bell* was not a resounding financial success. Thompson questions whether it may have even lost money, despite an 1843 claim that the gift book "always doubles the money invested in it" (158, 158 n.11). Its poor circulation beyond pre-established abolitionists underscores the comparative effectiveness and subtlety of British annuals as abolitionist works.

62. Thompson 160–161, 164.

63. Elizabeth Barrett Browning, "The Runaway Slave," *The Liberty Bell. By Friends of Freedom,* ed. Maria Weston Chapman (Boston: American Anti-Slavery Society, 1848): 29–44; see page 29 line 2. Subsequent references refer to line numbers from this edition of the poem.

64. As Herbert F. Tucker has argued, the Victorian dramatic monologue is not "overheard" in precisely the manner that we "overhear" the solitary, lyrical poet. See "Dramatic Monologue and the Overhearing of Lyric," in *Lyric Poetry: Beyond New Criticism,* ed. Chaviva Hosek and Patricia Parker (Ithaca: Cornell University Press, 1985): 226–243, 228, 233; E. Warwick Slinn, "Dramatic Monologue" in *A Companion to Victorian Poetry,* ed. Richard Cronin, Ali-son Chapman, and Antony H. Harrison (Malden and Oxford: Blackwell, 2002): 80–98, 81.

65. It also illustrates dramatic monologues' emphasis on the separation of reader from speaker. See, for instance, Slinn 82. Even the fact that Barrett Browning speaks through and for the slave underscores the way that abolitionist activity here is an exchange between abolitionists, not between slave and abolitionists.

66. The tale that precedes Barrett Browning's poem—"The Insurrection and Its Hero. A Tale of the South. By a Southron" (1–28)—similarly places action firmly in the hands of the

abolitionists. In this story, a slave's plotted rebellion is foiled; he is sentenced to death but still manages to win over the minister who attempts to make him turn in the other rebels. Despite the story's sympathy with this heroic rebel, it ends his life and leaves the onus for change on readers, implying that neither rebellion nor "pray[er] to God as our common father" is as effective as abolitionist work.

67. Eliza F. Meriam to Caroline Weston, January 16, 1843, quoted in Chambers-Schiller (259).

68. The voluntary servitude that "Daddy Davy" gives his long-lost master follows the history Boulukos traces of ameliorating, rather than abolishing, slavery through depictions of gratitude (e.g., 21–22; 235).

69. This volume's impressive list of contributors, which included Coleridge, Hemans, Landon, Scott, Southey, Wordsworth, and the late P. B. Shelley in addition to "The Author of Frankenstein," made it noteworthy not only then but again for twenty-first-century readers: it is the first of the annuals to be reproduced for classroom use.

70. The Italian setting and tragic ending authorize a Catholic theme in a story published shortly before Catholic Emancipation (1829), but the distinction between contemplative and active orders was also important. Shelley borrows from and contributes to a rich literary tradition that appropriated Catholic institutions for English tales. (Gothic fiction frequently employed convents, and women from Mary Astell in 1694 through Anna Jameson in 1855 focused their literary visions on sisterhoods and their occupants.) The mid-century proliferation of Anglican sisterhoods, which I discuss in Chapter 4 of this volume, comes out of this tradition.

71. The cruel aunt is an important instance of a "bad woman" as benefactress; *Jane Eyre*'s Aunt Reed is another example of the same type. Such figures served to underscore the failures of "cold" charity and their contrast with more successful models of egalitarian exchange.

Chapter 2

1. Charlotte Brontë, *Jane Eyre: An Authoritative Text, Contexts, Criticism*, 3rd ed., ed. Richard J. Dunn (New York and London: W. W. Norton, 2001): 103. Subsequent citations in parentheses.

2. Heather Glen, *Charlotte Brontë: The Imagination in History* (Oxford and New York: Oxford University Press, 2002): 108; see also Christine Alexander, "'That Kingdom of Gloom': Charlotte Brontë, the Annuals, and the Gothic," *Nineteenth-Century Literature* 47: 4 (March 1993): 409–436, 414–415.

3. For Jane's development in terms of anger and psychological doubles, see Sandra M. Gilbert and Susan Gubar, *The Madwoman in the Attic: The Woman Writer and the Nineteenth-Century Literary Imagination*, 2nd ed. (New Haven: Yale University Press, 1984, 2000): 339, 360–361; Elaine Showalter, "Charlotte Brontë: Feminine Heroine," *New Casebooks: Jane Eyre*, ed. Heather Glen (Houndmills: Macmillan, 1997): 68–77, 68; Mary Poovey, *Uneven Developments: The Ideological Work of Gender in Mid-Victorian England* (Chicago: University of Chicago Press, 1988): 140–141. For her ambiguous class status, see Poovey 127, 137; Jina Politi, "*Jane Eyre* Class-ified," *New Casebooks: Jane Eyre*. Ed. Heather Glen (Houndmills: Macmillan, 1997): 78–91, 79; and Susan Fraiman, *Unbecoming Women: British Women Writers and the Novel of Development* (New York: Columbia University Press, 1993): 96. The status of Rochester's creole wife Bertha Mason is central to debates about the novel's racial politics and often paired with Jane's own references to harems and slaves. See Gayatri Chakravorty Spivak, "Three Women's Texts and a Critique of Imperialism," *Critical Inquiry* 12:1 (Autumn 1985): 243–261, 247–248; Jenny Sharpe, *Allegories of Empire: The Figure of the Woman in the Colonial Context* (Minneapolis: University of Minnesota Press, 1993): 28; Susan Meyer, *Imperialism at Home: Race and Victorian Women's Fiction* (Ithaca: Cornell University Press, 1996): 74, 86; and Carolyn Vellenga Berman, "Undomesticating the Domestic Novel: Creole Madness in *Jane Eyre*," *Genre: Forms of Discourse and Culture* 32:4 (Winter 1999): 267–296, 276. Many critics see Jane as complicit with conservative disciplinary systems of

middle-class, patriarchal, and imperialist ideology. See Deirdre David, *Rule Britannia: Women, Empire, and Victorian Writing* (Ithaca: Cornell University Press, 1995): 110; Politi 90; Joseph A. Dupras, "Tying the Knot in the Economic Warp of *Jane Eyre*," *Victorian Literature and Culture* 26:2 (1998): 395–408, 399; and Elaine Freedgood, *The Ideas in Things: Fugitive Meaning in the Victorian Novel* (Chicago: University of Chicago Press, 2006): e.g., 32, 35, 50. Work on *Aurora Leigh* focusing on individual genius and the conflicting development of poet and woman includes Ellen Moers, *Literary Women* (New York: Oxford University Press, 1985): 182; Gilbert and Gubar 576–577; and Alison Case, "Gender and Narration in *Aurora Leigh*," *Victorian Poetry* 29:1 (Spring 1991): 17–18, 25. For the intimate, political, class-fraught, and maternal relationships between women, see, respectively, Sharon Marcus, *Between Women: Friendship, Desire, and Marriage in Victorian England* (Princeton: Princeton University Press, 2007): 91–96; Angela Leighton, *Elizabeth Barrett Browning* (Bloomington: Indiana University Press, 1986): 147, 154–155; Cora Kaplan, ed., "Introduction," *Aurora Leigh and Other Poems* (London: The Women's Press, 1978): 11–12; and Dorothy Mermin, *Elizabeth Barrett Browning: The Origins of a New Poetry* (Chicago: University of Chicago Press, 1989): 190–196.

4. Many scholars attribute the novel's narration to "1818 or 1819" and claim that it "describes events taking place between 1798 and 1808." See Judith Raiskin, ed., Jean Rhys, *Wide Sargasso Sea* (New York: W. W. Norton, 1999): 31 n.7. Scholars also date the novel through its references to publications such as Scott's *Marmion* in 1808 or the second volume of Bewick's *The History of British Birds*, in 1804.

5. We saw this in Chapter 1's discussion of "The Orphan Family," when Alice's husband, not Alice, transfers her money to Elizabeth. For coverture, see Mary Lyndon Shanley, *Feminism, Marriage, and the Law in Victorian England* (Princeton: Princeton University Press, 1989): 8, 22. As Joanne Bailey and others have noted, however, "in practice coverture was often ignored or bypassed." See "Favoured or Oppressed? Married Women, Property, and 'Coverture' in England, 1660–1800," *Continuity and Change* 17:3 (2002): 351–372, 353, 366, 368; Margot C. Finn, "Women, Consumption and Coverture in England, c. 1760–1860," *The Historical Journal* 39:3 (September 1996): 703–722, 707. Courts of equity offered one exception by making it possible for wealthy families to secure trusts to women as their "separate estates" (Shanley 25;); as Finn has shown, "Other, less familiar legal practices that expanded women's economic agency were [...] arguably more important on a daily basis to the bulk of married women than was equity." See Finn, "Women" 705–706.

6. Ruth Perry has recently suggested that women's economic standing in the family and in society diminished over the past 100 years, as primogeniture increasingly cut them off from family land and wealth and made them more dependent on new, marital ties. *Novel Relations: The Transformation of Kinship in English Literature and Culture 1748–1818* (Cambridge: Cambridge University Press, 2004): 64, 4, 34, 40, 47, 212. For the way that common law diminished women's claims to property, see also Susan Staves, *Married Women's Separate Property in England, 1660–1833* (Cambridge: Harvard University Press, 1990): e.g., 27–36, 129–130, 217. Other historians have argued, however, that this focus on common law obscures continuity and even possible growth in women's economic standing during this period. See Amanda Vickery, *The Gentleman's Daughter: Women's Lives in Georgian England* (New Haven: Yale University Press, 1998): 4; Vickery, "Golden Age to Separate Spheres? A Review of the Categories and Chronology of English Women's History," *The Historical Journal* 36:2 (June, 1993): 383–414, 405; Finn, "Women" 720. Moreover, Amy Louise Erickson points out that even though men increasingly inherited family land, "primogeniture" fails to adequately describe "the 'grid of inheritance' among ordinary people," partly because younger children, male and female alike, would often receive "the equivalent value in moveables"; see *Women and Property in Early Modern England* (London: Routledge, 1993): 78, 77, also 26–27.

7. See Fraiman 90 and Poovey 126–128.

8. The first petition for Married Women's Property was submitted in March 1856; Elizabeth Barrett Browning and Elizabeth Gaskell wrote 2 of its 26,000 signatures. Coverture was not the last word on women's economic position. In addition to the settlements that wealthy women made through courts of equity, women from "all levels of society" protected their interests through "different types of pre-nuptial settlements [. . .]." See Erickson 150. Finn details women's ability to control their husbands' property through the strategic use of the "law of necessaries," and their economic agency in small claims courts: "Women" 707–709, 719.

9. See Margaret Reynolds, "Editorial Introduction," in *Aurora Leigh* (Athens: Ohio University Press, 1992): 78–156, esp. 84–91. Robert Browning acknowledges his wife's influence in helping him publish his work (84) but nevertheless writes to publishers on her behalf (88).

10. "A gift that is not returned can become a debt [. . .]; the only recognized power [. . .] is obtained by giving" (Pierre Bourdieu, *The Logic of Practice*, trans. Richard Nice [Cambridge: Polity Press, 1990]: 126). Linda Schlossberg notes the doubly-dependent status of nineteenth-century orphan children; see "'The Low, Vague Hum of Numbers': The Malthusian Economies of *Jane Eyre*," *Victorian Literature and Culture* 29:2 (2001): 489–506, 497–498.

11. For the significance of symbolic capital, including honor and prestige, see Bourdieu 118. See also Daniel Jeremy Siegel, "The Failure of Condescension," *Victorian Literature and Culture* 33.2 (September 2005): 398, 409.

12. The heroine of Anne Brontë's *Tenant of Wildfell Hall*, published approximately eight months after *Jane Eyre*, also learns to reject gifts that put her "under obligations that I can never repay" (Oxford: Oxford University Press, 2008): 64.

13. Mariana Valverde, "The Love of Finery: Fashion and the Fallen Woman in Nineteenth-Century Social Discourse," *Victorian Studies* 32:2 (Winter 1989): 169–188, 170–172, 175–176; Kate Washington, "Rochester's Mistresses: Marriage, Sex, and Economic Exchange in *Jane Eyre*," *Michigan Feminist Studies* 12 (1997–1998): 47–66, 55.

14. "*Gabe* can be either a gift or a dose and [. . .] *Gift*, which now means poison, once had the sense of our English 'gift' [. . .]." See Gary Shapiro, "The Metaphysics of Presents: Nietzsche's Gift, the Debt to Emerson, Heidegger's Values" in *The Logic of the Gift: Toward an Ethic of Generosity*, ed. Alan D. Schrift (New York: Routledge, 1997): 274–291. See also Marcel Mauss, *The Gift: The Form and Reason for Exchange in Archaic Societies*, trans. W. D. Hall (London: Routledge, 1990): 62–63 and "Gift, Gift," in *The Logic of the Gift: Toward an Ethic of Generosity*, ed. Alan D. Schrift (New York: Routledge, 1997): 28–32.

15. See Elizabeth Gaskell, *The Life of Charlotte Brontë* (1857) (London: Penguin, 1997): 157, 185, 192, 194. Brontë studied German during her two years at Madame Héger's school in Brussels. Whether or not Brontë intended the etymological play, these textual moments signal the double and dangerous valence of presents.

16. As Amit S. Rai notes, Jane does receive other affective gifts earlier (from Helen and Miss Temple); I disagree that these can "not [. . .] be returned through a calculus of exchange" (*Rule of Sympathy: Sentiment, Race, and Power, 1750–1850* [New York: Palgrave, 2002]: 250); Rai's note on 265 is more to the point.

17. John Reed's violent book-throwing and Mr. Brocklehurst's disciplinary use of pamphlets contrast with the Riverses' more sympathetic reading practices. As Spivak notes, reading unites the reader and Jane (246). It similarly unites Jane with her new cousins.

18. For other similarities between *Jane Eyre* and the annuals, see Glen 108–109, 116, 124 and Katherine D. Harris, "Borrowing, Altering and Perfecting the Literary Annual Form—or What It Is Not: Emblems, Almanacs, Pocket-books, Albums, Scrapbooks and Gift Books," *Poetess Archive Journal* 1:1 (April 12, 2007): 5.

19. Perry 98, 95. For Perry, this emphasis on blood in fiction coincides with an attenuation of those relations in life. Joanne Bailey argues, in contrast, that families of origin remain significant to women long after their marriage; see "Review of Perry, Ruth, *Novel Relations: The Transformation of Kinship in English Literature and Culture 1748–1818*," *H-Albion*, *H-Net Reviews*, http://www.h-net.org/reviews/showrev.php?id=11824.

20. Eliza Reed's final words to her sister: "'if the whole human race, ourselves excepted, were swept away, and we two stood alone on the earth, I would leave you in the old world, and betake myself to the new'" (201). See Mary Jean Corbett, *Family Likeness: Sex, Marriage, and Incest from Jane Austen to Virginia Woolf* (Ithaca: Cornell University Press, 2008): 107.

21. Their offer does not extend to the housekeeper who is performing the kitchen labor they stop Jane from assisting; recognition of similar class status precedes and also follows from this gift transaction.

22. In contrast to Helena Michie, I find this episode in Jane's life to be of utmost importance. See *Sororophobia: Differences Among Women in Literature and Culture* (Oxford: Oxford University Press, 1992): 17. See also Corbett 107.

23. See, for instance, Gilbert and Gubar 366–368 and Dianne F. Sadoff, "The Father, Castration, and Female Fantasy in *Jane Eyre*," in *Jane Eyre*, ed. Beth Newman (Boston: Bedford/St. Martin's, 1996): 533.

24. Edward W. Said, *Orientalism* (New York: Vintage Books, 1978): 188. See also Poovey 142; Dupras 399.

25. Corbett 108. Corbett's argument, by distinguishing between Jane's matrilineal and patrilineal relations, emphasizes the dispossession of mothers and maternal kin (107–108).

26. See, for instance, Sadoff 525–526.

27. For the colonialist significance of the "Indian ink" she uses, see Meyer 93–94. For Eyre as "heir" see Nina Schwartz, "No Place Like Home: The Logic of the Supplement in *Jane Eyre*," in *Jane Eyre*, ed. Beth Newman (Boston: Bedford/St. Martin's, 1996): 551–552 and Janet Gezari, *Charlotte Brontë and Defensive Conduct: The Author and the Body at Risk* (Philadelphia: University of Pennsylvania Press, 1992): 61. Other homonymic associations with Eyre include "air," "eyer," and, most frequently, "ire." See Gezari, 61–62.

28. No evidence suggests that Jane's uncle settled the money on her as her separate estate.

29. The vast majority of women's wills before the nineteenth century were made by widows and single women (Erickson 204).

30. See "Capabilities and Disabilities of Women," *The Westminster and Foreign Quarterly Review* (January 1, 1857): 51.

31. See Shanley 103. The 1870 Act covered only legacies of less than £200 (Shanley 74); even the Act of 1882 did not give wives full contractual or testamentary powers (Shanley 127). See also Perry 200; Erickson 229. However, Erickson finds that more women enjoyed "premarital property settlements" than previously thought (226).

32. Shanley 25–26.

33. Meyer 93; Freedgood 34–35, 50; Corbett 103, 108.

34. Perry 24, 47, 49, 212. Although other scholars have argued that women continued to receive more equitable divisions of family wealth (Erickson 63, 78), cases of intestacy favored eldest sons, and "[t]he wealthier a man was, the smaller the proportion of his estate left to his widow, and also to his daughters" (Erickson, 26, 19). According to Janette Rutterford and Josephine Maltby, "in 1875 [...] one-quarter of all land in England was held by only 710 individuals." See "Women and Wealth in Fiction in the Long Nineteenth Century 1800–1914," *Women and Their Money, 1700–1950: Essays on Women and Finance*, ed. Anne Laurence, Josephine Maltby, and Janette Rutterford (London and New York: Routledge, 2009): 151–164, 153. As David R. Green notes, "Wills [...] offer a way of unraveling and understanding a set of social relationships through the disposal of property and as such they provide a rare glimpse into the complex relationships between money, emotion, and duty." "To do the Right Thing: Gender, Wealth, Inheritance and the London Middle Class," *Women and Their Money, 1700–1950: Essays on Women and Finance*, ed. Anne Laurence, Josephine Maltby, and Janette Rutterford (London and New York: Routledge, 2009): 133–150, 134.

35. Entailed estates and primogeniture mean that "neither [Blanche] nor her sister have very large fortunes" (136), a fact which troubles Elsie B. Michie's recent division of rich and poor women in fiction, especially in reference to *Jane Eyre*. See "Rich Woman, Poor Woman:

Toward an Anthropology of the Nineteenth-Century Marriage Plot," *PMLA* 124:2 (March 2009): 421–436, 421.

36. See Erickson 77.

37. Vickery, "Women and the World of Goods: A Lancashire Consumer and Her Possessions, 1751–1781," *Consumption and the World of Goods*, ed. John Brewer and Roy Porter (London: Routledge, 1993): 294.

38. This is only one of many secrets Jane does not share with Rochester. See Lisa Sternlieb, "*Jane Eyre*: 'Hazarding Confidences,'" *Nineteenth-Century Literature*, 53:4 (March 1999): 473, 475, 477; Richard Menke, *Telegraphic Realism: Victorian Fiction and Other Information Systems* (Stanford: Stanford University Press, 2008): 85–86.

39. Corbett 108.

40. Corbett 103.

41. See 337, 339. The obvious explanation for St. John's fraternal inadequacy is that he wants her to go to India with him as his wife, a relation that would secure him a helpmeet and double his wealth. But it is also part of his larger mistrust of contentment in blood kinship, his desire for Jane to look "beyond [. . .] sisterly society" (333).

42. As Corbett notes, "kinship is and has always been a made thing, a human artifact, rather than (as some Victorian anthropologists would argue) a naturally occurring phenomenon based in blood" (60). See Naomi Tadmor, *Family and Friends in Eighteenth-Century England: Household, Kinship, and Patronage* (Cambridge: Cambridge University Press, 2001): 152. According to Tadmor, individuals used kinship titles to "incorporate new members into his or her kinship group and announce their incorporation" (139); however, despite gesturing toward "much broader relationships of amity, sympathy, and fellowship" (159), Tadmor's examples focus primarily on "whether [. . .] the 'brother' was a brother by full blood, half-blood, by marriage only, or by both blood and marriage" (144)—a different case from Jane's transformation of cousins into siblings. For erotic uses of "sister," see Martha Vicinus, *Intimate Friends: Women who Loved Women, 1778–1928* (Chicago: The University of Chicago Press, 2004): xxvii, 50.

43. Glen 108; Alexander 414–415.

44. The novel is most likely set between 1798 and 1808 and narrated a decade later. See Raiskin 31 n.7. During this time, new income taxes were also levied in order to create wartime revenue: Stephen Dowell, *A History of Taxation and Taxes in England from the Earliest Times to the Year 1885, Vol. II: Taxation, From the Civil War to the Present Day*, 2nd ed. (London: Longmans, Green, and Co. and New York: 15 East 16th Street, 1888): 230, 262, 325; Martin Daunton, *Trusting Leviathan: The Politics of Taxation in Britain, 1799–1914* (Cambridge: Cambridge University Press, 2001): 32–33.

45. "Inheritance" or "death" duties encompassed separate probate, legacy, and succession taxes until they were consolidated in a single Estate Account Duty in 1880–1881 (Dowell Vol. 3:131; Daunton 225). Probate duty preceded distribution; legacy and succession duties were paid by the estate's heirs. Max West, *The Inheritance Tax*, in *Studies in History Economics and Public Law, Vol. 4*, ed. The University Faculty of Political Science of Columbia College (New York: Columbia College, 1893–1894): 171–310, 185.

46. See West 181. British acts from 1694 through 1780 taxed only the documentation, and were frequently evaded through failures to record the transfer (West 207; Daunton 226). See also Jeremy Bentham, "Supply without Burden" (1795), *The Works of Jeremy Bentham*, Published under the Superintendence of his Executor, John Bowring, Vol. II (Edinburgh: William Tait, and London: Simpkin, Marshall, & Co., 1843): 592.

47. The new law taxed transfers of moveable property (not merely its documentation), at different rates depending on the relation of testator and heir. In 1805 the tax was extended to include direct descendants (Dowell 3:134–135).

48. Nieces paid higher rates than daughters. The rate for cousins was even greater. (In 1796, a niece or sister would pay 2 percent, but a cousin would pay 3 percent. See Dowell 3:133.) Jane lessens her cousins' extra duty, if only rhetorically, by simultaneously shifting their

degree of kinship and their tax bracket. By gifting her property during her life, she may have found a way for them to evade legacy taxes entirely. To prevent similar evasion through deathbed gifts, gifts of personal property made within a year of the donor's death were also taxed. See West 209; also Dowell 3:131–133. Gifts in general were not taxed; several taxes on transfers of property were proposed but not passed in the first decades of the century (see Dowell 2: 218, 232, and 296–297).

49. Bentham 586. Bentham defines "near relations" as those "within the *degrees* termed *prohibited* with reference to marriage." See Corbett (esp. ch. 3) for Victorian debates about those prohibited degrees. See also West 280–281.

50. Mill, *Principles of Political Economy with Some of their Applications to Social Philosophy, Vol. II* (1848), 5th ed. (London: Parker, Son, and Bourn, 1862): 387 (book 5, ch. 2, sec. 3). Mill favors inheritance tax over income tax, reinstated in 1842 after twenty-six years. See also Daunton 224, 229–232; West 290.

51. St. John, who cannot conceive of exchange among equals, associates Christian sacrifice with unrepayable debts. Critics have generally joined St. John and Rochester in attributing self-sacrifice to Jane. See, for example, Ilana M. Blumberg, "'Love Yourself as Your Neighbor': The Limits of Altruism and the Ethics of Personal Benefit in *Adam Bede*," *Victorian Literature and Culture* 37:2 (2009): 543–560, 545, 558 n. 15. However, Blumberg's work generally offers an important and nuanced corrective to "the notion [. . .] that sacrificing oneself on someone else's behalf must not generate any personal reward." See Blumberg, "'Unnatural Self-Sacrifice': Trollope's Ethic of Mutual Benefit," *Nineteenth-Century Literature* 58:4 (March, 2004): 506–546, 507, 524.

52. Mill 384.

53. Mill 380.

54. Mill 380.

55. Charles Dickens, *Oliver Twist* (1837–1839), ed. Peter Fairclough (London: Penguin Books, 1966): 422.

56. Citations are from Elizabeth Barrett Browning, *Aurora Leigh*, ed. Margaret Reynolds (New York and London: W. W. Norton, 1996). Subsequent references refer to book and line numbers from this edition of the poem.

57. Gilbert and Gubar see the distinction in terms of identity—"Jane had to learn to be herself. Aurora has to learn not to be herself"—but this formulation mistakenly conflates receptiveness to gifts with self-abnegation (576).

58. See Perry, e.g., 40, 47; Staves 33–34, 128–129.

59. See Angela Leighton, "'Because Men Made the Laws': The Fallen Woman and the Woman Poet," in *Victorian Women Poets: Emily Brontë, Elizabeth Barrett Browning, Christina Rossetti*, ed. Joseph Bristow (New York: St. Martin's Press, 1995): 228.

60. Although legal reform was still decades away, this petition, submitted in March 1856, gained 26,000 signatures. See Shanley 31–33; Cheri Larsen Hoeckley, "Anomalous Ownership: Copyright, Coverture, and *Aurora Leigh*," *Victorian Poetry* 35:2 (Summer 1998): 135–161, esp. 142–143, 149; and Lana L. Dalley, "'The Least "Angelical" Poem in the Language': Political Economy, Gender, and the Heritage of *Aurora Leigh*," *Victorian Poetry* 44:4 (Winter 2006): 525–542, esp. 526–527, 529, 534.

61. Hoeckley claims that Aurora will receive £300 *annually* (see 149), but a flat sum seems far more likely, since the interest from Jane's £5000 (£250/year at a yield of 5 percent) allows her to live in comfort. Aurora's admission that she must "work with one hand for the booksellers" (III: 303), along with her decision to sell her father's books, suggests that her inheritance provides her with something closer to £15 per year, half of Jane's salary at Thornfield. For calculations of "competence" at 5 percent, see Rutterford and Maltby, "Women and Wealth," 152.

62. Aunt Leigh's situation is not unusual; according to David R. Green, even wives frequently inherited only "rights of use but not of disposal [. . .] merely bec[oming] the vehicle by which property was transferred to the next generation." See "To Do the Right Thing: Gender, Wealth, Inheritance and the London Middle Class," *Women and Their Money*, 142.

63. See Shanley 15, 25. As Hoeckley notes, however, "equity settlements often simply allowed a father to preserve family property [...] for future male heirs" (149).

64. See, for instance, Jacques Derrida, *Given Time: 1. Counterfeit Money*, trans. Peggy Kamuf (Chicago: University of Chicago Press, 1992): 7, 23.

65. According to English property law since the early seventeenth century, gifts require both delivery and acceptance. Although this law "presumes acceptance [...] whether or not the donee has learned of the gift," one may disclaim a "repugnant gift [...] by way of avoidance." See Richard Hyland, *Gifts: A Study in Comparative Law* (Oxford: Oxford University Press, 2009): 493. It is unclear how English law handles the death of a potential recipient, but in French and Italian law "acceptance is permitted only while both parties are alive" (Hyland 484, 488). See also Aubrey L. Diamond, "When is a Gift . . .?" *The Modern Law Review* 27:3 (May 1964): 357–360, and Hoeckley 149.

66. See, for instance, Lewis Hyde, *The Gift: Imagination and the Erotic Life of Property* (New York: Random House, 1983): xv; Marcel Mauss, *The Gift: The Form and Reason for Exchange in Archaic Societies*, trans. W. D. Halls (New York: W. W. Norton, 1990): 39–41.

67. For an extended discussion of Marian's insistence that she was raped rather than "seduced" after being deceived and then drugged, see Leighton, *Elizabeth Barrett Browning*, ch. 7, esp. 144–145, 148–151. Dalley argues that Barrett Browning's revision of "'man-made law'" includes not only questions of sexual morality but also of "women's economic autonomy" (530). I agree; economic *interdependence* through gift exchange is part of this legal revision.

68. Authorial negotiations proved more difficult for women than men. See Reynolds, "Editorial Introduction" 78–156, esp. 84–91.

69. See Dalley 532; Hoeckley 152.

70. Bentham 586, 589.

71. See Dowell 3:105, 109; Daunton 46, 82, 88, 90, 229–232.

72. [Edmund Saul Dixon], "Taxes," *Household Words, Conducted by Charles Dickens* 14:337 (6 September 1856): 181–185, see 183.

73. "Speech of Sir Robert Peel, on The Financial Condition of the Country, on Friday, March 11, 1842" (London: William Strange, 1842): 10. Daunton notes that despite its rocky start, the income tax became "a source of pride and celebration" to British national identity by the end of the nineteenth century (183).

74. Margaret Reynolds glosses the line's "ironic allusion to Matthew 6.3," but the difference between "alms" and "tax" seems significant. See *Aurora Leigh* 7 n.6. Women were far less likely to pay income tax than men; married women's income augmented their husbands', and single women rarely earned more than the £150 exempted from the tax. Jane's annual income at Thornfield is £30; working-class women made much less. In 1850, for instance, female workers employed in cotton manufacture made roughly 7 s. weekly. See Leone Levi, *Wages and Earnings of the Working Classes. Report to Sir Arthur Bass, M.P.* (London: John Murray, 1885): 119, 121–123.

75. Aurora helps Romney indirectly, echoing the partial blindness of the biblical "left hand" she invokes.

76. Jane's comments come after she has doused the fire Bertha set to Rochester's bed, preventing him from being burned alive.

77. Despite this cross-class "sisterhood," the narrative is not finally interested in and even perpetuates class conflict in its depictions of the poor. See Kaplan 11–12.

78. For more on a gift poetics that appears also in works by Christina Rossetti and Letitia Elizabeth Landon, see the conclusion of Chapter 4 in this volume and Rappoport, "Buyer Beware: The Gift Poetics of Letitia Elizabeth Landon," *Nineteenth-Century Literature* 58:4 (March, 2004): 441–473, 454, 457–458.

79. See, for instance, Marcus 93, 94.

80. See, for instance, Gilbert and Gubar 578; Rachel Blau DuPlessis, *Writing Beyond the Ending: Narrative Strategies of Twentieth-Century Women Writers* (Bloomington: Indiana University Press, 1985): 87; Case 29–30.

81. Reciprocity of gifts is often indirect, "deferred and different" from the original transaction. See Bourdieu 105.

82. See *Aurora Leigh* 301 n.8. In her December 26, 1856, letter to Anna Jameson, Barrett Browning distinguishes between Rochester's "hideously scarred" visage and the post-conflagration demise of Romney's optic nerve. See *The Letters of Elizabeth Barrett Browning, Vol. II*, ed. Frederic G. Kenyon (New York: The Macmillan Company, 1897): 245–246. An anonymous review of *Aurora Leigh*, attributed to George Eliot, deplores the "lavish mutilation of heroes' bodies" then popular. See *The Westminster and Foreign Quarterly Review* (January 1, 1857): 307.

83. See Elaine Showalter, *A Literature of Their Own: British Women Novelists from Brontë to Lessing* (Princeton: Princeton University Press, 1977): 152. Mary Wilson Carpenter discusses the common reading of Romney's blinding as "a metaphor for feminist vengeance directed at masculinist power" (55) in "Blinding the Hero," *Differences* 17:3 (Fall 2006): 52–68. For Fraiman as for others, the ending of *Jane Eyre* is ambivalent (116–118).

84. For a more sacrificial reading of Aurora's art, see DuPlessis 87.

85. Mauss 16; see also Derrida, *Given Time* 138.

86. See René Girard, "Mimesis and Violence," in *The Girard Reader*, ed. James G. Williams (New York: Crossroad, 1996): 11–12; Georges Bataille, *The Accursed Share: An Essay on General Economy, Vol. 1: Consumption*, trans. Robert Hurley (New York: Zone Books, 1991): 58.

87. For the history and ideal of the "companionate" marriage, see Lawrence Stone, *The Family, Sex, and Marriage in England, 1500–1800* (London: Weidenfeld and Nicolson, 1977): especially ch. 8, "The Companionate Marriage," 325–404, e.g. 392. See also Randolph Trumbach, *The Rise of the Egalitarian Family: Aristocratic Kinship and Domestic Relations in Eighteenth-Century England* (New York: Academic Press, 1978): 3–4, 119–124.

88. See also Carpenter 64–65.

89. See, for instance, Carpenter 62.

90. Jacques Derrida, *The Gift of Death*, trans. David Wills (Chicago: University of Chicago Press, 1995): 96, 107. See also 97–109.

91. Derrida, *Gift* 101, 109.

92. Even St. John, who—to the confusion of many readers—gets the final words of Jane's narrative, is granted partial access to its economy by the end, as the letter he sends Jane, which moves her to tears, speaks of his "anticipated [. . .] sure reward, his incorruptible crown" (385). Despite earlier rejecting her intended gift of a painting (320), he enters into reciprocal transactions with her. As the recipient of Jane's wealth, he sends her accounts of the work it funds. Also, like Rochester and Romney at the end of their stories, he sees himself as engaging in heavenly transactions that grant him divine returns on his sacrifices. If, unlike them, he "eagerly" foresees his own "reward," he has participated in this particular economy with clearer vision all along (385).

93. Alfred, Lord Tennyson, *In Memoriam*, 2nd ed., ed. Erik Gray (New York: W. W. Norton, 2003): line 6.

94. This recognition is limited to the system of exchange that the texts explicitly endorse; it does not include the larger systems that produced their wealth in the first place.

95. Derrida, *Given Time* 23.

96. For these (separate) insights about the dissolution of selfhood in *Aurora Leigh* and *Jane Eyre*, I am indebted to Hoeckley 156 and Gezari 82.

Chapter 3

1. Ruth Perry, *Novel Relations: The Transformation of Kinship in English Literature and Culture 1748–1818* (Cambridge: Cambridge University Press, 2004): 64. See also Mary Lyndon Shanley, *Feminism, Marriage, and the Law in Victorian England* (Princeton: Princeton University Press, 1989): esp. 103–104, 124–130.

2. Single women, of whom an 1851 census revealed a disproportionate number, were considered "redundant." Solutions offered for these middle-class women included emigration and religious sisterhoods. (Working-class women, of course, were no strangers to employment, though they took home less pay than men for comparable work. Factory girls such as *North and South's* Bessy figure prominently in Gaskell's more "industrial" fiction.) Some women addressed these concerns by seeking higher education for middle- and upper-class women; such arguments were taken up at mid-century by Anglican Sisterhoods, as I discuss in Chapter 4 of this volume. Whereas I read *Cranford's* hermetic community of women as a secular vision of these contemporary religious movements, Tonya McArthur aligns Gaskell's work even more closely with them. See "Unwed Orders: Religious Communities for Women in the Works of Elizabeth Gaskell," *The Gaskell Society Journal* 17 (2003): 59–76.

3. See, for example, Beth Fowkes Tobin, *Superintending the Poor: Charitable Ladies and Paternal Landlords in British Fiction, 1770–1860* (New Haven: Yale University Press, 1993): 3. The recent BBC film adaptation of *Cranford* calls attention to the contrast between Cranford's sympathetic, egalitarian exchange and upper-class condescension by including characters and plot lines from Gaskell's *My Lady Ludlow*.

4. Scrooge demonstrates his famous emotional transformation by buying a turkey for the Cratchits (Charles Dickens, *The Christmas Books, Volume 1: A Christmas Carol/The Chimes* [1843] [London: Penguin Books, 1971]: 129).

5. For example: Winifred Gérin, *Elizabeth Gaskell: A Biography* (Oxford: Clarendon Press, 1976): 123–125; Andrew H. Miller, *Novels Behind Glass: Commodity Culture and Victorian Narrative* (Cambridge: Cambridge University Press, 1995): 95, 101.

6. See Patricia A. Wolfe, "Structure and Movement in *Cranford,*" *Nineteenth-Century Fiction* 23:2 (September 1968): 161–176; Rae Rosenthal, "Gaskell's Feminist Utopia: The Cranfordians and the Reign of Goodwill," *Utopian and Science Fiction by Women: Worlds of Difference*, ed. Jane L. Donawerth and Carol A. Kolmerten (Syracuse: Syracuse University Press, 1994): 73–92. Mark Mossman presents a different binary, contrasting the Jenkyns sisters rather than the towns, in "Speech, Behavior, and the Function of Utopia: Restraint and Resistance in Elizabeth Gaskell's *Cranford,*" *Nineteenth-Century Feminisms* 5 (Fall/Winter 2001): 78–87. For Nina Auerbach, Cranford is a "homely little village . . . a sadly withering root of English kindness and community" (77), but one that triumphs over masculine "reality" (*Communities of Women: An Idea in Fiction* [Cambridge: Harvard University Press, 1978]: 82, 86). More recent complications of these oppositions examine gender construction (see Margaret Case Croskery, "Mothers Without Children, Unity Without Plot: *Cranford's* Radical Charm," *Nineteenth-Century Literature* 52:2 [September, 1997]: 198–220) or consider Cranford's economies in the context of contemporary culture. See Andrew H. Miller, "Subjectivity, Ltd: The Discourse of Liability in the Joint Stock Companies Act of 1856 and Gaskell's *Cranford,*" *English Literary History* (*ELH*) 61:1 (Spring 1994): 139–157; Lorna Huett, "Commodity and Collectivity: *Cranford* in the Context of *Household Words,*" *The Gaskell Society Journal* 17 (2003)· 34–49, and McArthur 59–76.

7. Despite disagreeing with his emphasis on *Cranford's* individualism, I join Amanpal Garcha in reading Gaskell's novella as far more "modern" than it is commonly seen to be. See *From Sketch to Novel: The Development of Victorian Fiction* (Cambridge: Cambridge University Press, 2009): 201, 210.

8. I agree with the first part of Auerbach's similar observation that "the ladies of Cranford are too involved with each other to interest themselves in their larger charitable mission" (85); in fact, however, the ladies' "larger mission," though sympathetic, is not actually charitable. Along similar lines, Garcha emphasizes "a social world functioning with a near-absence of feminine sympathy" (201) but reads "feminine sympathy" as a monolithic entity, rather than as diverse transactions, each directed toward particular recipients, for specific ends.

9. Elizabeth Gaskell, *Cranford* (Oxford: Oxford University Press, 1998); subsequent citations refer to this edition.

10. Newcomer Captain Brown offers his aid to an old, poor woman unable to carry her own dinner, shocking the ladies, who expect him to apologize for this deviation from their communal norms (10). See also Miss Pole's terror at an "Irish beggar-woman" who "all but forced herself in [. . .], saying her children were starving" (91).

11. Nursing has a similar function in the case of Captain Brown. The ladies become reconciled to him mainly through the illness of his daughter, whose state permits their rendering of "many little kindnesses" (16).

12. Auerbach 80.

13. See also Auerbach 84.

14. Gift theories largely reject the idea of a "free gift"—or the possibility of any pure "gift" at all—because of the implicit reciprocity that the gift demands. For discussions of the obligation entailed by gifts, see Marcel Mauss, *The Gift: The Form and Reason for Exchange in Archaic Societies*, trans. W. D. Hall (London: Routledge, 1990): 5, as well as subsequent discussions from theological, sociological, philosophical, and literary camps: John Milbank, "Can a Gift be Given? Prolegomena to a Future Trinitarian Metaphysic," *Modern Theology* 11:1 (January 1995): 122, 123; Pierre Bourdieu, *The Logic of Practice*, trans. Richard Nice (Cambridge: Polity Press, 1990): 105; Jacques Derrida, *Given Time: I. Counterfeit Money*, trans. Peggy Kamuf (Chicago: University of Chicago Press, 1992): 13; and Jill Rappoport, "Buyer Beware: The Gift Poetics of Letitia Elizabeth Landon," *Nineteenth-Century Literature* 58:4 (March 2004): 452–453, 456.

15. Garcha 209 (emphasis in original). Garcha considers self-interested individualism characteristic of the Cranfordians, whereas I see the novella as far more invested in communal effort and communal benefit. Self-interest, that is, does not have to occur at the expense of community.

16. See Thomas S. Kuhn, "Energy Conservation as an Example of Simultaneous Discovery," *Critical Problems in the History of Science: Proceedings of the Institute for the History of Science at the University of Wisconsin, September 1–11, 1957*, ed. Marshall Clagett (Madison: The University of Wisconsin Press, 1962): 321–356, 321–323. Kuhn's interest lies in the simultaneity of these discoveries: "Why, in the years 1830 to 1850 did so many of the experiments and concepts required for a full statement of energy conservation lie so close to the surface of scientific consciousness?" (323). See also Anson Rabinbach, *The Human Motor: Energy, Fatigue, and the Origins of Modernity* (Basic Books, 1990): 54. Carl B. Boyer, criticizing Kuhn's essay for what he sees as insufficient emphasis on quantitative elements, nevertheless agrees that the scientists' simultaneous suggestions were significant ("Commentary on the Papers of Thomas S. Kuhn and I. Bernard Cohen," *Critical Problems in the History of Science: Proceedings of the Institute for the History of Science at the University of Wisconsin, September 1–11, 1957*, ed. Marshall Clagett [Madison: The University of Wisconsin Press, 1962]: 384–390, 386–387). See also Donald Cardwell, "Science and Technology: The Work of James Prescott Joule," *Technology and Culture* 17:4 (October, 1976): 674–687, 682; J. T. Lloyd, "Background to the Joule-Mayer Controversy," *Notes and Records of the Royal Society of London* 25:2 (December, 1970): 211–225, 212, 219. For a nineteenth-century perspective on this simultaneity of discovery, see Edward L. Youmans, "Introduction," *The Correlation and Conservation of Forces: A Series of Expositions, by Prof. Grove, Prof. Helmholtz, Dr. Mayer, Dr. Faraday, Prof. Liebig and Dr. Carpenter*, ed. Edward L. Youmans (New York: D. Appleton and Company, 1865): xi–xlii: "The discoverer is . . . in a great degree, but the mouthpiece of his time" (xvi, also xxvi–xxviii). Youmans ranks the work of Joule, Mayer, and Grove highest among those engaged in similar scientific pursuits. For the relationship of these newer theories to earlier "belief in the interconversion of natural powers and the unity of nature," see P. M. Harman, *Energy, Force, and Matter: The Conceptual Development of Nineteenth-Century Physics* (Cambridge: Cambridge University Press, 1982): 21, 33–37.

17. Harman (51) attributes the "first use of the term 'energy' as a general and fundamental physical concept" to Thomson.

18. Kuhn 321. William Thomson (later Lord Kelvin) first coined the term *thermo-dynamics* in 1854. See Harman 45. Philip Mirowski sees this discovery as "the event that eventually recast the entire content of nineteenth-century physics." See *More Heat than Light: Economics as Social Physics: Physics as Nature's Economics* (Cambridge: Cambridge University Press, 1989): 35.

19. James Prescott Joule, *The Scientific Papers of James Prescott Joule, Published by Permission of The Physical Society of London* (London: Dawsons of Pall Mall, 1963). In this volume, see "On the Calorific Effects of Magneto-Electricity, and on the Mechanical Value of Heat" (1843): 149–159, 158 and "On the Changes of Temperature produced by the Rarefaction and Condensation of Air" (1845): 172–189, 172. For a detailed overview of various scientists' contributions to theories of conservation and later thermodynamics, see Harman 33–71.

20. Thomas Stone, "A Shilling's Worth of Science," *Household Words* 1:22 (August 1850): 510.

21. Dickens repaid Faraday in the currency that this project describes, making a gift of a book to thank the scientist for "so generously lending [. . .] his valuable notes." See his letter to Michael Faraday, December 11, 1850, *The Letters of Charles Dickens, Vol. Six, 1850–1852*, ed. Graham Storey, Kathleen Tillotson, and Nina Burgis (Oxford: Clarendon Press, 1988): 230. For other correspondence between Dickens and Faraday, see 105–106 (May 28, 1850); 108–109 (May 31, 1850); and 110 (June 6, 1850). See also George Levine, *Darwin and the Novelists: Patterns of Science in Victorian Fiction* (Chicago: University of Chicago Press, 1988): 124, 157.

22. In *The Letters of Charles Dickens*, editors Storey, Tillotson, and Burgis note that a later article by Percival Leigh, "The Chemistry of a Pint of Beer" (*Household Words* 2:47 [February 15, 1851]: 498–502) "was obviously suggested by" Faraday's lectures as well (230 n.1). *ProQuest British Periodicals* database, <http://gateway.proquest.com/openurl?url_ver=Z39.88-2004&res_dat=xri:bp-us:&rft_dat=xri:bp:article:x164-1851-002-47-000075:4>.

23. Levine 3. Cf. Jay Clayton, *Charles Dickens in Cyberspace: The Afterlife of the Nineteenth Century in Postmodern Culture* (Oxford: Oxford University Press, 2003): 8.

24. Gaskell saw the Exhibition a few months before *Cranford's* serialization began; her repeated visits contradict her professed lack of interest. See her letter to Anne Robson, September 1, 1851 (*The Letters of Mrs. Gaskell*, ed. J. A.V. Chapple and Arthur Pollard [Cambridge: Harvard University Press, 1967]: 159): "Of course we did the Exhibition. I went 3 times, & should never care to go again; but then I'm *not* scientific nor mechanical. Meta and Wm went often, but not enough they say."

25. Youmans, in 1865, considers the social application of correlation and conversion (xxxvi). Critical accounts of thermodynamics' social implications favor its second law (entropy), but, as Greg Myers shows, ideas about the conservation of energy also borrowed from and found their way into economic and political discourses. See "Nineteenth-Century Popularizations of Thermodynamics and the Rhetoric of Social Prophecy," in Patrick Brantlinger, ed., *Energy and Entropy: Science and Culture in Victorian Britain* (Bloomington: Indiana University Press, 1989): 307–338, esp. 326, 328–329.

26. Rabinbach 69–83, esp. 72–74, 76–81.

27. Nicholas Georgescu-Roegen, *Energy and Economic Myths: Institutional and Analytical Economic Essays* (New York: Pergamon Press, 1976): 8; cf. 4, 6–7. Mirowski further argues that "the economic theory used in the West [. . .] was essentially a simulacrum of the physics of the mid-nineteenth century" (3). See also 396. Myers similarly demonstrates that financial metaphors in later nineteenth-century textbooks on thermodynamics suggest widespread conviction that "value, like energy, cannot be produced, but only exchanged" (328).

28. Barri J. Gold, "The Consolation of Physics: Tennyson's Thermodynamic Solution," *PMLA* 117:3 (May 2002): 454–456; Stephen C. Brush, *The Temperature of History: Phases of Science and Culture in the Nineteenth Century* (New York: Burt Franklin & Co., 1978): 20. See also 24–26 for Brush's idea of science as "part of a cultural movement" (24).

29. Levine 156.

30. Levine 157, 269 n.9. Gold notes that mid-century uses of thermodynamics merged "physical and spiritual" interests (456). Stuart Peterfreund claims that interest in energy re-emerged "for reasons primarily metaphysical, and especially religious, rather than physical"; see "The Re-Emergence of Energy in the Discourse of Literature and Science," *Annals of Scholarship* 4:1 (1986): 24. See also Gold 455. For William Thomson's similar attribution of mechanical energy to "Creative Power alone," see "On a Universal Tendency in Nature to the Dissipation of Mechanical Energy" (from the Proceedings of the Royal Society of Edinburgh for April 19, 1852), reprinted in *Mathematical and Physical Papers by Sir William Thomson*, Vol. 1 (Cambridge: Cambridge University Press, 1882): 511.

31. Joule, "Calorific Effects" 158; see also Joule, "Changes of Temperature": "the power to destroy belongs to the Creator alone" (189).

32. William Robert Grove, *On the Correlation of Physical Forces: Being the Substance of a Course of Lectures Delivered in the London Institute in the Year 1843* (London: C. Skipper and East, 1846): 50. See also William B. Carpenter, "On the Mutual Relations of the Vital and Physical Forces," *Philosophical Transactions of the Royal Society of London* 140 (1850): 727–757, 730, <http://links.jstor.org/sici?sici=02610523%281850%29140%3C727%3AOTMROT%3E 2.0.CO%3B2-4>.

33. Gérin 52.

34. Walter M. Kendrick, *The Novel Machine: The Theory and Fiction of Anthony Trollope* (Baltimore: The Johns Hopkins University Press, 1980): 6–7.

35. Margaret Flanders Darby, "*Unnatural History: Ward's Glass Cases*," *Victorian Literature and Culture* 35 (2007): 635–647, 637.

36. Fern collecting became extremely popular for Victorians. See Lynn Barber, *The Heyday of Natural History 1820–1890* (Garden City: Doubleday, 1980): 111–115; Judith Flanders, *Inside the Victorian Home: A Portrait of Domestic Life in Victorian England* (New York: W. W. Norton, 2004): 162–166; David Elliston Allen, *The Victorian Fern Craze: A History of Pteridomania* (London: Hutchinson, 1969): 24, 43.

37. See Clayton 30–31, 35.

38. Darby 643.

39. See "Climates for All Nations," *Punch, or the London Charivari* (November 30, 1850): 229 (from *Gale 19th-Century UK Periodicals* database [Villanova University, Villanova, PA]), <http://find.galegroup.com/ukpc/basicSearch.do;jsessionid=47770154FEADEF3EF9 E321577C4F546A>, accessed March 8, 2009). More serious meditations on climate control suggested the benefits of these cases for controlling the air that tuberculosis patients breathed (Darby 641).

40. See, for instance, Byron, *Don Juan* Canto IV, Verses 113–114, in Jerome McGann, ed., *Lord Byron: The Major Works* (Oxford: Oxford University Press, 1986): 547.

41. In contrast with Cranford's conservation of sympathy, Matthew Rowlinson notes that diminishment is inherent to capitalism: "while money can transform itself into commodities and back again without losing value, it cannot do so without suffering the continual wear of its material substance and eventually becoming the residue of its own repeated use" ("Reading Capital with Little Nell," *The Yale Journal of Criticism* 9 [1996]: 347–380, 357). This idea is more consistent with the dissipation inherent to thermodynamics' second law.

42. For a good discussion of thermodynamics and form in later mid-century Victorian narrative, see Tina Young Choi, "Forms of Closure: The First Law of Thermodynamics and Victorian Narrative," *ELH* 74 (2007): 301–322, esp. 305–307, 316. While Choi is interested in how novels reflect tension between conservation's circulation and the overall linear plot of thermodynamics' second law of entropy, *Cranford* non-linear plot suggests a work even more firmly in line with conservation both thematically and formally.

43. See Gayle Rubin, "The Traffic in Women: Notes on the 'Political Economy' of Sex," *Toward an Anthology of Women*, ed. Rayna R. Reiter (New York: Monthly Review Press, 1975): 174, 183 and Luce Irigaray, "Women on the Market," *The Logic of the Gift: Toward an Ethic of*

Generosity, ed. Alan D. Schrift (New York: Routledge, 1997): 175, for discussions of how patriarchal kinship structures use gift exchange at the expense of women. By limiting participation in its community, however, Cranford in effect overturns these kinship structures, insisting that women can both join in and contribute to the organization of relationships. One key difference is the gift object: if, in the structures that Rubin and Irigaray denounce, women are the gifts exchanged between men, in *Cranford* women exchange sympathies in order to form and reinforce their own alliances. Annette B. Weiner suggests that women also participate in gift exchange by producing and protecting "inalienable possessions," a point to which I return in the next section of this chapter (*Inalienable Possessions: The Paradox of Keeping-While-Giving* [Berkeley: University of California Press, 1992]: 11, *passim*).

44. Miller, *Novels* 113.

45. Grove's similar point about the "reciprocal dependence" of forces in experimental physics is "[t]hat neither, taken abstractedly, can be said to be the essential or proximate cause of the others, but that either may, as a force, produce or be convertible into the other" (8).

46. For James Mulvihill, who is interested in economy more as management than as exchange, Matty's "happy returns" are a function of her moral and material management ("Economies of Living in Mrs. Gaskell's *Cranford*," *Nineteenth-Century Literature* 50:3 [December 1995]: 337–356, 355). See also Auerbach 85–87 and Miller, "Subjectivity" 151–154 for Matty's communal ethos.

47. Even sacrificial transactions have two sides; anthropological analyses of vast expenditures reveal the debt accrued through these often antagonistic displays of wealth. See, e.g., Mark Osteen, "Introduction: Questions of the Gift," *The Question of the Gift: Essays across Disciplines*, ed. Mark Osteen (London: Routledge, 2002): 1–41, 4.

48. As Auerbach notes, these returns—such as the gifts brought to "the old rector's daughter" in the shop—constitute part of Matty's "triumph" (87). While Auerbach attributes such returns simply to "Matty's innocent generosity," however, I see them as an element of *Cranford*'s larger structure of sympathetic conservation. The triumph thus belongs to the town, for maintaining itself by aligning "generosity" with forms of two-way exchange.

49. See, for instance, Lewis Hyde, *The Gift: Imagination and the Erotic Life of Property* (New York: Random House, 1983): 16: "Circular giving differs from reciprocal giving in several ways. First, when the gift moves in a circle no one ever receives it from the same person he gives it to. [...] I have to give blindly. And I will feel a sort of blind gratitude as well. The smaller the circle is—and particularly if it involves just two people—the more a man can keep his eye on things and the more likely it is that he will start to think like a salesman."

50. Reversing Matty's and Martha's fortunes and roles as giver/receiver may attempt to replace class alienation with affection (see Veena Singh, "Women Without Men: Family Patterns in *Cranford*," *Women's Writing: Text and Context*, ed. Jasbir Jain [Jaipur: Rawat Publications, 1996]: 76–83, 78). But the exchange serves Matty's class, not Martha's, by representing a servant's life as indistinguishable from her mistress's interests. Martha is never granted equal status in the exchange. Her plotline, more traditionally linear through matrimony, also sets her apart from the "ladies" of Cranford.

51. Garcha, too, notes that this aid comes from a "dispersed, concealed network"; I disagree with his reading that this network consequently limits the support that Miss Matty receives and allows her benefactors to avoid "feel[ing] fully responsible for her" (213).

52. Hilary M. Schor, *Scheherezade in the Marketplace: Elizabeth Gaskell and the Victorian Novel* (Oxford: Oxford University Press, 1992): 115–116; Mulvihill 354. Auerbach notes that Matty's "feminine and corporate" response (85) helps Cranford to "triumph over the failure of economic and masculine reality outside" (86).

53. Consider, for example, Karl Marx's equation for surplus value: M_1-C-M_2, where $M_2 > M_1$, or, in other words, where a commodity (C) is sold for more money (M_2) than the money that originally purchased it (M_1) ("The General Formula for Capital" from *Capital*, Vol. One, in *The Marx-Engels Reader*, ed. Robert C. Tucker, 2nd ed. [New York: W. W. Norton, 1978]:

329–336). Giovanni Arrighi offers a corrective to views of capitalism as simple accumulation in his discussion of systemic cycles of accumulation and diminished returns. See *The Long Twentieth Century: Money, Power, and the Origins of Our Times* (London and New York: Verso, 1994): 6–9, 214–215, 226.

54. Levine (160) contrasts this "stingy" law with the "abundance, excess, and multitudinousness" of evolutionary theories.

55. One exception is the ladies' miserly practice of hoarding butter, string, or candles—a form of conservation removed from circulation, and, as Marx notes, more akin to the capitalist's drive to accumulate. See Rowlinson 355–356. But hoarding is also antithetical to capitalism. The actual interest that presumably comprises a source of income for some of the ladies—their "genteel competency" (136)—is passed over almost entirely. *Cranford* ignores the capitalist exchanges that guarantee that continual interest, in favor of the conservationist activities it describes.

56. Miller, "Subjectivity" 151–154. See also Auerbach (85–86) for the element of "communality" in Miss Matty's dealings and Schor (6) for how this novel without a heroine models collective heroineship.

57. The (well-documented) interpenetration of "public" and "private" spheres, and the instability of the gender codes they purport to regulate, offers one way of seeing Cranford as inflected by Drumble, and helps to show why Cranford's "public" and "private" are interdependent. See, for instance, Jürgen Habermas, *The Structural Transformation of the Public Sphere: An Inquiry into a Category of Bourgeois Society*, trans. Thomas Burger (Cambridge: MIT Press, 1989); Mary Poovey, *Uneven Developments: The Ideological Work of Gender in Mid-Victorian England* (Chicago: University of Chicago Press, 1988); William Cohen, *Sex Scandal: The Private Parts of Victorian Fiction* (Durham: Duke University Press, 1996); and Karen Chase and Michael Levenson, *The Spectacle of Intimacy: A Public Life for the Victorian Family* (Princeton: Princeton University Press, 2000). But Cranford—a town that limits both domesticity and its supposed counterpart—is a unique case, as are the alternate public and private spheres it creates.

58. See Weiner, especially 6, 40–42, 150. Although most of the properties that Weiner describes are material objects, she also suggests that oral tradition and knowledge may be inalienable possessions (37, 64). Osteen explicitly compares the ways in which inalienable possessions and secrets are withheld from exchange: "they are given only in privileged circumstances, and given only to Others who are part of ourselves" ("Gift or Commodity?" *The Question of the Gift: Essays across Disciplines*, ed. Mark Osteen [London: Routledge, 2002]: 229–247, 244).

59. My discussion of secrets as a form of ownership extends Auerbach's observation that "white lies" and "the female error of discreet falsity, the code that is secret message rather than ethical imperative" (87, 89) play a powerful part in preserving Miss Matty. Miller also notes that "deceit encourage[s] a communal spirit" among the ladies (*Novels* 114).

60. According to Weiner, possessions become inalienable through their "exclusive and cumulative identity with a particular series of owners through time" (33). See also Weiner 6.

61. Jacques Derrida and Maurizio Ferraris, *A Taste for the Secret*, trans. Giacomo Donis, ed. Giacomo Donis and David Webb (Cambridge: Polity Press, 2001): 58.

62. Derrida, *Taste* 57.

63. Derrida argues that the secret is key to "the history of the responsible self" because the "other" (God, or ultimately any *other* "other") is secret, unknown—we are able to know only that we *don't* know. Our responsibility to that other *as fully other* from us entails a sacrifice of our responsibility to every *other* "other"—essentially a sacrifice of ethics to this one responsibility. See *The Gift of Death*, trans. David Wills (Chicago: University of Chicago Press, 1995): 7, 57–70, esp. 68–70. *Cranford* suggests an alternative model: an ethics that depends upon shared responsibility to *each* other's otherness, to the secrets that individuate each woman. I return to the idea of sacrifice in Part II of this volume.

64. D. A. Miller, *The Novel and the Police* (Berkeley: University of California Press, 1988): 207, 195. Miller's emphasis on the construction of subjectivity misses the possibility of social relationships not based on "subjection" (220).

65. Patricia Meyer Spacks, *Privacy: Concealing the Eighteenth-Century Self* (Chicago: The University of Chicago Press, 2003): 12, 15.

66. D. A. Miller 207.

67. Raymond Williams, *Keywords: A Vocabulary of Culture and Society* (New York: Oxford University Press, 1976): 243.

68. Indeed, the gendered nature of these secrets and their power within Cranford underscore how women's production and maintenance of "inalienable possessions" can shape gift communities as much as the exchanges brought about between men. See Weiner 2–4, 12.

69. Margot C. Finn, too, distinguishes between the individualism of capitalism and the "fictional descriptions of gifting [that] instead prized social groups" (*Character of Credit: Personal Debt in English Culture, 1740–1914* [Cambridge: Cambridge University Press, 2003]: 45). See also Finn 67.

70. Jeff Nunokawa usefully notes a paradox of the capitalist marketplace when he describes the model of ownership set forth in Dickens's *Dombey and Son* (1848): to share property is to lose it, but capital's symbolic value as communication makes such sharing inevitable. *Cranford*, a book that self-consciously recalls *Dombey* in the railway death that Captain Brown suffers (à la Carker) while reading Dickens, inverts the relationship between sharing and loss. See *The Afterlife of Property: Domestic Security and the Victorian Novel* (Princeton: Princeton University Press, 1994): 40–76, esp. 44–49, 56.

71. This does not imply that the ladies are not sexual. "Sucking" oranges—a practice that Miss Jenkyns associates with breastfeeding (26)—is eroticized; the ladies habitually withdraw to their bedrooms to indulge in it privately.

72. A number of the novel's critics describe its female community in terms of its vertical axes of relation. For motherhood, see Wolfe, esp. 170–172; Julie M. Fenwick, "Mothers of Empire in Elizabeth Gaskell's *Cranford*," *English Studies in Canada* 23:4 (December 1997): 409–426; and Croskery 198–220. Eileen Gillooly analyzes Cranford's daughters; see "Humor as Daughterly Defense in *Cranford*," *ELH* 59:4 (Winter 1992): 883–910, esp. 893, 887. I'm interested instead in the lateral bonds that constitute community through exchange. Unlike the relational direction of motherhood, horizontal affiliations can be directed outward, beyond the text to the reader's (and Gaskell's) "*we*."

73. Darby 641.

74. As Bruce Clarke notes, according to "classical thermodynamic laws [...] the material world is not only fallen, it is still and continuously falling"; "in some circles," he adds, "the second law [...] was interpreted as God's withdrawal [...]." See "Allegories of Victorian Thermodynamics," *Configurations* 4.1 (1996): 73, 76.

75. See Thomson's 1852 "On a Universal Tendency in Nature to the Dissipation of Mechanical Energy," 511–514. See also Clarke 76; Harman 66–67.

76. Gold 451, also 452–454. The term *entropy* itself was not used until 1865, by Rudolf Clausius (see Harman 65). See also Georgescu-Roegen 8–9.

77. Gold 451; Levine 159.

78. Here, I share Choi's conviction that "conservation" depends upon narrative (Choi 320), but the emphasis on recruitment rather than dispersal in Gaskell's novella underscores its *pre-entropic* depiction of the fragility of conservation; failures of conservation are not yet uniformly seen in terms of dissipation and decline.

79. Weiner 11. In Weiner's study, the passing of inalienable possessions from generation to generation, over time, increases their power to authenticate status. While time is certainly important to many of the secrets circulating in Cranford—the secrecy of Miss Matty's romance depends on the lapse of time since her youth—these secrets are transmitted laterally as much as vertically, spread among friends as much as passed down to generations.

80. Lauren M. E. Goodlad, *Victorian Literature and the Victorian State: Character and Governance in a Liberal Society* (Baltimore: The Johns Hopkins University Press, 2003): 11; Michel Foucault, *Discipline and Punish: The Birth of the Prison*, trans. Alan Sheridan (New York: Vintage Books, 1977): 193.

81. Ilana M. Blumberg suggests, with regard to Wilkie Collins's *The Moonstone*, that "not-offering information" can be a productive sacrifice—one that, in her argument, perpetuates both mystery and novel; along similar lines, Mary's gift of "not-offering information" helps to produce her narrative. See Ilana M. Blumberg, "Collins's *Moonstone*: The Victorian Novel as Sacrifice, Theft, Gift and Debt," *Studies in the Novel* 37:2 (Summer 2005): 162–186, 175.

82. Carpenter, working on the physiological ramifications of theories of conservation, notes "the extraordinary force developed under the influence of emotional excitement, which often calls forth a much greater measure of muscular power than the will can command" (746). Youmans, adding that "Dr. Carpenter, in his Physiology, has brought forward numerous exemplifications of this principle of the conversion of emotion into movement" suggests that "[a]s the emotions rise in strength . . . the various systems of muscles are thrown into action; and when they reach a certain pitch of intensity, violent convulsive movements ensue. Anger frowns and stamps; grief wrings its hands; joy dances and leaps—the amount of sensation determining the quantity of correlative movement" (xxxiv; see also xxxi–xxxv). See also Rabinbach's discussion of "labor power" as a way for nineteenth-century theorists to view the body's energy; it "was not merely analogous to other natural physical forces, it became one among them" (46). For D. A. Miller, such physical expression of emotion is often the counterpoint to repression (205); yet repression is a private activity, while concealment requires interaction. Focusing too firmly on the individual makes us lose sight of the communities so important to works by Gaskell, Barrett Browning, Brontë, and others.

83. Rosenthal 88. Rosenthal similarly attributes this transition to gained knowledge, but focuses on spoken transmissions. I consider Mary's most important education silent—the public knowledge of private secrets that initiates her is as much from her own tacit observations as from any statements told to her.

84. Schor, quoted from 87; see also 118.

85. Garrett Stewart, *Dear Reader: The Conscripted Audience in Nineteenth-Century British Fiction* (Baltimore: The Johns Hopkins University Press, 1996): 8.

86. Miss Betty Barker dresses her Alderney cow in flannel after it loses its hair in a lime-pit (5).

87. *The Letters of Mrs Gaskell.* See, respectively, 174, 290, and 747.

88. For the varied political stakes of conservation itself, see Choi 308–309.

89. See Weiner 8, for her astute comment that "The paradox inherent in the process of keeping-while-giving creates an illusion of conservatism, of refashioning the same things, of status quo. The problems inherent in 'keeping' nurture the seeds of change." We might also consider Youmans's earlier formulation of a similar thought: "Although at each stage of individual growth the forces of the organism [. . .] have each a certain definite amount of strength, yet these ratios are constantly changing, and it is in this change that development essentially consists. So with society" (xxxviii).

Chapter 4

1. Christina Rossetti, "A Safe Investment," *Commonplace and Other Short Stories* (London: F. S. Ellis, 1870): 241. The story was first published in the *Churchman's Shilling Magazine* 2 (1867): 287–292; my thanks to Simon Humphries for directing me to the story's original publication date. See also *The Letters of Christina Rossetti, Vol. 1: 1843–1873*, ed. Antony H. Harrison (Charlottesville: The University Press of Virginia, 1997): 305 n.2.

2. Jan Marsh, *Christina Rossetti: A Writer's Life* (New York: Viking Penguin, 1995): 367; see also "Banking and the Bank Act," *The Times*, December 26, 1866 (Issue 25691; col. E): 4.

3. Ilana M. Blumberg describes "Christian charity [. . . as] bedeviled by its inescapable effects: its givers automatically amass spiritual 'credit'" ("Collins's *Moonstone*: The Victorian Novel as Sacrifice, Theft, Gift and Debt," *Studies in the Novel* 37:2 [Summer 2005]: 162–186, 166, also 172). For Blumberg's excellent analysis of "a 'purist' view of sacrifice: the notion common among Victorians that sacrificing oneself on someone else's behalf must not generate any personal reward"—see "'Unnatural Self-Sacrifice': Trollope's Ethic of Mutual Benefit," *Nineteenth-Century Literature* 58:4 (March, 2004): 506–546, 507. Like Blumberg, I'm interested in the Victorian works that afford their sacrificial subjects a return; "whatever a person gives up in 'sacrifice' must ultimately be worth less to him or her than whatever he or she stands to receive in return" ("'Unnatural'" 525).

4. See Elizabeth K. Helsinger, "Consumer Power and the Utopia of Desire: Christina Rossetti's *Goblin Market*," *English Literary History (ELH)* 58:4 (Winter 1991): 903–933; Elizabeth Campbell, "Of Mothers and Merchants: Female Economics in Christina Rossetti's *Goblin Market*," *Victorian Studies* 33 (Spring 1990): 393–410; Terrence Holt, "'Men Sell Not Such in Any Town': Exchange in *Goblin Market*," *Victorian Poetry* 28 (1990): 51–67; Richard Menke, "The Political Economy of Fruit: *Goblin Market*," in *The Culture of Christina Rossetti: Female Poetics and Victorian Contexts*, ed. Mary Arseneau, Antony H. Harrison, and Lorraine Janzen Kooistra (Athens: Ohio University Press, 1999): 105–136; Catherine Maxwell, "Tasting the 'Fruit Forbidden': Gender, Intertextuality, and Christina Rossetti's *Goblin Market*," *The Culture of Christina Rossetti*, 75–102; Herbert F. Tucker, "Rossetti's Goblin Marketing: Sweet to Tongue and Sound to Eye," *Representations* 82 (Spring 2003): 117–133; and Krista Lysack, *Come Buy, Come Buy: Shopping and the Culture of Consumption in Victorian Women's Writing* (Athens: Ohio University Press, 2008): 15–43.

5. Christina Rossetti, "Goblin Market" (1862), *Victorian Literature 1830–1900*, ed. Dorothy Mermin and Herbert F. Tucker (Orlando: Harcourt College Publishers, 2002): 847, line 115. Subsequent references to the poem will refer to this edition, using line numbers rather than pages.

6. Menke 127.

7. See Dorothy Mermin, "Heroic Sisterhood in *Goblin Market*," *Victorian Poetry* 21:2 (Summer 1983): 117, and Helena Michie, *Sororophobia: Differences Among Women in Literature and Culture* (New York and Oxford: Oxford University Press, 1992): 32–37 for sisterhood and desire. Other treatments of sisterhood include Mary Arseneau, *Recovering Christina Rossetti: Female Community and Incarnational Poetics* (Houndmills: Palgrave Macmillan, 2004): 17–38; Janet Galligani Casey, "The Potential of Sisterhood: Christina Rossetti's *Goblin Market*," *Victorian Poetry* 29:1 (Spring 1991): 63–78; and Marjorie Stone, "Sisters in Art: Christina Rossetti and Elizabeth Barrett Browning," *Victorian Poetry* 32:3–4 (Autumn-Winter 1994): 339–364.

8. *The Gift: The Form and Reason for Exchange in Archaic Societies* (1954), trans. W. D. Halls (London: Routledge, 1990). Also Marshall Sahlins, *Stone Age Economics* (Chicago: Aldine Atherton, 1972): 133; Tucker 120.

9. Marsh, *Christina Rossetti* 234. D. G. Rossetti's "Jenny" also links golden coins and hair with prostituted sexuality (lines 340–342, 378). See Tucker 125 for Laura's exchange as a loss of imagination.

10. See Holt 52–54; Helsinger 907, 928. Margot C. Finn notes the confluence of nineteenth-century gift and retail practices in *The Character of Credit: Personal Debt in English Culture, 1740–1914* (Cambridge: Cambridge University Press, 2003): 88, 105.

11. Tucker 128. For Ruskin's interest in economics' roots (*oikonomos*, or household management) see Menke 118. During the late nineteenth century, economists' emphasis shifted from production to consumption. See Regenia Gagnier, *The Insatiability of Human Wants: Economics and Aesthetics in Market Society* (Chicago: University of Chicago Press, 2000): 40–48. Erika Rappaport addresses the Victorian "assumption that [shopping] was a 'natural'

feminine pastime" in *Shopping for Pleasure: Women in the Making of London's West End* (Princeton: Princeton University Press, 2000): 5, also 49–52, 106.

12. Mary Jean Corbett, *Family Likeness: Sex, Marriage, and Incest from Jane Austen to Virginia Woolf* (Ithaca: Cornell University Press, 2008): 60.

13. Helsinger 927; Arseneau, "Recovering" 32.

14. Jan Marsh, "Christina Rossetti's Vocation: The Importance of *Goblin Market*," *Victorian Poetry* 32 (1994): 238–239, 245; Marsh, *Christina Rossetti*, 218–228; Jerome J. McGann, "Introduction," *The Achievement of Christina Rossetti*, ed. David A. Kent (Ithaca: Cornell University Press, 1987): 4; Diane D'Amico, "Eve, Mary, and Mary Magdalene: Christina Rossetti's Feminine Triptych," *The Achievement of Christina Rossetti* 186; Casey 72–73; and Mary Wilson Carpenter, "'Eat me, drink me, love me': The Consumable Female Body in Christina Rossetti's *Goblin Market*," *Victorian Poetry* 29:4 (Winter 1991): 417–422.

15. See Marsh, "Vocation" 239–240. D. M. R. Bentley hypothesizes that Rossetti read to penitents in "The Meretricious and the Meritorious in *Goblin Market*: A Conjecture and an Analysis," *The Achievement of Christina Rossetti* 58, 69. Diane D'Amico treats Lizzie as a Christ figure in *Christina Rossetti: Faith, Gender, and Time* (Baton Rouge: Louisiana State University Press, 1999): 75–79. Arseneau treats the poem's relationship to Rossetti's devotional works; see *Recovering*, esp. 96–107, 121–128.

16. Eighteenth-century convents were fictional sites for Gothic intrigues and narrative resolutions. See, for instance, Ann Radcliffe, *The Mysteries of Udolpho* (1794), ed. Bonamy Dobrée (Oxford: Oxford University Press, 1998); Samuel Richardson, *Sir Charles Grandison* (1754), ed. Jocelyn Harris (London: Oxford University Press, 1972).

17. For example, Mary Shelley, "The Sisters of Albano," *The Keepsake for 1829*, ed. Frederic Mansel Reynolds (London: Hurst, Chance, and Co., 1828): 80–100.

18. Mary Astell is a notable forerunner in her advocacy of similar establishments in *A Serious Proposal to the Ladies, for the Advancement of their True and Greatest Interest by a Lover of her Sex* (London: R. Wilkin, 1694). *Early English Books Online (EEBO)*, <%3ca href=http://gateway.proquest.com.ps2.villanova.edu/openurl?ctx_ver=Z39.88-2003&res_id=xri:eebo&;rft_id=xri:eebo:citation:11665663>, accessed June 20, 2008.

19. England saw its first Protestant sisterhood in 1845 and at least twenty-five more by 1865. Susan Mumm's discovery of "approximately 10,000 women [. . . who] passed through ninety-odd communities between 1845 and 1900" (*Stolen Daughters, Virgin Mothers: Anglican Sisterhoods in Victorian Britain* [London: Leicester University Press, 1999]: 213, 214) increases earlier counts in Martha Vicinus, *Independent Women: Work and Community for Single Women, 1850–1920* (Chicago: University of Chicago Press, 1985): 50; and Elaine Showalter, ed. "Introduction," *Christina Rossetti: Maude* and *Dinah Mulock Craik: "On Sisterhoods"* and *A Woman's Thoughts About Women* (New York: New York University Press, 1995): xii.

20. See *Letters*. For correspondence with Jameson, see 226; 322; 407; for Parthenope Nightingale (Florence's sister): 358; 382; for F. Nightingale: 522. For discussion of sisterhoods' merits, see 158 and 115–118. Tonya Moutray McArthur, commenting on the "traditional Christian underpinning" of *Cranford*, has called it a "flexible version [of such a sisterhood,] in which single women maintain a domestic household while interacting in a corporate manner." See McArthur, "Unwed Orders: Religious Communities for Women in the Works of Elizabeth Gaskell," *The Gaskell Society Journal* 17 (2003): 67, 66. In *Cranford*, however, the paired display of Mrs. Jamieson's Bible and Peerage (75) suggests that Christianity was only one of many important traditions in this community. Whereas McArthur claims that the women of *Cranford* "subordinate individuality" in the interests of corporate life (67), I have argued that secrets allow them to preserve their own differences. Gaskell's allegiances were torn between religious and domestic sisterhoods. (See *Letters* 322.)

21. See, for instance, "Art. VI.-1. Miss Sellon and the Sisters of Mercy. An Exposure of the Constitution, Rules, Religious Views, and Practical Working of their Society, obtained through a 'Sister' who has recently seceded," [Review] *Dublin Review* 32:64 (June 1852): 436–464. *ProQuest British Periodicals* database, <http://gateway.proquest.com/openurl?url_ver=Z39.88-2004&res_dat=xri:bp-us:&rft_dat=xri:bp:article:6389-1852-032-64-000023>.

22. Jane comments that Eliza's "sense [. . .] will be walled up alive in a French convent" (206). Such views of nunneries were common. See, for example, "Taking the Veil," *The Achill Missionary Herald, and Western Witness* (Dublin, Ireland) 132 (June 26, 1848): 77. *Gale 19th Century UK Periodicals* database: *Empire* collection, <http://find.galegroup.com.ezp1.villanova.edu/ukpc/infomark.do?docType=LTO&contentSet=LTO&sort=DateAscend&tabID=T012&docId=CC1903348199&prodId=NCUK&searchId=R5&callistoContentSet=NCUP&docLevel=FASCIMILE&qrySerId=Locale(en,,):FQE=(tx,None,15)taking the veil:And:LQE=(MB,None,16)NCUK-1 OR NCUK-2$$&type=multipage&retrieveFormat=MULTIPAGE>_DOCUMENT&currentPosition=127&version=1.0&userGroupName=vill_main&searchType=BasicSearchForm&docPage=article&source=gale>. For a contemporary defense of the cloister see "Art. VII.—*Sisters of Charity Catholic and Protestant, Abroad and at Home*," [Review] *Dublin Review* 38:76 (June 1855): 442–460, esp. 459–460. *ProQuest British Periodicals* database, <http://gateway.proquest.com/openurl?url_ver=Z39.88-2004&res_dat=xri:bp-us:&rft_dat=xri:bp:article:6389-1855-038-76-000051>.

23. For Sisterhoods' relationships to Church hierarchy, see Showalter xii; Vicinus 58, 50; and Mumm 137–165, esp. 145–147, 153–157.

24. Mumm 18. See also Anna Jameson, *Sisters of Charity, Catholic and Protestant, and The Communion of Labor* (Boston: Ticknor and Fields, 1857): 70, 119; [Dinah Mulock Craik], "The Author of 'John Halifax, Gentleman,'" "About Sisterhoods," *Longman's Magazine* (London: Longmans, Green, and Co., January 1883): 308, 309; Dorice Williams Elliott, *The Angel out of the House: Philanthropy and Gender in Nineteenth-Century England* (Charlottesville: University of Virginia Press, 2002): 129; and Mumm 190–194.

25. Jameson 80.

26. See Frances Power Cobbe, "What Shall We Do with Our Old Maids?" (*Fraser's Magazine*, November, 1862), reprinted in *Prose by Victorian Women: An Anthology*. ed. Andrea Broomfield and Sally Mitchell (New York: Garland, 1996): 244–245. See Jameson 91; Florence Nightingale, *Cassandra and Suggestions for Thought* (New York: New York University Press, 1992): 219.

27. Jameson 275.

28. See Marsh, "Vocation" 238; Stone 356; Elliott 133.

29. These lectures sold well (Elliott 115) see "*Sisters of Charity, Catholic and Protestant, Abroad and at Home*," [Review] *Athenaeum* 1432 (April 7, 1855): 399–400. *ProQuest British Periodicals* database, <http://gateway.proquest.com/openurl?url_ver=Z39.88-2004&res_dat=xri:bp-us:&rft_dat=xri:bp:article:e932-1e855-000-32-028277>.

30. Jameson 169, 25–26, 30, 268 (emphasis in original).

31. Jameson 150–151, 187.

32. See note 10; Holt 52–54; Helsinger 907, 928.

33. A notice about the Sisters of Mercy in Plymouth notes that "the Sisters are contemplating the erection of 'A Home.' The appeals for pecuniary aid [. . .] have been responded to by donations exceeding 14,000*l.*" See *John Bull* (London, England) 1,504 (October 6, 1849): 627. *Gale 19th Century UK Periodicals* database: *New Readerships* collection, http://find.galegroup.com.ezp1.villanova.edu/ukpc/infomark.do?docType=LTO&contentSet=LTO&sort=DateAscend&tabID=T012&docId=DX1900704967&prodId=NCUK&searchId=R7&callistoContentSet=NCUP&docLevel=FASCIMILE&qrySerId=Locale(en,,):FQE=(tx,None,33)miscellaneous church intelligence:And:LQE=(jn,None,9)john bull:And:LQE=(da,None,4)1849:And:LQE=(MB,None,16)NCUK-1 OR NCUK-2$$&type=multipage&retrieveFormat=MULTIPAGE_DOCUMENT&currentPosition=114&version=1.0&userGroupName=vill_main&searchType=BasicSearchForm&enlarge=true&docPage=page&source=gale.

34. Elliott 130, 129.

35. "The Unseen Charities of London," *Fraser's Magazine for Town and Country* 39:234 (June 1849): 639–647, 640. *ProQuest British Periodicals* database, <http://gateway.proquest.com/openurl?url_ver=Z39.88-2004&res_dat=xri:bp-us:&rft_dat=xri:bp:article:e513-1849-039-34-000103>.

36. Alison Booth, *How to Make It as a Woman: Collective Biographical History from Victoria to the Present* (Chicago: University of Chicago Press, 2004): 136, 146–147. For a discussion of Victorian "ambivalence toward direct remuneration," see Monica F. Cohen, *Professional*

Domesticity in the Victorian Novel: Women, Work and Home (Cambridge: Cambridge University Press, 1998): 4, also 5, 23. Without wages, Sisterhoods could be paid in admiration. See "The Protestant Nuns of Devonport," *The Bengal Catholic Herald* (Calcutta, India), 22 (June 2, 1849): 30. *Gale 19th Century UK Periodicals* database: *Empire* collection, <http://find. galegroup.com.ezp1.villanova.edu/ukpc/infomark.do?docType=LTO&contentSet=LTO&s ort=DateAscend&tabID=T012&docId=CC1903327666&prodId=NCUK&searchId=R6& callistoContentSet=NCUP&docLevel=FASCIMILE&qrySerId=Locale(en,,):FQE=(tx,Non e,28)protestant nuns of devonport:And:LQE=(MB,None,16)NCUK-1 OR NCUK-2$$typ e=multipage&retrieveFormat=MULTIPAGE_DOCUMENT&currentPosition=1&version =1.0&userGroupName=vill_main&searchType=BasicSearchForm&docPage=article&sour ce=gale>; "The Sisters of Mercy," *The Lady's Newspaper* 140 (September 1, 1849): 114. *Gale 19th Century UK Periodicals* database: *New Readerships* collection, <http://find.galegroup.com. ezp1.villanova.edu/ukpc/infomark.do?docType=LTO&contentSet=LTO&sort=DateAscen d&tabID=T012&docId=DX1900457662&prodId=NCUK&searchId=R8&callistoContent Set=NCUP&docLevel=FASCIMILE&qrySerId=Locale(en,,):FQE=(tx,None,16)sisters   of mercy:And:LQE=(MB,None,16)NCUK-1 OR NCUK-2$$&type=multipage&retrieveForma t=MULTIPAGE_DOCUMENT&currentPosition=174&version=1.0&userGroupName=vi ll_main&searchType=BasicSearchForm&docPage=article&source=gale>.

37. Elliott 130.

38. Jameson 185, 187, 194, 289–290, 194. For the sisters' finances and "remunerative" laundries, see Mumm 82–85, 87.

39. "The Protestant Nuns of Devonport" 305.

40. "The Sisters of Mercy at Plymouth," *The Lady's Newspaper* 114 (March 3, 1849): 115. *Gale 19th Century UK Periodicals* database: *New Readerships* collection, <http://find.galegroup. com.ezp1.villanova.edu/ukpc/infomark.do?docType=LTO&contentSet=LTO&sort=Dat eAscend&tabID=T012&docId=DX1900456512&prodId=NCUK&searchId=R8&callisto ContentSet=NCUP&docLevel=FASCIMILE&qrySerId=Locale(en,,):FQE=(tx,None,28) sisters of mercy at plymouth:And:LQE=(MB,None,16)NCUK-1 OR NCUK-2$$&type=m ultipage&retrieveFormat=MULTIPAGE_DOCUMENT&currentPosition=2&version=1. 0&userGroupName=vill_main&searchType=BasicSearchForm&docPage=article&sourc e=gale>. See also A. Booth 146.

41. Craik 309.

42. Jameson 287. Unlike many women before the Married Women's Property Act of 1882, sisters were able to choose the communities that would benefit from their dowries.

43. Jameson 274, 278, 275.

44. "Unseen Charities" 640: "[S]uch is the result of the efforts of a few ladies, who *might* have devoted their time to needle-work and party-going, but whose energies were thus nobly directed." See also "The Sisters of Mercy (September 1, 1849): 114.

45. See Mumm 82, 42–43 and 35–36.

46. Jameson 276.

47. Craik similarly distinguishes between the "useful" "Low Church Bible-woman" and the "grace" of the lady in a nun's dress (312).

48. See also Krista Lysack, "Goblin Markets: Victorian Women Shoppers at Liberty's Oriental Bazaar," *Nineteenth-Century Contexts* 27: 2 (June 2005): 159; Lysack, *Come Buy, Come Buy* 41.

49. Carpenter 428; Tucker 126; Menke 127–128; and Helsinger 923.

50. Menke 127.

51. Holt 58.

52. See Linda E. Marshall, "'Transfigured to His Likeness': Sensible Transcendentalism in Christina Rossetti's *Goblin Market*," *University of Toronto Quarterly* 63:3 (Spring 1994): 436; Arseneau, *Recovering* 128. Marylu Hill also suggests similarities between Lizzie and Christ in "'Eat Me, Drink Me, Love Me': Eucharist and the Erotic Body in Christina Rossetti's *Goblin Market*," *Victorian Poetry* 43:4 (Winter 2005): 462. Menke 128; Tucker 128–129; and Maxwell 85 offer explanations of the juice's restorative powers.

53. For Eucharistic cravings, see Caroline Walker Bynum, *Holy Feast and Holy Fast: The Religious Significance of Food to Medieval Women* (Berkeley: University of California Press, 1987): 58–59, 116, 119, 137, 157. For the saving power of women's bodily excretions and the tradition of a lactating Christ, see also the chapters "Food in the Lives of Women Saints" (113-49) and "Food in the Writings of Women Mystics" (150-86).

54. Lysack notes that the goblins seek "endless consumer desire more than curls or coins" (159). Victor Roman Mendoza emphasizes the abstracted status of Lizzie's silver penny as fetish in "'Come Buy': The Crossing of Sexual and Consumer Desire in Christina Rossetti's *Goblin Market*," *English Literary History* 73:4 (2006): 930.

55. Gayle Rubin and Luce Irigaray were among the first to argue that gift economies operate solely at the expense of women. Since their influential work, theorists including Annette B. Weiner (*Inalienable Possessions: The Paradox of Keeping-While-Giving* [Berkeley: University of California Press, 1992]) and Aafke E. Komter (*Social Solidarity and the Gift* [Cambridge: Cambridge University Press, 2005]: 8, 76) have shown how women have also benefited from gift economies. Kathy Psomiades, Mary Jean Corbett, and Sharon Marcus have all argued for forms of Victorian kinship based on models of relation other than heterosexual exchange. See Gayle Rubin, "The Traffic in Women: Notes on the 'Political Economy' of Sex," *Toward an Anthology of Women*, ed. Rayna R. Reiter (New York: Monthly Review Press, 1975): 157–210; Luce Irigaray, "Women on the Market," ed. Alan D. Schrift, *The Logic of the Gift: Toward an Ethic of Generosity* (New York: Routledge, 1997), 174–189.

56. Anna Eliza Bray, *A Peep at the Pixies; or, Legends of the West* (London: Grant and Griffith, 1854); Anna Eliza Bray, *Traditions, Legends, Superstitions, and Sketches of Devonshire on the Borders of The Tamar and the Tavy, Illustrative of Its Manners, Customs, History, Antiquities, Scenery, and Natural History, In a Series of Letters to Robert Southey, Esq.,* 3 vols. (London: John Murray, 1838); and Thomas Keightley, *The Fairy Mythology, Illustrative of the Romance and Superstition of Various Countries, a New Edition, Revised and Greatly Enlarged,* (London: H. G. Bohn, 1850). See also Marsh, "Vocation" 235–137; Marsh, *Christina Rossetti* 230–231; and Maxwell 89.

57. Molly Clark Hillard reminds us that a goblin itself was "quite literally money," the Victorian "slang for a sovereign"; see "Dangerous Exchange: Fairy Footsteps, Goblin Economies, and *The Old Curiosity Shop*," *Dickens Studies Annual* 35 (2005): 75.

58. Pixies "pinch the maids" who neglect household duties and reward them with coin or "silver pennies" for setting water basins by chimneys (Bray, *Traditions* 174–175; 188–189). Keightley describes punitive pinching and rewards of pennies (289, 291, 342, 344) or silver pennies (348). These penny-pinching goblins deliver pinches in lieu of pennies.

59. Roles shift in other fairy traditions. Though Shakespeare's puck Robin Goodfellow interferes with butter churning, Milton's "L'Allegro" tells "how the drudging goblin sweat / To earn his cream-bowl duly set" (*John Milton: A Critical Edition of the Major Works*, ed. Stephen Orgel and Jonathan Goldberg [Oxford: Oxford University Press, 1991]: 22–25, lines 105–106). More recently, *Harry Potter's* enslaved house elves partake in this second, more labor-intensive tradition.

60. Hillard suggests that commercial, market transactions with fairies and goblins similarly entailed danger (72–73). Ellen Moers attributes the goblins' violence to the rough physicality of siblings. See *Literary Women* (Garden City: Doubleday, 1976): 105–106.

61. "Peter's penny, n." OED Online. Oxford University Press, <http://www.oed.com/view/Entry/141833?redirectedFrom=Peter%20pence>, accessed May 16, 2011.

62. Keightley 291.

63. Many thanks to Michael Hargreave Mawson and Hugh MacDougall for their responses to my initial VICTORIA listserv query about silver pennies (December 5, 2005). See also "The Penny," *Coins of England and Great Britain*, ed. Tony Clayton, 46 (June 22, 2005, December 6, 2005), <http://www.tclayton.demon.co.uk/penny.html>.

64. Ted Wilson, *Battles for the Standard: Bimetallism and the Spread of the Gold Standard in the Nineteenth-Century* (Burlington: Ashgate, 2000): 28. For the valuation and fetishization of gold in "Goblin Market," see Mendoza 923–927.

65. See Brian Robinson, *Silver Pennies and Linen Towels: The Story of the Royal Maundy* (London: Spink & Son, 1992): 67–68; see also 69–73. My thanks to Karen Selesky for this reference. Since the reign of Queen Elizabeth I, the pennies were distributed in purses not unlike Lizzie's (line 324). See Robinson 32–33.

66. See "St. John 13:5-16" in "The New Testament" of *The Bible: Authorized King James Version*, ed. Robert Carroll and Stephen Prickett (Oxford: Oxford University Press, 1997): 135; Frank Prochaska, *Royal Bounty: The Making of a Welfare Monarchy* (New Haven: Yale University Press, 1995): 5. "Maundy" derives from "commandment."

67. "Maundy, n." OED Online. Oxford University Press, <http://www.oed.com/view/Entry/115188?redirectedFrom=Maundy>, accessed May 16, 2011.

68. See Robinson 120; 126–127; and Tony Clayton, "Maundy Money," *Coins of England and Great Britain*, ed. Tony Clayton, 6, 24 (October 2003, December 6, 2005), <http://www.tclayton.demon.co.uk/maund.html>.

69. Menke 107.

70. Robert W. Ackerman, "The Pearl-Maiden and the Penny," *Romance Philology* 17:3 (1964): 621–623; Jill Mann, "Satisfaction and Payment in Middle English Literature," *Studies in the Age of Chaucer* 5 (1983): 26; Mendoza 929. For Christ as host, see Anne Howland Schotter, "The Paradox of Equality and Hierarchy of Reward in *Pearl*," *Renascence* 33 (1981): 174.

71. See Mendoza 931. No evidence suggests that sovereigns participated actively in the service for 233 years after 1698 (Robinson 42, 48–49). See also Prochaska 6–7, 209.

72. The silver of her penny is also a "white" metal.

73. Lysack, *Come Buy* 31–33. See also Susan Meyer, *Imperialism at Home: Race and Victorian Women's Fiction* (Ithaca: Cornell University Press, 1996): 17, 89, 119–120. As Moers observes, the crossing of species was a particularly Victorian fantasy (102).

74. The goblins' relationship to Lizzie is one of "negative reciprocity," at the socially distant end of a spectrum of reciprocities tying generosity to kinship. See Sahlins 193–199.

75. Mermin 109; James Eli Adams, *Dandies and Desert Saints: Styles of Victorian Manhood*, (Ithaca: Cornell University Press, 1995): 61–65; Seth Koven, *Slumming: Sexual and Social Politics in Victorian London* (Princeton: Princeton University Press, 2004): 231–236; and Lysack, *Come Buy* 33–34.

76. Sharon Marcus argues that the female intimacy frequently associated with sisterhood-by-affiliation was central to, rather than in conflict with, those family ties. See *Between Women: Friendship, Desire, and Marriage in Victorian England* (Princeton: Princeton University Press, 2007): 78–79, 99, 102. Mary Jean Corbett also explores the significance of first-family ties of sisterhood to the constitution of conjugal (or second-family) relations; see *Family Likeness* 80–84.

77. Jameson 219, 224.

78. For the hierarchical relationship of sister to penitent, see Mumm 106, 108, and Vicinus 78.

79. For Lizzie and Laura's mutual redemption, see Casey 68; Carpenter 427–428.

80. This accords with the foot-washing ceremony (*pedilavium*) that predated Maundy money. Temporarily reversing clerical hierarchies, senior clergy served the lower clergy as well as the poor (Robinson 19).

81. This is the redemption that, according to the speaker of D. G. Rossetti's "Jenny," could not be effected by another woman; see Mermin 111; Maxwell 94; Marsh, "Vocation" 244.

82. In contrast with the (limited, but strong) intimacy between women that works like "Goblin Market" and *Cranford* highlight, one review of Jameson's *Sisters of Charity* emphasizes women's discord as the price of the marriage market: "It is scant measure of generosity, and still less of justice, that women mete out towards women,—each of them seeks to make her own terms secretly with the world [. . .]." See "*Sisters of Charity, Catholic and Protestant, Abroad and at* Home," [Review] *The Athenaeum* 1432 (April 5, 1855): 399–400, 400.

83. For "fallenness" as "attenuated agency," see Amanda Anderson 14–15. D'Amico stresses the spiritual nature of sexual fall (*Christina Rossetti* 70–71) and Rossetti's refusal to see women as "forever fallen" ("Eve" 188).

84. See also Michie 33–37. The importance of sin or a fall to salvation is consistent with other Victorian religious doctrine, including that of the Salvation Army. For sisterhood as constructed by difference, by envy that demands intimacy, see Mary Ann O'Farrell, "Sister Acts," *Women's Studies Quarterly* 34:3/4 (Fall–Winter, 2006): 154–173.

85. Lysack, *Come Buy* 30, notes the role of visuality in markets' production of desire. A donor's "return" on a gift often comes from sources other than the initial recipient. See Lewis Hyde, *The Gift: Imagination and the Erotic Life of Property* (New York: Vintage Books, 1983): 16.

86. Constance W. Hassett, *Christina Rossetti: The Patience of Style* (Charlottesville: University of Virginia Press, 2005): 25, 28, 27. For Rossetti's euphoric *silence*, see 53–63.

87. Tucker 119.

88. McGann 8.

89. For a rich discussion of how "a self-preserving, self-appreciating ethic" (545) merged with and countered traditions of sacrifice, see Blumberg, "'Love Yourself as Your Neighbor': The Limits of Altruism and the Ethics of Personal Benefit in *Adam Bede,*" *Victorian Literature and Culture* 37 (2009): 543–560, esp. 545–553.

90. Rappaport 28; Lysack, *Come Buy* 6–7.

Chapter 5

1. Mrs. [Sarah Stickney] Ellis, *The Women of England, Their Social Duties, and Domestic Habits* (London: Fisher, Son, & Co., 1839): 155.

2. See Introduction, nn.4 and 5.

3. Ilana M. Blumberg, "'Unnatural Self-Sacrifice': Trollope's Ethic of Mutual Benefit," *Nineteenth-Century Literature* 58:4 (March 2004): 524. See also 509.

4. Judith Walkowitz, *City of Dreadful Delight: Narratives of Sexual Danger in Late-Victorian London* (Chicago: University of Chicago Press, 1992): 53, also 52–59; Seth Koven, *Slumming: Sexual and Social Politics in Victorian London* (Princeton: Princeton University Press, 2004): 236–248. For a good overview see Ellen Ross, "Introduction: Adventures among the Poor," *Slum Travelers: Ladies and London Poverty, 1860–1920,* ed. Ellen Ross (Berkeley: University of California Press, 2007): 1–39.

5. See, for example, Norman H. Murdoch, *Origins of the Salvation Army* (Knoxville: University of Tennessee Press, 1994): 132; Andrew Mark Eason, *Women in God's Army: Gender and Equality in the Early Salvation Army* (Ontario: Wilfrid Laurier University Press, 2003): 52–53, 90–91.

6. See Eason; Pamela J. Walker, *Pulling the Devil's Kingdom Down: The Salvation Army in Victorian Britain* (Berkeley: University of California Press, 2001); Roger J. Green, "Settled Views: Catherine Booth and Female Ministry," *Methodist History* 31:3 (April 1993): 131–147, 134; Christine Parkin, "Pioneer in Female Ministry," *Christian History* 26 (1990): 10–13. For Army women in the United States, see Diane Winston, *Red-Hot and Righteous: The Urban Religion of the Salvation Army* (Cambridge: Harvard University Press, 1999); Daphne Spain, *How Women Saved the City* (Minneapolis: University of Minneapolis Press, 2001). See also "Capt. Bessie Wilkins, of Seven-Dials Slum Post," *War Cry (WC),* October 20, 1888, 5. In "London Slum Work," *WC,* April 6, 1889, Major Cooke took "much pleasure in correcting a wrong impression made in the 'War Cry' lately [...] that there are only two women District Officers in The Army. For over ten months, Adjutant Isabel Cartner has been one of our Slum D.O.s. Since then we have had Mrs. Major Rapkin and Mrs. Staff-Capt. Hall as Slum D.O.s" (13). While "Mrs. Major" and "Mrs. Staff-Capt." illustrate the precedence of men's titles in the Army (see also Eason 53, 90–91), the correction shows the Army's emphasis on providing, and appearing to provide, leadership roles to women. The *War Cry* takes pride in Cartner's subsequent promotion ("Adjutant Isa Cartner, of the Slum Work," *WC,* July 13, 1889, 3). Cooke adds that "every Slum-post [...] ought to have at least two men, and two women soldiers, transferred from the corps [....] our difficulty is to keep the men, as we have so few men soldiers." "Our Slum Work," *WC,* March 29, 1890, 4. Glenn K. Horridge notes records

of "723 male and 746 female officers" in 1883 ("William Booth's Officers," *Christian History* 26 (9:2) 1990: 14–17, 15). See also Emma Booth, [chapter] "IV," *Called Out!*: "Through the clamour of tongues pronouncing this way and that, for a woman's feet, He points her still to the narrow road of service and sacrifice, which, without respect of sex or persons, He calls us each to tread" (Herbert H. Booth and Emma M. Booth, ed., *Called Out!* 30).

7. Eason 138. Slum work was "heavily in women's hands," records Ellen Ross (*Slum Travelers* 3). A notice for the first annual meeting of the London Slum Work, to be conducted by Colonel Nicol, Staff-Captain and Mrs. Cooke, advertises over forty Slum Sisters; a subsequent write-up calls attention to details of their costume: "At the foot of their aprons was worked in red letters, 'Slum Saviour.'" See *WC*, February 11, 1888, 16, and February 25, 1888, 10.

8. Winston and Eason offer more substantial treatments of Salvation Army Slum Sisters. Most literary critics and historians favor more "literary" representatives—George Bernard Shaw's *Major Barbara* (1907) and Margaret Harkness's *Captain Lobe* (1889), later renamed *In Darkest London*. See Deborah Epstein Nord, *Walking the Victorian Streets: Women, Representation, and the City* (Ithaca: Cornell University Press, 1995): 194–195. Nord's is a key study of female exploration and social investigation, but her claim that "Harkness's [. . .] middle-class slum workers, Salvation Army officers, and Fabians reflect a contemporary reality that had as yet no literary existence" passes over a significant literature created by Army slum workers.

9. While the slum work with which I am concerned first appeared in print in November 1884, the work had been going on for months, and emerged from other Army projects and divisions, including its Midnight Rescue Brigade and Women's Training Home. Similarly, the work does not cease with Booth's *In Darkest England*. Reports on Slum Sisters persist into the early decades of the twentieth century; Blanche B. Cox, an important figure in the early "Cellar, Gutter, Garret Brigade," published "Reminiscences" in 1932. But the period between the work's inauguration in print in 1884 and the publication of *In Darkest England* in late 1890 offers the largest concentration of material on this work, as well as the opportunity to see it as it emerged, shaped by those involved in the slum work rather than by their General in promotion of his larger plan. The monthlies *All the World* (*AW*) and *The Deliverer* (*Del*) began circulation during this period as well, in 1884 and 1889, respectively.

10. Staff-Capt. and Mrs. Cooke refer to the merger in "London Slum Work," *WC*, February 18, 1888, 10.

11. All images in this chapter were digitized for me courtesy of The Salvation Army International Heritage Centre at the William Booth College in London. I am indebted to archivist Gordon Taylor, archive assistant Karen Thompson, and photographic archivist Alex von der Becke at the Centre for their generous assistance.

12. By the 1880s, of course, not only Catholics, Methodists, and Quakers alike but also Anglican women used the term *sister* to refer to religious workers and community members, and Slum Sisters note the precedence. See, for example, Kathleen Barrington, *Four Years' Slumming* 3; "Ensign Polly Redmead," *WC*, February 21, 1891, 3; Ross, *Slum Travelers* 9. But the extent to which this term becomes a means for writing about charitable activity—becoming both description and appeal for such a large audience—is significant.

13. "Sisters of the People," *AW* 25:10 (October 1904): 556; [George] R[ailton], "Our Murdered Sisters," *Del* 1:2 (August 1889): 19.

14. S[uzie] F. Swift, *In the Slums!* 13; Harriette Field, "My Sister and Yours," *Del* 1:9 (March 1890): 115. The longer quote notes that the girls were "mothered by Captain Polly and sistered by her lassies." Maternal titles and phrases were reserved for unique cases, such as "Mother" Harriet Webb (see *WC*, December 25, 1888, 10) and "Mother" Booth. "Sistered," here, is the action of many slum workers.

15. Blanche B. Cox, "[Chapter] VI," (Herbert H. Booth and Emma M. Booth, ed., *Called Out!* 45).

16. Ross, *Slum Travelers* 16, 17.

17. Ross, *Slum Travelers* 18.

18. Ross, *Slum Travelers* 17.

19. Ballington Booth, "Why Wear the Uniform?" *WC*, August 22, 1883, 1.

20. "Staff-Captain Blanche B. Cox: (For India)," *WC*, July 30, 1887, 3. "Miss Booth" was also credited with initiating the workers' dress (*AW* 1:9 [July 1885]: 165).

21. B. B. Cox, "Cellar, Gutter, and Garret,'" *WC*, December 25, 1884, 1.

22. The term *sister* was interchangeable, but even this is a matter of sheer rhetorical force; "real" sisters, as Helena Michie and others have discussed, would not be simply interchangeable. This attempt to claim sisters across cultural difference, and to speak for them, is similar to that rejected by late-twentieth-century feminists, but it is important to note that the attempt—certainly not new to the 1970s—is a significant act of production and obfuscation, not merely a gloss over difference.

23. Ellen Ranyard's working-class bible women and nurses, like the Slum Sisters, traveled in uniform and took on housekeeping duties. Her program began in 1858. See Ross, *Love and Toil: Motherhood in Outcast London, 1870–1918* (Oxford: Oxford University Press, 1993): 172–173; F. K. Prochaska, *Women and Philanthropy in Nineteenth-Century England* (Oxford: Clarendon Press, 1980): 126–129.

24. Ross, *Love* 12, 14; "'Fierce Questions and Taunts': Married Life in Working-Class London, 1870–1914," *Feminist Studies* 8:3 (Autumn 1982): 575–602, 577; "Hungry Children: Housewives and London Charity, 1870–1918," *The Uses of Charity: The Poor on Relief in the Nineteenth-Century Metropolis*, ed. Peter Mandler (Philadelphia: University of Pennsylvania Press, 1990):161–196, 171; Koven 11.

25. For analyses of neighborhood support and working-class charity, see Ellen Ross, "Fierce" 576, 578, 587–588; "Hungry" 166–167; *Love* 116, 134–135, 156, 178.

26. Railton, "To the Editor of the Times," *The Times*, January 10, 1889, 6.

27. Ross, *Slum Travelers* 5, 23. As Ross notes, many upper-class "ladies" also pushed far beyond this pejorative label in their diverse philanthropic efforts. See my introduction to *Giving Women* for a description of Dickens's paradigmatically problematic middle-class visitor, Mrs. Pardiggle.

28. As Nord suggests of Webb's "slumming," disguise may have enabled the Slum Sisters themselves, as well as slum inhabitants, to enjoy the idea of sisterhood (Nord, *Walking* 192).

29. Emma M. Booth and Ballington Booth, "Our Christmas Training Home Barracks Appeal," *WC*, December 23, 1882, 1.

30. Mrs. [Lydia Corbett] Cooke, "The London Slum Corps," *WC*, January 8, 1887, 14.

31. Such doubled portraits were popular entryways to discussions of the Slum Sisters. See the images "Slum Saviours," *WC*, December 24, 1887, 1 and "Slum Evangels," the cover image of the Third Annual Slum Report.

32. Koven 198–204. See also Anne McClintock's study of Arthur Munby's photographs of his wife, working-class Hannah Cullwick (*Imperial Leather: Race, Gender and Sexuality in the Colonial Contest* [New York: Routledge, 1995]: 132–139).

33. The Army published many accounts of its growth: see [Army Commissioner George] R[ailton], *The Salvation War 1883*, 64; R[ailton],"Four Years Ago and Now," *AW* IV:11 (November 1888): 363; R[ailton], "The Army Going Down!" *WC*, August 10, 1882, 1; and William Booth's "General Order," *WC*, August 17, 1882, 2.

34. B[lanche] B. Cox, T.H.S., "Please Read This, and Help!" *WC*, November 8, 1884, 2.

35. S[uzie] F. S[wift], *In the Slums!* 7; Kathleen Barrington, *Four Years' Slumming* 34.

36. "£. s. d. Can Our Soldiers Be Bought? How Much a Week?" *WC*, September 14, 1882, 2.

37. Books and pamphlets combine descriptive reports with financial statements, as in [James Cooke, attrib.,] *Slum Evangels*. See also Helen Irvine, "The Legitimizing Power of Financial Statements in the Salvation Army in England, 1865–1892," *The Accounting Historians Journal* 29:1 (2002): 1–36, 31. William Booth's "General Order" stresses the Army's need to "be beyond the suspicion of being influenced by selfish motives" and emphasizes "the interests of the Army," attempting to distinguish between personal and communal good (*WC*, August 17, 1882, 2); see also Staff-Captain [James J.] Cooke, "The London Slum Work," *WC*, July 2, 1887, 3 and Major [James J.] Cooke, "London Slum Work," *WC*, April 6, 1889, 13.

Swift offers descriptions as well as "accounts" in the form of figures—hours spent visiting, families visited, persons prayed with, persons rescued (S. F. S., *In the Slums!* 9). See also W. Bramwell Booth, *Light in Darkest England* 47; Railton, "Four Years Ago and Now" 363; Cox, "Celler, Gutter and Garret," *WC*, March 26, 1887, 15; and *What Is Being Done by the "Darkest England" Social Scheme* 24. The interest in precise and accountable observations overlaps with the growing emphasis on scientific analysis that Beatrice Webb and others used in their social investigations. See Nord, *Walking* 190–191 and Elliott 142–143.

38. George Bernard Shaw, *Major Barbara* (London: Penguin Books, 1957): Act II: 109; Winston 223. Shaw's preface speculates on the Army's "economic deadlock"—the necessity of using money earned through (in his example) Bodger's distillery and Undershaft's cannon foundry—but calls "[t]he notion that you can earmark certain coins as tainted [. . .] an unpractical individualist superstition," as his eponymous heroine must learn (Shaw 25, 26).

39. [Cooke, attrib.] *Slum Evangels* 18.

40. Florence Kinton, Lieutenant, "One Little Sister," *AW* 5:11 (November 1889): 514.

41. Mrs. Captain G., "A Word to God's Women. A Plea for the Rescue Work," *WC*, May 6, 1885, 1; Cooke, "Easter in the Slums," *WC*, April 19, 1890, 12; B[lanche] C[ox], "Special Appeal," *WC*, March 21, 1885, 4.

42. ["A sister engaged in the Cellar, Gutter, and Garret work," qtd.] "Our Household Troops," *WC*, January 23, 1886, 2.

43. S. F. S., *In the Slums!* 5; S.F. S., "Hidden Woes," *WC*, February 27, 1886, 4; Kathleen Barrington, *Four Years' Slumming* 14.

44. J. J. Cooke, Staff-Captain, "Life in the London Slums," *WC*, April 9, 1887, 15. See also Tim Macquiban, "Soup and Salvation: Social Service as an Emerging Motif for the British Methodist Response to Poverty in the Late 19th Century," *Methodist History* 39:1 (2000): 28–43 and Shaw's dramatic representation of this theory (79, 100).

45. See Louise A. Jackson, "'Singing Birds as well as Soap Suds': The Salvation Army's Work with Sexually Abused Girls in Edwardian England," *Gender & History* 12:1 (April 2000): 107–126, 112; McClintock 210–211; Captain Harriett Charterie, "Back Room and Garret Work at Exeter," *WC*, March 14, 1885, 2.

46. E. Harriman, "A Cellar, Gutter, and Garret Lass," "Cellar, Gutter and Garret Work (Whitechapel Branch), *WC*, September 10, 1887, 6.

47. See, for instance, Capt. Myers, "(*Original for the War Cry.*) Precious Cleansing," *WC*, March 7, 1883, 4; A Sister at Worthing, "Make Me Clean," *WC*, February 18, 1885, 2; F. G. Roadway, "The Cleansing River," *WC*, February 18, 1885, 4; *Slum Evangels* 30.

48. [Staff-Captain Cooke], "The London Slum Work," *WC*, July 9, 1887, 4; "The Slum Work in the Provinces. An Interview with Mrs. Major Cooke," *WC*, March 2, 1889, 10; James J. Cooke, Staff-Captain, "Deeper Down, or The London Slums," *WC*, March 19, 1887, 13.

49. "Sisters of the People," *AW* 25:10 (October 1904): 555.

50. Judith Flanders, *Inside the Victorian Home: A Portrait of Domestic Life in Victorian England* (New York: W. W. Norton, 2004): 114. Isabella Beeton's popular *Book of Household Management* (1861) recommends that the "mistress" of a household use her superior knowledge to visit and instruct the poor "in cleanliness, industry, cookery, and good management." See Nicola Humble, ed., *Mrs. Beeton's Book of Household Management* (Oxford: Oxford University Press, 2000): 13. For their erotic and imperialist readings of Victorian dirt and social housekeeping, see Koven (esp. ch. 4, 183–227); McClintock (ch. 5, 207–231). See also Spain's discussion of public, "redemptive spaces"—rescue homes, shelters, and infant hospitals—opened by Slum Sisters in the United States (xii, 24–25, 106–110, 121).

51. See, for example, Gaskell, *Mary Barton: A Tale of Manchester Life*, ed. Macdonald Daly (London: Penguin Books, 1996): 61–62; *North and South*, ed. Patricia Ingham (London: Penguin Books, 1995): 289; Friedrich Engels, *The Condition of the Working Class in England* (Oxford: Oxford University Press, 1993): *passim*, e.g., 140. Jane Eyre shares this focus on cleanliness; after receiving the inheritance discussed in Chapter 2 of this volume she claims that her "first

aim will be [...] to *clean down* Moor House from chamber to cellar; my next to rub it up with beeswax, oil, and an indefinite number of cloths, till it glitters again" (332).

52. H. E. Govan, "Slumdom in Glasgow," *AW* 6:2 (February 1890): 70.

53. "£. s. d. Can Our Soldiers Be Bought? How Much a Week?" *WC*, September 14, 1882, 2.

54. Cooke, "Slumdom's Bitter Cry," *Del* 2:10 (April 1891): 158.

55. Elaine Freedgood, *The Ideas in Things: Fugitive Meaning in the Victorian Novel* (Chicago: University of Chicago Press, 2006): 61; Engels e.g., 77.

56. Freedgood 72.

57. Cox, "Please Read This, and Help!" *WC*, November 8, 1884, 2. See also "Cellar, Gutter, and Garret Work. (By one of the lasses engaged in it.)" *WC*, August 19, 1885, 1; Cadet Theresa Garner, "A Cellar, Gutter and Garret Lass," "Cellar, Gutter & Garret. Every Day Scenes," *WC*, March 5, 1887, 4; and "Cellar, Gutter and Garret Work," *WC*, December 4, 1886, 3.

58. Other slum workers relied upon ethnographic language as well. See Ross, *Love* 14, 16–17.

59. Ross, *Love* 42–44.

60. Nineteenth-century ethnographers, according to Christopher Herbert, increasingly considered culture not as a system of controls imposed upon free, natural desire but rather as a system of desire (*Culture and Anomie: Ethnographic Imagination in the Nineteenth Century* [Chicago: The University of Chicago Press, 1991] 51–53).

61. See Deborah Cohen's discussion of how the middle classes came to associate moral virtue with home furnishings, 1–31, esp. 1–3, 19–25, 30.

62. For conversion narratives, see Koven 114. The Army shared its focus on domestic space with others writing about female visitors. See, for example, Nord, *Walking* 207, and Elliott 144. While these literary critics emphasize workers' maternalism, however, Slum Sisters make the domestic space available not to mothers but to sisters—who were to be, according to *War Cry* advertisements, "young, healthy women, able to sing, speak, and take hold of God in prayer, whose hearts are full of compassion for souls; ages from twenty-one to about twenty-eight or twenty-nine." "Wanted, Slum Officers," *WC*, January 5, 1889, 11. See also Staff-Capt. and Mrs. Cooke, "London Slum Work," *WC*, August 4, 1888, 7.

63. See, for example, James J. Cooke, Major, "To Slum Candidates," *WC*, December 7, 1889, 6; Staff-Captain and Mrs. Cooke, "London Slum Work," *WC*, March 24, 1888, 12; and J[ames] J. Cooke, Major, "Christmas in the London Slums," *WC*, January 12, 1889, 12.

64. *WC*, May 7, 1884, 1.

65. "Cellar, Gutter and Garrett Work," *WC*, December 4, 1886, 3.

66. Although middle-class men were initially the primary furnishers of the homes over which they enjoyed ultimate control, women acquired greater prerogative over their domestic space by the end of the century; "feminism and home decoration," Cohen notes, "were complementary pursuits" (105, also 95–101).

67. Cohen 12–13, 25. "Incarnationalism," which preached forgiveness and the alleviation of suffering, offered a less punitive model of God and Christianity than older evangelical models of self-denial. Cohen notes that "[i]n this new schema, sackcloth and ashes were neither necessary nor inherently virtuous" (25). Slum Sisters' pairing of sacrifice with acquisition seems a tense negotiation of these models.

68. Cohen 19. Whereas Cohen discusses the cultivation of good *taste* among the middle classes, this category is absent from Slum Sisters' frantic efforts to fill the destitute slum homes of the lower classes.

69. Mrs. Onslow, "First Annual Meeting of the London Slum Work," *WC*, February 25, 1888, 10.

70. Ibid.

71. Ibid.; Mahlah, "Odd Leaves From My Note-Book: Down Slumdom," *WC*, February 19, 1887, 12.

72. Major J[ames] J. Cooke, "Plums for the Slums," *WC*, November 2, 1889, 11.

73. Cf. Cohen 116.

74. Finn, *Character* 9, 12. Freedgood's insistence on a "thing" culture that pre-dated and informed commodity culture is a related, though not identical, mingling of systems. See, for instance, 8, 157.

75. See Cox, "Cellar, Gutter, and Garret," *WC*, December 25, 1884, 1; "A Week in the Slums. By a Hospital Nurse," *WC*, October 4, 1890, 13; H. E. Govan, "Slumdom in Glasgow," *AW* 6:2 (February 1890): 70; Sergeant-Major M. Giles, "A Story of Seven Dials. Told by a Hallelujah Lass at Bristol VI," *WC*, April 2, 1887, 2.

76. S. F. S., "Cellar, Gutter, and Garret," *AW* 1:10 (August 1885): 189.

77. See also Walkowitz, *City* 194: "Even the police hesitated to enter the notorious Wentworth and Dorset streets alone." Biographies of English prison reformer Elizabeth Fry and others suggest that the fearless woman ministering was a common nineteenth-century trope (Alison Booth 149).

78. See, for instance, Cohen 86.

79. [George] R[ailton], *Twenty-one Years' Salvation Army* 202. See also "Slummers & Slumdom. Celebration of the Second Anniversary," *WC*, March 9, 1889, 4.

80. Barrington 14.

81. "Sisters of the People," *AW* 25:10 (October 1904): 556; and [George] R[ailton], "Our Murdered Sisters," *Del* 1:2 (August 1889): 19. References to the Whitechapel murders make explicit the sexual nature of the danger to which the Slum Sisters exposed themselves. See Walkowitz, *City* esp. 206 (also 207–227) for an important discussion of these murders.

82. S. F. S., "Within the Circle of the Whitechapel Murders," *WC*, October 13, 1888, 4; Staff-Captain Cooke, D.O., "London Slum Work. The Latest Whitechapel Murder," *WC*, December 1, 1888, 4; and "Our Year's Retrospect," *WC*, January 5, 1889, 9.

83. Other Army work, such as its "Midnight Rescue Brigades," involved rescuing prostitutes off of the streets.

84. See Nord, *Walking* e.g., 12, for a wonderful discussion of the *flâneuse*.

85. For the attenuated agency of prostitutes in nineteenth-century representations, see A. Anderson 41.

86. *Slum Evangels* 18.

87. Booth, "General Order," *WC*, August 17, 1882, 2; *Slum Evangels* 33.

88. Cox, "Cellar, Gutter and Garret," *WC*, February 3, 1886, 4; S.F.S., "For Body and Soul," *WC*, January 26, 1889, 1.

89. S.F.S., "Glimpses of East End Life," *WC*, December 25, 1889, 18.

90. S.F.S., "For Body and Soul," *WC*, January 26, 1889, 1; S.F.S., "Cellar, Gutter, and Garret," *AW* 1:9 (July 1885): 164; Govan, "Slumdom in Glasgow," *AW* 6:2 (February 1890): 70; "Ebb Tide in the East End," *Del* 1:4 (October 1889): 38.

91. *Slum Evangels* 33.

92. James Campbell, "Combat Gnosticism: The Ideology of First World War Poetry Criticism," *New Literary History* 30:1 (1999): 203–215, 207. Slum Sisters' claims to military knowledge are particularly interesting in light of what Campbell calls "combat gnosticism" because, as he notes, in the World War I poetry he describes such knowledge is limited to male combatants and pitted against the ignorance of female civilians (Campbell 204–207). Thus Slum Sisters' military designations give them more than rank and uniform, and pre-World War I Army writing offers some interesting literary precursors to the later "trench lyric."

93. J. Campbell 203–208.

94. Major [James J. Cooke], "London Slum Work," *WC*, April 6, 1889, 13. See also Blumberg, "Collins's *Moonstone*" 166, 172.

95. Koven 151–154, 334 n.30.

96. Cf. Murdoch, 118–119; [George] R[ailton], *The Salvation War 1883* 63–64; R[ailton], *Twenty-one Years' Salvation Army* 70; and S. F. S., "For Body and Soul," *WC*, January 26, 1889, 1.

97. R[ailton], *The Salvation War 1883* 63; R[ailton], *Twenty-one Years' Salvation Army* 71.

98. See R[ailton], *Salvation War 1883* 64, and "Office Notes," *AW* 5:8 (August 1889): 385.

99. "Ensign Polly Redmead," *WC*, February 21, 1891, 3. See also Major Eileen Douglas, "The Slums," *AW* 21:1 (January 1900): 44; and "The New Slum Report," *WC*, March 9, 1889, 6.

100. Slum Sisters accumulate stories that build upon each other to emphasize the vastness of the work: "We know of scores of similar cases, but what are they to what we don't know?" The stories are similar not only because of the similar plights many inhabitants faced but also because their cumulative value is greater than that of any individual story. The repetition of risky stairways, for example, underscores the risks the Sisters take and their ubiquity, the need for help and the daily climbing that makes the Slum Sisters fit to determine solutions. Staff-Capt. Cooke, "London Slum Work," *WC*, January 28, 1888, 6. See also "Rescue Work in East London. [. . .] A Letter from Mrs. [Lizzie S.] Hodgson," *WC*, January 14, 1885, 2: "If I had space, and could tell the history of these dear sisters [. . .]"; Cadet Sarah E. Owen, "Cellar, Gutter, and Garret Work in Seven Dials," *WC*, January 17, 1885, 4: "Out of many cases which might be given [. . .] we cannot find space or time to mention more than two."

101. Laurel Brake, *Subjugated Knowledges: Journalism, Gender and Literature in the Nineteenth Century* (New York: New York University Press, 1994): 86.

102. Brake 86–91.

103. Brake 91. For an important complication of this trajectory, see Rachel Sagner Buurma, "Anonymity, Corporate Authority, and the Archive: The Production of Authorship in Late-Victorian England," *Victorian Studies* 50:1 (Autumn 2007): 26–27. According to Buurma, and borne out in the work of the Army, the narrative of individuation existed in tandem with other persisting ideas of corporate authorship.

104. Buurma 19.

105. Buurma 20.

106. For instance: "Cellar, Gutter, and Garret Work. (By one of the lasses engaged in it.)," *WC*, August 19, 1885, 1.

107. B[lanche] B. Cox, "Cellar, Gutter, and Garret; or, our Training Home at Work on 'Outcast London,'" *WC*, December 25, 1884, 1.

108. See, for instance, Ross, *Slum Travelers* 12.

109. "An Afternoon with the Slum Officers," *AW* 3:7 (July 1887): 210.

110. "Midnight Rescue Brigade, Glasgow. Letters from our Girls," *WC*, June 13, 1883, 3.

111. *Slum Evangels* 25–26.

112. James J. Cooke, "The London Slums," *WC*, January 22, 1887, 2.

113. See, for example, Major J[ames] J. Cooke, "Easter in the Slums," *WC*, April 19, 1890, 12; "Angel of the Slums," *Del* 2:6 (December 1890): 102–103; "Between the Poles," *WC*, March 22, 1890, 4.

114. W. Bramwell Booth, *Light in Darkest England in 1895* 46.

115. This rewriting was not unique to Army publication practices. As Laurel Brake notes of the "old journalism" that attempted to create a unified periodical style, "[t]o some extent then, and probably particularly in the early contributions of a young critic, the published piece was the result of a collaboration between contributor and editor, sometimes with the cooperation of the author and sometimes without it" (Brake 16). In the *War Cry*, collaboration evidently effaces class as well as individual authorial style.

116. C., "The '*War Cry*.' A Peep Between the Scenes," *WC*, April 10, 1886, 7.

117. See, for example, S. F. S., "Life As It Is," *AW* 2:12 (December 1886): 295, 299.

118. S. F. S., "Cellar, Gutter, and Garret," *AW* 1:9 (July 1885): 164.

119. "Hell is a city much like London," is line 147 of Shelley's "Peter Bell the Third" (the first line of the third part, "Hell.") Despite the importance she places on her citations, Swift actually misquotes Shelley, adding the "very."

120. See John Plotz, *Portable Property: Victorian Culture on the Move* (Princeton: Princeton University Press, 2008): 57, 63.

121. S. F. S., "Lower Still!" *AW* 2:3 (March 1886): 56.

122.   From December 1886 through December 8, 1888, the *War Cry* refers to and contains regular articles on the slums by Staff-Captain, sometimes with Mrs. Staff-Captain [Lydia Corbett] Cooke; on December. 15, 1888 his title becomes Major (10).
123.   Sometimes spelled "Readmead."
124.   J[ames J.] Cooke, "Our Third Birthday," *AW* 5:11 (November 1889): 502.
125.   S. F. S., "For Body and Soul," *WC*, January 26, 1889, 1. George Railton also expresses interest in the *War Cry*'s production history. See R[ailton], *Twenty-one Years' Salvation Army* 70–73.
126.   "Sisters of the People," *AW* 25:10 (October 1904): 555.

Chapter 6

1.   Daniel J. Kevles, *In the Name of Eugenics: Genetics and the Uses of Human Heredity* (New York: Alfred A. Knopf, 1985): ix.
2.   Angelique Richardson, "The Eugenization of Love: Sarah Grand and the Morality of Genealogy," *Victorian Studies* 42:2 (Winter 1999/2000): 227–255, 231.
3.   Erika Diane Rappaport, *Shopping for Pleasure: Women in the Making of London's West End* (Princeton: Princeton University Press, 2000): 38, 52. Although the advent of department stores and public spaces for women fueled such anxieties in the late nineteenth century, the anxieties themselves were not new. See Amanda Vickery, *The Gentleman's Daughter: Women's Lives in Georgian England* (New Haven: Yale University Press, 1998): 5.
4.   Rappaport 82.
5.   Sir Edward Bulwer-Lytton, *The Coming Race* (1871) (Orchard Park: Broadview Press, 2002).
6.   The years immediately preceding *The Coming Race* saw significant public activism by and for women. In 1869, female ratepayers gained the right to vote in local elections (Mary Lyndon Shanley, *Feminism, Marriage, and the Law in Victorian England* [Princeton: Princeton University Press, 1989]: 109). The year 1869 also saw the petition of the Ladies' National Association for the Repeal of the Contagious Diseases Act, signed by 128 women. Bills for suffrage, married women's property rights, and the repeal of the CDAs all appeared before Parliament in 1870 (Shanley 76, 85). See also Judith R. Walkowitz, *Prostitution and Victorian Society: Women, Class, and the State* (Cambridge: Cambridge University Press, 1980): 69–147. For another contemporary reaction against women's political activism, see Eliza Lynn Linton's "The Shrieking Sisterhood" (*Saturday Review*, May 12, 1870): 341–342.

7.   For similar observations on the sexes' relative sizes in the natural world, see Olive Schreiner, *Woman and Labour* (1911) (Charleston: BiblioBazaar, 2007): 11 [hereafter *WL*].
8.   In England, the Matrimonial Causes Act of 1878 finally allowed women to apply for separation from abusive husbands, increasing women's bodily autonomy but ultimately leaving their rights up to "the discretionary judgment of a male magistrate" (Shanley 169). Legal debates about married women's bodily rights continued through the important 1891 case, *Regina v. Jackson*. See Shanley 156–188. In the United States, judges more readily saw marital violence as legitimate grounds for divorce (Elizabeth Pleck, *Domestic Tyranny: The Making of Social Policy Against Family Violence from Colonial Times to the Present* [New York: Oxford University Press, 1987]: 91–94).
9.   The etymological similarity between "vril" and "virile" implies that women's evolutionary prowess appropriates masculine virility.
10.   Richardson, "Eugenization" 231.
11.   The one American among other British "New Women" of this chapter, Gilman was an internationally acclaimed writer, referred to familiarly and frequently as "Mrs. Stetson" in British papers of the day. The two-way flow between writers on both sides of the ocean is evident in her acknowledgment of transatlantic influences (citing *Bleak House*, for instance). See also Beth Sutton-Ramspeck, *Raising the Dust: The Literary Housekeeping of Mary Ward, Sarah Grand, and Charlotte Perkins Gilman* (Athens: Ohio University Press, 2004): 13–14. Despite

significant national differences in eugenic attitudes and practices, Gilman locates herself within a transatlantic literary tradition.

12. For new-woman discourses of sexual and moral "difference," see Seth Koven, "Borderlands: Women, Voluntary Action, and Child Welfare in Britain, 1840 to 1914," *Mothers of a New World: Maternalist Politics and the Origins of Welfare States*, ed. Seth Koven and Sonya Michel (New York: Routledge, 1993): 94–135, 107–108; Richardson, *Love and Eugenics in the Late Nineteenth Century: Rational Reproduction and the New Woman* (Oxford: Oxford University Press, 2003): 26, 68; Patricia Murphy, *Time Is of the Essence: Temporality, Gender, and the New Woman* (Albany: State University of New York Press, 2001): 113; and Talia Schaffer, "'Nothing But Foolscap and Ink': Inventing the New Woman," *The New Woman in Fiction and in Fact: Fin-de-Siècle Feminisms*, ed. Angelique Richardson and Chris Willis (Houndmills: Palgrave, 2001): 39–52, 41.

13. Supporters of the eugenics movement were known as "eugenists" in England and "eugenicists" in America.

14. E. Rappaport notes that although the Married Women's Property Acts of 1870 and 1882 allowed women to become property owners, they ironically made her "less liable for her debts" (57). See also 64.

15. The "new woman" of late-century fiction was a useful creation both for writers who supported and condemned the growing women's movement. She had as many identities as the writers who described her: sexual anarchist, spinster, Amazon, marriage-reformer; she could be earnest or ridiculous, severely moral or unchaste, "radical" or "conservative." See Schaffer 39–50; Gail Cunningham, "Introduction," *The New Woman and the Victorian Novel* (London: Macmillan, 1978): 1–19; Elaine Showalter, *Sexual Anarchy: Gender and Culture at the Fin de Siècle* (New York: Penguin Books USA, 1990): 38–46. Endorsements of "divided skirts" over corsets include William Thomas Stead, "Rational Dress for Women," *Review of Reviews* (March 1894): 291–292. See also Schaffer 39; 43–44; Angelique Richardson and Chris Willis, "Introduction," *The New Woman in Fiction and Fact: Fin-de-Siècle Feminisms*, ed. Angelique Richardson and Chris Willis (Houndmills: Palgrave, 2001): 1–38, 23–24.

16. Charlotte Perkins Gilman, *Herland* (1915) (Mineola, NY: Dover, 1998).

17. Linda Dowling, "The Decadent and the New Woman in the 1890s," *Nineteenth-Century Fiction* 33:4 (March 1979): 434–453, 445. Iveta Jusová notes that late-century military defeats were detrimental to Britain's imperial confidence. See *The New Woman and the Empire* (Columbus: The Ohio State University Press, 2005): 3–4.

18. Sarah Grand, *The Heavenly Twins*, Vols. 1 and 2 (Charleston: Bibliobazaar, 2007). For the reception history of this popular, remunerative novel, see Lucy Bland, *Banishing the Beast: Feminism, Sex and Morality* (London: I. B. Tauris, 2002): 147; Teresa Mangum, *Married, Middlebrow, and Militant: Sarah Grand and the New Woman Novel* (Ann Arbor: The University of Michigan Press, 1998): 88–89, 112; and Richardson, *Love* 95, 98, 100–103.

19. Mangum notes that this episode suggests "the tremendous anxiety provoked when sexual identities are unsettled" ("Sex, Siblings, and the Fin De Siecle," *The Significance of Sibling Relationships in Literature*, ed. JoAnna Stephens Mink and Janet Doubler Ward (Bowling Green: Bowling Green State University Popular Press, 1993): 70–82, 79; also Mangum, *Married* 136–137).

20. See Dowling 439; and Showalter, *Anarchy* 41.

21. Charlotte Perkins Gilman, *Women and Economics* (New York: Cosimo, 2006) [hereafter *WE*].

22. Patrick Geddes and J. Arthur Thomson, *The Evolution of Sex* (1889), revised ed. (London: Walter Scott, 1901). See Helen Meller, *Patrick Geddes: Social Evolutionist and City Planner* (London: Routledge, 1990): 192, 2. Geddes wore many hats, from Professor of Botany in 1889 to Chair of Sociology in 1918 (6, 224). His joint emphasis on sexual and environmental factors granted women important but biologically limited roles in social evolution (82–83). For the connections he drew between urbanization and racial degeneration, see Meller 141, 143.

23. This difference parallels the distinct visions presented by the first two laws of thermodynamics. The first, positing that energy cannot be destroyed, offers a positive image of preservation; the second, suggesting that energy systems tend toward chaos, may be a better fit for late-Victorian attitudes toward women. See Barri J. Gold, "The Consolation of Physics: Tennyson's Thermodynamic Solution," *Publications of the Modern Language Association* (*PMLA*) 117:3 (May, 2002): 449–464, 451–452.

24. For a feminist revision of Geddes and Thomson's biological doctrine, see Richardson, *Love* 50. Gail Bederman notes its importance to Gilman and calls it "a far more positive view of female biology" than other authorities held (*Manliness and Civilization: A Cultural History of Gender and Race in the United States, 1880–1917* [Chicago: University of Chicago Press, 1995]: 153). Vickery points out that the idea of "female parasitism" was also prevalent in the 1690s (*Gentleman's Daughter* 5).

25. For the genesis of Schreiner's argument about "parasitism" as a suggestion that women's value was not *solely* reproductive, see Carolyn Burdett, *Olive Schreiner and the Progress of Feminism: Evolution, Gender, Empire* (Houndmills: Palgrave, 2001): 61–65. Showalter locates Schreiner's "parasites" among the "monstrous, swollen, and destructive" women of her fiction (*A Literature of Their Own: British Women Novelists from Brontë to Lessing*, expanded ed. [Princeton: Princeton University Press, 1999]: 196), while John Kucich interprets Schreiner's aversion to gain, along with her self-sacrificing desires, as part of a structure of masochism feeding into fantasies of omnipotence ("Olive Schreiner, Masochism, and Omnipotence: Strategies of a Preoedipal Politics," *Novel: A Forum on Fiction* 36:1 [Autumn, 2002]: 79–102; 90–92). Working-class women, of course, did not have the luxury of parasitism, as many middle-class women were well aware.

26. See Burdett 60.

27. Ménie Muriel Dowie, *Gallia* (London: Orion Publishing Group, 1995). See Helen Small, "Introduction," Ménie Muriel Dowie, *Gallia* (London: Orion, 1995): xxv–xxvi, xxviii, xxxi.

28. For instance, Lady Cook [Tennessee C. Claflin], "Modesty," in *Evils of Society and Their Remedies. First Series of Essays* (London: The Universal Publishing Company, 1895): 15: "It may be they have suffered vicariously, and that your purity has been preserved at the cost of theirs." (John Johnson Collection on Sex, Population, and Eugenics [hereafter JJCSPE], Box 2, Folder: "Vice.")

29. Sheila Jeffreys, *The Spinster and her Enemies: Feminism and Sexuality 1880–1930* (London: Pandora, 1985): 15. Ellice Hopkins advocated men's chastity leagues. See Jeffreys 12–13; 18–19. See also the Church of England Purity Society Pamphlets, e.g., "Papers for Men No. 3" (1885), in the JJCSPE, Box I.

30. See Francis Galton, "Hereditary Improvement," *Fraser's Magazine* 7:37 (January 1873): 116–130, 17. For British alarm at the prospect of degeneracy or "race suicide," see Donald J. Childs, *Modernism and Eugenics: Woolf, Eliot, Yeats, and the Culture of Degeneration* (Cambridge: Cambridge University Press, 2001): 1–5; Lyndsay Andrew Farrall, *The Origins and Growth of the English Eugenics Movement, 1865–1925* (New York: Garland, 1985): 21. As Farrall points out, similar problems were discussed between 1860 and 1890 without using the word *eugenics* (34, 37); the doctrine had become "commonplace" by the early 1890s (38). Evolutionary theory was so popular that an 1878 edition of *Encyclopaedia Britannica* favored it with twice as many pages as "Christianity" (Lois A. Cuddy and Claire M. Roche, "Introduction," *Evolution and Eugenics in American Literature and Culture, 1880–1940: Essays on Ideological Conflict and Complicity*, ed. Cuddy and Roche [Lewisburg: Bucknell University Press, 2003]: 9–53, 11). Eugenics proposed that human beings could intervene in and accelerate their own evolution (12).

31. In 1894, Pearson connected women's solidarity and emancipation to eugenics ideology. See "Woman and Labour," *Fortnightly Review*, 61 (1894), 561–577, reproduced in *The Chances of Death*, 2 vols. (London: Edward Arnold, 1897), quoted in Richardson xiv.

32. Pres. Dr. Chas. R. Drysdale, *Annual Report for 1903–4 of the Malthusian League (Founded 1877)* (London: George Standring, 1904): 12; Richardson, *Love* 58–60; 64; Christine

Rosen, *Preaching Eugenics: Religious Leaders and the American Eugenics Movement* (Oxford: Oxford University Press, 2004): 13–14, 29, 35. Eugenics shared its emphasis on motherhood with other discourses on health and welfare at the end of the century (Koven 3–5).

33. Karl Pearson, *The Scope and Importance to the State of National Eugenics* (1907), 2nd ed. (London: Dulau and Co., 1909): 25.

34. Pearson, "Nature and Nurture: The Problem of the Future." *A Presidential Address Delivered by Karl Pearson, F.R.S., at the Annual Meeting of the Social and Political Education League* (London: Dulau and Co., 1910): 12; Pearson, *The Academic Aspect of the Science of National Eugenics* (London: Dulau and Co., 1911): 18. See also Galton, *Eugenics as a Factor in Religion* 70. Eugenists who wished to establish eugenics as a science, represented by the Francis Galton Laboratory for the Study of National Eugenics (directed by Karl Pearson from 1907–1933), split from those who attempted to make its ideology more widespread, such as the Eugenics Education Society, several of whose pamphlets I quote here (Farrall 103–104, 108).

35. Malthusian Leaflets No. 7, "The Cry of the Poor," n.d. (JJCSPE, Box 1).

36. Annie Besant, *The Law of Population: Its Consequences, and Its Bearing Upon Human Conduct and Morals* (London: Freethought Publishing Company, 1878 ed.): 30, 33–35, 26, 43. Mr. Justice Windeyer's "Extracts from a Judgment Delivered in the Supreme Court of New South Wales," (Malthusian Leaflet No. 9, n.d.): 2 advertises Besant's *Law of Population* and notes that the volume has already sold more than 100,000 copies.

37. Mrs. Mary Sowden, "Wedded Life: As It Is, and As It Should Be" (London: G. Standring, Printer, n.d.): 5; Dr. Alice Drysdale Vickery, "Appeal for Funds," *The Malthusian* 33:5 (May 15, 1909): 33.

38. Pearson, *Scope* 37. Daniel J. Kevles records the prominence of women among the members, officers, and audiences of British and American eugenics societies in their early years (64). See also Mangum, *Married* 200–201. Other women found eugenics antagonistic to women's advancement along non-maternal lines (Childs 7).

39. Richardson's discussion of eugenic feminism stresses its essentializing construction of "civic motherhood" and women's rational selection of sexual partners (9, 49, 68, and *passim*). See also Alisa Klaus, "Depopulation and Race Suicide: Maternalism and Pronatalist Ideologies in France and the United States," in *Mothers of a New World: Maternalist Politics and the Origins of Welfare States*, ed. Seth Koven and Sonya Michel (New York: Routledge, 1993): 188–212, 191. For women's financial contributions to the movement, see Kevles 55. Koven and Michel, noting the importance of maternalism to women's public activism at this historical moment (29), also stress its limits in pre-WWI welfare systems (Koven 96; Michel 279). Berg, too, notes that maternalism racialized, rather than unifying, the women's movement (4).

40. Caleb Williams Saleeby, *Parenthood and Race Culture: An Outline of Eugenics* (London: Cassell and Company, 1909): 182. See also Richardson, *Love* 76.

41. In a discussion of financial incentives for eugenic birth, Pearson attempts to "differentiate between the economic values of good and bad parentage" (*Problem* 21, also 22, 28). See also Sybil Gotto, *The Eugenic Principle in Social Reconstruction* (Kingsway: Eugenics Education Society [Reprinted from *The Eugenics Review*, October 1917]): 5; Galton, *Possible Improvement* 11, 29; Galton, *Local* 108. For a historical discussion of such incentives, see Kevles 91.

42. John Russell, *Can the School Prepare for Parenthood?* (Eugenics Education Society, 1909 [Reprinted from *The Eugenics Review*, July 1909]): 3; Russell, *Eugenics and Education* (Kingsway: Eugenics Education Society, 1912): 4; W. H. Bishop, Jr., *Education and Heredity; or, Eugenics: a Mental, Moral, and Social Force* (London: A. & F. Denny, 1909): 21, 23. The eugenic education of women and girls was thought to be of particular importance. See Alice Ravenhill, *Eugenic Education for Women and Girls*, 2nd ed., rev. (Kingsway: Eugenics Education Society, 1914 [First published in *The Eugenics Review*, 1909]): 10–12; Elsie Clews Parsons, Ph.D., *The Family: An Ethnographical and Historical Outline with Descriptive Notes, Planned as a Textbook for the Use of College Lecturers and of Directors of Home-reading Clubs* (New York and

London: G. P. Putnam's Sons, 1906): 343, 346; Bland 143. However, Saleeby and others worried that women's higher education could "be carried to the point at which motherhood is compromised" (*Parenthood* xiv, 93).

43. *The Vanguard. The Monthly Paper of the Church of England Purity Society* 4:10 (October 1887): 75; Edward and Eleanor Marx Aveling, "The Woman Question" (London: Swan Sonnenschein, Lowrey, & Co., 1887): 11.

44. The Manageress, The Hygienic Stores, Advertisement for the Anti-Geniture ("for use by married ladies desiring to regulate the number of their offspring"). In *Private and Confidential. (To the Married Only.)* (The Hygienic Store, 95 Charing Cross Road, n.d.): 3. JJCSPE, Box I.

45. Austin Holyoake, "Large or Small Families? On Which Side Lies the Balance of Comfort?" n.d., 5, JJCSPE, Box 1.

46. See "Illustrated List of Domestic and Surgical Specialties supplied by J. Greevz Fisher," n.d., JJCSPE, Box I.

47. Lady Cook [Tennessee C. Claflin], "Maternity," in *Evils of Society and their Remedies. First Series of Essays* (London: The Universal Publishing Company, 1895): 19; "The Ideal Woman," *Evils of Society and their Remedies. First Series of Essays* (London: The Universal Publishing Company, 1895): 6.

48. Lillian Harman offers an example of a "friend" who appears to follow Evadne's example; after discovering "a defect in her husband's nature," she resolved to protect "possible offspring" by "never incur[ring] the risk of maternity again [. . .]." "Eve and her Eden," *The Adult: The Journal of Sex* 2:2 (March 1898): 33.

49. Syphilis received special attention in essays on women's sex education. See, for instance, Lady Cook [Tennessee C. Claflin], "A Short History of Marriage," in *Evils of Society and their Remedies. Second Series of Essays* (London: The Universal Publishing Company, 1895): 27; Mrs. [Edith] H[avelock] Ellis, "A Noviciate for Marriage," n.d., 13. For an opposing view of the spread of syphilis and other venereal diseases, see James Stuart, M.P., and Henry J. Wilson, M.P., "Facts *versus* Panic: Being a Reply to certain Alarmist Statements and Proposals recently made" (London: The British Committee, 1898), JJCSPE, Box 2, Folder: Vice. Emma Liggins discusses new-woman fears of syphilis ("Writing Against the 'Husband-Fiend': Syphilis and Male Sexual Vice in the New Woman Novel," *Women's Writing* 7:2 [2000]: 175–195, 185), while Marilyn Bonnell discusses Grand's decision to "[break] the silence" about men's sexual contagion ("Sarah Grand and the Critical Establishment: Art for [Wo]man's Sake," *Tulsa Studies in Women's Literature* 14:1 [Spring 1995]: 123–148, 126).

50. For the racist and classist sides of Gilman's evolutionary concerns, see Allison Berg, *Mothering the Race: Women's Narratives of Reproduction, 1890–1930* (Urbana: University of Illinois Press, 2002): 56–57; Bederman, esp. 122–123, 135–150; Lisa Ganobcsik-Williams, "The Intellectualism of Charlotte Perkins Gilman: Evolutionary Perspectives on Race, Ethnicity, and Class," *Charlotte Perkins Gilman: Optimist Reformer*, ed. Jill Rudd and Val Gough (Iowa City: University of Iowa Press, 1999): 16–41, 18–36; Gary Scharnhorst, "Historicizing Gilman: A Bibliographer's View," *The Mixed Legacy of Charlotte Perkins Gilman*, ed. Catherine J. Golden and Joanna Schneider Zangrando (Newark: University of Delaware Press, 2000): 65–73, 68–69.

51. Richardson, "Eugenization" 235.

52. Adeline Champney, "The Woman Question. An Address Delivered Before the Boston Social Science Club," *The Agitator* 11:1 (September 1903. New York: Comrade Cooperative Company): 3. From the JJCSPE, d. 3029.

53. Richardson, *Love* 93, 121. Grand and other new women believed that rigorous education would help women's reproductive choices, reversing earlier doctrines that found reading antagonistic to their reproductive abilities (Murphy 141). Gail Cunningham provocatively and persuasively suggests that Gallia (against custom and Evadne) selects her husband "not *despite* but *because* of his sexual history," which proves his fertility ("'He-Notes': Reconstructing

Masculinity," *The New Woman in Fiction and in Fact: Fin-de-Siècle Feminisms,* ed. Angelique Richardson and Chris Willis [Houndmills: Palgrave, 2001]: 94–106, 99).

54. The religious sermons of Protestants, Catholics, and Jews alike incorporated eugenics (Rosen 3–4, 8, 18–19). See also Kevles 61. Richardson emphasizes the theological tradition of treating love as sacrifice (76).

55. Here, Gallia explicitly remarks on the risk of sacrificing oneself merely "to fly in the face of custom" (180); she suggests that the costs of eschewing romantic love for eugenic sacrifice are high, especially if motivated not by spiritual impulse but by show. Annette Weiner's theory that the items withheld from circulation are as important as those items exchanged in gift economies reminds us that one can give too much, that keeping-while-giving is the key to social status and power.

56. Gail Cunningham reports that "*Gallia* was on the whole sympathetically received" by contemporaries (*New Woman* 76).

57. Geddes and Thomson 183–185, 186–188.

58. Gilman, *Women and Economics* 65. Cynthia J. Davis attributes Gilman's interest in parthenogenesis to an additional source, the Gynaecocentric Theory of Lester Frank Ward (Cynthia J. Davis, "His and Herland: Charlotte Perkins Gilman 'Re-presents' Lester F. Ward," *Evolution and Eugenics in American Literature and Culture, 1880–1940: Essays on Ideological Conflict and Complicity,* ed. Lois A. Cuddy and Claire M. Roche [Lewisburg: Bucknell University Press, 2003]: 73–88, 77). See also Berg 151 n.5; and Bederman 150.

59. Pope, *Dunciad* II:156; Shelley, "Preface" to 1831 edition of *Frankenstein* (ed. J. Paul Hunter, New York: W. W. Norton & Company, 1996): 173.

60. Sutton-Ramspeck also draws parallels between late-century approaches to motherhood and writing (42–43).

61. "Negative" eugenics "disfavour[s] the production of those who are unfit for citizenship," "interfering as far as may be with [their] parentage" (Saleeby, *Parenthood* 68, 183). To this end, Parsons proposes that "marriage licenses [include] data about the personal and family health and character [. . . as] *partial* proof of [. . .] matrimonial eligibility or non-eligibility" (344).

62. Childs notes that "sterilization laws had already been enacted in thirty American states, as well as a number of other countries" *before* the Nazi Eugenic Sterilization Law (15). See also Cuddy and Roche 14; Edwin Black, *War Against the Weak: Eugenics and America's Campaign to Create a Master Race* (New York: Four Walls Eight Windows, 2003): 87–93. Kevles 94–111 discusses immigration restrictions and sterilization in detail, noting that by the mid-1930s, 20,000 people had been legally sterilized in the United States alone.

63. Richard A. Soloway's 1996 Galton Lecture discusses the eugenic roots of the birth control movement (see 54–55). See also Black 127. Both Marie Stopes and Margaret Sanger were advocates of eugenics.

64. See Walkowitz, *City* ch. 5, esp. 138, 140, 148–151, 165; Bland 11–14, 20–21, 29, 38–39.

65. See, for instance, August Forel, M.D., Ph.D., LLD, *The Sexual Question: A Scientific, Psychological, Hygienic and Sociological Study (1906, 1908)*, English Adaptation from the 2nd German Ed., Revised and Enlarged by C.F. Marshall, M.D., F.R.C.S. (London: William Heinemann [Medical Books], 1927): 512.

66. Popular belief held that "Nature sterilizes women of immoral lives," and Lady Cook, reflecting on this point, adds that "Immoral men should be sterilized also [. . .]." See Cook, "Maternity," 24. In the Herlanders' distinction between childbearing and childrearing (70–71), Gilman concurs with Schreiner that maternity alone will not benefit the race. See Burdett 66.

67. Quoted in Shanley 185. See also Jeffreys 29–30.

68. Cook, "The Regeneration of Society," in *Evils of Society and Their Remedies. First Series of Essays* (London: The Universal Publishing Company, 1895): 39.

69. In calling Galbraith's authority into question, I differ from popular readings expressed by Richardson, *Love* 100, 125 and Jusová, especially in the latter's insistence that "Evadne ends up as a conventional housewife" (17), rewarded "with a happy marriage to Dr. Galbraith"

and "happily accept[ing] her husband as the agent of her life" (20, 24). Liggins calls Evadne "the slave to Dr Galbraith's first-person narrative" and reminds us that Galbraith serves as one of the representative members of society who enabled Edith's marital tragedy (186). Liggins forgets her own observations, however, when she too describes the narrative's "conventional happy ending" (187). Ann Heilmann's reading of Galbraith underscores this doctor/husband's similarity to the husband in Gilman's "The Yellow Wallpaper," and draws attention to the prefatory note, though in reference to his misdiagnosis, not to Evadne's suicide attempt ("Narrating the Hysteric: *Fin-de-Siècle* Medical Discourse and Sarah Grand's *The Heavenly Twins* [1893]," *The New Woman in Fiction and in Fact: Fin-de-Siècle Feminisms*, ed. Angelique Richardson and Chris Willis [Houndmills: Palgrave, 2001]: 123–135, 126–130). See also Mangum's discussion of the "suspicion" that other critics express regarding his unreliable "limited perspective" (*Married* 116) as well as of the "troubling [. . .] connection between [Galbraith's] love and [Evadne's] madness" (120).

70. Liggins notes that many Victorian doctors still encouraged wives' sexual ignorance (177).

71. In case the reader should miss this point, the novel draws our attention to the fact that Colquhoun and Galbraith are both called George on 2:371—more than a "coincidence," according to Evadne's aunt.

72. Sutton-Ramspeck 74.

73. Shanley 148–150. For an earlier novel that takes up the imbalance of parental power in the face of adultery and abuse, see Anne Brontë's *The Tenant of Wildfell Hall*.

74. Norma Clarke notes that "Grand attacks the Victorian ideal of womanly submission, ignorance and self-sacrifice" (99), but I'm interested in the way that Grand and other new women transform the self-sacrifice of women who hope to change or "save" their delinquent husbands into other forms of sacrifice, presumably capable of saving the race.

75. As Jusová argues, Grand and others were "personally invested in the maintenance of the empire" (14). However, where she finds that "the subversiveness of Grand's feminism was diminished by the emphasis that her writing placed on racial, social, and cultural purity" (15), the feminism that I have been discussing is actually constituted by these social inequalities.

76. See Introduction, n.37.

Epilogue

1. L. Ormiston Chant, "Friendly Words to Women on Religion and Politics" (London: Central National Society for Women's Suffrage, n.d.): 4.

2. Israel Zangwill, "'One and One are Two.' (Being a verbatim report of the speech delivered at Exeter Hall, on February 9th, and the Demonstration of Women's Suffrage Societies.)" (London: Women's Social and Political Union): 3. Suffrage papers are interested in property rights, and note that, despite some recent improvements, "The laws of inheritance, both as to land and goods, give preference to males over females." See H. Musk Beattie, "The Law Relating to Inheritance and Devolution as it Affects Women. Part II," *Votes for Women* (*VFW*), October 11, 1912, 22.

3. A Looker On, "Women's Rights as Preached by Women Past and Present," new ed. (London: Kegan Paul, Trench, & Co., 1881): 15.

4. Lady Constance Lytton, "'No Votes for Women.' A Reply to Some Recent Anti-Suffrage Publications" (London: A. C. Fifield, 1909): 4.

5. Robert F. Cholmeley, "Women's Suffrage: The Demand & Its Meaning" (London: The Athenaeum Press, 1909): 9.

6. A Looker On 29 (emphasis in original).

7. For the idea that women should have the vote precisely because, as women, they addressed an important but unrepresented side of politics, see Lisa Tickner, *The Spectacle of Women: Imagery of the Suffrage Campaign, 1907–14* (Chicago: University of Chicago Press, 1988): 153, 156, 215; for the hunger-stricken and forcibly fed bodies of suffrage campaigners as

"stitch[ing] together a community via sentimentality and domestic feeling," see Barbara Green, *Spectacular Confessions: Autobiography, Performative Activism, and the Sites of Suffrage, 1905–1938* (New York: St. Martin's Press, 1997): 25. More recently, Laura E. Nym Mayhall has suggested that we move away from these bodies in order to focus on militants' use of legal discourses for citizenship; for their "rational political calculus," see *The Militant Suffrage Movement: Citizenship and Resistance in Britain, 1860–1930* (Oxford: Oxford University Press, 2003): 7.

8. Mayhall 8.

9. Amanda Vickery's comment that "equal rights feminism was less a reflex response to a newly imposed model of stifling passivity, than the fruition of a political tradition" refers to a different set of traditions from the ones I investigate here, but offers a parallel way to rethink the "before" of women's late-century campaigns as continuous with earlier efforts. See "Golden Age to Separate Spheres? A Review of the Categories and Chronology of English Women's History," *The Historical Journal* 36:2 (June, 1993): 392.

10. *Votes for Women* had a circulation of over 30,000 in 1909, according to Tickner 60.

11. Krista Lysack, *Come Buy, Come Buy: Shopping and the Culture of Consumption in Victorian Women's Writing* (Athens: Ohio University Press, 2008): 145; Michel de Certeau, *The Practice of Everyday Life*, xvii, cited in Lysack 141.

12. Lysack 145–147; Erika Diane Rappaport, *Shopping for Pleasure: Women in the Making of London's West End* (Princeton: Princeton University Press, 2000): 219; see also "The World We Live In. At the Time of the Sales," *VFW*, January 14, 1910, 247; "Campaign Throughout the Country," *VFW*, October 4, 1912, 852; "For Christmas Presents," *VFW*, December 18, 1912, 174.

13. Lysack 155, 154.

14. Lysack 155; for appeals for volunteers to staff the shops, see *VFW*, October 15, 1909, 45; *VFW*, November 26, 1909, 142.

15. "Campaign Throughout the Country," *VFW*, October 4, 1912, 853.

16. E. Sylvia Pankhurst, "East End Campaign," *The Suffragette*, October 18, 1912, 9.

17. "Campaign Throughout the County," *VFW*, October 4, 1912, 853.

18. *VFW*, November 5, 1909, 94.

19. *VFW*, November 12, 1909, 110.

20. E. Rappaport, e.g., 18. See also Leslee Thorne-Murphy, "Women, Free Trade, and Harriet Martineau's *Dawn Island* at the 1845 Anti-Corn Law League Bazaar," in *Economic Women: Essays on Desire and Dispossession in Nineteenth-Century British Culture*, ed. Lana Dalley and Jill Rappoport (unpublished manuscript).

21. "The Christmas Presents Sale," *VFW*, October 11, 1912, 19 (emphasis in original).

22. "Local Notes," *VFW*, November 26, 1909, 142; "Christmas Gifts at the W.S.P.U. Shops," *VFW*, December 10, 1909, 174; "Christmas Sale," *The Suffragette*, October 25, 1912, 22; "Christmas Presents Sale," *The Suffragette*, November 15, 1912, 73.

23. *VFW*, December 17, 1909, 178.

24. "Christmas Gifts at the W.S.P.U. Shops," *VFW*, December 10, 1909, 170.

25. "Come to Our Christmas Fair," *The Suffragette*, December 13, 1912, 128.

26. Susan L. Mizruchi differentiates between "self-denial" ("what isolated individuals must give up in order to gain spiritual efficacy") and "sacrifice" ("a collective ritual"), but the texts I examine call into question this opposition by making self-denial a collective pursuit and by finding in sacrifice some of the "optimism in asceticism" that she attributes to self-denial as a "positive good, strengthening and supporting the self." See 29, 30. Mizruchi, like Girard, writes primarily of sacrificial rites in which the victim is other than oneself.

27. Emmeline Pethick Lawrence, "In Quest of Freedom," *VFW*, April 29, 1910, 499.

28. Mrs. [Emmeline] Pankhurst, "Self-Denial Week. Special Message from Mrs. Pankhurst," *The Suffragette*, February 28, 1913, 304.

29. Christabel Pankhurst, "Unshackled: The Story of How We Won the Vote [1959]," in *The Militant*, ed. Marie Mulvey Roberts, Tamae Mizuta (London: Routledge, 1995): 70.

30. Tickner 42.
31. Margaret Haley, "Greetings from Prisoners," *The Suffragette*, February 28, 1913, 304.
32. Tickner describes some of the portrait photographs as establishing a martyrology (27). See also the Women's Library Postcard Album 1, 7JCC/0/1/02 ("Suffragette Procession" with signs advertising "690 Imprisonments to Win Freedom for Women"); 7JCC/0/1/22 ("Arrest of Mrs. Pankhurst, Miss Pankhurst, and Mrs. Drummond. Mr. Jarvis Reading the Warrant at Clement's Inn, October 13, 1908"); 7JCC/0/1/115 ("The Imprisoned Suffragist Leaders"); 7JCC/01/1/99 ("2nd Division Cell Allotted to Suffragettes"); 7JCC/0/1/46 ("Showing cells where Mrs. Pankhurst & other hunger strikers have been imprisoned [. . . .] With best wishes for Christmas and the New Year"; and 7JCC/0/1/45 ("After a Hunger Strike").
33. Suffragettes protested their "2nd Division" imprisonment, arguing that they should be afforded the status and treatment of political prisoners instead.
34. "The Scottish Exhibition," *VFW*, April 29, 1910, 494.
35. "Local Notes," *VFW*, November 26, 1909, 142.
36. "W.S.P.U. Announcements," *VFW*, February 25, 1910, 384.
37. Pankhurst, *The Militant* 48–49, 288. Campaigns for suffrage were split on the question of militancy. See, for example, Mayhall 98, 104–105.
38. Annie P. Budgett, "Facts Behind the Press. Paper read at a meeting of the 'Bromley Women's League for the Discussion of Social and Ethical Subjects' on November 15, 1906" (London: Women's Social and Political Union): 6; Pankhurst, "America and the War" 8.
39. Winifred Mayo [Winifred Alice Monck-Mason], "Prison Experiences of a Suffragette," *Idler: An Illustrated Monthly Magazine* 33:67 (April 1908): 85–99, 85. *ProQuest British Periodicals* database, <http://gateway.proquest.com/openurl?url_ver=Z39.88-2004&res_dat=xri:bp-us:&rft_dat=xri:bp:article:e597-1908-033-67-002882:1>.
40. Mayo 85, 86.
41. Mayo 86, 87, 88.
42. Mayo 93, 97, 91. See also Beth Sutton-Ramspeck, *Raising the Dust: The Literary Housekeeping of Mary Ward, Sarah Grand, and Charlotte Perkins Gilman* (Athens: Ohio University Press, 2004): 8.
43. Mayo 89.
44. Mayo 95.
45. Elizabeth Crawford, "Women's Social and Political Union," *The Women's Suffrage Movement: A Reference Guide 1866–1928* (London: University College London Press, 1999): 740.
46. See, for instance, Crawford, "Pankhurst, [Estelle] Sylvia," *The Women's Suffrage Movement: A Reference Guide 1866–1928* (London: University College London Press, 1999): 515–525, e.g., 520–521, 523.
47. Tickner 6. See also see *VFW*, October 25, 1912, 50; Crawford, "Women's Social and Political Union," in *The Women's Suffrage Movement* 726–755, 748.
48. Millicent Garrett Fawcett, "Constitutional Suffragists and the Militants. Mrs. Fawcett's Position. To the Editor of The Times," *The Times*, March 9, 1912, 7.
49. Fawcett, "Constitutional Suffragists and Sentences of Militants. To the Editor of the Times," *The Times*, June 8, 1912, 7.
50. Haldane of Cloan, E. Gray, Alfred Lyttelton, F. D. Acland, et al., "Women Suffrage and Militancy," *The Times*, July 23, 1912, 9.
51. Fawcett, "Constitutional Suffragists and the Militants. Mrs. Fawcett's Position. To the Editor of The Times," *The Times*, March 9, 1912, 7; Fawcett, "Constitutional Suffragists and Sentences of Militants. To the Editor of The Times," *The Times*, June 8, 1912, 7. See also Fawcett, "The Suffrage Prisoners and Forcible Feeding. To the Editor of The Times," *The Times*, June 24, 1912, 7.
52. Emmeline Pethick Lawrence, "Our Policy," *VFW*, October 25, 1912, 56.
53. "Our Policy" 56.
54. Tickner 104.

55. "Forcible Feeding. Opinions of Medical Experts. Grave Danger to Life Involved," *VFW*, October 1, 1909, 2.

56. E. Sylvia Pankhurst, "The Hunger and Thirst Strike and its Effects" (issued by The East London Federation of the Suffragettes, 319 East India Dock Road, Poplar, E., and printed by E. H. Williams [T. U.], 232 Devons Road, Bow, E., n.d.,): 2.

57. Green 17.

58. For instance, "Forcible Feeding. Opinions of Medical Experts. Grave Danger to Life Involved," *VFW*, October 1, 1909, 2; "The Dangers of Forcible Feeding. Opinions of Medical Experts. Memorial Signed by One Hundred and Sixteen Doctors," *VFW*, October 8, 1909, 19.

59. E[mmeline] P[ethick] L[awrence], "Treasurer's Note," *VFW*, October 1, 1909, 9; see also Emmeline Pankhurst, "The Fiery Cross," *VFW*, October 1, 1909, 8. The experience of forcible feeding was often compared to rape.

60. "Forcible Feeding. Statement by Mrs. Mary Leigh to Her Solicitor," *VFW*, October 15, 1909; Constance Lytton, "Prison Experiences of Lady Constance Lytton," *VFW*, January 28, 1910, 276; Sylvia Pankhurst, "They Tortured Me," *The Suffragette*, March 28, 1913, 385; see also "Statement from Miss Annie Wheeler. Forcibly Fed for Seven Weeks. News of Mary Richardson. Heart-Breaking Screams," *The Suffragette*, July 17, 1914, 249.

61. "A Speech by Lady Constance Lytton. Delivered at the Queen's Hall, January 31, 1910," *VFW*, February 4, 1910, 292; E[mmeline] P[ethick] L[awrence], "Treasurer's Note," *VFW*, October 1, 1909, 9; see also Christabel Pankhurst, "Methods of Violence," *VFW*, October 8, 1909, 24; Constance Lytton, "Prison Experiences of Lady Constance Lytton," *VFW*, January 28, 1910, 276; letter from *The Christian Commonwealth*, *VFW*, February 7, 1913, 278; Emmeline Pethick Lawrence, "The Spirit of Sacrifice," *VFW*, May 9, 1913, 459. Green notes that the repetitive accounts "turned the dwindling body into an excessive textuality" (88).

62. Green 13; Tickner 38.

63. Mayhall 84, 100.

64. Christabel Pankhurst, "'The War.' A Speech Delivered at the London Opera House on September 8, 1914" (London: The Women's Social and Political Union, 1914): 15.

65. "Self-Denial Week. Special Message from Mrs. Pankhurst," *The Suffragette*, February 28, 1913, 304; *VFW*, October 1, 1909, 8.

66. "Votes for Women—One Penny!" *VFW*, February 4, 1910, 297.

67. "Increasing the Sale of 'Votes for Women,'" *VFW*, October 8, 1909, 29; E[mmeline] P[ethick] L[awrence], "Treasurer's Note," *VFW*, October 1, 1909, 9.

68. E[mmeline] P[ethick] L[awrence], "Treasurer's Note." *VFW*, October 15, 1909, 41.

69. "Treasurer's Note," *VFW*, October 22, 1909. See also *VFW*, January 24, 1913, 243: "where the best gift of all—personal service—is for any reason impossible, we must be thankful that money (which is stored-up human labour) is available as a substitute."

70. E[mmeline] Pankhurst, "The Fighting Fund and Self-Denial Week. Treasurer's Note," *The Suffragette*, February 21, 1913, 287.

71. Constance Lytton, "Prison Experiences of Lady Constance Lytton," *VFW*, January 28, 1910, 276.

72. Annie P. Budgett, "'Facts Behind the Press.' Paper read at a meeting of the 'Bromley Women's League for the Discussion of Social and Ethical Subjects,' on November 15, 1906" (London: Women's Social and Political Union): 3.

73. Budgett 5–6.

74. *VFW*, January 24, 1913, 243.

75. See, for instance, Crawford, "Women's Social and Political Union" 736: "On 16 December Dora Montefiore warned Adelaide Knight that working women should not rely on the WSPU. 'It was perhaps foolish to believe that the W.S. & Pol. Union was *really* democratic [. . .].'" Crawford suggests that after it began to attract "women of substance," the W.S.P.U. could "dispense with the women from Canning Town and West Ham who, although raising

the body count, could not contribute to what Christabel deemed necessary to influence the government." See Crawford, "Christabel Harriette Pankhurst" 490. For an overview of the W.S.P.U. and its relationship to socialism, see Krista Cowman, "'Incipient Toryism'? The Women's Social and Political Union and the Independent Labour Party, 1903–1914," *History Workshop Journal* 53 (Spring, 2002): 128–148; for the shifts in representational strategy, see esp. 132; for the common understanding that the W.S.P.U. moved away from its early ties with the Independent Labour Party (ILP), see 133; for an argument regarding its continued sympathies with socialist concerns despite its independence from the political party, see 134, 139–144.

76. "Women and Legislation: A Series of Articles by Mrs. [Elizabeth C.] Wolstenholme Elmy." Revised and Enlarged from *Shafts* of April, May, June and July, 1896. (Women's Emancipation Union. Appendix, September 1896): 19. See also Mayhall's discussion of militancy as a "civic republican ideal of the citizen in action" (11).

77. Israel Zangwill, "One and One are Two. (Being a verbatim report of the speech delivered at Exeter Hall, on February 9th, at the Demonstration of Women's Suffrage Societies)" (London: Women's Social and Political Union, n.d.): 5. See also Tickner 38.

78. Mayhall 118.

79. See Timothy Larsen, *Christabel Pankhurst: Feminism and Fundamentalism in Coalition* (Rochester: Boydell Press, 2002): 9; Martin Pugh, *The Pankhursts* (London: Penguin, 2001): 299–304; "Miss Pankhurst Here Unheralded," *The New York Times* (Oct. 15, 1914): 9. *ProQuest Historical Newspapers* database, *The New York Times* (1851-2007) <http://proquest. umi.com.ezp1.villanova.edu/pqdweb?did=100329409&sis=1&Fmt=10&clinetId=3260& RQT=309&VName=HNP>.

80. "Release of the Suffragists: Mr. McKenna's Wise Decision Received with Universal Approval," *VFW*, August 14, 1914, 697; *VFW*, August 21, 1914, 708. On August 21, 1914, *VFW* left the editorship of the Pethick Lawrences and became the official organ of the United Suffragists.

81. "Release of the Suffragists: Mr. McKenna's Wise Decision Received with Universal Approval," *VFW*, August 14, 1914, 697.

82. "Press Opinions," *VFW*, August 14, 1914, 697.

83. "Women Suffrage 'On Account,'" *VFW*, September 18, 1914, 736.

84. For the "service model of citizenship," see Mayhall 117, 121. For sacrifice as the indication of a greater value, see Ilana M. Blumberg, "'Unnatural Self-Sacrifice': Trollope's Ethic of Mutual Benefit," *Nineteenth-Century Literature* 58:4 (March 2004): 506–546, 525.

85. Pankhurst, "'The War.' A Speech Delivered at the London Opera House on September 8, 1914" (London: W.S.P.U.).

86. Not all W.S.P.U. members endorsed this "jingoist" approach, which occasioned further divisions. See Crawford, "Women's Social and Political Union" 755.

87. Pankhurst, "Speech" 2, 3; Pankhurst, "America and the War" 5.

88. "America" 4. See also "Miss Pankhurst Attacks Germans," *The New York Times* (Oct. 25, 1914): C3. *ProQuest Historical Newspapers* database, *The New York Times* (1851-2007) <http://proquest.umi.com.ezp1.villanova.edu/pqdweb?did=100109390&sid=3&Fmt=10 &clientId=3260&RQT=309&VName=HNP>.

89. "America" 6–7. Tickner notes that motherhood was a selling point for pro-and anti-suffrage camps alike (217).

90. For instance, the Women's Library Box FL 337 includes a typed letter, dated November 1916, from the President of the Eugenics Education Society to the Secretary of the London Society for Women's Suffrage, thanking her for the "sympathetic interest you have already shown in our efforts" and promising to notify her regarding an upcoming meeting.

91. Robert F. Cholmeley, "Women's Suffrage: The Demand & Its Meaning" (London: Women Citizen Publishing Society, 1909): 9; "The Outlook," *VFW*, August 7, 1914, 678. See also

Christabel Pankhurst, "The War," *The Suffragette*, August 7, 1914, 301. Mayo also notes that "motherhood" awakened some of her companions to the need for women's suffrage (86).

92. "America" 19.
93. Olive Schreiner, *Woman and Labour* (1911) (Charleston: BiblioBazaar, 2007): 90.
94. S. D. Shallard, "Women in War," *VFW*, August 7, 1914, 679; "From Miss Annie Kenney," *The Suffragette*, May 28, 1915, 107.
95. Pankhurst, "America" 19.
96. "Women Suffrage 'On Account,'" *VFW*, September 18, 1914, 736.
97. Margaret Kilroy Kenyon, "Correspondence," *VFW*, August 14, 1914, 698.
98. Special to *The Christian Science Monitor*, "Women's Vote Not as Reward," *The Christian Science Monitor*, July 6, 1917, 2; John Massie, "Partisan Suffragism and The National Crisis: To the Editor of the 'Oxford Chronicle,'" *The Oxford Chronicle*, letter written June 19, 1915 [clipping from John Johnson Collection, n.d.]. See also Mayhall 119.
99. "Miss Pankhurst Here Unheralded" 9. See also "America" 7: "do you suppose that it is going to be so easy when this war is over to refuse to acknowledge the rights and duties of British women [...]?"
100. The age limit was lowered to twenty-one in 1928.
101. Mayhall points out that "women's electoral concerns had become marginal within the overall scheme of franchise reform" (134).
102. Mayo 87.

WORKS CITED

Newspapers and Periodicals

All the World: A Monthly Record of the Operations of The Salvation Army in All Lands [AW].
The Deliverer [Del] & Record of Salvation Army Rescue Work.
The Suffragette.
Votes for Women [VFW].
The War Cry and Official Gazette of the Salvation Army [WC].

Other Primary Sources and Criticism

Ablow, Rachel. *The Marriage of Minds: Reading Sympathy in the Victorian Marriage Plot*. Stanford: Stanford University Press, 2007.

Ackerman, Robert W. "The Pearl-Maiden and the Penny." *Romance Philology* 17:3 (1964): 615–623.

Adams, James Eli. *Dandies and Desert Saints: Styles of Victorian Manhood*. Ithaca: Cornell University Press, 1995.

Alexander, Christine. "'That Kingdom of Gloom': Charlotte Brontë, the Annuals, and the Gothic." *Nineteenth-Century Literature* 47:4 (March 1993): 409–436.

Allen, David Elliston. *The Victorian Fern Craze: A History of Pteridomania*. London: Hutchinson, 1969.

Anderson, Amanda. *Tainted Souls and Painted Faces: The Rhetoric of Fallenness in Victorian Culture*. Ithaca: Cornell University Press, 1993.

Anderson, Benedict. *Imagined Communities: Reflections on the Origin and Spread of Nationalism*. Revised ed., London: Verso, 1991.

Appadurai, Arjun, ed. *The Social Life of Things: Commodities in Cultural Perspective*. Cambridge: Cambridge University Press, 1986.

Arrighi, Giovanni. *The Long Twentieth Century: Money, Power, and the Origins of Our Times*. London and New York: Verso, 1994.

Arsenau, Mary. "Incarnation and Interpretation: Christina Rossetti, the Oxford Movement, and *Goblin Market*." *Victorian Poetry* 31 (1993): 79–93.

———. *Recovering Christina Rossetti: Female Community and Incarnational Poetics*. Houndmills: Palgrave Macmillan, 2004.

———. "Recovering Female Community: Frances, Maria, and Christina Rossetti." *Journal of Pre-Raphaelite Studies* 12 (Fall 2003): 17–38.

"ART. VI.-1. Miss Sellon and the Sisters of Mercy. An Exposure of the Constitution, Rules, Religious Views, and Practical Working of Their Society, Obtained through a 'Sister' Who Has Recently Seceded." *Dublin Review* 32.64 (June 1852): 436–464. *ProQuest British Periodicals* database,

<http://gateway.proquest.com/openurl?url_ver=Z39.88-2004&res_dat=xri:bp-us:&rft_dat=xri:bp:article:6389-1852-032-64-000023>.

"ART. VII. Sisters of Charity: Catholic and Protestant, Abroad and at Home. By Mrs. Jameson." [Review] *Dublin Review* 38.76 (June 1855): 442–460. *ProQuest British Periodicals* database, <http://gateway.proquest.com/openurl?url_ver=Z39.88-2004&res_dat=xri:bp-us:&rft_dat=xri:bp:article:6389-1855-038-76-000051>.

Astell, Mary. *A Serious Proposal to the Ladies, for the Advancement of their True and Greatest Interest by a Lover of her Sex.* London: R. Wilkin, 1694. *Early English Books Online (EEBO)*, <http://gateway.proquest.com.ps2.villanova.edu/openurl?ctx_ver=Z39.88-2003&res_id=xri:eebo&rft_id=xri:eebo:citation:11665663>.

Auerbach, Nina. *Communities of Women: An Idea in Fiction.* Cambridge: Harvard University Press, 1978.

Bailey, Joanne. "Favoured or Oppressed? Married Women, Property, and 'Coverture' in England, 1660–1800." *Continuity and Change* 17:3 (2002): 351–372.

"Review of Perry, Ruth, *Novel Relations: The Transformation of Kinship in English Literature and Culture 1748–1818.*" *H-Albion, H-Net Reviews,* <http://www.h-net.org/reviews/showrev.php?id=11824>.

"Banking and the Bank Act." *The Times,* December 26, 1866 (Issue 25691; col. E): 4.

Barber, Lynn. *The Heyday of Natural History 1820–1890.* Garden City: Doubleday, 1980.

Barrington, Kathleen. *Four Years' Slumming. Being the Fourth Report of the Work of the Salvation Army in The Slums, also Statement of Accounts from February 1st, 1890, to January 31st, 1891.* London: International Headquarters, 1891.

Bataille, Georges. *The Accursed Share: An Essay on General Economy Vol. 1: Consumption.* Trans. Robert Hurley. New York: Zone Books, 1991.

Batchelor, Jennie. "Fictions of the Gift in Sarah Scott's Millenium Hall." *The Culture of the Gift in Eighteenth-Century England.* Ed. Linda Zionkowski and Cynthia Klekar. New York and Houndmills: Palgrave Macmillan, 2009, 159–175.

Baucom, Ian. *Out of Place: Englishness, Empire, and the Locations of Identity.* Princeton: Princeton University Press, 1999.

Beaver, Donald deB. "Writing Natural History for Survival, 1820–1856: The Case of Sarah Bowdich, Later Sarah Lee." *Archives of Natural History* 26:1 (1999): 19–31.

Bederman, Gail. *Manliness and Civilization: A Cultural History of Gender and Race in the United States, 1880–1917.* Chicago: University of Chicago Press, 1995.

"Belles Lettres." [Review of *Aurora Leigh.*] *The Westminster and Foreign Quarterly Review* (January 1, 1857): 306–310.

Bentham, Jeremy. "Supply Without Burden; or Escheat *vice* Taxation: Being a Proposal for a Saving of Taxes by an Extension of the Law of Escheat, including Strictures on the Taxes on Collateral Succession comprised in the Budget of December 7th, 1795" (1795). *The Works of Jeremy Bentham.* Published under the Superintendence of his Executor, John Bowring, Vol. II. Edinburgh: William Tait, and London: Simpkin, Marshall, & Co., 1843, 585–598.

Bentley, D. M. R. "The Meretricious and the Meritorious in *Goblin Market.*" *The Achievement of Christina Rossetti.* Ed. David A. Kent. Ithaca: Cornell University Press, 1987, 57-81.

Berg, Allison. *Mothering the Race: Women's Narratives of Reproduction, 1890–1930.* Urbana: University of Illinois Press, 2002.

Berman, Carolyn Vellenga. "Undomesticating the Domestic Novel: Creole Madness in *Jane Eyre.*" *Genre: Forms of Discourse and Culture* 32:4 (Winter, 1999): 267–296.

Besant, Annie. *The Law of Population: Its Consequences, and Its Bearing Upon Human Conduct and Morals.* London: Freethought Publishing Company, 1878 ed.

Bishop, W. H., Jr. *Education and Heredity; or, Eugenics: a Mental, Moral, and Social Force.* London: A. & F. Denny, 1909.

Black, Edwin. *War Against the Weak: Eugenics and America's Campaign to Create a Master Race.* New York: Four Walls Eight Windows, 2003.

Blake, Kathleen. "Between Economies in *The Mill on the Floss*: Loans Versus Gifts, Or, Auditing Mr. Tulliver's Accounts." *Victorian Literature and Culture* 33:1 (2005): 219–237.

Bland, Lucy. *Banishing the Beast: Feminism, Sex and Morality*. London: I. B. Tauris, 2002.

Blumberg, Ilana M. "Collins's *Moonstone*: The Victorian Novel as Sacrifice, Theft, Gift and Debt." *Studies in the Novel* 37:2 (Summer 2005): 162–186.

———. "'Love Yourself as Your Neighbor': The Limits of Altruism and the Ethics of Personal Benefit in *Adam Bede*." *Victorian Literature and Culture* 37:2 (2009): 543–560.

———. "'Unnatural Self-Sacrifice': Trollope's Ethic of Mutual Benefit." *Nineteenth-Century Literature* 58:4 (March 2004): 506–546.

Bonnell, Marilyn. "Sarah Grand and the Critical Establishment: Art for [Wo]man's Sake." *Tulsa Studies in Women's Literature* 14:1 (Spring 1995): 123–148.

Booth, Alison. *How to Make It as a Woman: Collective Biographical History from Victoria to the Present*. Chicago: University of Chicago Press, 2004.

Booth, Bradford Allen, ed. *A Cabinet of Gems: Short Stories from the English Annuals*. Berkeley: University of California Press, 1938.

Booth, Herbert H., and Emma M. Booth. *Called Out! and What Comes of It*. London: International Headquarters, 1886.

Booth, W. Bramwell. *Light in Darkest England in 1895. A Review of the Social Operations of The Salvation Army, with Annual Statement of Accounts of the Darkest England Fund*. London: International Headquarters, 1895.

Boulukos, George. *The Grateful Slave: The Emergence of Race in Eighteenth-Century British and American Culture*. Cambridge: Cambridge University Press, 2008.

Bourdieu, Pierre. *The Logic of Practice*. Trans. Richard Nice. Cambridge: Polity Press, 1990.

Boyer, Carl B. "Commentary on the Papers of Thomas S. Kuhn and I. Bernard Cohen." *Critical Problems in the History of Science: Proceedings of the Institute for the History of Science at the University of Wisconsin, September 1–11, 1957*. Ed. Marshall Clagett. Madison: University of Wisconsin Press, 1962, 384–390.

Brake, Laurel. *Subjugated Knowledges: Journalism, Gender and Literature in the Nineteenth Century*. New York: New York University Press, 1994.

Bray, Mrs. [Anna Eliza]. *A Peep at the Pixies; or, Legends of the West*, London: Grant and Griffith, 1854.

———. *Traditions, Legends, Superstitions, and Sketches of Devonshire on the Borders of The Tamar and the Tavy, Illustrative of Its Manners, Customs, History, Antiquities, Scenery, and Natural History, In a Series of Letters to Robert Southey, Esq.*, Volume 1, London: John Murray, 1838.

Brontë, Anne. *Tenant of Wildfell Hall* (1848). Oxford: Oxford University Press, 2008.

Brontë, Charlotte. *Jane Eyre* (1847). New York: W. W. Norton, 2001.

Brown, Sarah Annes. *Devoted Sisters: Representations of the Sister Relationship in Nineteenth-Century British and American Literature*. Burlington: Ashgate, 2003.

Browning, Elizabeth Barrett. *Aurora Leigh* (1857). Ed. Margaret Reynolds. W.W. Norton, 1996.

———. *The Letters of Elizabeth Barrett Browning, Vol. II*. Ed. Frederic G. Kenyon. New York: The Macmillan Company, 1897.

———. "The Runaway Slave." *The Liberty Bell. By Friends of Freedom*. Ed. Maria Weston Chapman. Boston: American Anti-Slavery Society, 1848, 29–44.

Brush, Stephen C. *The Temperature of History: Phases of Science and Culture in the Nineteenth Century*. New York: Burt Franklin & Co., 1978.

Bulwer-Lytton, Sir Edward. *The Coming Race* (1871). Orchard Park: Broadview Press, 2002.

Burdett, Carolyn. *Olive Schreiner and the Progress of Feminism: Evolution, Gender, Empire*. Houndmills: Palgrave, 2001.

Burton, Antoinette. *Burdens of History: British Feminists, Indian Women, and Imperial Culture, 1865–1915*. Chapel Hill: University of North Carolina Press, 1994.

Butts, Dennis. *Mistress of Our Tears: A Literary and Bibliographical Study of Barbara Hofland*. Aldershot: Scolar Press, 1992.

Buurma, Rachel Sagner. "Anonymity, Corporate Authority, and the Archive: The Production of Authorship in Late-Victorian England." *Victorian Studies* 50:1 (Autumn 2007): 15-42.

Bynum, Caroline Walker. *Holy Feast and Holy Fast: The Religious Significance of Food to Medieval Women*. Berkeley: University of California Press, 1987.

Byron, Lord. *Don Juan. Lord Byron: The Major Works*. Ed. Jerome McGann. Oxford: Oxford University Press, 1986.

Campbell, Elizabeth. "Of Mothers and Merchants: Female Economics in Christina Rossetti's 'Goblin Market.'" *Victorian Studies* 33 (Spring 1990): 393–410.

Campbell, James. "Combat Gnosticism: The Ideology of First World War Poetry Criticism." *New Literary History* 30:1 (1999): 203–215.

"Capabilities and Disabilities of Women." *The Westminster and Foreign Quarterly Review* (January 1, 1857): 42–72.

Carby, Hazel V. *Reconstructing Womanhood: The Emergence of the Afro-American Woman Novelist*. Oxford: Oxford University Press, 1987.

Cardwell, Donald. "Science and Technology: The Work of James Prescott Joule." *Technology and Culture* 17:4 (October 1976): 674–687.

Carlyle, Thomas. *Chartism* (London: James Fraser, 1840). *The Making of the Modern World*. Cengage Learning, <http://galenet.galegroup.com.ezp1.villanova.edu/servlet/MOME?af=RN&ae=U106023541&srchtp=a&ste=14>.

Carpenter, Mary Wilson. "Blinding the Hero." *Differences* 17:3 (Fall 2006): 52–68.

———. "'Eat me, drink me, love me': The Consumable Female Body in Christina Rossetti's *Goblin Market*." *Victorian Poetry* 29:4 (Winter 1991): 415–434.

Carpenter, William B. "On the Mutual Relations of the Vital and Physical Forces." *Philosophical Transactions of the Royal Society of London* 140 (1850): 727–757, <http://links.jstor.org/sici?sici=02610523%281850%29140%3C727%3AOTMROT%3E2.0.CO%3B2–4>.

Carrier, James G. *Gifts and Commodities: Exchange and Western Capitalism Since 1700*. London: Routledge, 1995.

Carroll, Robert and Stephen Prickett, ed. *The Bible: Authorized King James Version*. Oxford: Oxford University Press, 1997.

Case, Alison. "Gender and Narration in *Aurora Leigh*." *Victorian Poetry* 29:1 (Spring 1991): 17–32.

Casey, Janet Galligani. "The Potential of Sisterhood: Christina Rossetti's *Goblin Market*." *Victorian Poetry* 29:1 (Spring 1991): 63–78.

Chambers, Diane M. "Triangular Desire and The Sororal Bond: The 'Deceased Wife's Sister Bill.'" *Mosaic: A Journal for the Interdisciplinary Study of Literature* 29:1 (March 1996): 19–36.

Chambers-Schiller, Lee. "'A Good Work among the People': The Political Culture of the Boston Antislavery Fair." *The Abolitionist Sisterhood: Women's Political Culture in Antebellum America*. Ed. Jean Fagan Yellin and John C. Van Horne. Ithaca: Cornell University Press, 1994, 249–274.

Champney, Adeline. "The Woman Question. An Address Delivered Before the Boston Social Science Club." *The Agitator* 11:1 (September 1903) New York: Comrade Cooperative Company. John Johnson Collection d. 3029.

Chant, L. Ormiston. "Friendly Words to Women on Religion and Politics." London: Central National Society for Women's Suffrage, n.d.

Chase, Karen, and Michael Levenson. *The Spectacle of Intimacy: A Public Life for the Victorian Family*. Princeton: Princeton University Press, 2000.

Cheal, David. "Moral Economy." *The Gift: An Interdisciplinary Perspective*. Ed. Aafke E. Komter. Amsterdam: Amsterdam University Press, 1996, 81–94.

Childs, Donald J. *Modernism and Eugenics: Woolf, Eliot, Yeats, and the Culture of Degeneration*. Cambridge: Cambridge University Press, 2001.

Cholmeley, Robert F. "Women's Suffrage: The Demand & Its Meaning." London: Athenaeum Press, 1909.

Cixous, Hélène. "The Laugh of the Medusa." *Feminisms: an Anthology of Literary Theory and Criticism.* Ed. Robyn R. Warhol and Diane Price Herndl. New Brunswick: Rutgers University Press, 1997, 347–362.

Clarke, Bruce. "Allegories of Victorian Thermodynamics." *Configurations* 4:1 (1996): 67–90.

Clarke, Norma. "Feminism and the Popular Novel of the 1890s: A Brief Consideration of a Forgotten Feminist Novelist." *Feminist Review* 20 (Summer 1985): 91–104.

Clayton, Jay. *Charles Dickens in Cyberspace: The Afterlife of the Nineteenth Century in Postmodern Culture.* Oxford: Oxford University Press, 2003.

Clayton, Tony. "Maundy Money." *Coins of England and Great Britain.* Ed. Tony Clayton, v6 October 24, 2003, December 6, 2005, <http://www.tclayton.demon.co.uk/maund.html>.

———. "The Penny." *Coins of England and Great Britain.* Ed. Tony Clayton, 46:22 (June 2005, December 6, 2005), <http://www.tclayton.demon.co.uk/penny.html>

"Climates for All Nations." *Punch, or the London Charivari*, November 30, 1850, 229. *Gale 19th Century UK Periodicals* database (Villanova University, Villanova, PA), <http://find.galegroup.com/ukpc/basicSearch.do;jsessionid=47770154FEADEF3EF9E321577C4F546A>.

Cobbe, Frances Power. "What Shall We Do with Our Old Maids?" (*Fraser's Magazine*, November, 1862) reprinted in *Prose by Victorian Women: An Anthology.* Ed. Andrea Broomfield and Sally Mitchell. New York: Garland, 1996, 236–261.

Cohen, Deborah. *Household Gods: The British and Their Possessions.* New Haven: Yale University Press, 2006.

Cohen, Monica F. *Professional Domesticity in the Victorian Novel: Women, Work and Home.* Cambridge: Cambridge University Press, 1998.

Cohen, William. *Sex Scandal: The Private Parts of Victorian Fiction.* Durham: Duke University Press, 1996.

Cook, Lady [Tennessee C. Claflin]. "The Ideal Woman." *Evils of Society and Their Remedies. First Series of Essays.* London: The Universal Publishing Company, 1895, 5–7.

———. "Maternity." *Evils of Society and their Remedies. First Series of Essays.* London: The Universal Publishing Company, 1895, 16–25.

———. "Modesty." *Evils of Society and their Remedies. First Series of Essays.* London: The Universal Publishing Company, 1895, 12–15.

———. "The Regeneration of Society." *Evils of Society and Their Remedies. First Series of Essays.* London: The Universal Publishing Company, 1895, 35–42.

———. "A Short History of Marriage." *Evils of Society and Their Remedies. Second Series of Essays.* London: The Universal Publishing Company, 1895, 3–28.

[Cooke, Major James, attrib.] *Slum Evangels. Being the Third Report of the Work of the Salvation Army in The Slums, also Statement of Accounts from February 1st, 1889, to January 31st, 1890.* London, E.C.: International Headquarters, 1890.

Corbett, Mary Jean. *Family Likeness: Sex, Marriage, and Incest from Jane Austen to Virginia Woolf.* Ithaca: Cornell University Press, 2008.

Cowell, Andrew. "The Pleasures and Pains of the Gift." *The Question of the Gift: Essays Across Disciplines.* Ed. Mark Osteen. London: Routledge, 2002, 280–297.

Cowman, Krista. "'Incipient Toryism'? The Women's Social and Political Union and the Independent Labour Party, 1903–14." *History Workshop Journal* 53 (Spring 2002): 128–148.

Cox, Blanche B., Lieut.-Colonel. "Reminiscences of Early-Day Fighting: Salvation Army History Viewed from a Personal Angle." *The Officer's Review* 1:4 (July–August 1932): 333–336.

[Craik, Dinah Mulock] The Author of 'John Halifax, Gentleman.' "About Sisterhoods." *Longman's Magazine*, London: Longmans, Green, and Co., January 1883, 303–313.

Croskery, Margaret Case. "Mothers Without Children, Unity Without Plot: *Cranford's* Radical Charm." *Nineteenth-Century Literature* 52:2 (September 1997): 198–220.

Cuddy, Lois A., and Claire M. Roche. "Introduction." *Evolution and Eugenics in American Literature and Culture, 1880–1940: Essays on Ideological Conflict and Complicity.* Ed. Lois A. Cuddy and Claire M. Roche. Lewisburg: Bucknell University Press, 2003, 9–53.

Cunningham, Gail. "'He-Notes': Reconstructing Masculinity." *The New Woman in Fiction and in Fact: Fin-de-Siècle Feminisms.* Ed. Angelique Richardson and Chris Willis. Houndmills: Palgrave, 2001, 94–106.

———. *The New Woman and the Victorian Novel.* London: Macmillan, 1978.

Dalley, Lana L. "'The Least "Angelical" Poem in the Language': Political Economy, Gender, and the Heritage of *Aurora Leigh.*" *Victorian Poetry* 44:4 (Winter 2006): 525–542.

D'Amico, Diane. *Christina Rossetti: Faith, Gender, and Time.* Baton Rouge: Louisiana State University Press, 1999.

———. "Eve, Mary, and Mary Magdalene: Christina Rossetti's Feminine Triptych." *The Achievement of Christina Rossetti.* Ed. David A. Kent. Ithaca: Cornell University Press, 1987, 175–191.

Darby, Margaret Flanders. "*Un*natural History: Ward's Glass Cases." *Victorian Literature and Culture* 35 (2007): 635–647.

Daunton, Martin. *Trusting Leviathan: The Politics of Taxation in Britain, 1799–1914.* Cambridge: Cambridge University Press, 2001.

David, Deirdre. *Rule Britannia: Women, Empire, and Victorian Writing.* Ithaca: Cornell University Press, 1995.

Davidoff, Leonore, and Catherine Hall. *Family Fortunes: Men and Women of the English Middle Class 1780–1850,* 2nd ed. London: Routledge, 2002.

Davies, Kate. "A Moral Purchase: Femininity, Commerce, and Abolition, 1788–1792." *Women, Writing and the Public Sphere, 1770–1830.* Ed. Elizabeth Eger, Charlotte Grant, et al. Cambridge: Cambridge University Press, 2001, 133–159.

Davis, Cynthia J. "His and Herland: Charlotte Perkins Gilman 'Re-presents' Lester F. Ward." *Evolution and Eugenics in American Literature and Culture, 1880–1940: Essays on Ideological Conflict and Complicity.* Ed. Lois A. Cuddy and Claire M. Roche. Lewisburg: Bucknell University Press, 2003, 73–88.

Dellamora, Richard. "Book Review Forum: Friendship, Marriage, and *Between Women.*" *Victorian Studies* 50:1 (Autumn 2007): 67–74.

Derrida, Jacques. *The Gift of Death.* Trans. David Wills. Chicago: University of Chicago Press, 1995.

———. *Given Time: I. Counterfeit Money.* Trans. Peggy Kamuf. Chicago: University of Chicago Press, 1992.

Derrida, Jacques, and Ferraris, Maurizio. *A Taste for the Secret.* Trans. Giacomo Donis. Ed. Giacomo Donis and David Webb. Cambridge: Polity Press, 2001.

Diamond, Aubrey L. "When Is a Gift . . . ?" *The Modern Law Review* 27:3 (May 1964): 357–360.

Dickens, Charles. *Bleak House* (1853). Ed. Nicola Bradbury. London: Penguin Books, 1996.

———. *The Christmas Books, Volume 1: A Christmas Carol/The Chimes* (1843). London: Penguin Books, 1971.

———. *The Letters of Charles Dickens, Vol. Six, 1850–1852.* Ed. Graham Storey, Kathleen Tillotson, and Nina Burgis. Oxford: Clarendon Press, 1988.

———. *Oliver Twist* (1837–1839). Ed. Peter Fairclough. London: Penguin Books, 1966.

Dickinson, Cindy. "Creating a World of Books, Friends, and Flowers: Gift Books and Inscriptions, 1825–60." *Winterthur Portfolio* 31:1 (Spring 1996): 53–66.

Dill, Bonnie Thornton. "Race, Class, and Gender: Prospects for an All-Inclusive Sisterhood." *Feminist Studies* 9:1 (Spring 1983): 131–150.

[Dixon, Edmund Saul]. "Taxes." *Household Words* 14:337 (September 6, 1856): 181–185.

Dowell, Stephen. *A History of Taxation and Taxes in England from the Earliest Times to the Year 1885. Vol. II: Taxation, From the Civil War to the Present Day.* 2nd ed. London: Longmans, Green, and Co., 1888.

———. *A History of Taxation and Taxes in England from the Earliest Times to the Year 1885. Vol. III: Direct Taxes and Stamp Duties.* 2nd ed., Revised and Altered. London: Longmans, Green, and Co., 1888.

Dowie, Ménie Muriel. *Gallia* (1895). London: Orion, 1995.

Dowling, Linda. "The Decadent and the New Woman in the 1890s." *Nineteenth-Century Fiction* 33:4 (March 1979): 434–453.

Drysdale, Pres. Dr. Chas. R. *Annual Report for 1903–4 of the Malthusian League (Founded 1877).* London: George Standring, 1904.

Drysdale-Vickery, Dr. Alice. "Appeal for Funds." *The Malthusian* 33:5 (15 May, 1909).

Dunfee, Susan Nelson. "The Sin of Hiding: A Feminist Critique of Reinhold Niebuhr's Account of the Sin of Pride." *Soundings* 65:3 (1982): 316–327.

DuPlessis, Rachel Blau. *Writing Beyond the Ending: Narrative Strategies of Twentieth-Century Women Writers.* Bloomington: Indiana University Press, 1985.

Dupras, Joseph A. "Tying the Knot in the Economic Warp of *Jane Eyre*." *Victorian Literature and Culture* 26:2 (1998): 395–408.

Eason, Andrew Mark. *Women in God's Army: Gender and Equality in the Early Salvation Army.* Ontario: Wilfrid Laurier University Press, 2003.

Egenolf, Susan B. "Josiah Wedgwood's Goodwill Marketing." *The Culture of the Gift in Eighteenth-Century England.* Ed. Linda Zionkowski and Cynthia Klekar. New York and Houndmills: Palgrave Macmillan, 2009, 197–213.

[Eliot, George]. "The Natural History of German Life." *The Westminster and Foreign Quarterly Review* 10 (July 1856): 51–79.

Elliott, Dorice Williams. *The Angel Out of the House: Philanthropy and Gender in Nineteenth-Century England.* Charlottesville: University of Virginia Press, 2002.

Ellis, Mrs. [Sarah Stickney]. *The Women of England, Their Social Duties, and Domestic Habits.* London: Fisher, Son, & Co., 1839.

Emerson, Ralph Waldo. "Gifts" (1844). *The Logic of the Gift: Toward an Ethic of Generosity.* Ed. Alan D. Schrift. London: Routledge, 1997, 25–27.

Engels, Friedrich. *The Condition of the Working Class in England* (1845). Oxford: Oxford University Press, 1993.

England, Paula. "The Separative Self: Andocentric Bias in Neoclassical Assumptions." *Beyond Economic Man: Feminist Theory and Economics.* Ed. Marianne A. Ferber and Julie A. Nelson. Chicago: University of Chicago Press, 1993, 37–53.

Erickson, Amy Louise. *Women and Property in Early Modern England.* London: Routledge, 1993.

Farrall, Lyndsay Andrew. *The Origins and Growth of the English Eugenics Movement, 1865–1925.* New York: Garland, 1985.

Feiner, Susan F. "Reading Neoclassical Economics: Toward an Erotic Economy of Sharing." *Out of the Margins: Feminist Perspectives on Economics.* Ed. Edith Kuiper and Jolande Sap. London: Routledge, 1995, 151–166.

Feldman, Paula R. "Introduction." *The Keepsake for 1829.* (Ed. Frederick Mansel Reynolds.) Orchard Park: Broadview Press, 2006, 7–32.

———. "The Poet and the Profits: Felicia Hemans and the Literary Marketplace." *Women's Poetry, Late Romantic to Late Victorian: Gender and Genre, 1830–1900.* Ed. Isobel Armstrong and Virginia Blain. New York: St. Martin's Press, 1999, 71–101.

———. "Women, Literary Annuals, and the Evidence of Inscriptions." *Keats-Shelley Journal* 55 (2006): 54–62.

Fennell, Lee Anne. "Unpacking the Gift: Illiquid Goods and Empathetic Dialogue." Ed. Mark Osteen. *The Question of the Gift: Essays Across Disciplines.* London: Routledge, 2002, 85–101.

Fenwick, Julie M. "Mothers of Empire in Elizabeth Gaskell's *Cranford*." *English Studies in Canada* 23:4 (December 1997): 409–426.

Ferguson, Moira. "Introduction to the Revised Edition." *The History of Mary Prince, a West Indian Slave. Related by Herself.* Revised ed. Ed. Moira Ferguson. Ann Arbor: University of Michigan Press, 1997, 1–51.

———. *Subject to Others: British Women Writers and Colonial Slavery, 1670–1834.* New York: Routledge, 1992.

Finn, Margot C. *The Character of Credit: Personal Debt in English Culture, 1740–1914*. Cambridge: Cambridge University Press, 2003.

———. "Women, Consumption and Coverture in England, c. 1760–1860." *The Historical Journal* 39:3 (September 1996): 703–722.

Flanders, Judith. *Inside the Victorian Home: A Portrait of Domestic Life in Victorian England*. New York: W. W. Norton and Company, 2004.

Flint, Kate. *The Woman Reader 1837–1914*. Oxford: Oxford University Press, 1993.

Folbre, Nancy, and Heidi Hartman. "The Rhetoric of Self-Interest: Ideology and Gender in Economic Theory." *The Consequences of Economic Rhetoric*. Ed. Arjo Klamer, Donald N. McCloskey, Robert M. Solow. Cambridge: Cambridge University Press, 1988, 184–203.

Forel, August, M.D., Ph.D., LLD. *The Sexual Question: A Scientific, Psychological, Hygienic and Sociological Study* (1906, 1908). English Adaptation from the 2nd German Ed., Revised and Enlarged by C. F. Marshall, M.D., F.R.C.S. London: William Heinemann (Medical Books), 1927.

Foucault, Michel. *Discipline and Punish: The Birth of the Prison*. Trans. Alan Sheridan. New York: Vintage Books, 1977.

Fox-Genovese, Elizabeth. "The Personal Is Not Political Enough." *Marxist Perspectives* 8 (Winter 1979/80): 94–113.

Fraiman, Susan. "Review of *Devoted Sisters: Representations of the Sister Relationship in Nineteenth-Century British and American Literature* by Sarah Annes Brown." *Victorian Studies* 48:1 (Autumn 2005): 177–179.

———. *Unbecoming Women: British Women Writers and the Novel of Development*. New York: Columbia University Press, 1993.

Freedgood, Elaine. *The Ideas in Things: Fugitive Meaning in the Victorian Novel*. Chicago: University of Chicago Press, 2006.

Freyhan, R. "The Evolution of the Caritas Figure in the Thirteenth and Fourteenth Centuries." *Journal of the Warburg and Courtauld Institutes* 11 (1948): 68–86.

Friendship's Offering; and Winter's Wreath: A Christmas and New Year's Present. London: Smith, Elder and Co., 1830, 1831, 1832, 1835, 1836, 1837.

Gagnier, Regenia. *The Insatiability of Human Wants: Economic and Aesthetics in Market Society*. Chicago: University of Chicago Press, 2000.

Gallagher, Catherine. *The Body Economic: Life, Death, and Sensation in Political Economy and the Victorian Novel*. Princeton: Princeton University Press, 2006.

Galton, Francis. "Eugenics as a Factor in Religion." *Essays in Eugenics*. London: The Eugenics Education Society, 1909, 68–70.

———. "Hereditary Improvement." *Fraser's Magazine* 7:37 (January 1873): 116–130.

———. "Local Associations for Promoting Eugenics" (1908). *Essays in Eugenics*. London: The Eugenics Education Society, 1909, 100–109.

———. "The Possible Improvement of the Human Breed Under the Existing Conditions of Law and Sentiment" (1901). *Essays in Eugenics*. London: The Eugenics Education Society, 1909, 1–34.

Ganobcsik-Williams, Lisa. "The Intellectualism of Charlotte Perkins Gilman: Evolutionary Perspectives on Race, Ethnicity, and Class." *Charlotte Perkins Gilman: Optimist Reformer*. Ed. Jill Rudd and Val Gough. Iowa City: University of Iowa Press, 1999, 16–41.

Garcha, Amanpal. *From Sketch to Novel: The Development of Victorian Fiction*. Cambridge: Cambridge University Press, 2009.

Gaskell, Elizabeth. *Cranford* (1851-1853). Oxford: Oxford University Press, 1998.

———. *The Letters of Mrs Gaskell*. Ed. J.A.V. Chapple and Arthur Pollard. Cambridge: Harvard University Press, 1967.

———. *The Life of Charlotte Brontë* (1857). London: Penguin Books, 1997.

———. *Mary Barton: A Tale of Manchester Life* (1848). Ed. Macdonald Daly. London: Penguin Books, 1996.

———. *North and South* (1854–1855). Ed. Patricia Ingham. London: Penguin Books, 1995.

Geddes, Patrick, and J. Arthur Thomson. *The Evolution of Sex* (1889). Revised ed. London: Walter Scott, 1901.

Genette, Gérard. *Paratexts: Thresholds of Interpretations*. Trans. Jane E. Lewin. Cambridge: Cambridge University Press, 1997.

Georgescu-Roegen, Nicholas. *Energy and Economic Myths*. Oxford: Pergamon, 1976.

Gérin, Winifred. *Elizabeth Gaskell: A Biography*. Oxford: Clarendon Press, 1976.

Gezari, Janet. *Charlotte Brontë and Defensive Conduct: The Author and the Body at Risk*. Philadelphia: University of Pennsylvania Press, 1992.

Gilbert, Sandra M., and Susan Gubar. *The Madwoman in the Attic: The Woman Writer and the Nineteenth-Century Literary Imagination*. 2nd ed. New Haven: Yale University Press, 2000.

Gillooly, Eileen. "Humor as Daughterly Defense in *Cranford*." *English Literary History (ELH)* 59:4 (Winter 1992): 883–910.

Gilman, Charlotte Perkins. *Herland* (1915). Mineola: Dover Publications, 1998.

———. *Women and Economics* (1898). New York: Cosimo Classics, 2006.

Girard, René. "Mimesis and Violence." *The Girard Reader*. Ed. James G. Williams. New York: Crossroad, 1996, 9-19.

Glen, Heather. *Charlotte Brontë: The Imagination in History*. Oxford and New York: Oxford University Press, 2002.

Godelier, Maurice. *The Enigma of the Gift*. Trans. Nora Scott. Chicago: University of Chicago Press, 1999.

Gold, Barri J. "The Consolation of Physics: Tennyson's Thermodynamic Solution." *Publications of the Modern Language Association* 117:3 (May, 2002): 449–464.

Goodlad, Lauren M.E. *Victorian Literature and the Victorian State: Character and Governance in a Liberal Society*. Baltimore: The Johns Hopkins University Press, 2003.

Gotto, Sybil. *The Eugenic Principle in Social Reconstruction*. Kingsway: Eugenics Education Society. (Reprinted from *The Eugenics Review*, October 1917.)

Goux, Jean-Joseph. "Seneca Against Derrida: Gift and Alterity." *The Enigma of Gift and Sacrifice*. Ed. Edith Wyschogrod, Jean-Joseph Goux, and Eric Boynton. New York: Fordham University Press, 2002, 148–160.

Grand, Sarah. *The Heavenly Twins, Vols. I and II* (1893). Charleston: BiblioBazaar, 2007.

Green, Barbara. *Spectacular Confessions: Autobiography, Performative Activism, and the Sites of Suffrage, 1905–1938*. New York: St. Martin's Press, 1997.

Green, David R. "To do the Right Thing: Gender, Wealth, Inheritance and the London Middle Class." *Women and Their Money, 1700–1950: Essays on Women and Finance*. Ed. Anne Laurence, Josephine Maltby, and Janette Rutterford. London and New York: Routledge, 2009, 133–150.

Green, Roger J. "Settled Views: Catherine Booth and Female Ministry." *Methodist History* 31:3 (April 1993): 131–147.

Grove, W[illiam] R[obert]. *On the Correlation of Physical Forces: Being the Substance of a Course of Lectures Delivered in the London Institute in the Year 1843*. London: C. Skipper and East, 1846.

Gruner, Elisabeth Rose. "Born and Made: Sisters, Brothers, and the Deceased Wife's Sister Bill." *Signs* 24:2 (Winter 1999): 423–447.

Gubar, Susan. "What Ails Feminist Criticism?" *Critical Inquiry* 24:4 (Summer 1998): 878–902.

Habermas, Jürgen. *The Structural Transformation of the Public Sphere: An Inquiry into a Category of Bourgeois Society*. Trans. Thomas Burger. Cambridge: MIT Press, 1989.

Hall, S. C., ed. *The Amulet. A Christian and Literary Remembrancer*. London: Frederick Westley and A. H. Davis, 1833, 1835.

Harman, Lillian. "Eve and Eden." *The Adult: The Journal of Sex* 2:2 (March 1898): 32 35.

Harman, P. M. *Energy, Force, and Matter: The Conceptual Development of Nineteenth-Century Physics*. Cambridge: Cambridge University Press, 1982.

Harris, Katherine D. "Borrowing, Altering and Perfecting the Literary Annual Form—or What It Is Not: Emblems, Almanacs, Pocket-books, Albums, Scrapbooks and Gift Books." *Poetess Archive Journal* 1:1 (April 12, 2007).

———. "Feminizing the Textual Body: Female Readers Consuming the Literary Annual." *The Papers of the Bibliographical Society of America* 99:4 (2005): 573–622.

Hassett, Constance W. *Christina Rossetti: The Patience of Style*. Charlottesville: University of Virginia Press, 2005.

Heilmann, Ann. "Narrating the Hysteric: Fin-de-Siècle Medical Discourse and Sarah Grand's *The Heavenly Twins* (1893)." *The New Woman in Fiction and in Fact: Fin-de-Siècle Feminisms*. Ed. Angelique Richardson and Chris Willis. Houndmills: Palgrave, 2001, 123–135.

Helsinger, Elizabeth K. "Consumer Power and the Utopia of Desire: Christina Rossetti's 'Goblin Market.'" *ELH* 58:4 (Winter 1991): 903–933.

Herbert, Christopher. *Culture and Anomie: Ethnographic Imagination in the Nineteenth Century*. Chicago: University of Chicago Press, 1991.

Hill, Marylu. "'Eat Me, Drink Me, Love Me': Eucharist and the Erotic Body in Christina Rossetti's *Goblin Market.*" *Victorian Poetry* 43:4 (Winter 2005): 455–472.

Hillard, Molly Clark. "Dangerous Exchange: Fairy Footsteps, Goblin Economies, and *The Old Curiosity Shop.*" *Dickens Studies Annual* 35 (2005): 63–86.

Himmelfarb, Gertrude. *Poverty and Compassion: The Moral Imagination of the Late Victorians*. New York: Random House, 1991.

Hoeckley, Cheri Larsen. "Anomalous Ownership: Copyright, Coverture, and *Aurora Leigh.*" *Victorian Poetry* 35:2 (Summer 1998): 135–161.

Holt, Terrence. "'Men sell not such in any town': Exchange in *Goblin Market.*" *Victorian Poetry* 28 (1990): 51–67.

hooks, bell. *Ain't I a Woman: Black Women and Feminism*. Boston: South End Press, 1981.

Horridge, Glenn K. "William Booth's Officers." *Christian History Issue* 26 (9:2) 1990: 14–17.

Huett, Lorna. "Commodity and Collectivity: *Cranford* in the Context of *Household Words.*" *The Gaskell Society Journal* 17 (2003): 34–49.

Humble, Nicola, ed. *Mrs. Beeton's Book of Household Management*. Oxford: Oxford University Press, 2000.

Humphrey, Mrs. "Women on Wheels." *Idler: An Illustrated Monthly Magazine* 8:43 (August 1895): 71–74.

Hunt, Lynn. *Inventing Human Rights: A History*. New York: W.W. Norton, 2007.

Hunter, J. Paul. *Before Novels: The Cultural Contexts of Eighteenth-Century English Fiction*. New York: W.W. Norton, 1990.

Hyde, Lewis. *The Gift: Imagination and the Erotic Life of Property*. New York: Random House, 1983.

Hyland, Richard. *Gifts: A Study in Comparative Law*. Oxford: Oxford University Press, 2009.

The Imperial: A Christmas and New-Year's Present for 1839. London: W. Tombleson & Company, 1839.

Irigaray, Luce. "Women on the Market." *The Logic of the Gift: Toward an Ethic of Generosity*. Ed. Alan D. Schrift. New York: Routledge, 1997, 174–189.

Irvine, Helen. "The Legitimizing Power of Financial Statements in the Salvation Army in England, 1865–1892." *The Accounting Historians Journal* 29:1 (2002): 1–36.

Jackson, Louise A. "'Singing Birds as well as Soap Suds': The Salvation Army's Work with Sexually Abused Girls in Edwardian England." *Gender & History* 12:1 (April 2000): 107–126.

Jaffe, Audrey. *Scenes of Sympathy: Identity and Representation in Victorian Fiction*. Ithaca: Cornell University Press, 2000.

Jameson, Anna. *Sisters of Charity, Catholic and Protestant. And The Communion of Labor* (London: 1855). Boston: Ticknor and Fields, 1857.

Jeffreys, Sheila. *The Spinster and her Enemies: Feminism and Sexuality 1880–1930*. London: Pandora Press, 1985.

Joule, James Prescott. *The Scientific Papers of James Prescott Joule*. London: Dawsons of Pall Mall, 1963.

———. "On the Calorific Effects of Magneto-Electricity, and on the Mechanical Value of Heat" (1843): 123–159.

————. "On the Changes of Temperature produced by the Rarefaction and Condensation of Air" (1845): 172–189.

————. "On the Heat disengaged in Chemical Combinations" (1852): 205–207.

Jusová, Iveta. *The New Woman and the Empire*. Columbus: Ohio State University Press, 2005.

Kaplan, Cora, ed. "Introduction." *Aurora Leigh and Other Poems*. London: The Women's Press, 1978.

Keen, Suzanne. *Empathy and the Novel*. Oxford: Oxford University Press, 2007.

The Keepsake for 1837. London: Longman, Rees, Orme, Brown, Green, and Longman, 1836.

Keightley, Thomas. *The Fairy Mythology, Illustrative of the Romance and Superstition of Various Countries, a New Edition, Revised and Greatly Enlarged*. London: H.G. Bohn, 1850.

Kendrick, Walter M. *The Novel Machine: The Theory and Fiction of Anthony Trollope*. Baltimore: The Johns Hopkins University Press, 1980.

Kevles, Daniel J. *In the Name of Eugenics: Genetics and the Uses of Human Heredity*. New York: Alfred A. Knopf, 1985.

Klaus, Alisa. "Depopulation and Race Suicide: Maternalism and Pronatalist Ideologies in France and the United States." *Mothers of a New World: Maternalist Politics and the Origins of Welfare States*. Ed. Seth Koven and Sonya Michel. New York: Routledge, 1993, 188–212.

Komter, Aafke E., ed. *The Gift: An Interdisciplinary Perspective*. Amsterdam: Amsterdam University Press, 1996.

————. *Social Solidarity and the Gift*. Cambridge: Cambridge University Press, 2005.

Kooistra, Lorraine Janzen. "Modern Markets for *Goblin Market*." *Victorian Poetry* 32 (1994): 249–277.

Koven, Seth. "Borderlands: Women, Voluntary Action, and Child Welfare in Britain, 1840 to 1914." *Mothers of a New World: Maternalist Politics and the Origins of Welfare States*. Ed. Seth Koven and Sonya Michel. New York: Routledge, 1993, 94–135.

————. *Slumming: Sexual and Social Politics in Victorian London*. Princeton: Princeton University Press, 2004.

Koven, Seth, and Sonya Michel. "Introduction: 'Mother Worlds.'" *Mothers of a New World: Maternalist Politics and the Origins of Welfare States*. Ed. Seth Koven and Sonya Michel. New York: Routledge, 1993, 1–42.

Kucich, John. "Olive Schreiner, Masochism, and Omnipotence: Strategies of a Preoedipal Politics." *Novel: A Forum on Fiction* 36:1 (Autumn 2002): 79–109.

Kuhn, Thomas S. "Energy Conservation as an Example of Simultaneous Discovery." *Critical Problems in the History of Science: Proceedings of the Institute for the History of Science at the University of Wisconsin, September 1–11, 1957*. Ed. Marshall Clagett. Madison: University of Wisconsin Press, 1962, 321–356.

Larsen, Timothy. *Christabel Pankhurst: Feminism and Fundamentalism in Coalition*. Rochester: Boydell Press, 2002.

Ledbetter, Kathryn Ruth. "'BeGemmed and beAmuletted': Tennyson and Those 'Vapid' Gift Books." *Victorian Poetry* 34:2 (Summer 1996): 235–245.

————. *British Victorian Women's Periodicals: Beauty, Civilization, and Poetry*. New York and Houndmills: Palgrave Macmillan, 2009.

————. *Tennyson and Victorian Periodicals: Commodities in Context*. Aldershot: Ashgate Publishing Limited, 2007.

————. "'White Vellum and Gilt Edges': Imaging *The Keepsake*." *Studies in the Literary Imagination* 30:1 (Spring 1997): 35–47.

Leigh, Percival. "The Chemistry of a Candle." *Household Words conducted by Charles Dickens* 1:19 (August 1850): 439–444.

————. "The Mysteries of a Tea Kettle." *Household Words conducted by Charles Dickens* 2:34 (November 1850): 176–181.

Leighton, Angela. "'Because Men Made the Laws': The Fallen Woman and the Woman Poet." *Victorian Women Poets: Emily Brontë, Elizabeth Barrett Browning, Christina Rossetti*. Ed. Joseph Bristow. New York: St. Martin's Press, 1995, 223–245.

————. *Elizabeth Barrett Browning.* Bloomington: Indiana University Press, 1986.

Levi, Leone. *Wages and Earnings of the Working Classes. Report to Sir Arthur Bass, M.P.* London: John Murray, 1885.

Levine, George. *Darwin and the Novelists: Patterns of Science in Victorian Fiction.* Chicago: University of Chicago Press, 1988.

Lévi-Strauss, Claude. "The Principle of Reciprocity." *The Gift: An Interdisciplinary Perspective.* Ed. Aafke E. Komter. Amsterdam: Amsterdam University Press, 1996, 18–25.

Liggins, Emma. "Writing Against the 'Husband-Fiend': Syphilis and Male Sexual Vice in the New Woman Novel." *Women's Writing* 7:2 (2000): 175–195.

Linton, E[liza] Lynn. "The Shrieking Sisterhood" (1870). *The Girl of the Period and Other Social Essays, in Two Volumes.* London: Richard Bentley & Son, 1883, 2: 64–71.

Lloyd, J.T. "Background to the Joule-Mayer Controversy." *Notes and Records of the Royal Society of London* 25:2 (December 1970): 211–225.

A Looker On. "Women's Rights as Preached by Women Past and Present." New ed. London: Kegan Paul, Trench, & Co., 1881.

Lysack, Krista. *Come Buy, Come Buy: Shopping and the Culture of Consumption in Victorian Women's Writing.* Athens: Ohio University Press, 2008.

————. "Goblin Markets: Victorian Women Shoppers at Liberty's Oriental Bazaar." *Nineteenth-Century Contexts* 27:2 (June 2005): 139–165.

Lytton, Lady Constance. "'No Votes for Women.' A Reply to Some Recent Anti-Suffrage Publications." London: A.C. Fifield, 1909.

Macquiban, Tim. "Soup and Salvation: Social Service as an Emerging Motif for the British Methodist Response to Poverty in the Late 19th Century." *Methodist History* 39:1 (2000): 28–43.

Mandler, Peter. "Poverty and Charity in the Nineteenth-Century Metropolis: An Introduction." *The Uses of Charity: The Poor on Relief in the Nineteenth-Century Metropolis.* Ed. Peter Mandler. Philadelphia: University of Pennsylvania Press, 1990, 1–37.

Mangum, Teresa. *Married, Middlebrow, and Militant: Sarah Grand and the New Woman Novel.* Ann Arbor: University of Michigan Press, 1998.

————. "Sex, Siblings, and the Fin De Siecle." *The Significance of Sibling Relationships in Literature.* Ed. JoAnna Stephens Mink and Janet Doubler Ward. Bowling Green: Bowling Green State University Popular Press, 1993, 70–82.

Mann, Jill. "Satisfaction and Payment in Middle English Literature." *Studies in the Age of Chaucer* 5 (1983): 17–48.

Manning, Peter J. "Wordsworth in the *Keepsake*, 1829." *Literature in the Marketplace: Nineteenth-Century British Publishing and Reading Practices.* Ed. John O. Jordan and Robert L. Patten. Cambridge: Cambridge University Press, 1995, 44–73.

Marcus, Sharon. *Between Women: Friendship, Desire, and Marriage in Victorian England.* Princeton: Princeton University Press, 2007.

Marsh, Jan. *Christina Rossetti: A Writer's Life.* New York: Viking Penguin, 1995.

————. "Christina Rossetti's Vocation: The Importance of *Goblin Market*." *Victorian Poetry* 32 (1994): 233–248.

Marshall, David. *The Surprising Effects of Sympathy: Marivaux, Diderot, Rousseau, and Mary Shelley.* Chicago: University of Chicago Press, 1988.

Marshall, Linda E. "'Transfigured to His Likeness': Sensible Transcendentalism in Christina Rossetti's 'Goblin Market.'" *University of Toronto Quarterly* 63:3 (Spring 1994): 429–450.

Marx, Karl, "The General Formula for Capital." *The Marx-Engels Reader.* Ed. Robert C. Tucker. 2nd ed. New York: W.W. Norton, 1978, 329–336.

Marx, Karl, and Friedrich Engels. *The Communist Manifesto.* London: Penguin Books, 1967.

"Maundy, n." OED online. Oxford University Press, <http://www.oed.com/view/Entry/115188?redirected From=Maundy>, accessed May 16, 2011.

Mauss, Marcel. *The Gift: The Form and Reason for Exchange in Archaic Societies.* Trans. W.D. Hall. London: Routledge, 1990.

————. "Gift, Gift." *The Logic of the Gift: Toward an Ethic of Generosity*. Ed. Alan D. Schrift. New York: Routledge, 1997, 28–32.

Maxwell, Catherine. "Tasting the 'Fruit Forbidden': Gender, Intertextuality, and Christina Rossetti's *Goblin Market*." *The Culture of Christina Rossetti: Female Poetics and Victorian Contexts*. Ed. Mary Arseneau, Antony H. Harrison, and Lorraine Janzen Kooistra. Athens: Ohio University Press, 1999, 75–102.

May, Leila Silvana. *Disorderly Sisters: Sibling Relations and Sororal Resistance in Nineteenth-Century British Literature*. Lewisburg: Bucknell University Press, 2001.

Mayhall, Laura E. Nym. *The Militant Suffrage Movement: Citizenship and Resistance in Britain, 1860–1930*. Oxford: Oxford University Press, 2003.

Mayo, Winifred [Winifred Alice Monck-Mason]. "Prison Experiences of a Suffragette." *Idler: An Illustrated Monthly Magazine* 33:67 (April 1908): 85–99. *ProQuest British Periodicals* database, <http://gateway.proquest.com/openurl?url_ver=Z39.88-2004&res_dat=xri:bp-us:&rft_dat=xri:bp:article:e597-1908-033-67-002882:1>.

McArthur, Tonya Moutray. "Unwed Orders: Religious Communities for Women in the Works of Elizabeth Gaskell." *The Gaskell Society Journal* 17 (2003): 59–76.

McClintock, Anne. *Imperial Leather: Race, Gender and Sexuality in the Colonial Contest*. New York: Routledge, 1995.

McGann, Jerome J. "Introduction." *The Achievement of Christina Rossetti*. Ed. David A. Kent. Ithaca: Cornell University Press, 1987, 1-19.

Meller, Helen. *Patrick Geddes: Social Evolutionist and City Planner*. London: Routledge, 1990.

Mellor, Anne K. "'Am I Not a Woman, and a Sister?': Slavery, Romanticism, and Gender." *Romanticism, Race, and Imperial Culture, 1780–1834*. Ed. Alan Richardson and Sonia Hofkosh. Bloomington: Indiana University Press, 1996, 311–326.

Mendoza, Victor Roman. "'Come Buy': The Crossing of Sexual and Consumer Desire in Christina Rossetti's *Goblin Market*." *ELH* 73:4 (2006): 913–947.

Menke, Richard. "The Political Economy of Fruit: *Goblin Market*." *The Culture of Christina Rossetti: Female Poetics and Victorian Contexts*. Ed. Mary Arseneau, Antony H. Harrison, and Lorraine Janzen Kooistra. Athens: Ohio University Press, 1999, 105–136.

————. *Telegraphic Realism: Victorian Fiction and Other Information Systems*. Stanford: Stanford University Press, 2008.

Mermin, Dorothy. *Elizabeth Barrett Browning: The Origins of a New Poetry*. Chicago: University of Chicago Press, 1989.

————. "Heroic Sisterhood in *Goblin Market*." *Victorian Poetry* 21:2 (Summer 1983): 107–118.

Meyer, Susan. *Imperialism at Home: Race and Victorian Women's Fiction*. Ithaca: Cornell University Press, 1996.

Michel, Sonya. "The Limits of Maternalism: Policies Toward American Wage-Earning Mothers During the Progressive Era." *Mothers of a New World: Maternalist Politics and the Origins of Welfare States*. Ed. Seth Koven and Sonya Michel. New York: Routledge, 1993, 277–320.

Michie, Elsie B. "Rich Woman, Poor Woman: Toward an Anthropology of the Nineteenth-Century Marriage Plot." *PMLA* 124:2 (March 2009): 421–436.

Michie, Helena. *Sororophobia: Differences Among Women in Literature and Culture*. Oxford: Oxford University Press, 1992.

Midgley, Clare. *Women Against Slavery: The British Campaigns, 1780–1870*. London: Routledge, 1992.

Milbank, John. "Can a Gift Be Given? Prolegomena to a Future Trinitarian Metaphysic." *Modern Theology* 11:1 (January 1995): 119–161.

Mill, John Stuart. *Principles of Political Economy with Some of their Applications to Social Philosophy. Vol. II* (1848). 5th ed. London: Parker, Son, and Bourn, 1862.

Miller, Andrew H. *Novels Behind Glass: Commodity Culture and Victorian Narrative*. Cambridge: Cambridge University Press, 1995.

————. "Subjectivity, Ltd: The Discourse of Liability in the Joint Stock Companies Act of 1856 and Gaskell's *Cranford*." *ELH* 61:1 (Spring 1994): 139–157.

Miller, D.A. *The Novel and the Police*. Berkeley: University of California Press, 1988.

Milton, "L'Allegro." *John Milton: A Critical Edition of the Major Works*. Ed. Stephen Orgel and Jonathan Goldberg. Oxford: Oxford University Press, 1991, 22–25.

Mirowski, Philip. *More Heat than Light: Economics as Social Physics: Physics as Nature's Economics*. Cambridge: Cambridge University Press, 1989.

"Miscellaneous Church Intelligence." *John Bull* 1,504 (October 6, 1849): 626–627. *Gale 19th Century UK Periodicals* database: *New Readerships* collection, <http://find.galegroup.com. ezp1.villanova.edu/ukpc/infomark.do?docType=LTO&contentSet=LTO&sort=DateAscen d&tabID=T012&docId=DX1900704967&prodId=NCUK&searchId=R7&callistoContentS et=NCUP&docLevel=FASCIMILE&qrySerId=Locale(en,,):FQE=(tx,None,33)miscellane- ous church intelligence:And:LQE=(jn,None,9)john bull:And:LQE=(da,None,4)1849:And :LQE=(MB,None,16)NCUK-1 OR NCUK-2$&type=multipage&retrieveFormat=MULTIP AGE_DOCUMENT&currentPosition=114&version=1.0&userGroupName=vill_main&se archType=BasicSearchForm&enlarge=true&docPage=page&source=gale>.

"Miss Pankhurst Here Unheralded," *The New York Times* (Oct. 15, 1914): 9. *ProQuest Historical Newspapers* database, *The New York Times* (1851-2007) <http://proquest.umi.com.ezp1.vil- lanova.edu/pqdweb?did=100329409&sis=1&Fmt=10&clinetId=3260&RQT=309&VName =HNP>.

See also "Miss Pankhurst Attacks Germans," *The New York Times* (Oct. 25, 1914): C3. *ProQuest Historical Newspapers* database, *The New York Times* (1851-2007) <http://proquest.umi.com. ezp1.villanova.edu/pqdweb?did=100109390&sid=3&Fmt=10&clientId=3260&RQT=309 &VName=HNP>.

Mitchell, David J. *The Fighting Pankhursts: A Study in Tenacity*. New York: Macmillan, 1967.

Mizruchi, Susan L. *The Science of Sacrifice: American Literature and Modern Social Theory*. Princeton: Princeton University Press, 1998.

Moers, Ellen. *Literary Women*. Garden City: Doubleday, 1976.

Mossman, Mark. "Speech, Behavior, and the Function of Utopia: Restraint and Resistance in Eliza- beth Gaskell's *Cranford*." *Nineteenth-Century Feminisms* 5 (Fall/Winter 2001): 78–87.

Mullan, John. *Sentiment and Sociability: The Language of Feeling in the Eighteenth Century*. Oxford: Clarendon Press, 1988.

Mulvihill, James. "Economies of Living in Mrs. Gaskell's *Cranford*." *Nineteenth-Century Literature* 50:3 (December 1995): 337–356.

Mumm, Susan. *Stolen Daughters, Virgin Mothers: Anglican Sisterhoods in Victorian Britain*, London: Leicester University Press, 1999.

Murdoch, Norman H. *Origins of the Salvation Army*. Knoxville: University of Tennessee Press, 1994.

Murphy, Margueritte. "The Ethic of the Gift in George Eliot's *Daniel Deronda*." *Victorian Literature and Culture* 34:1 (2006): 187–207.

Murphy, Patricia. *Time Is of the Essence: Temporality, Gender, and the New Woman*. Albany: State University of New York Press, 2001.

Myers, Greg. "Nineteenth-Century Popularizations of Thermodynamics and the Rhetoric of Social Prophecy." *Energy and Entropy: Science and Culture in Victorian Britain*. Ed. Patrick Brantlinger. Bloomington: Indiana University Press, 1989.

Newman, Louise Michele. *White Women's Rights: The Racial Origins of Feminism in the United States*. Oxford: Oxford University Press, 1999.

Nightingale, C.A. *Fifteenth Annual Report of The Salvation Army Slum Work in Bristol*. Bristol: Divi- sion Headquarters, 1904.

Nightingale, Florence. *Cassandra and Suggestions for Thought* (1860). Ed. Mary Poovey. New York: New York University Press, 1992.

Nord, Deborah Epstein. *Gypsies and the British Imagination, 1807–1930*. New York: Columbia Uni- versity Press, 2006.

———. *Walking the Victorian Streets: Women, Representation, and the City*. Ithaca: Cornell University Press, 1995.

Nunokawa, Jeff. *The Afterlife of Property: Domestic Security and the Victorian Novel.* Princeton: Princeton University Press, 1994.

O'Dea, Gregory. "'Perhaps a Tale You'll Make It': Mary Shelley's Tales for *The Keepsake.*" *Iconoclastic Departures: Mary Shelley after Frankenstein–Essays in Honor of the Bicentenary of Mary Shelley's Birth.* Ed. Syndy M. Conger, Frederick S. Frank, and Gregory O'Dea. London: Associated University Presses, 1997, 62–78.

O'Farrell, Mary Ann. "Sister Acts." *Women's Studies Quarterly* 34:3/4 (Fall-Winter, 2006): 154–173.

Osteen, Mark. "Gift or Commodity?" *The Question of the Gift: Essays across Disciplines.* Ed. Mark Osteen. London: Routledge, 2002, 229–247.

———. "Introduction: Questions of the Gift." *The Question of the Gift: Essays across Disciplines.* Ed. Mark Osteen. London: Routledge, 2002, 1–41.

Pankhurst, Christabel. "America and the War: A Speech Delivered at Carnegie Hall, New York, October 24th, 1914." London: The Women's Social and Political Union, 1914.

———. "Speech in Washington, January 24, 1915." *Appeal to America.* London: Charles Jones & Co., 1915.

———. *Unshackled: The Story of How We Won the Vote* (1959). *The Militant.* Ed. Marie Mulvey Roberts, Tamae Mizuta. London: Routledge, 1995.

Parkin, Christine. "Pioneer in Female Ministry." *Christian History* 26 (1990): 10–13.

Parsons, Elsie Clews, Ph.D. *The Family: An Ethnographical and Historical Outline with Descriptive Notes, Planned as a Text-book for the Use of College Lecturers and of Directors of Home-reading Clubs.* New York and London: G.P. Putnam's Sons, 1906.

Pascoe, Judith. "Poetry as Souvenir: Mary Shelley in the Annuals." *Mary Shelley in Her Times.* Ed. Betty T. Bennett and Stuart Curran. Baltimore: The Johns Hopkins University Press, 2000, 173–184.

The Pearl; or, Affection's Gift. A Christmas and New Year's Present. Philadelphia: Thomas T. Ash, 1830.

Pearson, Karl. *The Academic Aspect of the Science of National Eugenics.* London: Dulau and Co., 1911.

———. "Nature and Nurture: The Problem of the Future." *A Presidential Address Delivered by Karl Pearson, F.R.S., at the Annual Meeting of the Social and Political Education League.* London: Dulau and Co., 1910.

———. *The Problem of Practical Eugenics.* London: Dulau and Co., 1909.

———. *The Scope and Importance to the State of National Eugenics* (1907). 2nd ed. London: Dulau and Co., 1909.

———. "Women and Labor." *Fortnightly Review* 61 (1894): 561–577.

Perkin, Harold. *The Origins of Modern English Society.* 2nd ed. London: Routledge, 1969, 2002.

Perry, Ruth. *Novel Relations: The Transformation of Kinship in English Literature and Culture 1748–1818.* Cambridge: Cambridge University Press, 2004.

Peterfreund, Stuart. "The Re-Emergence of Energy in the Discourse of Literature and Science." *Annals of Scholarship* 4:1 (1986): 22–53.

"Peter's penny, n." OED online. Oxford University Press, http://www.oed.com/view/Entry/131833? redirectedFrom=Peter%20pence, accessed May 16, 2011.

Plaskow, Judith. *Sex, Sin and Grace: Women's Experience and the Theologies of Reinhold and Paul Tillich.* Boston: University Press of America, 1980.

Pleck, Elizabeth. *Domestic Tyranny: The Making of Social Policy Against Family Violence from Colonial Times to the Present.* New York: Oxford University Press, 1987.

Plotz, John. *Portable Property: Victorian Culture on the Move.* Princeton: Princeton University Press, 2008.

Politi, Jina. "*Jane Eyre* Class-ified." *New Casebooks: Jane Eyre.* Ed. Heather Glen. Houndmills. Macmillan, 1997, 78–91.

Poovey, Mary. *Uneven Developments: The Ideological Work of Gender in Mid-Victorian England.* Chicago: University of Chicago Press, 1988.

Prochaska, F. K. *Royal Bounty: The Making of a Welfare Monarchy.* New Haven: Yale University Press, 1995.

————. *Women and Philanthropy in Nineteenth-Century England.* Oxford: Clarendon Press, 1980.

"The Protestant Nuns of Devonport." *The Bengal Catholic Herald* 22 (June 2, 1849): 305. *Gale 19th Century UK Periodicals* database: *Empire* collection, <http://find.galegroup.com. ezp1.villanova.edu/ukpc/infomark.do?docType=LTO&contentSet=LTO&sort=DateAs cend&tabID=T012&docId=CC1903327666&prodId=NCUK&searchId=R6&callistoC ontentSet=NCUP&docLevel=FASCIMILE&qrySerId=Locale(en,,):FQE=(tx,None,28) protestant nuns of devonport:And:LQE=(MB,None,16)NCUK-1 OR NCUK-2$&type =multipage&retrieveFormat=MULTIPAGE_DOCUMENT&currentPosition=1&versio n=1.0&userGroupName=vill_main&searchType=BasicSearchForm&docPage=article& source=gale>.

Psomiades, Kathy. "Heterosexual Exchange and Other Victorian Fictions: *The Eustace Diamonds* and Victorian Anthropology." *NOVEL: A Forum on Fiction* 33:1 (Autumn 1999): 93–118.

Pugh, Martin. *The Pankhursts.* London: Penguin, 2001.

Pujol, Michèle. "Into the Margin!" *Out of the Margins: Feminist Perspectives on Economics.* Ed. Edith Kuiper and Jolande Sap. London: Routledge, 1995, 17–34.

R. [George Railton]. *The Salvation War 1883.* London: Salvation Army Book Depôt, 1883.

————. *The Salvation War 1884.* London: Salvation Army Book Depôt, 1884.

————. *The Salvation War 1885.* London: Salvation Army Book Depôt, 1885.

————. *Twenty-one Years' Salvation Army,* London: International Headquarters, 1889.

Rabinbach, Anson. *The Human Motor: Energy, Fatigue, and the Origins of Modernity.* New York: Basic Books, 1990.

Radcliffe, Ann. *The Mysteries of Udolpho* (1794). Ed. Bonamy Dobrée. Oxford: Oxford University Press, 1998.

Rai, Amit S. *Rule of Sympathy: Sentiment, Race, and Power, 1750–1850.* New York: Palgrave, 2002.

Rappaport, Erika Diane. *Shopping for Pleasure: Women in the Making of London's West End.* Princeton: Princeton University Press, 2000.

Rappoport, Jill. "Buyer Beware: The Gift Poetics of Letitia Elizabeth Landon." *Nineteenth-Century Literature* 58:4 (March, 2004): 441–473.

Ravenhill, Alice. *Eugenic Education for Women and Girls* (1909). 2nd ed., rev. Kingsway: Eugenics Education Society, 1914.

Remember Me! New Years Gift or Christmas Present, 1825. London: J. Poole, 1825.

Renier, Anne. *Friendship's Offering: An Essay on the Annuals and Gift Books of the 19th Century.* London: Private Libraries Association, 1964.

Reynolds, Frederic Mansel, ed. *The Keepsake for 1829.* London: Hurst, Chance, and Co., 1828.

Reynolds, Margaret, ed. "Editorial Introduction." *Aurora Leigh.* Athens: Ohio University Press, 1992, 78-156.

Rhys, Jean. *Wide Sargasso Sea.* Ed. Judith Raiskin. New York: W.W. Norton, 1999.

Richardson, Angelique. "The Eugenization of Love: Sarah Grand and the Morality of Genealogy." *Victorian Studies* 42:2 (Winter 1999/2000): 227–255.

————. *Love and Eugenics in the Late Nineteenth Century: Rational Reproduction and the New Woman.* Oxford: Oxford University Press, 2003.

Richardson, Angelique, and Chris Willis. "Introduction." *The New Woman in Fiction and Fact: Fin-de-Siècle Feminisms.* Ed. Angelique Richardson and Chris Willis. Houndmills: Palgrave, 2001, 1–38.

Richardson, Samuel. *Sir Charles Grandison* (1754). Ed. Jocelyn Harris. London: Oxford University Press, 1972.

Robinson, Brian. *Silver Pennies and Linen Towels: The Story of the Royal Maundy.* London: Spink & Son, 1992.

Rosen, Christine. *Preaching Eugenics: Religious Leaders and the American Eugenics Movement.* Oxford: Oxford University Press, 2004.

Rosenthal, Rae. "Gaskell's Feminist Utopia: The Cranfordians and the Reign of Goodwill." *Utopian and Science Fiction by Women: Worlds of Difference.* Ed. Jane L. Donawerth and Carol A. Kolmerten. Syracuse: Syracuse University Press, 1994, 73–92.

Ross, Ellen. "'Fierce Questions and Taunts': Married Life in Working-Class London, 1870–1914." *Feminist Studies* 8:3 (Autumn 1982): 575–602.

———. "Hungry Children: Housewives and London Charity, 1870–1918." *The Uses of Charity: The Poor on Relief in the Nineteenth-Century Metropolis*. Ed. Peter Mandler. Philadelphia: University of Pennsylvania Press, 1990, 161–196.

———. "Introduction: Adventures among the Poor." *Slum Travelers: Ladies and London Poverty, 1860–1920*. Ed. Ellen Ross. Berkeley: University of California Press, 2007, 1–39.

———. *Love and Toil: Motherhood in Outcast London, 1870–1918*. Oxford: Oxford University Press, 1993.

———. "New Thoughts on 'The Oldest Vocation': Mothers and Motherhood in Recent Feminist Scholarship." *Signs* 20:2 (Winter 1995): 397–413.

Rossetti, Christina. "Goblin Market" (1862). *Victorian Literature 1830–1900*, ed. Dorothy Mermin and Herbert F. Tucker. Orlando: Harcourt College Publishers, 2002: 846–852.

———. "A Safe Investment" (1867). *Commonplace and Other Short Stories*. London: F.S. Ellis, 1870, 241–253.

Rowlinson, Matthew. "Reading Capital with Little Nell." *The Yale Journal of Criticism* 9 (1996): 347–380.

Rubin, Gayle. "The Traffic in Women: Notes on the 'Political Economy' of Sex." *Toward an Anthology of Women*. Ed. Rayna R. Reiter. New York: Monthly Review Press, 1975, 157–210.

Russell, John. *Can the School Prepare for Parenthood?* Eugenics Education Society, 1909. [Reprinted from *Eugenics Review*, July 1909.]

———. *Eugenics and Education*. Kingsway: Eugenics Education Society, 1912.

Rutterford, Janette, and Josephine Maltby. "Women and Wealth in Fiction in the Long Nineteenth Century 1800–1914." *Women and Their Money, 1700–1950: Essays on Women and Finance*. Ed. Anne Laurence, Josephine Maltby, and Janette Rutterford. London and New York: Routledge, 2009, 151–164.

Sadoff, Dianne F. "The Father, Castration, and Female Fantasy in *Jane Eyre*." *Jane Eyre*. Ed. Beth Newman. Boston: Bedford/St. Martin's, 1996, 518–535.

Sahlins, Marshall. *Stone Age Economics*. Chicago: Aldine Atherton, 1972.

Said, Edward W. *Orientalism*. New York: Vintage Books, 1978.

Saleeby, Caleb Williams. *Parenthood and Race Culture: An Outline of Eugenics*. London: Cassell and Company, 1909.

Sánchez-Eppler, Karen. "Bodily Bonds: The Intersecting Rhetorics of Feminism and Abolition." *Interracialism: Black-White Intermarriage in American History, Literature, and Law*. Ed. Werner Sollors. Oxford: Oxford University Press, 2000, 408–437.

Schaffer, Talia. "'Nothing But Foolscap and Ink': Inventing the New Woman." *The New Woman in Fiction and in Fact: Fin-de-Siècle Feminisms*. Ed. Angelique Richardson and Chris Willis. Houndmills: Palgrave, 2001, 39–52.

Scharnhorst, Gary. "Historicizing Gilman: A Bibliographer's View." *The Mixed Legacy of Charlotte Perkins Gilman*. Ed. Catherine J. Golden and Joanna Schneider Zangrando. Newark: University of Delaware Press, 2000, 65–73.

Schlossberg, Linda. "'The Low, Vague Hum of Numbers': The Malthusian Economies of *Jane Eyre*." *Victorian Literature and Culture* 29:2 (2001): 489–506.

Schor, Hilary M. *Scheherezade in the Marketplace: Elizabeth Gaskell and the Victorian Novel*. Oxford: Oxford University Press, 1992.

Schotter, Anne Howland. "The Paradox of Equality and Hierarchy of Reward in *Pearl*." *Renascence* 33 (1981): 172–179.

Schreiner, Olive. *Woman and Labour* (1911). Charleston: BiblioBazaar, 2007.

Schwartz, Nina. "No Place Like Home: The Logic of the Supplement in *Jane Eyre*." *Jane Eyre*. Ed. Beth Newman. Boston: Bedford/St. Martin's, 1996, 549–564.

Scott, Walter. *Ivanhoe* (1819). London: Penguin Books, 2000.

Sedgwick, Eve Kosofsky. *Between Men: English Literature and Male Homosocial Desire*. New York: Columbia University Press, 1985.

Shakespeare, William. *A Midsummer Night's Dream* (c. 1594–1596). *The Norton Shakespeare: Comedies*. Ed. Stephen Greenblatt. New York: W.W. Norton, 1997, 327–385.

Shanley, Mary Lyndon. *Feminism, Marriage, and the Law in Victorian England*. Princeton: Princeton University Press, 1989.

Shapiro, Gary. "The Metaphysics of Presents: Nietzsche's Gift, the Debt to Emerson, Heidegger's Values." *The Logic of the Gift: Toward an Ethic of Generosity*. Ed. Alan D. Schrift. New York: Routledge, 1997, 274–291.

Sharpe, Jenny. *Allegories of Empire: The Figure of the Woman in the Colonial Context*. Minneapolis: University of Minnesota Press, 1993.

Shaw, George Bernard. *Major Barbara* (1907). London: Penguin Books, 1957.

Shelley, Mary. "The Sisters of Albano." *The Keepsake for 1829*. Ed. Frederic Mansel Reynolds. London: Hurst, Chance, and Co., 1828, 80–100.

Shelley, Percy Bysshe. "Peter Bell the Third" (1819/1839). *The Poetical Works of Shelley, Cambridge Edition*. Ed. Newell F. Ford. Boston: Houghton Mifflin, 1974, 258–271.

Shoberl, Frederic, ed. *Forget Me Not; A Christmas, New Year's, and Birthday Present*. London: R. Ackermann & Co., 1828, 1830, 1831, 1833, 1842.

Showalter, Elaine. "Charlotte Brontë: Feminine Heroine." *New Casebooks: Jane Eyre*. Ed. Heather Glen. Houndmills: Macmillan, 1997, 68–77.

———, ed. "Introduction." *Christina Rossetti: Maude and Dinah Mulock Craik: "On Sisterhoods" and A Woman's Thoughts About Women*. New York: New York University Press, 1995, vii–xxvi.

———. *A Literature of Their Own: British Women Novelists from Brontë to Lessing*. Expanded ed. Princeton: Princeton University Press, 1999.

———. *Sexual Anarchy: Gender and Culture at the Fin de Siècle*. New York: Penguin Books USA, 1990.

Siegel, Daniel Jeremy. "The Failure of Condescension." *Victorian Literature and Culture* 33:2 (September 2005): 395–414.

Simons, Margaret A. "Racism and Feminism: A Schism in the Sisterhood." *Feminist Studies* 5:2 (Summer 1979): 384–401.

Singh, Veena. "Women Without Men: Family Patterns in *Cranford*." *Women's Writing: Text and Context*. Ed. Jasbir Jain. Jaipur: Rawat Publications, 1996, 76–83.

"Sisters of Charity, Catholic and Protestant, Abroad and at Home." [Review] *Athenaeum* 1432 (April 7, 1855): 399–400. ProQuest British Periodicals database, <http://gateway.proquest.com/openurl?url_ver=Z39.88-2004&res_dat=xri:bp-us:&rft_dat=xri:bp:article:e932-1e855-000-32-028277>.

"The Sisters of Mercy." *The Lady's Newspaper* 140 (September 1, 1849): 114. Gale 19th Century UK Periodicals database: *New Readerships* collection, <http://find.galegroup.com.ezp1.villanova.edu/ukpc/infomark.do?docType=LTO&contentSet=LTO&sort=DateAscend&tabID=T012&docId=DX1900457662&prodId=NCUK&searchId=R8&callistoContentSet=NCUP&docLevel=FASCIMILE&qrySerId=Locale(en,,):FQE=(tx,None,16)sisters of mercy:And:LQE=(MB,None,16)NCUK-1 OR NCUK-2$$&type=multipage&retrieveFormat=MULTIPAGE_DOCUMENT&currentPosition=174&version=1.0&userGroupName=vill_main&searchType=BasicSearchForm&docPage=article&source=gale>.

"The Sisters of Mercy at Plymouth." *The Lady's Newspaper* 114 (March 3, 1849): 115. Gale 19th Century UK Periodicals database: *New Readerships* collection, <http://find.galegroup.com.ezp1.villanova.edu/ukpc/infomark.do?docType=LTO&contentSet=LTO&sort=DateAscend&tabID=T012&docId=DX1900456512&prodId=NCUK&searchId=R10&callistoContentSet=NCUP&docLevel=FASCIMILE&qrySerId=Locale(en,,):FQE=(tx,None,28)sisters of mercy at plymouth:And:LQE=(MB,None,16)NCUK-1 OR NCUK-2$$&type=multipage&retrieveFormat=MULTIPAGE_DOCUMENT&currentPosition=2&version=1.0&userGroupName=vill_main&searchType=BasicSearchForm&docPage=article&source=gale>.

Slinn, E. Warwick. "Dramatic Monologue." *A Companion to Victorian Poetry*. Ed. Richard Cronin, Alison Chapman, and Antony H. Harrison. Malden and Oxford: Blackwell, 2002, 80–98.

Small, Helen, ed. "Introduction." In Ménie Muriel Dowie, *Gallia* (1895). London: J.M. Dent, 1995, xxv–xlii.

Smith-Rosenberg, Carroll. "The Female World of Love and Ritual: Relations Between Women in Nineteenth-Century America." *Signs* 1:1 (Autumn 1975): 1–29.

Soloway, Richard A. "The Galton Lecture 1996: Marie Stopes, Eugenics, and the Birth Control Movement." *Marie Stopes, Eugenics and the English Birth Control Movement: Proceedings of a Conference Organised by the Galton Institute, London, 1996.* Ed. Robert A. Peel. London: The Galton Institute, 1997, 49–76.

Spacks, Patricia Meyer. *Privacy: Concealing the Eighteenth-Century Self.* Chicago: University of Chicago Press, 2003.

Spain, Daphne. *How Women Saved the City.* Minneapolis: University of Minneapolis Press, 2001.

Speech of Sir Robert Peel, on The Financial Condition of the Country, on Friday, March 11, 1842; with The Schedules Containing the New Customs Duties, and the Tax Upon Property and Income. Carefully Revised. London: William Strange, 1842.

Spivak, Gayatri Chakravorty. "Three Women's Texts and a Critique of Imperialism." *Critical Inquiry* 12:1 (Autumn 1985): 243–261.

Staves, Susan. *Married Women's Separate Property in England, 1660–1833.* Cambridge: Harvard University Press, 1990.

Stead, William Thomas. "Rational Dress for Women." *Review of Reviews* (March 1894): 291–292.

Sternlieb, Lisa. "Jane Eyre: 'Hazarding Confidences.'" *Nineteenth-Century Literature* 53:4 (March 1999): 452–479.

Stewart, Garrett. *Dear Reader: The Conscripted Audience in Nineteenth-Century British Fiction.* Baltimore: The Johns Hopkins University Press, 1996.

Stone, Lawrence. *The Family, Sex, and Marriage in England, 1500-1800.* London: Weidenfeld and Nicolson, 1977.

Stone, Marjorie. "Sisters in Art: Christina Rossetti and Elizabeth Barrett Browning." *Victorian Poetry* 32:3–4 (Autumn–Winter 1994): 339–364.

[Stone, Thomas.] "A Shilling's Worth of Science." *Household Words* 1:22 (1850 August): 507–510.

Strassmann, Diana. "Not a Free Market: The Rhetoric of Disciplinary Authority in Economics." *Beyond Economic Man: Feminist Theory and Economics.* Ed. Marianne A. Ferber and Julie A. Nelson. Chicago: University of Chicago Press, 1993, 54–68.

Strathern, Marilyn. *The Gender of the Gift: Problems with Women and Problems with Society in Melanesia.* Berkeley: University of California Press, 1988.

Sutton-Ramspeck, Beth. *Raising the Dust: The Literary Housekeeping of Mary Ward, Sarah Grand, and Charlotte Perkins Gilman.* Athens: Ohio University Press, 2004.

[Swift, Suzie F.? Author listed as "already known to many [. . .] as Editor of 'All the World.'"] *The "Darkest England" Social Scheme. A Brief Review of the First Year's Work.* London, E.C.: International Headquarters, 1891.

Swift, S[uzie] F. *In the Slums! An Account of Salvation Army Warfare in the Dark Courts and Alleys of Modern Babylon, and other Great Cities.* London, E.C.: International Headquarters, 1889.

Tadmor, Naomi. *Family and Friends in Eighteenth-Century England: Household, Kinship, and Patronage.* Cambridge: Cambridge University Press, 2001.

"Taking the Veil." *The Achill Missionary Herald, and Western Witness* 132 (June 26, 1848): 77. *Gale 19th Century UK Periodicals* database: *Empire* collection, <http://find.galegroup.com.ezp1. villanova.edu/ukpc/infomark.do?docType=LTO&contentSet=LTO&sort=DateAscend &tabID=T012&docId=CC1903348199&prodId=NCUK&searchId=R5&callistoConten tSet=NCUP&docLevel=FASCIMILE&qryScrId=Locale(en,,).FQE=(tx,None,15)taking the veil:And:LQE=(MB,None,16)NCUK-1 OR NCUK-2$$&type=multipage&retrieveFor mat=MULTIPAGE_DOCUMENT&currentPosition=127&version=1.0&userGroupNam e=vill_main&searchType=BasicSearchForm&docPage=article&source=gale>.

Taylor, Beverly. "Elizabeth Barrett Browning's Subversion of the Gift Book Model." *Studies in Browning and His Circle* 20 (1993): 62–69.

Tennyson, Alfred, Lord. *In Memoriam*. Ed. Erik Gray. 2nd ed. New York: W.W. Norton, 2003.

[Thackeray, William Makepeace.] *Vanity Fair: A Novel without a Hero* (1847–8). Ed. John Sutherland. Oxford: Oxford University Press, 1983.

———. "A Word on the Annuals." *Fraser's Magazine* 16 (December 1837): 758.

Thompson, Ralph. "*The Liberty Bell* and Other Anti-Slavery Gift-Books." *The New England Quarterly* 7:1 (March 1934): 154–168.

Thomson, William. "On a Universal Tendency in Nature to the Dissipation of Mechanical Energy." *Mathematical and Physical Papers by Sir William Thomson*. Vol. 1. Cambridge: Cambridge University Press, 1882.

Tickner, Lisa. *The Spectacle of Women: Imagery of the Suffrage Campaign, 1907–14*. Chicago: University of Chicago Press, 1988.

Tobin, Beth Fowkes. *Superintending the Poor: Charitable Ladies and Paternal Landlords in British Fiction, 1770–1860*. New Haven: Yale University Press, 1993.

Todd, Janet. *Sensibility: An Introduction*. London: Methuen, 1986.

Trollope, Anthony. *The Eustace Diamonds* (1871–1873). Oxford: Oxford University Press, 2008.

Trumbach, Randolph. *The Rise of the Egalitarian Family: Aristocratic Kinship and Domestic Relations in Eighteenth-Century England*. New York: Academic Press, 1978.

Tucker, Herbert F. "Dramatic Monologue and the Overhearing of Lyric." *Lyric Poetry: Beyond New Criticism*. Ed. Chaviva Hosek and Patricia Parker. Ithaca: Cornell University Press, 1985, 226–243.

———. "Rossetti's Goblin Marketing: Sweet to Tongue and Sound to Eye." *Representations* 82 (Spring 2003): 117–133.

Twells, Alison. "'Happy English Children': Class, Ethnicity, and the Making of Missionary Women in the Early Nineteenth Century." *Women's Studies International Forum* 21:3 (1998): 235–245.

"The Unseen Charities of London." *Fraser's Magazine for Town and Country* 39.234 (June 1849): 639–647. *ProQuest British Periodicals* database, <http://gateway.proquest.com/openurl?url_ver=Z39.88-2004&res_dat=xri:bp-us:&rft_dat=xri:bp:article:e513-1849-039-34-000103>.

Valverde, Mariana. "The Love of Finery: Fashion and the Fallen Woman in Nineteenth- Century Social Discourse." *Victorian Studies* 32:2 (Winter 1989): 169–188.

Vicinus, Martha. "Book Review Forum: Normalizing Female Friendship." *Victorian Studies* 50:1 (Autumn 2007): 81–86.

———. *Independent Women: Work and Community for Single Women, 1850–1920*. Chicago: University of Chicago Press, 1985.

———. *Intimate Friends: Women who Loved Women, 1778–1928*. Chicago: University of Chicago Press, 2004.

Vickery, Amanda. *The Gentleman's Daughter: Women's Lives in Georgian England*. New Haven: Yale University Press, 1998.

———. "Golden Age to Separate Spheres? A Review of the Categories and Chronology of English Women's History." *The Historical Journal* 36:2 (June 1993): 383–414.

———. "Women and the World of Goods: A Lancashire Consumer and Her Possessions, 1751–81." *Consumption and the World of Goods*. Ed. John Brewer and Roy Porter. London: Routledge, 1993, 274–301.

Walker, Pamela J. *Pulling the Devil's Kingdom Down: The Salvation Army in Victorian Britain*. Berkeley: University of California Press, 2001.

Walkowitz, Judith. *City of Dreadful Delight: Narratives of Sexual Danger in Late-Victorian London*. Chicago: University of Chicago Press, 1992.

———. *Prostitution and Victorian Society: Women, Class, and the State*. Cambridge: Cambridge University Press, 1980.

Walvin, James. *Britain's Slave Empire*. Stroud: Tempus, 2000.

———. *England, Slaves and Freedom, 1776–1838*. Houndmills: Macmillan, 1986.

Warhol, Robyn R. "Toward a Theory of the Engaging Narrator: Earnest Interventions in Gaskell, Stowe, and Eliot." *PMLA* 101:5 (October 1986): 811–818.

Washington, Kate. "Rochester's Mistresses: Marriage, Sex, and Economic Exchange in *Jane Eyre*." *Michigan Feminist Studies* 12 (1997–8): 47–66.

Watts, Alaric A., ed. *The Literary Souvenir; or, Cabinet of Poetry and Romance*. London: Hurst, Robinson, and Co., 1826.

Weiner, Annette B. *Inalienable Possessions: The Paradox of Keeping-While-Giving*. Berkeley: University of California Press, 1992.

West, Max. "The Inheritance Tax." *Studies in History Economics and Public Law*, Vol. 4. Ed. The University Faculty of Political Science of Columbia College. New York: Columbia College, 1893–1894, 171–310.

What Is Being Done by the "Darkest England" Social Scheme. London, E.C.: International Headquarters of The Salvation Army, Christmas, 1891.

Williams, Raymond. *Keywords: A Vocabulary of Culture and Society*. New York: Oxford University Press, 1976.

Wilson, Ted. *Battles for the Standard: Bimetallism and the Spread of the Gold Standard in the Nineteenth-Century*. Burlington: Ashgate, 2000.

Winston, Diane. *Red-Hot and Righteous: The Urban Religion of the Salvation Army*. Cambridge: Harvard University Press, 1999.

Wolfe, Patricia A. "Structure and Movement in *Cranford*." *Nineteenth-Century Fiction* 23:2 (September 1968): 161–176.

Woodmansee, Martha, and Mark Osteen ed. *The New Economic Criticism: Studies at the Intersection of Literature and Economics*. London: Routledge, 1999.

Yellin, Jean Fagan. *Women and Sisters: The Antislavery Feminists in American Culture*. New Haven: Yale University Press, 1989.

Yellin, Jean Fagan, and John C. Van Horne. "Introduction." *The Abolitionist Sisterhood: Women's Political Culture in Antebellum America*. Ed. Jean Fagan Yellin and John C. Van Horne. Ithaca: Cornell University Press, 1994, 1–19.

Youmans, Edward L. "Introduction." *The Correlation and Conservation of Forces: A Series of Expositions, by Prof. Grove, Prof. Helmholtz, Dr. Mayer, Dr. Faraday, Prof. Liebig and Dr. Carpenter*. Ed. Edward L. Youmans. New York: D. Appleton and Company, 1865, xi–xlii.

Zangwill, Israel. "'One and One Are Two.' (Being a verbatim report of the speech delivered at Exeter Hall, on February 9th, and the Demonstration of Women's Suffrage Societies.)" London: Women's Social and Political Union. n.d.

Zionkowski, Linda. "The Nation, the Gift, and the Market in *The Wanderer*." *The Culture of the Gift in Eighteenth-Century England*. Ed. Linda Zionkowski and Cynthia Klekar. New York and Houndmills: Palgrave Macmillan, 2009, 177–194.

INDEX

abolition
    female campaigners for, 31, 35, 187nn50,55, 188n65
    as gift, 28–29, 186nn42–43, 187n49
    gradual vs. immediate, 30–31, 187nn48, 50–51, 189n68
    of slave trade, 31, 187n44
    of slavery, 37, 187n44
activism, *passim*
    continuity between print and social movements, 12, 181n45
altruism, 5–6, 13, 175n4, 176n9
The Amulet. See literary annuals
Anglican sisterhood. *See* sisterhood, Anglican
Aurora Leigh. See Browning, Elizabeth Barrett
authorship. *See* writing
Aveling, Eleanor Marx and Edward, 147

bank failure, 73, 75–76, 78, 89, 90
Barrett Browning, Elizabeth. *See* Browning, Elizabeth Barrett
Bataille, Georges, 64
Bentham, Jeremy, 53–54
Besant, Annie, 146
biological altruism. *See* eugenics, as charity
birth control, 146–147, 151, 222n48, 223n63. *See also* eugenics *entries*; sex education
blindness
    regarding gift circulation, 65–66, 76, 195n75, 201n49
    as visual impairment, 62–66, 196n82
body, 29–30, 83, 127, 142, 227n61
    economic significance of, 91, 98, 139–140, 159, 168–170
    vulnerability of, 63, 124–128, 164–165, 167–168, 216n77, 224–225n7
    See also blindness; forcible feeding; hunger strike; syphilis; violence
Booth, William. *See* Salvation Army, Booth, General William

Bourdieu, Pierre, 191n10, 191n11, 196n81
Bowdich, Sarah, "The Booroom Slave," 33–35, 37–38, 188n58
Bray, Anna Eliza, 99–100
breastfeeding. *See* motherhood, breastfeeding and
bribe, 3
Brontë, Anne, 191n12, 224n73
Brontë, Charlotte
    Jane Eyre, 3, 6, 9, 14–15, 26, 45–68, 71, 76, 77, 80, 90, 109, 126, 128, 142, 189–190nn3–4, 214–215n51
    and literary annuals, 45, 48, 53
brotherhood, 102–103
Browning, Elizabeth Barrett, 133
    Aurora Leigh, 6, 9, 14, 26, 45–47, 54–68, 77, 90, 109, 171, 190n3, 195n67
    "The Runaway Slave at Pilgrim's Point," 35–37
Bulwer-Lytton, Sir Edward, *The Coming Race*, 140–142, 144, 150, 152, 155–156, 168

capitalism, 82, 177n16, 203n70
    as accumulation, 77–78, 201–202n53, 202n55
    contrasted with gift exchange. *See* gift exchange, distinct from market transactions
    as incomplete vision of economics, 7
    See also consumerism *entries*; market *entries*;
Carpenter, William B., 72, 83
castration, symbolic, 63, 196n83
Catholicism, anti-, 93, 189n70, 207n22
census, 1851. *See* women, as redundant
Chapman, Maria Weston, 35
charity, 14, 42, 46–48, 75–76, 100, 115, 123, 139, 198n10
    bazaar, 35, 159–161, 188n61
    classifications of poor for. *See* recipient, classification as deserving or undeserving
    coldness of, 47, 54–55, 69–70, 189n71
    dangers of, 47–48, 128–129

giving, *passim*
  as distinct from the gift, 7
  men and, 55–57, 181n43
  pleasure of, 29, 104–105, 162
  politics of, 15, 28, 171–173
  as sacrifice, 4, 14–15. *See also* sacrifice
"Goblin Market." *See* Rossetti, Christina, "Goblin Market."
Grand, Sarah (Frances Elizabeth Bellenden Clarke), 14, 141, 144
  The Heavenly Twins, 142–143, 146, 148–149, 153–157, 162, 167–168
The Great Exhibition of 1851, 72–74, 199n24
Grove, William Robert, 72, 201n45
gypsy, 115, 184n21, 185nn32–33
  erasure of, 24–26
  prejudice against, 23
  See also Hofland, Barbara, "The Gipsy Mother."

hair, symbolic value of, 91, 205n9
Hawthorne, Nathaniel, 73
Hemans, Felicia, 19, 182n3
  literary profits of. *See* profit, literary
  "The Sister's Dream," 38
heterosexual exchange. *See* marriage, as exchange of women
Hill, Octavia, 132
hoarding, 202n55
Hofland, Barbara, 184n20
  "The Gipsy Mother," 22–27, 30, 35, 38, 103
  "The Orphan Family," 42–44
homoeroticism, 11, 98, 104–105, 114–115, 203n71
Hopkins, Ellice, 146
horizontal exchange. *See* gift exchange, balanced
hunger strike, 15, 163, 167–170
Hyde, Lewis, 23, 176n2, 178n24, 201n49

inalienable possession, 78, 81, 83, 98–99, 201n43, 202nn58,60, 203nn68,79, 223n55
income, 14, 59–60, 63, 194n61, 195n74, 202n55. *See also* property law, income tax in; profit
individualism, overemphasis on, 46, 58, 66–67, 71, 79, 107, 130–131, 197n7, 198n15, 217n103
inheritance, 14, 48–57, 59–60
  poetic, 59–60
  redistribution of, 48–54, 55
  See also property law, inheritance in; property law, doctrine of primogeniture in
Irigaray, Luce, 9, 179n33, 200–201n43, 209n55

Jack the Ripper. *See* Slum Sisters, Jack the Ripper and
Jameson, Anna, 14, 90, 93–98, 103, 106, 115
Jane Eyre. See Brontë, Charlotte, *Jane Eyre*
Jewsbury, Geraldine, 27, 42
Joule, James Prescott, 69, 72–73

The Keepsake. See literary annuals
Keightley, Thomas, 99–100
Kenney, Annie, 162, 170–171
kinship
  children and, 10, 59, 61
  consanguineal vs. marital, 51, 185n34, 191n19, 193n41, 210n76
  elective, 10, 59, 67
  fatherhood and, 148–150, 154
  as a human artifact, 193n42
  by marriage. *See* marriage *entries*
  outside of marriage, 10, 13–14, 49, 51, 59, 62, 68, 201n43, 209n55
  motherhood. *See* motherhood *entries*
  orphanhood and, 38, 42, 47, 191n10
  parthenogenesis and, 150, 152, 223n58
  and taxation. *See* property law, inheritance in
  See also eugenics *entries*

lady bountiful, 114, 213n27
Landon, Letitia Elizabeth, 19, 182n3
  "The Black Seal," 38–40
lateral transaction. *See* gift exchange, balanced
L. E. L. *See* Landon, Letitia Elizabeth
Leslie, Eliza, 22, 184n18
Lévi-Strauss, Claude, 4, 177n18, 179n33
The Liberty Bell, 35–37, 188nn60–61. *See also* literary annuals
literary annuals, 8, 14, 19–44, 45, 48, 53, 61, 182nn1–2, 189n69
  vs. gift-books, 19, 183n6
  as gifts, 21–22, 183nn5, 7–9
  ethos of generosity in, 20–23, 29, 148, 183n13
  expectation to circulate, 20–24, 37, 161, 184n17
  as political, 28
  sales of, 19, 182n3
  See also reading, as basis for community
Literary Souvenir. See literary annuals
loss. *See* sacrifice
Lytton, Lady Constance, 170–171

Malthusian
  neo-, 146
  League, 146–147
market, 106, 177n16
  criticism of the, 8, 98, 178n26
  gendered dangers of the, 90–91, 97–98, 102–105, 115
  as engine of growth, 121
  literary, 19
  See also consumerism *entries*; gift exchange, distinct from market transactions
marriage
  companionate, 65, 67, 196n87
  cross-class, 9, 24, 58